Advance Praise for W

A collection of inspiring interviews with warrior l. ... .world. Their
stories should serve as a call to action in Canada and the U.S., which are woefully
behind the rest of the world in recognizing the rights of all to live in a healthy
environment.

  William Deverell, award-winning novelist, lawyer and environmentalist

In the face of the most significant crises of humankind, a global movement is
emerging to transform human consciousness. Silver Donald Cameron shares the
provocative stories of frontline *Warrior Lawyers* around the world. These bold warriors are standing up to redesign legal systems to recognize and value the rights of
all life to thrive. A powerful read for anyone who cares about our planet.

  Robin R. Milam, Global Alliance for the Rights of Nature

There really are heroes and heroines. In *Warrior Lawyers*, Cameron has gathered
some of the best together in one place. Moving, terrifying, inspirational — their
stories stand as a beacon of hope in our troubled world.

  Maude Barlow, The Council of Canadians

An intriguing, inspiring and optimistic book. All those lawyers, judges, activists
— spiritual warriors, as Silver Donald Cameron calls them — fighting to save
our environment, not in the trenches, but in courts of law, with the visionary idea
of the basic human right to a healthy environment as their weapon. Cameron, a
green warrior himself, and a great storyteller, deftly writes of legal battles won and
those to come.

  Maggie Siggins, Governor-General's Award-winning author of
  Revenge of the Land

A romp with some of the finest legal minds on the planet as they force governments
and businesses to honour the environment. You get to the end and realize you have
feasted on both revolution and hope.

  Alanna Mitchell, named by the Reuters Foundation as "the world's
  best environmental journalist"

WARRIOR
LAWYERS

WARRIOR LAWYERS

From Manila to Manhattan, Attorneys for the Earth

SILVER DONALD CAMERON

Green Interview Books
www.TheGreenInterview.com
An imprint of Paper Tiger Enterprises Ltd.
Halifax, Nova Scotia

Published in Canada by Paper Tiger Enterprises Ltd. ,
287 Lacewood Drive - Unit 103, Halifax, NS B3M 1Y7

ISBN 978-0-9952338-0-5 (book); 978-0-9952338-
2-9 (e-book); 978-0-9952338-1-2 (PDF)

Printed in Canada by Marquis Livres Books, Montmagny, QC

Cover design: Denise Saulnier
Text design and layout: Brenda Conroy
Editorial consultant: Elizabeth Eve

Cataloguing in Publication is available from
Library and Archives Canada, Ottawa.

For Erika Beatty, Chris Beckett — and, always, for Marjorie

Also by
Silver Donald Cameron

Faces of Leacock (Ryerson Press, 1967)

Conversations with Canadian Novelists (Macmillan Canada, 1973)

The Education of Everett Richardson (McClelland and Stewart, 1977)

Seasons in the Rain: An Expatriate's Notes on British Columbia (McClelland and Stewart, 1978)

Dragon Lady: A Novel (McClelland and Stewart, 1980; Seal, 1981)

The Baitchopper (James Lorimer, 1982)

Schooner: Bluenose and Bluenose II (Seal, 1984), rev. *Once Upon a Schooner* (Formac, 1992)

Outhouses of the West (Nimbus, 1988) (with Sherman Hines)

Wind, Whales and Whisky: A Cape Breton Voyage (Macmillan Canada, 1991)

Lifetime: A Treasury of Uncommon Wisdoms (Macmillan Canada; co-author; 1992)

An Illustrated History of Marine Atlantic (Breakwater; co-author; 1992)

Sniffing the Coast: An Acadian Voyage (Macmillan Canada, 1993)

Sterling Silver: Rants, Raves and Revelations (Breton Books, 1994)

An Island Parish (St. Hyacinth's Parish; co-author; 1995)

The Living Beach: Life, Death and Politics Where the Land Meets the Sea (Macmillan Canada, 1998; 2nd edition, Red Deer Press, 2014)

Sailing Away from Winter: A Cruise from Nova Scotia to Florida and Beyond (McClelland and Stewart, 2008)

A Million Futures: The Remarkable Legacy of the Canada Millennium Scholarship Foundation (Douglas & McIntyre, 2010)

(For more information about Silver Donald Cameron and his work, please visit www.SilverDonaldCameron.ca)

Contents

Preface: The Green Rights Journey...9

Warrior Lawyers and the Quest for *Buen Vivir* 15

Meet the Warriors.. 45

    David Boyd.. 47

    John Borrows 67

    Cormac Cullinan 87

    Michelle Maloney 105

    Mumta Ito 119

    Pablo Fajardo and Steven Donziger 135

    Daniel Sallaberry... 157

    Antonio Oposa Jr. 165

    Thomas Linzey and Mari Margil 185

    Larry Kowalchuk 213

    Jan van de Venis.. 227

    Femke Wijdekop 247

    Marjan Minnesma.. 267

    Roger Cox 289

    Polly Higgins... 307

About The Green Interview 327

About Silver Donald Cameron.. 329

Thanks and Acknowledgments... 331

Preface

The Green Rights Journey

"Peer deeply into the sewage sludge of Tamaqua.
It may contain the future of the law."

Thus ended my first newspaper column of 2007. I was in the middle of a 13-year romp as a freelance commentator for the *Sunday Herald* in Halifax, NS. As the news about the state of the planet had grown steadily darker, I had found myself writing more frequently about environmental matters, particularly about people and organizations who were generating light — like the 7,000 people of Tamaqua, Pennsylvania, an hour's drive south of Scranton.

One of the most important events of 2006, I declared, might well have been the passage of the Tamaqua Borough Sewage Sludge Ordinance, which had gone largely unnoticed.

"Tamaqua's revolutionary ordinance does two things," I wrote. "It denies the right of corporations to spread sewage sludge as fertilizer on farmland, even when the farmer is willing, and it recognizes natural communities and ecosystems as legal 'persons' with legal rights. It is among the first 'wild laws' to be passed anywhere in the world."

The Tamaqua ordinance owed a great deal to the Community Environmental Legal Defence Fund, a Pennsylvania public-interest law firm headed by a visionary lawyer named *Thomas Linzey*. Elsewhere in the column (which is online at http://ow.ly/Fmig301bhlm), I cited a book called *Wild Law: A Manifesto for Earth Justice*, written by a South African attorney named *Cormac Cullinan*. I also noted that when I was researching *The Living Beach* (1998), I had discovered a brilliant essay by Christopher Stone, a Southern California law professor, entitled *Should Trees Have Standing? Towards Legal Rights for Natural Objects*. Both Cullinan and Stone argued that real things (like trees and rivers and ecosystems) should have at least the same legal recognition as imaginary entities like states and corporations. To me, that made perfect sense.

"Without rapid and radical change," I concluded, "the days of our own species may be numbered, and the fundamental justice and sanity of wild law is indisputable. Peer deeply into the sewage sludge of Tamaqua. It may contain the future of the law."

As I continued to write columns about trail-blazing environmental leaders, scientists and citizen activists, I found myself thinking, "Wouldn't it be wonderful to talk to these people, to help spread their ideas and to learn directly from them myself?" Interviews can be deeply revealing and engaging, as I had learned with my 1973 book *Conversations with Canadian Novelists*. In 2009, however, the logical medium might be the internet, not the printing press.

Aha! Why not do the interviews by phone, and enjoy free distribution worldwide, presenting the actual voices instead of transcripts? *As It Happens: The Green Edition. Green Democracy Now.* Something like that? Why not?

I know from many years of radio work that I'm not good at capturing crisp, clean sound, especially in the field. However, Mount Saint Vincent University had a great sound booth that it used for distance education. The nice guy in charge of it was Chris Beckett, whom I knew, though not well. Could I use the university's facilities?

"Of course," said Chris. "But I think you're crazy."

"Why am I crazy?"

"Because these are historic interviews with some of the most important people in the world. They're of archival importance. You're building a remarkable intellectual resource. It should be on video."

"But I have no capacity to do video."

"No," said Chris. "But I do."

And so began TheGreenInterview.com. Chris was still working for the university, which was very supportive, and many of our first interviews were recorded in Mount Saint Vincent's studio. I bought a small high-definition camera, and Chris showed me how to use it, which allowed me to capture interviews when I was travelling for other projects. I was invited to a conference in Bhutan, for instance, whose king long ago declared that Gross National Product was less important than Gross National Happiness; the conference was on the topic of Education for Gross National Happiness. In Thimphu I was able to interview people like *Vandana Shiva, Satish Kumar, Gregory Cajete* and *Prime Minister Jigme Thinley*. On other trips I was able to interview towering figures like *James Lovelock, Paul Watson, Robert Bateman* and *William Rees*. We posted the interviews in audio and text form as well as video. (I'm using *italics* to indicate the names of people we have interviewed for The Green Interview.)

TheGreenInterview.com was and is a membership site, supported by individual subscribers, but our most important market turned out to be educational distributors and aggregators. Gale Cengage Learning — bless them! — became a partner very early, and other content providers, like Films on Demand, Kanopy Streaming, Biblioboard and McIntyre Media, later incorporated our work into their collections, making it available in libraries and educational institutions all over the world. Now we had a modest travel budget, and Chris Beckett had retired from the university. We joked that we had become the OFIAS Film Collective. OFIAS stands for Old Farts In A Subaru.

Chris has spent most of his life in network television, and I have been writing and narrating TV and radio documentaries, dramas and commentaries since 1963. Between us we have more than a century of experience — but we could never have done this work prior to the digital revolution. We both remember vividly the days when the work we now do out of a Subaru Outback would have required sound trucks, massive generators, trained technicians to deal with sound and lighting, an octopoid network of fat black cables, script assistants, roadies and God knows what else. Today the whole production apparatus fits in a couple of fat plastic cases wheeled through the hotel lobby by two senior citizens.

Since TheGreenInterview.com was launched in 2010, we have amassed nearly 90 interviews with green giants from 18 countries. I have climbed to the Tiger's Nest, a Buddhist monastery that clings to a Himalayan cliffside in Bhutan, while Chris and I together have lived on a houseboat on an Amsterdam canal, stayed at the ultra-posh University Club in New York, and bounced around in an inflatable speedboat in a Pacific gale off Tofino, BC, to welcome the Greenpeace ship *Rainbow Warrior*. We have travelled a filthy urban river in Buenos Aires on a garbage barge, and stopped en route to a meeting in northern France to pay our respects at an impeccable cemetery for young Canadians killed in the First World War. We have crossed the Andes in a taxi from Quito to reach the Ecuadorian oil town of Lago Agrio, and interviewed a wounded Andean Aboriginal leader in a rectory in Lima, Peru.

We've had a wonderful time. It's been an education, a privilege and an inspiration.

Our documentary projects emerged by a process of evolution. Chris shaped the footage that I brought back from Bhutan — mostly stills — into a micro-documentary called *Bhutan: The Pursuit of Gross National Happiness*. When we interviewed composer *Scott Macmillan* and librettist *Jennyfer Brickenden* about *The Celtic Mass for the Sea,* we were able to present our subscribers with a video showing a performance on the Halifax waterfront of that powerful, beautiful work.

In 2011, I wrote a *Sunday Herald* column deploring the Nova Scotia govern-ment's decision to permit open net-pen salmon feedlots to foul the clean, cold waters of the province's coast. That column brought a call from Henry Hicks, a sport fisherman who loves wild salmon and wondered what could be done to keep the issue in the public eye. Well, I said, Chris and I could make a documentary about it, and that film could be shown in community halls, local theatres and church basements and aired on community cable TV. At Henry's request, Chris and I worked out a minimal budget; Henry enlisted some other salmon fishermen, and they raised the money. The result was a 75-minute film. *Salmon Wars: Wild Fish, Aquaculture and the Future of Communities* (2012) greatly raised awareness of the issue, may have influenced the subsequent provincial election, and has now been seen in classrooms and festivals as far away as Bangkok, Tokyo and Tasmania. You can see it on the Green Interview website.

This kind of work, we later discovered, is called "documentary activism" — we'd never even heard the phrase — and the documentaries had a symbiotic relationship with the interview site. The films included big interviews with major players in many locations; the projects covered our travel costs, and the conversations provided content for the Green Interview web site.

A few weeks after *Salmon Wars* was launched, we interviewed activist and legal scholar *David Boyd* — an interview that is included in this book. That conversation took me back to the theme of environmental rights that I had first encountered in Christopher Stone — but with an explosive difference. David had just published a scholarly book called *The Environmental Rights Revolution,* in which he reported that 177 (now 180) of the 193 countries in the United Nations had recognized the human right to a healthy environment, often in their constitutions. A few countries had even enacted laws recognizing the rights of Mother Nature herself. David told us stories from all over the globe about determined citizens and imaginative lawyers who had used those provisions to mount dramatic legal offensives against ecological aggressors and compliant governments.

Amazing! These rights might be the universal solvent for environmental issues, the Unified Field Theory of environmentalism. Foul air, poisoned water, reckless genetic engineering, salmon feedlots, deforestation, hydraulic fracturing — green rights provided a tool to tackle any of them. It is one of the most exciting ideas I've ever encountered.

Sixteen countries, however, did *not* recognize those rights, and one of them was ours. Another was our next-door neighbour, the United States. Chris and I didn't take long to imagine a new film — a film that would tell those inspiring stories to Canadians and Americans, adding momentum to the movement to embed green rights in the legal systems of North America. *Salmon Wars* had given us the model: raise the cost of the full-length movie from donors who shared our values, and make the film available for free. We could (and later did) make shorter versions for classroom use and for broadcast. (A one-hour TV show called *Defenders of the Dawn: Green Rights in the Maritimes* was broadcast in September 2015, by the Canadian Broadcasting Corporation.) The new project would have its own website — www.

GreenRights.com — but once again, we would incorporate the major full-length interviews into TheGreenInterview.com, allowing interested viewers to plunge much deeper into the material. Heavens, there could even be a book!

We found sympathetic ears in a number of environmental organizations, notably the Council of Canadians, Ecojustice and the David Suzuki Foundation. The Sierra Club Canada Foundation adopted GreenRights as a Foundation project, which meant that financial contributions could generate tax receipts. We attracted small contributions from as far away as Inuvik and Washington State, but most of the funds we raised came from the same small group of generous Nova Scotians who had financed *Salmon Wars*. The new film, *Green Rights: The Human Right to a Healthy World* was completed in August 2016. It would be distributed online, at conferences and festivals, and at screenings in universities and colleges during a national promotional tour that my wife, Marjorie Simmins and I would undertake in October 2016. Later, we hope, it will be shown by civil-society organizations at their own events and meetings.

So we've done the project, but there are plenty of great stories and magnificent individuals out there, and we didn't contrive to interview some of the people I had really hoped to include. I wanted to start with Christopher Stone, for example, and to incorporate his account of the steady extension of legal rights to entities formerly considered to be property, such as slaves, women and animals. Recognizing the rights of Mother Nature and her constituent parts is, for Stone, the logical continuation of a long evolution of civilized behaviour. I deeply regret that we didn't interview the astonishing Indian lawyer M.C. Mehta, who brought such a stream of ground-breaking environmental lawsuits that for a certain period, the New Delhi courts reserved a courtroom just for his use. His Goldman Environmental Prize citation lists more than 40 landmark judgments, including actions to clean up Delhi's air, preserve the Taj Mahal, and cleanse the Ganges.

I wish we could have included Vera Mischenko, the founder of Ecojuris, post-Communist Russia's first public-interest law organization, who (among other things) blocked Exxon from a reckless discharge of toxic chemicals into the sea at Sakhalin Island. I wanted to learn about the legal ban on hydraulic fracturing in France, the first nation ever to enact such a measure. I would love to hear, first-hand, how Costa Rica defied the oil barons by simply refusing to honour a trade agreement that would have permitted offshore drilling in sensitive waters. The lesson from that brave little nation is that destructive provisions in international trade agreements cannot actually be enforced on sovereign nations which place their commitment to their people and to the Earth ahead of an illusory corporate concept of wealth.

So we didn't get everything we wanted. One never does. But we're not finished. We continue to post a new full-length interview on the Green Interview site every month. We know how to make movies. We know how to make books. Who knows what comes next?

And sometime towards the end of the process we realized that just by following our noses, we had groped our way into something quite new: a multi-faceted narrative procedure for the digital age. The overall Green Rights project uses audio, video and text, and incorporates such traditional forms as book publication, TV broadcast and documentary film production — but it also includes such digital expansions as e-books, membership websites presenting stand-alone components of the books and films, and global electronic distribution through academic content providers. We had found a home-grown financing mechanism in the form of generous allies who believed passionately in the project, and in us. We had achieved an enviable working relationship with environmental NGOs, particularly the Sierra Club Canada Foundation. We had figured out how to distribute the finished products ourselves, self-publishing this book and showing the film online and in person. Even the structure of this book seems unique: a focussed collection of interviews set in the context of a long interpretive essay.

You can stream our film, *Green Rights: The Human Right to a Healthy World*, by going to the Green Interview site, www.TheGreenInterview.com and taking a free one-month trial subscription. That trial subscription also gives you access to the full-length audio and video versions of the interviews in this book. Subscribers are our life-blood and our security, so we ardently hope that you'll continue the subscription after your free trial — but that's up to you.

If you want to arrange for a screening of *GreenRights* with an audience, we'd be delighted. We may even be able to attend the screening — by Skype, or possibly in person. To arrange that, please write to info@TheGreenInterview.com. I'm also available for speaking engagements; please write me at sdc@silverdonaldcameron.ca.

Warrior Lawyers
and the
Quest for *Buen Vivir*

"You should be a lawyer," said my mother.

She meant it, and it was not a compliment. Her eldest son was argumentative and ungovernable, ingenious and glib. She was serious enough to arrange a meeting for me with an old friend of the family, George Curtis, then Dean of Law at the University of British Columbia. Dean Curtis was courteous and persuasive, and he encouraged me to consider law as a career.

Well, okay. And so, for my first two undergraduate years, I vaguely assumed that I was doing pre-law, although I had no real concept of what lawyers did. I discerned that they mostly wore three-piece suits, involved themselves in financial transactions, raked in tidy incomes, lived in prosperous neighbourhoods and thought well of themselves. They seemed to be servants of the establishment; indeed, to a large extent they *were* the establishment. Still, I had no better idea of what to do with my life, so I accepted that I was going to be a lawyer. In my second year, I fell in love with the study of philosophy, and I even tried to imagine a career at the intersection of philosophy and law.

And then I took a job as a high-school teacher, found that I loved teaching, and realized that one could actually make a living teaching literature in a university. Literature was always my most passionate love, but I had never thought of it as a career. With a roar like a rocket at lift-off, my heart and mind engaged. By the time the rocket had spent its first-stage fuel, I found myself a tenured professor with a PhD in English.

After a couple of tenured years, however, it occurred to me that instead of studying literature, I could possibly make a living producing it. I could be a professional writer. I had, at last, found my real destiny.

I didn't entirely lose touch with the law; I've since written about the law on many occasions, and I even served briefly as a Lay Bencher with the Nova Scotia Barristers Society. I have no complaints about the overall trajectory of my life; it's been a grand adventure. But if I had another lifetime, and if my silver self could counsel my callow self, I would tell him something that I only gradually learned about the law.

Getting a legal training, I would say, is like building a boat — which I've also had the pleasure of doing. There are certain basic requirements. The boat has to be tight, strong, stable and seaworthy. Beyond that, though, you can do whatever you like with it: rig it as you wish, paint it whatever colour pleases you, equip it according to your own preferences. Most important of all, you can sail it to almost any port on earth.

As a lawyer, you can make a ton of money working for corporate masters. You can use the law as a springboard to politics. You can teach, or you can help mend broken families. You can become an expert on copyright, international treaties or marine salvage. You can be a prosecutor, a defense attorney, a judge. You can shape the development of cities. You can go into some unrelated business for yourself. I know a lawyer who ships lobsters to China. You can transform yourself into a novelist, like Scott Turow or my friend Bill Deverell.

You can even become a warrior.

A warrior?

I don't mean a soldier — although you can become that, too; just ask the Judge Advocate General — but a spiritual warrior. I am an admirer of the Tantric Buddhist tradition, not a practitioner, but as I understand it, the spiritual warrior in that elegant philosophy is a compassionate person with a brave mind and a powerful sense of ethics, a person focussed not on individual salvation, but on alleviating the suffering of other beings, and helping them to find wisdom and liberation.

Note — "other beings," not just other persons. Buddhists commonly pray for the welfare of "all sentient beings." A spiritual warrior may act to defend any part of the living world — or all of it.

For such a person, I suspect, environmentalism becomes a spiritual practice, a form of worship. In Aboriginal societies, indeed, the responsibility of protecting the homeland and of stewarding all life within it belongs specifically to the warriors — and it is a sacred obligation. As Mi'kmaw warrior Sakej Ward writes, the warrior protects "life in all forms, including animals, birds, plants, fish, and insects; as well as the life of the lands, mountains, rivers, and skies." The warrior serves the harmony and balance of nature, and guards the interests of succeeding generations by upholding natural law.

And the warrior who is also a lawyer comes armed with what the formidable *Tony Oposa* calls "the sword of reason, the fire of passion, and the will, the force, and the power of the law."

The Power of Green Rights: The Philippines

Tony Oposa — formally "Antonio Oposa, Jr." — is one of the seventeen warrior lawyers from nine countries whom you'll meet in the following pages. He's known throughout the Philippines as "Attorney Oposa" and throughout the world as the source of "the Oposa doctrine," which established the legal right of future generations to inherit a healthy, life-sustaining environment.

Tony's journey began in 1990, when he went walking in the mountains of Cebu, in what used to be the forest — and the forest was gone. Erased. Clearcut. On inquiry, Oposa learned that only four percent of the country's original forest remained — 800,000 hectares — and the government had issued logging permits for an absurd 3.9 million hectares, five times as much forest as actually existed. If logging weren't halted immediately, the country would be completely denuded. Future generations would inherit a stripped and wasted landscape. At its heart, the pillage of the forests was an attack on posterity.

Three years earlier, however, after the Marcos dictatorship, the Philippines had adopted a new constitution, Section 16 of which provided that the State "shall protect and advance the right of the people to a balanced and healthful ecology in accord with the rhythm and harmony of nature." This provision, or one like it, is the essence of "environmental rights" — the right of human beings to a healthy environment, and also the right of Nature herself to thrive and flourish.

As *David Boyd* notes, rights derive from wrongs, and the human right to a healthy environment is the newest of human rights, inspired by the newest of human wrongs, namely the widespread degradation of the biosphere in the years after World War Two. The growing concern about the environment gained global attention in 1972, at the landmark United Nations Conference on the Human Environment held in Stockholm. The first country to recognize environmental rights in its legal system was Portugal, in 1976. Today the vast majority of nations — about 180 out of the 193 members of the United Nations — recognize that their citizens are entitled to a healthy environment, and in 110 countries, environmental rights are embedded in the Constitution. Only a dozen or so countries do not recognize those rights at all. Among the laggards, sadly, are the United States and Canada.

But the 1987 Constitution of the Philippines did recognize those rights, and if the government was failing to uphold them, then the government could be sued. If posterity was the offended party, thought Tony Oposa, then posterity should sue.

So, acting on behalf of 43 children (including his own), and on behalf of children not yet born, Oposa sued Fulgencio Factoran, then the Secretary of Environment and Natural Resources. The plaintiffs demanded that all existing timber concessions be cancelled, and that no new ones be issued. "Minors Oposa vs. Factoran," as the case is known, was Oposa's very first legal action. He lost, largely on the grounds that people who didn't yet exist had no "legal personality," and thus no right to sue.

He appealed, and ultimately he won. Ten of the 11 Supreme Court justices agreed that "the rhythm and harmony of nature" inescapably required the "management, renewal and conservation" of natural capital, and imposed on each generation a responsibility to preserve nature for succeeding generations. This duty to provide "intergenerational equity" is now known as "the Oposa Doctrine," and its echoes can be heard in courtrooms around the world. And, though it took some years, all logging in wild forests is now banned in the Philippines.

As it turned out, Fulgencio Factoran was delighted to lose. He accepted his legal obligation to steward the forests, but he was constrained by pressure from government and industry. So he actually welcomed Oposa's suit, which, says Oposa, "put the wind under his wings" and empowered Factoran to do what he wanted to do anyway.

Oposa went on to win a string of other landmark cases based on environmental rights, including a massive cleanup of Manila Bay. As this is being written, he is heading a movement to split all the country's roads along the centre line, reserving half of every road for the use of cyclists, pedestrians and public transit. This is, he says, simple justice: all Filipinos pay for the roads, but only two percent own cars. And the measure — which may actually be adopted — will dramatically reduce the country's carbon emissions.

"If you took in all the carbon footprint of the life cycle of the motor vehicle," says Oposa, "from the mining, refining of ore and oil to the making of steel, to the making of the car, to the making of aggregated cement, to the making of rubber, to wiping out forests — real forests, just to plant rubber trees — the manufacture of rubber tires and all of these, if you take it all into account, the carbon footprint is about half of all the climate forcing gasses."

Oposa's activism is not restricted to the courtroom. He has also played a robust role in enforcement, heading up raids on illegal logging operations, intercepting ships and arresting poachers who were fishing in the Visayan Sea with dynamite and cyanide. Once a poacher is convicted, however, Oposa uses a form of judicial judo which begins with a request that the court remand the offender into Oposa's custody.

"My former adversaries have become not only my allies, but have become my fellow advocates," he says. "And that is for me the highest achievement. It also springs from a belief that life is about redemption. We all commit mistakes, but if you get me an opportunity to correct myself then you restore my dignity. I am so tough in court against them! But after they are convicted, I tell this court, please, may I talk to them in advance?

"I say, do you want to go to jail or are you going to help our cause? I give them an offer they cannot refuse. Do you want to go to jail? That is going to take you at least 10 years. You have your wife here, you have your children there, and by the time you come home your wife will have another husband....

"Okay, when we go to court now, you plead guilty. And then I will talk to the judge that you'll be released on probation, on a suspended sentence for five years, whatever, six years. But as a condition of the probation you will work with my Sea School and serve to protect the sea. And that's what they're doing. It's something I'm really proud of."

If I had known that I could have gone to law school and developed into someone like Tony Oposa, I might well have made a different decision. As Stephen Leacock sadly noted, "many a man realizes late in life that if when he was a boy he had known what he knows now, instead of being what he is he might be what he won't; but how few boys stop to think that if they knew what they don't know instead of being what they will be, they wouldn't be?"

The Law as Storytelling

Tony Oposa doesn't actually regard himself as a lawyer but as a storyteller who uses the law to tell stories that the community needs to hear. If he held a press conference to tell his story, he says, nobody would come — and if they did come, they wouldn't really pay attention, and the story would soon be forgotten. But if he tells the story of the forests and the unborn generations in the form of a lawsuit, influential people will have to listen; the truth of the story will be established by the evidence; there will be an accurate record; and ultimately there will be a decision. And if the suit fails, he can appeal — and the story will be told all over again. A lawsuit undertaken in this spirit cannot really be lost. Any outcome will spread understanding by publicizing the story.

Which leads to the reflection that stories are the beating heart of law. *John Borrows*, the brilliant Anishinaabe legal scholar, points out that Canada has three legal traditions, all recognized in the Constitution: the English common law, the French civil law, and the legal systems of the First Nations. And all of them rest on stories. What are known as "cases" and "precedents" are fundamentally stories, and it is through the process of bringing stories together and negotiating meaning and priority between them that law emerges.

That said, European and Indigenous approaches to law are very different. In English, the word "law" can mean either of two quite different things. One is the bookish business of the legal system, human laws capable of being modified by government. The other describes the immutable principles that govern the natural world, like the law of gravity. These are never modified. No parliament can repeal the laws of thermodynamics.

In Aboriginal thought, the two kinds of law are closely related. As John Borrows describes it, human laws often derive from natural laws. For Borrows, law is what provides guidance to people, the principles or standards or observations that people use in making decisions and shaping their behaviour. In the European tradition, those principles are recorded in written statutes and precepts. Aboriginal thought, by contrast, finds that guidance in the living and shifting world around us, which transforms the concept of law into something dynamic and spiritual.

"If you see the Creator, or the trees, or the waters, or the animals, or people's own living interactions as being the source of authority — the criteria, the precedent — then you would obviously have another view of where you should look to find law," Borrows says. "In Anishinaabe, there's a different set of terms for thinking about law. One is called *Inaakinogewin*, which means 'the great guided ways of decision-making.' But another is *kinwezhiwewin*, and this word means 'to take guidance from the criteria that you find around you.' And so, Anishinaabe people themselves have ideas about law that are more organic, that are more embedded in interactions and relationships."

One afternoon many years ago, during my earliest days of sailing, I had perhaps the most profound learning experience of my life. Sensing how the boat moved, how the waves behaved, how the wind pulsed and faded, how my own actions fed into this complex dance between the boat and the elements, I had a sensation I had never encountered before. I felt as though I were listening with my skin, soaking up information through my hair and my sense of balance and my breath — paying attention so intently that my entire body virtually tingled. I never knew that learning could be a physical rush, a bit like being stoned.

Decades later, sitting in the sunlight on the shore of Georgian Bay, listening to John Borrows and his daughter Lindsay — a law student — my mind racing to keep up, ravenous for more, I had a similar sensation: sweeping landscapes and vistas of new insight and understanding, cascades of concepts and implications, a dawning realization that I was receiving a whole new lens through which to view the world.

I'll return to John Borrows later, but for now, the essential point is that all legal systems seem to be constructed around stories, and the purpose of legal action is not only to seek a favourable decision, but also to tell the story. In short, sue the bastards. Even if you lose, you win.

Finding the Warrior Lawyers

Easily said — but, says the long-suffering citizen, just exactly how do I do that? How do I find a lawyer? How do I pay the costs of a suit? All good questions. It takes research to find a lawyer. You talk to law schools, bar societies, environmental organizations, friends and colleagues. There are a lot more warrior lawyers out there than there used to be, and some lawyers and law firms will do a significant amount of legal work "pro bono" — for the public good. They work mainly for paying clients, but spend the remainder of their time on unpaid work for causes they believe in. The adventurous and innovative Dutch lawyer Jan van de Venis spends 50 percent of his time earning an income, and the other 50 percent working free for human rights and sustainability.

In addition, some fascinating new devices are being unveiled. Legal costs have always been a deterrent used by the rich and powerful to dissuade the poor and the weak from seeking justice, but the obvious unfairness created by that imbalance of power has stimulated a range of innovations. By now we are all familiar with the class action lawsuit, a device that allows whole groups or "classes" of people to launch joint lawsuits against governments, churches, corporations and other organizations. In the Netherlands, *Marjan Minnesma* of the Urgenda Foundation invented "crowd-pleading," analogous to crowd-funding, when she invited individual citizens to join with the organization in suing the Dutch government for its failure to protect citizens by taking timely and effective action on climate change. The foundation eventually went to court with more than 900 co-plaintiffs.

Urgenda itself actually functions as a successful business which applies its profits to environmental purposes rather than distributing them as dividends, so it covered all the costs of the legal action. But there's no reason that crowd-pleading couldn't be combined with crowd-funding to finance a lawsuit. Indeed, Jan van de Venis has created a crowd-funding website — TheCrowdversus.com — specifically to raise money for environmental purposes.

The Power of Green Rights: Argentina

In western nations, lawyers often work on a "contingency" basis, taking no fees up front, but receiving a generous share in the eventual cash settlement if they win. In Argentina, *Daniel Sallaberry* heads a group of lawyers who were offended by the fact that the environmental guarantees in the country's constitution weren't being respected in practice. The group took on a major test case on a contingency basis: the Riachuelo River in Buenos Aires. The river had been horribly despoiled since the Spaniards established tanneries on its banks in the sixteenth century. By the late twentieth century, the river was clotted with debris, including 53 abandoned ships, dead horses, great rafts of plastic containers, and innumerable mouldering trucks and cars, all of it bathed in the toxic run-off from tanneries, oil refineries, chemical industries, shanty-towns and farmlands. The Riachuelo basin was also home to about 3.5 million people, and it was considered one of the 10 most polluted spots on Earth.

Acting on behalf of the residents of a riverside slum called Villa Inflammable, Sallaberry and his associates sued the municipal, provincial and federal governments, and 44 industries, for infringing the environmental rights of the residents. On July 8, 2008, after four years of hearings and investigation, the Supreme Court handed down an astounding decision. In a judgment that David Boyd described as "sweeping and poetic," the court held that government and industry had indeed infringed the residents' right to a healthy environment, and were obliged to repair the damage. Furthermore, the court did not leave the matter to be resolved by other agencies. Instead, it declared that the clean-up would be supervised by a citizens' group and a new intergovernmental organization called Acumar, and by a judge. Acumar would create a timeline, file regular reports with the Supreme Court, and face heavy penalties if it failed to meet its own deadlines.

The remediation process has been complex and fitful, and a decade after the Supreme Court's landmark decision, the Riachuelo is far from clean. But the progress has been remarkable. In one recent year, Argentina spent more than a billion dollars on the cleanup. The Riachuelo-Matanza basin now has about 250 environmental inspectors — more than the entire nation of Canada. Landfills have been removed, most of the junk is out of the water, hundreds of families have been moved into new housing, and, where their shanties once stood, a linear riverbank park, planted with native trees, is giving the river back to the city and its citizens. The Riachuelo is still a dirty urban river, but it gets a little cleaner every day. And, as an example of what can be done, it has shifted the thinking of citizens and activists around the world.

Daniel Sallaberry was thrilled when the Supreme Court later ruled that keeping an orangutan caged in a zoo was an infringement of an animal's rights, and ordered that it be moved to a sanctuary. He was less thrilled when the court found that although the Riachuelo defendants had indeed infringed the plaintiffs' right to a healthy environment, the plaintiffs should nevertheless pay their own whopping legal costs. That finding is being appealed to the Inter-American Commission on Human Rights, which means that Sallaberry and his colleagues remain unpaid, and may never be paid. That's the risk that a lawyer takes in working on a contingency basis.

On the other hand, contingency fees are potentially enormous — which brings us to the lawsuit known throughout South America as the "Chevron Tóxico" case.

The Power of Green Rights: Ecuador

Join me at a pond in Ecuador's Amazon rain forest. I'm standing on a log. The pond is perhaps 20 meters long, 10 meters wide, 4 meters deep. My gloved hands plunge below the surface and come up full of dead plants dripping with thick, shiny black syrup. Crude oil.

A thousand such ponds have been seeping and spilling here for half a century, abandoned by an oil industry that also pumped at least 12 billion gallons of contaminated water into 1700 square miles of the Amazon watershed. The devastation, sometimes called the Amazonian Chernobyl, has spawned the second largest environment lawsuit ever mounted — a suit which may reach its finale, oddly, in the courts of Canada. Chris Beckett and I have taken a six-hour taxi ride over the Andes from Quito to the oil town of Lago Agrio to film the damage before interviewing *Pablo Fajardo*, the young mestizo lawyer who heads the legal team representing Los Afectados, "the affected ones" — 30,000 Aboriginals and farmers.

The basic facts are pretty clear. In 1972, as the operating partner in a consortium with the state oil company PetroEcuador, Texaco began drilling and pumping oil here, pouring its wastes into pits and waterways. The company knew better; it didn't do this back home in Texas. In 1992, Texaco sold its 37.5 percent share to PetroEcuador, and in 1994, it agreed to "remediate" 37.5 percent of the contaminated sites. It spent $40 million on a wholly inadequate partial clean-up, and in 1998 Ecuador's military government released it from further claims.

Texaco took that release to New York, where it had been fighting a class action suit from Los Afectados since 1993. Texaco argued that US courts had no jurisdiction, and with the release, it considered the matter settled. No, said the courts; the settlement ties the government's hands, but not the citizens'. Then, in 2002 a US appeal court agreed with Texaco that the case should indeed be heard in Ecuador, but insisted that Texaco agree in advance to accept the findings of the Ecuadorian courts and pay any penalties imposed. By then, Texaco had been swallowed by Chevron, so in Latin America the case is now known as "Chevron Tóxico."

In 2003, the plaintiffs re-filed the case in Ecuador. Enter Pablo Fajardo — skinny, young, intense, descended from native people who lived by drinking the river waters, eating the river fish, picking fruit. Once the oil industry had "developed" their territory, the only fish they could eat was canned tuna, and the only safe water came in plastic bottles. Fajardo himself grew up desperately poor, beside a filthy stream devoid of fish, where the very rain fell black with oil-industry soot. It was, he says, "a catastrophic landscape."

Fajardo became an oilfield labourer, a night-school student, a human-rights activist, a municipal councillor, an unpaid teacher. But what his people really needed was a lawyer. Aided by the Catholic church, and supported financially by eight friends, he took a six-year law course by correspondence. When he graduated in 2004, he was already on the Chevron Tóxico legal team. In 2005, he took over its direction. It was his very first case, and the effort succeeded. Los Afectados won a judgment of $18 billion, later reduced by Ecuador's Supreme Court to $9.5 billion.

Chevron had already agreed to abide by the Ecuadorian courts' decision, but when it lost, it refused to pay, alleging that the judgment had been obtained by fraud. It had already removed all its assets from Ecuador, so Los Afectados launched collection actions in Argentina, Brazil, and Ontario, Canada. The first Canadian court dismissed the action, ruling that Chevron and Chevron Canada were two different entities. The Ontario Court of Appeal, however, declared that Ontario could and should accept jurisdiction, and in 2015 the Supreme Court of Canada agreed. Chevron's case has now been dismissed by 18 appellate courts in Ecuador and Canada, but the company, incredibly, has filed yet another suit in Ontario denying Canadian jurisdiction. Chevron's strategy, said former general counsel Charles James, is to "fight this case until hell freezes over, and then fight it out on the ice."

They're in the right country for that. But this case has been going on for 23 years, in several countries. How is it possible for impoverished Third World farmers and natives to sustain such an action?

Enter Pablo Fajardo's American colleague, *Steven Donziger*, who was a journalist before attending Harvard Law School, where he played basketball with Barack Obama. He then became a public defender — a legal aid lawyer — and in 1993 he joined the legal team working on the Chevron Tóxico case. In the intervening twenty-odd years, he has raised millions of dollars and enlisted the support of powerful law firms and international financiers. Donziger has financed the suit by selling shares in the eventual settlement, an exponential extension of contingency fee-setting. Clearly, without Donziger's innovations, a crowd of poor people could never have sued the third-largest corporation in the world. *Business Week* summed up his achievement this way: "However the confrontation ends, it will have implications far beyond Latin America because Donziger has rewritten the rules for how to sustain far-flung environmental litigation."

Whole books have been written about Chevron Tóxico, and articles have appeared not only in the international business press, but also in major consumer magazines like *Vanity Fair*. In addition, the case was the subject of a feature documentary, *Crude* (2009), produced and directed by Joe Berlinger. The years go by, and Donziger, Fajardo and Los Afectados soldier on. Chevron Tóxico is no longer just a lawsuit: it is their life's work. Why?

"I live here," says Pablo Fajardo, in his bare little house in Lago Agrio. "This is my home. I could leave, take my children and go somewhere else. But what happens to the rest of the people who live here? What happens to the Indigenous people who have been here all their lives? I try to do my duty to the extent possible by respecting nature, people, life, and so that there is justice. I do what I must. What's at stake for Chevron is its reputation and a lot of money. For us, the stakes are about life."

Mandamus and Its Cousins

Chevron Tóxico is a spectacularly egregious example of a common legal problem: you win your case, and nothing changes. The losing party has no money, declares bankruptcy, moves to another jurisdiction, can't be found. Or he simply thumbs his nose at the court and its decision, which means the winner has to start another action, seeking an enforcement order which may or may not actually yield results.

One solution, which is part of many legal systems, is to seek a "writ of mandamus," a court order commanding a dilatory organization, lower court or individual to fulfill its legal duties and obligations or be penalized for contempt of court. This ought to be a powerful lever for upending "regulatory capture," the situation where an organization that's supposed to regulate an industry becomes instead a cheerleader for that industry. The National Energy Board comes to see itself as an enabler for the oil industry; the food inspectors become allies of the agrifood industry rather than protectors of public health. In these neoliberal times, regulatory capture is commonplace, like a genetic modification of government itself.

In North America, mandamus seems to be an under-utilized tool, but it could be a glorious instrument for the political toolkit of civil society. If the governing statute of the Department of Fisheries and Oceans, for example, requires that the department protect wild fish stocks, then the department has a legal obligation to review and, if need be, to stop anything that would adversely affect those stocks. It cannot legally ignore the erection of power dams, the issuance of far too many fishing licenses, the damage caused by intense unregulated aquaculture, or the release of toxic chemicals into fish habitat. It does, of course, routinely ignore all these things. By failing to challenge this dereliction of duty, we the people connive at both corruption and destruction.

By contrast, in the Riachuelo case, the Supreme Court of Argentina exercised a power of "continuing mandamus" — not simply making a ruling and hoping it would be enforced by some other body, but undertaking to supervise the enforcement itself. The Supreme Court of India also seems particularly enamoured of continuing mandamus, and has invoked it in several of the cases brought before it by the legendary M.C. Mehta.

Other societies have additional tools. Tony Oposa has made shrewd use of a legal instrument unique to the Philippines, the "writ of kalikasan" ("kalikasan" means "nature"), a court order intended to deal swiftly with environmental threats affecting life, health, or property in two or more municipalities or provinces. Many other Third World nations, particularly in Latin America, have developed creative approaches to the problem of access to the judicial system. Brazil and Colombia, for instance, have an independent agency called a Ministerio Publico, to protect public interests such as the environment; citizens can take their concerns to the agency, which in turn can bring a legal action.

Many other nations, including Costa Rica, Chile, Paraguay, Peru and Brazil, have adopted simplified procedures that allow citizens to bring constitutional and human rights issues directly to senior courts. Most use some version of a "writ of amparo" or a writ of protection, a Mexican innovation that provides citizens with a fast, simple, inexpensive route into the legal system. On matters of equal access to the law, North Americans could learn a lot from their Latin neighbours.

Defending the Defenders of Life

The need for mandamus — even continuing mandamus — is a vivid reminder that environmental issues are real-world issues, not merely courtroom exercises. Winning in the courtroom doesn't necessarily mean winning in the field or on the river, and people who take on powerful forces in industry and government often face serious consequences, up to and including death. Tony Oposa at one point had a million-peso price on his head, and in 2006 his closest friend and associate, Jojo de la Victoria, was shot dead in front of his own home.

Pablo Fajardo, too, has lived with death threats for decades. In fact, both Pablo's best friend and his brother have been murdered. The brother may have been killed because he was mistaken for Pablo, or as a warning to Pablo. Nobody knows. *Vanity Fair's* international correspondent William Langewiesche reports that the trial judge in the Chevron Tóxico case had been "ambushed and machine-gunned while driving his car. His companion was killed, but he himself escaped. The attackers were hired killers, of whom Lago Agrio has an ample supply." The police "did not investigate the attack, the judge believes, because they feared retribution." This work is not for the faint of heart.

The threats are not, of course, only directed towards judges and lawyers. As this is written, Honduran Goldman Prize winner Berta Cáceres and her associate Nelson Garcia have both been murdered. Globally, according to the human rights website Global Witness, at least 116 environmental activists were murdered in 2014 and 40 percent of victims were Indigenous. About 75 percent of the deaths were in Central and South America. Honduras is particularly shocking: at least 109 environmental defenders were killed in Honduras between 2010 and 2015. In 2016, Global Witness reported that the situation had worsened. Today, three environmental defenders are killed *every week.*

Dutch lawyer *Femke Wijdekop* has taken a particular interest in defending the green defenders. She identifies two main responses to their persecution. The first is public pressure, organized by groups like Greenpeace and Amnesty International. She says,

> Public opinion, pressure, and naming and shaming can have a real effect on the personal safety of those environmental defenders. When the Dutch Greenpeace crew was arrested in Russia because they boarded an oil tanker, the Arctic 30 they are called, there was a huge campaign to support them and to urge the Russian government to release them. In the end they were released. It was very professionally set up by Greenpeace. But the people who are suffering the most often don't have that organizational capacity, and they are not as well represented. So they need better representation, they need more of our support. I would like that to become bigger. I would like this to become more in the conscience of the people that these people need our solidarity and support.

Meanwhile, she sees a growing recognition at the official and international level that environmental rights are *human* rights, and are entitled to the same protections as other fundamental human rights.

"UN agents like the Special Rapporteur on Human Rights Defenders, the Special Rapporteur on Indigenous Rights, and the Committee for Economic Social and Cultural Rights," she says, increasingly recognize a state duty to protect environmental defenders under international human rights law. "Under the Universal Declaration of Human Rights, and under the International Covenant on Civil Political Rights," she notes, "we have the right of expression, we have the right of assembly, we have the right of association — and environmental defenders exercise those rights on behalf of the environment."

Tony Oposa likes to say that the environment "is not about the birds and the bees and the flowers and the trees. It is about life, and the sources of life: land, air and water. Easy to remember: L, A, W. If we don't have air for three minutes, we die. If we don't have water for three days, we die. If we don't have food for thirty days, we die."

That's what environmental defenders are defending: life, and the continuance of life. That is the fundamental truth that human beings began to grapple with at the Stockholm conference, in 1972. And since then the vast majority of the world's nations have embraced in their legal systems the rights of life — for that is the real meaning of "the right to a healthy environment."

Goosing the Laggards: Routes to Rights Recognition

Who exactly are the laggards? Legal scholar David Boyd says,

> If you add up all of the countries in the world that have recognized the right to a healthy environment, you get 180 out of the 193 members of the United Nations, which is truly extraordinary. It means there are only 13 countries left in the world that have not yet recognized this fundamental human right: Canada, the United States, Australia, New Zealand, China, Japan, Laos, Cambodia, North Korea, Brunei Darussalam, Lebanon, Oman, and Kuwait.

Quite a list. And what do we do in countries where those rights do not exist in the legal system?

As Femke Wijdekop notes, the attacks on environmental defenders don't only offend environmental laws; they offend human rights, which are, in principle, global and inalienable. If there's an inalienable human right to life, wouldn't that naturally include an inalienable human right to the sources of life, as Tony Oposa calls them? Furthermore, if the state has a duty of care to its citizens — a duty almost universally recognized — then the state has an obligation to deal with things that threaten the human rights, the health and the well-being of its citizens. And perhaps that obligation, in itself, is enough to support strong legal action in environmental matters.

In other words, new law often lies hidden in existing legislation; the law can evolve even if the text of the statute doesn't change. As University of New Mexico law professor Cliff Villa says, "There's a wonderful expression in military science: you go to war with the army you have. Around the world people are using the laws that they have to achieve the ends that they desire."

In Canada, for example, David Boyd notes,

> There are three pathways to recognition of the right to a healthy environment. One is through direct amendment of the Constitution, which requires Parliament's approval and the approval of seven of the 10 provincial governments. All of those approvals have to be secured in a three-year

time frame, so it's a politically daunting thing to achieve. But as Nelson Mandela said, things always seem impossible until they're done.

Boyd particularly likes this route because it involves the whole country in a discussion of national culture and values, which would give real democratic legitimacy to the new constitutional provisions.

The second pathway is a "judicial reference," which "basically allows governments to ask the courts hypothetical legal questions." The process has been used more than 100 times. The most famous was the "Persons case" in 1927, when five women, including the iconic Nellie McClung, petitioned the government for a declaration that women were "persons" within the meaning of the British North America Act, which would make them eligible for appointment to the Senate. The federal government referred the question to the Supreme Court of Canada — which, incredibly, said No. In those imperial days, however, Canadian Supreme Court decisions could be further appealed to the Privy Council in London, which metaphorically chuckled and said, "Oh, come on. Of course they are." As Boyd says, it was a transformative judgment for Canadian women.

More recently, Jean Chrétien made a judicial reference to the Supreme Court regarding the question of whether Québec could legally secede from Canada, and if so under what conditions. The Court's decision led to the Clarity Act, which laid out the process that Québec and Canada would have to follow.

The third pathway to constitutional change is the one Cliff Villa suggests, namely, going to war with the army you have by eliciting an appropriate provision from the existing laws. That's the route pursued by the Aamjiwnaang First Nation, located in Sarnia, in the heart of Ontario's notorious "Chemical Valley," which pumps out more air pollution than some entire provinces. Breathing the worst air in Canada, Aamjiwnaang's people suffer from really alarming health problems, including high levels of leukemia, Hodgkin's disease, asthma and miscarried pregnancies. In addition, far more girls than boys are born in Aamjiwnaang.

In 2010 two band members filed a trailblazing lawsuit arguing that their Charter rights to life, liberty and security of the person were being violated by the Ontario government's approval of the expansion of these toxic industries. In essence, *Ron Plain* and *Ada Lockridge* claimed that the right to life, which is guaranteed in Section 7 of Canada's Charter of Rights, logically includes the right to breathe. If that is so, then Canadians already do have environmental rights.

It will take a Supreme Court ruling to confirm that interpretation, but Aamjiwnaang had a powerful case. In 2016, however, a new provincial minister announced regulatory changes that would give Aamjiwnaang much of what it needed: better warnings and fuller information, and consideration in provincial decisions of the cumulative effects of all the pollution affecting the community. So the parties agreed to end the long-running litigation. Good news for Aamjiwnaang, but it meant the Charter issue was never adjudicated.

Goosing the Laggards: The Power of the Powerless

Aboriginal communities in Grassy Narrows, Ontario, and Invermere, BC, are bringing similar actions. But perhaps the most promising actions are taking shape in New Brunswick. In 2013, around Elsipogtog, NB, an apparently irresistible force met a genuinely immovable object. The force was the combined will of industry, government and the police. The immovable object was a defiant alliance of Aboriginals, Acadians and English-speaking citizens. The issue was hydraulic fracturing, or "fracking" — drilling wells into shale far below the surface, and then injecting a high-pressure cocktail of water, sand, diesel oil and various unspecified chemicals. The fluid shatters the shale and releases little pockets of gas and oil encapsulated in the rock. As a result, however, methane can escape, the fluid can pollute the groundwater, and intense fracking can trigger earthquakes.

The provincial government of David Alward had granted a lease allowing SWN Resources Canada — a subsidiary of a Texas oil company — to frack as much as 2.5 million acres for natural gas. The anti-fracking alliance tried all the usual avenues of democratic dissent — protests, delegations, publicity and so forth. When none of that worked, they moved to civil disobedience. They simply went out on the roads and sat down in front of the "thumper trucks" that were doing the seismic testing. The company called the cops, who arrived in large numbers, wearing riot gear.

Denise Melanson, a slight, feisty Acadian says, "The first time we saw this phalanx of cops arrive, we started to laugh because it was little old ladies like me, because who else is out in the middle of the day? Most people work. So when we saw this mass of officers, we thought: these people have lost their minds!"

She vividly remembers her shock at what happened on Aboriginal Day, June 21: "That day they decided they were only arresting First Nations people, and they literally dragged white people off the road, so they wouldn't have to arrest them," she recalls. "When that happened I thought, my gosh, the laws of Canada don't apply here."

As the summer went on, the fight intensified. Supported by the RCMP and the Alward government, SWN pushed forward with its testing — and the community pushed back. In late June, a SWN drilling truck went up in flames. At the end of July a convoy of thumper trucks emerging from the woods was ambushed and blocked by protesters. The united front of Natives, Acadians and anglophones faced down the police, went to jail, dove in front of trucks. They had one clear message: You will frack in New Brunswick — literally — *over our dead bodies.*

The crisis arrived on October 17 when hundreds of Mounties surrounded a sleeping encampment of protesters who were blocking a convoy of SWN trucks. The Mounties had dogs, snipers, aircraft and riot gear. Their guns were drawn. When the smoke cleared — literally — the trucks were gone, the jails were full, and four police cruisers were on fire.

And then the people won. New protesters arrived from across the country. When SWN tried to continue seismic testing, its equipment was smashed and burned. Eventually, the company gave up and left. The Alward government was trounced in the ensuing election, which also produced eastern Canada's first Green Party MLA, David Coon. Brian Gallant's new Liberal government announced a moratorium, with five requirements for any resumption of fracking, including a "social license" and proper consultations with First Nations.

All very well, but if the government had given, the government could also take away. So the people went to court in search of a permanent solution. Their advocate in two adventurous lawsuits is Saskatchewan environmental and human rights lawyer *Larry Kowalchuk*. The first suit, launched by the New Brunswick Anti Shale Gas Alliance, contends that the scientific evidence shows that fracking is so dangerous that it violates the Charter right of New Brunswickers to life, liberty and security of the person. NBASGA wants fracking banned completely and permanently.

A second suit, known as the People's Lawsuit, is largely driven by Aboriginal plaintiffs, and names SWN as well as the provincial and federal governments. It alleges that the company and the two governments have attacked their rights to freedom of speech and assembly, and have used police and malicious lawsuits to suppress and silence them. More importantly, it also contends that the governments have unlawfully permitted SWN to develop shale gas and ignore environmental protection laws. Unlawfully? Well, yes. The whole episode took place on unceded territory, over which the provincial government had no authority.

"The lawsuit says, based on the fact that this land was never ceded — I mean, there was a peace-and-friendship treaty, but that was to work in harmony with each other; it didn't surrender any land or rights to the Crown," says Larry Kowalchuk. "And because of that you can't come into this territory and do things without our consent. You're supposed to live sustainably with each other — the land, the animals, the water, the air — in a way that's respectful."

Like the abandoned Aamjiwnaang legal action, these two suits contain the seeds of fundamental legal changes that would apply to the whole country. If they succeed, all Canadians will have some version of environmental rights.

Goosing the Laggards: Urgenda in The Netherlands

Similar suits have succeeded elsewhere. In the Netherlands, a lawyer named *Roger Cox* had watched the progress of the international climate change talks with rising concern. In 2009, he observed with dismay the failure of the Copenhagen conference known as COP 15, the fifteenth annual "Conference of the Parties" to the UN Framework Convention on Climate Change. The next year, at COP 16, in Cancún, Mexico, the nations of the world reaffirmed their understanding that climate change directly threatens the human rights of all people and all societies. But the repeated failures to reach an effective accord on the matter showed clearly that political processes simply weren't capable of coping with the looming climate catastrophe. Climate is a long-term problem, and governments have short-term horizons, as do the corporations which have largely captured the world's governments.

"I thought, let's see if there is a way that we can use the law in pressuring governments into more climate action," says Cox, "because you will need nation states to take a coordinated and leading role in transforming our energy systems and transforming society. I think without them and without their lead and coordination, such a transformation is almost impossible."

He published a book on the subject in 2011 entitled *Revolution Justified: Why Only the Law Can Save Us Now*. The book caught the attention of *Marjan Minnesma*, director of the entrepreneurial Dutch organization called the Urgenda Foundation. The two conferred, and Urgenda developed a base of support; this is where Marjan created "crowd-pleading." In 2012, with a legal team led by Cox, Urgenda sued the government of the Netherlands, looking for a ruling that the government's duty of care towards its citizens required emissions cuts far more dramatic than the government was planning. Climate change, Cox argued, was fundamentally a human rights issue.

"If that duty of care is not complied with by nation states, the effect of climate change within every region of the world is so drastic that the consequences will indeed be the infringement of basic human rights such as the right to life, the right to water, the right to an undisturbed private life, etcetera," Cox explains. And all the 195 countries signatory to the UN climate convention — including the Netherlands — had already acknowledged this in Cancún.

"Maybe one of the best reasons to go to court is to get rid of this silly media discussion around climate change and climate science," Cox smiles. "I already said in my book that the climate science is clear and courts are the best organizations that we have in society to look at evidence. That's what courts do: they look at evidence. So I always said, let's bring the climate science to court because in the courts the climate science will be accepted as it is. The certainties around climate change are at a very, very high level. And indeed there was no room for our state to deny the climate science."

At Cancún the nations had agreed on the need to reduce carbon emissions by 25 percent to 40 percent from 1990 levels by 2020. Denmark and Germany had set 40 percent targets and were well on the way to achieving them, which showed that such reductions were possible. But the Dutch government was only expecting to achieve 16 percent, maybe not even that much. It argued that the Netherlands' share of the problem was so small as to be insignificant. It also argued that the matter was a political question, and not within the purview of the courts.

The court disagreed. In June 2015 it ruled that the government had to reduce emissions by at least 25 percent. Urgenda had posted its documents and arguments on the web in English as well as Dutch — and the judge also handed down his ruling in both languages. Marjan Minnesma had called the suit "a court case out of love," filed on behalf of future generations. When Urgenda won, it turned out to be a court case full of hope as well.

"When we won," she said, "within half an hour it was all over the world. I was really surprised how quickly news travels in this case and that we received thousands of phone calls, emails, letters from people that said, 'Oh, I really thought that we would never get the change, but now I have hope that it will happen. I will go on now.' It gave people hope to continue because they thought finally there's a judge that sees that this is a real big problem, and if there is one judge there might be more."

Since then a farmer in Pakistan and a group of young people in Washington state have successfully sued their governments for failing to act on climate change. Similar suits are before the courts in Oregon, Belgium and Norway, and before the federal courts in the United States.

The Urgenda victory was truly an historic event — based, once again, on new law hiding in familiar legislation. But there is something slightly unsatisfying about teasing out law from unexpected crannies as opposed to making a deliberate and bold decision as a community to institute essential changes. David Boyd is not alone in preferring an open and widely supported approach to constitutional change; such a process would involve the whole community in a discussion of values, and would generate widespread understanding not only of the legal change, but of the reasons for it, and of the cultural shift the change would signify.

Goosing the Laggards: Fertilizing the Grassroots

In recent years, however, senior governments in both the United States and Canada have shown remarkably little enthusiasm for such adventures. In Canada, the late unlamented regime of Stephen Harper was openly at war with environmental organizations and perspectives. In the US, non-profit environmental attorneys Monique Harden and Nathalie Walker filed a suit charging that the citizens of the African-American community Mossville, LA, located in the heart of Louisiana's "Chemical Alley," had a right to a healthy environment and to a decent quality of life, but that those rights were being systematically violated by this concentration of heavy industry. This was the first American case ever to be accepted by the Inter American Commission on Human Rights. The suit demanded fundamental change to the U.S. environmental regulatory system. In response, the US government took the spectacularly disheartening position that there is no such thing as a right to a healthy environment, and alternatively, if there *is* such a right, it doesn't apply to Americans. So there.

Mossville is a classic example of environmental racism, a vivid reminder that although white Americans and Canadians may not have much in the way of environmental rights, our Black and Native brothers and sisters have even less. In Nova Scotia, Dr Ingrid Waldron of Dalhousie University has overseen the creation of a provincial map showing the locations of garbage dumps, toxic waste sites and similar facilities, and also showing the locations of black and native communities. Unsurprisingly, dumps and communities of colour commonly occur together — all over the province, and indeed, all over the continent.

The lack of enthusiasm of North America's senior governments doesn't mean that nothing is being done. Edmonton MP Linda Duncan introduced an Environmental Bill of Rights in Parliament in 2014 as a private member's bill. That same year, Canada's iconic environmentalist *David Suzuki* launched his "Blue Dot movement," organizing citizens to demand that their municipal governments pass aspirational declarations asserting the environmental rights of citizens. Once the movement had achieved enough momentum, Suzuki planned to move his focus to provincial governments and ultimately to the federal government, thus securing not only environmental rights legislation, but also an educated and committed body of supporters. Less than two years later, 133 municipalities and nearly 100,000 citizens had affirmed their support for Blue Dot declarations. Years earlier, the provinces of Ontario and Quebec had recognized the environmental rights of their citizens, and in 2015, stimulated by the Blue Dot initiative, the Province of Manitoba introduced an environmental bill of rights. With the defeat of Manitoba's NDP government, however, the measure died. Similar bills have been introduced in BC and Nova Scotia, but their fate remains to be determined.

In addition, smaller groups were insisting on their own environmental rights. In New Brunswick, a unique alliance of parents, educators, health workers and civil servants was pressing their provincial government to adopt a Bill of Rights to Protect Children's Health from Environmental Hazards. Why just for children? Public health consultant Bonnie Hamilton-Bogart, one of the leaders of the alliance, smiles when that question arises.

"Well, it's not only children," she says. "When we do it for the children, we wind up creating a world that is fit for everyone." But the children are the most vulnerable. The bill, she says, "is essentially based on the notion of child-honouring, because that is a kind of an ethic that combines the ethic of respecting the child's development with the ethic of respecting the Earth."

And Inverness County, Nova Scotia, population 19,000, has boldly embedded environmental rights in its own bylaws. The process started in 2010, when Petroworth Resources proposed to drill for oil near Lake Ainslie, the largest freshwater lake in the province. But whatever oil and gas lies beneath Lake Ainslie can only be recovered by fracking.

The local chapter of the Council of Canadians allied themselves with the nearby Waycobah First Nation and the two groups waged a very effective campaign against the proposal. By February 2011, the opposition was strong enough for the Council of Canadians' Coralie Cameron to ask the Inverness county council to pass a resolution calling for a ban on fracking in Nova Scotia. The council did so, and Petroworth's partners withdrew, discouraged particularly by the opposition from Waycobah.

The anti-fracking alliance went on to propose an actual by-law banning fracking in the county. The council agreed that if the alliance drafted a bylaw, the council would consider it. So the citizens probed and researched, and eventually drafted a unique bylaw carefully rooted in the Supreme Court's rulings on the Charter of Rights and the "precautionary principle," the principle that if an action can be reliably foreseen to do serious harm, the action should not take place. The provincial government wasn't happy about the bylaw, but it tidily bypassed the province's jurisdiction.

"The province has jurisdiction over land use," explains Joanna Padelt of the Council of Canadians, "but they don't have jurisdiction over human rights issues." In addition, "the precautionary principle holds that if something can be foreseen to do harm, then one has a right to be protected from that. And so that put the whole bylaw on a different kind of legal ground."

In May 2013, the Inverness county council passed Bylaw #45, forbidding fracking within its jurisdiction as a matter of human rights, notably "a fundamental right to pure water." Two months later, Petroworth's drilling lease expired, and Petroworth was essentially bankrupt. County councillor Jim Mustard points out that even a small municipality has one huge resource which governments are rarely willing to use, namely the skill, energy and dedication of its own citizens.

"We don't have the expertise with our six municipal staff and our elected officials," says Mustard, "but we can *convene* the expertise, and in bringing that together, you don't think we can have better conversations? I do think."

In the United States, that same municipal activism is vigorously supported by our old friends, the Community Environmental Legal Defense Fund. CELDF organizes, educates and nurtures local groups of ordinary citizens who have discovered, to their shock and horror, that their democratic communities are the playthings of corporations, which have rights that mere citizens don't have. CELDF has assisted more than 110 local governments, not to mention the governments of Nepal, India and Ecuador. Originally, CELDF helped local communities to resist the incursions of factory farms, fracking, sludge dumping, toxic incinerators and so forth. Probing more deeply, they discovered that under US law, communities actually don't have the right to refuse such "developments." To begin with, municipalities are forbidden to adopt legislation that conflicts with state or provincial laws, and those laws are designed to facilitate commerce and industry. The system, says *Thomas Linzey*, CELDF's visionary founder, actually makes sustainability — and democracy — illegal.

"If you can't stop fracking, you can't say 'yes' to a sustainable energy future," Linzey says, "because if you can't stop the bad things from coming in, then you can't define the future of your community. The system has nothing to do with environmental protection. It has to do with something different, which is about legalizing harm. That's what the permit system is about."

Even the best regulatory regime, says Linzey's colleague *Mari Margil*, "still leads to ecosystem destruction. It may delay it a little bit, but it still means we're getting fracked, and we're getting factory farmed and so on. Communities are beginning to see the reframing that we don't just have a fracking problem, or a factory farm problem, we have a democracy problem."

When CELDF is invited into a community, its first priority is an intense educational initiative called a "Democracy School." Community members look at previous movements that enlarged or defended democracy and human rights, such as the abolition of slavery, the suffragette movement, the civil rights movement, the labour movement. All these movements grew from the grassroots. If the community chooses to take further action, CELDF helps them to draft a local "Community Bill of Rights." The bill can take many different forms, but its core is the assertion of the right of the community to govern itself democratically, and to strip corporations of the power to deny the rights of citizens within their own communities.

The Community Bill of Rights is all part of a larger plan, which is to put the environmental movement on the offensive, actively working for a green and democratic future.

"We need a plan," says Linzey, "And the plan is a grassroots revolt that redefines communities as not just the people who live there but also the nature and ecosystems within those communities, and then builds a structure of law that actually elevates those rights above the rights of corporations and commerce. It's pretty simple when you lay it out on paper. It's just that most people believe they live in a system that they don't live in. They believe that some of those things are already there. Our job over the past 10 years has been to prove that they're not there. That system of law doesn't exist. It has to be created."

As in Canada, local communities in the US are now coming together in statewide organizations, and considering national organizations. Their intention is to replace a corporate oligarchy with a genuine, profound democracy — which is why the recent documentary about CELDF and its work is entitled, "We the People 2.0: The Second American Revolution."

Above the Nations: The Rights of Pachamama

Suppose every single nation on Earth did recognize environmental rights. How would we deal with the fact that environmental issues pay no heed to national boundaries? Airborne pollution flowing eastward on the jet stream from the pulp mills and generating plants of Nova Scotia contributes to lung disease in Cornwall, Kazakhstan and California. What redress do the downstream victims have? How do we deal with problems whose sources are entirely within national boundaries — the burning forests in Indonesia, the Canadian tar sands, coal-fired power generation in China — but whose effects are global? Or with environmental crimes committed in international spaces, like bilge flushing by ships in the open sea, or Japanese whaling in the ostensible sanctuary of the Southern Ocean?

Offences like those aren't only offences against other human beings; they're offences against Nature herself, which brings us to the deepest level of the environmental-rights movement. Is it only humans that have rights? Some nations, notably Ecuador and Bolivia, recognize the legal rights not just of their citizens, but also of Mother Nature in all her manifestations. To the Indigenous people of the Andes, Mother Nature is known as "Pachamama" — a rich and profound concept of the living world as the Earth/time Mother, the cosmos, the giver and sustainer of life, the creative force that drives the universe. And although the name "Pachamama" comes from the Andes, its understanding of the natural world as the fundamental, sacred reality is shared by Indigenous people everywhere. In recent years, a broader movement to recognize the inherent rights of Pachamama has spread internationally. In early 2014, my colleague Chris Beckett and I attended and filmed a conference of the Global Alliance for the Rights of Nature in Otavalo, Ecuador. The meeting was inspiring, a gathering of brilliant and dedicated devotees of Pachamama from a dozen countries or more. The Alliance itself had emerged from the 2010 World People's Conference on Climate Change organized in response to the failure of Copenhagen. That conference, held in Bolivia, also produced the eloquent and beautiful *Universal Declaration of the Rights of Mother Earth*. The declaration isn't a legally binding document, but that doesn't mean it isn't important, says *Cormac Cullinan*, author of the seminal book *Wild Law*, and co-author of the Declaration itself.

"If one looks at an analogous document — *the Universal Declaration of Human Rights* — that also wasn't a legally binding document, but it shifted the norms of acceptable behaviour in society in a way that's been quite extraordinary and it's now completely accepted," he says. "If a government is criticized or an organization is criticized on the basis that they're violating human rights it really means something in the world."

Cullinan feels very lucky to have been a South African during the struggle against apartheid, because he has seen a peaceful revolution, and taken part in it. One of the most powerful tools of the anti-apartheid movement was a document of dreams called the "Freedom Charter," generated directly by the people. Cullinan remembers,

> People got together and said we need a vision, a positive vision that we can work towards, of a society that isn't like this. They went around and they gathered submissions all over the country. It ended up in a conference in Kliptown which adopted the Freedom Charter, an aspirational document describing the society — the dream — that we aspire to. They had to take statements like, 'the doors of learning and culture shall be open' and 'people shall have peace and security in their homes,' and 'it is a non-racial society of justice,' etcetera.
>
> That vision was an articulation of the voice of the people that were suppressed by the official system. It became an inspirational vision which roused and guided all kinds of actions — protests for equal education, for example. You would see people holding up banners saying 'The doors of learning and culture shall be open.' And that was one of the visions that took us into the new South Africa. That was a document that had no legal status. The government tried to suppress it as much as possible. But because it was authentic, because it had a legitimacy coming from

the people, because it was an expression of their dream, it was extraordinarily influential.

Could the same thing happen with the Universal Declaration of the Rights of Pachamama? For Cullinan, that evolution has already started: change begins in our conversations about it. "The mere fact of having the conversation is incredibly subversive to the existing system," he explains. "As soon as people start talking about a different future, the old starts being whittled away. It's partially getting people to think in a new way and to imagine a new future. But if you can pull it together into a cohesive vision that is shared by many people, it sets in motion a chain of actions that's like a strange attraction towards a vortex. The dream pulls the action towards us."

The Otavalo conference ended by convening the first-ever International Tribunal for the Rights of Nature, which heard nine charges of alleged violations of the Universal Declaration. The cases included climate change, the Chevron Tóxico case, open pit mining, the Deepwater Horizon oil spill, genetically modified organisms, and hydraulic fracturing. That first tribunal was chaired by *Vandana Shiva*, and included judges from seven nations; Cormac Cullinan was one of them. It was followed by a second sitting of the tribunal in Lima and a third at the Paris climate talks in 2015.

The tribunal is the world's first draft of an international court for the environment. It can't make binding rulings; its only authority is moral and ethical. Like the Universal Declaration of the Rights of Nature, it's an expression of responsible citizenship at a global level. But, as Cullinan would remind us, it's an acorn. That's how oak trees begin.

For now, the Universal Declaration remains a persuasive moral declaration that can in time give rise to a body of law. It's a political document, a multi-national manifesto. Its authority will grow as its support grows. Growing that support is the mission of *Mumta Ito*, formerly a corporate lawyer in the City of London, who founded the International Centre for Wholistic Law in Scotland. She is now engaged in a European Citizens' Initiative designed to embed the rights of Pachamama in the legal system of the European Union. This modest little task starts by obtaining a million signatures across at least seven member states. If she and her colleagues can do that, then the European Commission has to consider adopting the law that the citizens are calling for.

In the meantime, another British lawyer is lobbying for a super-law that would make "ecocide" a new UN-recognized crime against peace, ranking equally with crimes against humanity, war crimes and genocide. *Polly Higgins* is the award-winning author of *Eradicating Ecocide* and other works. She has been variously described as "the lawyer for the Earth" and — by an American magazine — as "one of the top ten most unreasonable people in the world." This delights her because "if you remain reasonable you remain complicit in an existing system that is causing harm."

Ecocide, she explains, is damage, destruction or loss of ecosystems such that the peaceful enjoyment of a territory by the inhabitants is severely diminished or lost. That means all the inhabitants, not just the human ones. Examples of ecocide could include deforestation, the destruction of world-scale fish stocks like the Atlantic cod, and large-scale nuclear accidents. Higgins proposed such a law to the UN in 2010, arguing that ecocide is not only a crime against peace but also a crime against humanity, against Nature and against future generations. An international ecocide law would trump national laws that give the highest priority to profit; it would substitute — globally — an overriding duty of care for people and the planet. Will international corporations accept such limitations?

"In one way, it's a limitation," Higgins explains, "but in another way it's an enabler, because if you really want to go beyond petroleum today, it's almost impossible. You're stuck in a legal framework that says that you have to put the interests of the shareholders first, which is to maximize profit. So of course it becomes a huge hindrance that you have to deal with environmental issues that fundamentally undermine your profit margins. But if you start with an overriding legal duty of care that puts the health and well-being of people and planet first, then it frees you up to make fundamentally different decisions at the boardroom level."

Buen Vivir: What's the Country You Dream of?

The western understanding of law is intimately interwoven with concepts of control, conflict, prevention and penalties. The environmental movement, because it has been so preoccupied with revealing and resisting harm, has developed a similar preoccupation with prohibition, retrenchment, restriction. Nobody is inspired by visions like that. As some wise wag once remarked, the civil rights movement would have slumped like a deflated balloon if Martin Luther King had cried, "I have a nightmare today!"

So, when we go beyond prohibition and restriction, when we try to imagine a future that is free, flowing, regenerative and fun, what is our green dream? In Montecristi, Ecuador, in 2008, a constituent assembly debated that very question. The group was charged with creating a new constitution for the country. Its chairman was a remarkable economist named *Alberto Acosta*, formerly the country's minister of energy and later a candidate for its presidency. One of his closest associates was a remarkable young woman named *Natalia Greene*.

The question put before the assembly, says Greene, was "What's the country you dream of?" And the answer was "A country where life was respected in all its forms, where people were respected in all their forms." Before long, the assembly was debating the very foundations of national life, the character of Ecuador's economic and social relationships, and deciding "we needed a different model of development away from a socialist model or a capitalist model. A model based on Ecuador. And that model is what we call well-being or *buen vivir*, or good living, or *'sumak kawsay'* in Quechua."

Sumak kawsay is deeply rooted in Indigenous Andean culture, and it was ultimately incorporated into the Montecristi constitution, which became the first constitution on earth to incorporate the rights of Pachamama. "We hereby decide to build a new form of public coexistence," says the document, "in diversity and in harmony with nature, to achieve the good way of living." The good way of life — "*buen vivir*" in Spanish — elevates human development above economic development, focusing on fundamental values, spirituality, ethics and an ever more complex and harmonious connection with Pachamama. Harmony lies at the heart of *buen vivir*.

As Alberto Acosta says,

> We have to move towards a world that is much more in harmony with nature. First, human beings must be in harmony with themselves. Humans must be in harmony with other people, with individuals and communities, and all must live in harmony with nature. We also have to understand that there is another type of economy. The extractivist capitalist economy is a necro-economy, an economy of death. We have to understand that there is an economy of life, a living economy, and this is what we should work toward.

The 2010 conference that gave birth to the Universal Declaration of the Rights of Pachamama was convened by *Pablo Solón*, a long-time social and environmental activist who served as Bolivia's Ambassador to the United Nations after the election of the Evo Morales government in 2006.

"The principle of *buen vivir* is you don't want to be better than the other," he explains. "You just want to live well, have enough, enough to solve problems of health, of education, of food, but not try to accumulate and have more and more because if you try to have more and more, you are going to exploit your neighbour and exploit nature."

Yes, exactly. Exploitation is precisely what they do teach you at the Harvard Business School.

One fascinating result of the philosophy of *buen vivir* is the decision of both

Ecuador and Bolivia to call themselves *"plurinational statesó"* — "plurinational states" — that respect human diversity as well as biodiversity. As Pablo Solón explains,

> Bolivia is home to many different Indigenous nations: Aymaras, Quechuas, Guaranis, Mojenos, and they wanted to be recognized as nations. So when the Constitution was being written, many said, "Oh, no, if you recognize these as nations that means you're going to split the country into tiny states." The Constitution was a challenge because the agreement was, no, this is going to be a 'plurinational state' — one state that recognizes different nations. And Bolivia has not split in different Indigenous nations, not at all, and they can all live together. I think it's very important for other countries where there are different nationalities or Indigenous groups. It's very good to recognize those different identities, cultures, and at the same time bring them together.

Canada, America — are you listening?

For a society organized on the principles of *buen vivir*, the law itself should become not a device for control, but an instrument to promote harmony. What Cormac Cullinan describes as "wildness" seems to yield a concept of law completely consonant with *buen vivir*. Wildness, for Cullinan, is "the juice that drives the universe."

> Wild law sounds strange, it sounds paradoxical, because our current conceptions of law reflect a controlling mindset. But imagine if we had a legal system with laws that facilitated the flow of the fundamental juices, the creative juices that run the universe. If we had a legal system specifically designed to enable us to participate and to contribute to the health and integrity of the whole. If our technologies were driven not just by the desire for profit, but the desire to contribute to the beauty, integrity, and health of the whole community, not just the human community. Wouldn't that be incredible?

What is that country that you dream of? What is that shimmering future that you long for?

All of which returns us to John Borrows, and to a fresh understanding of reality. If authority, and thus land title, for instance, derives from human sources like the Crown, as British law assumes, then the land and all the rest of the natural world becomes property. But if authority derives from Pachamama, the creative, organizing force in the universe, then humans are one with all the rest of creation, and the idea of owning land literally makes no sense. When presented with a treaty to sign, and told that his people would receive land, the great Cree leader Big Bear replied in bewilderment, "How can a man receive land? From whom would he receive it?"

Our inquiry thus takes us into fascinating and powerful alternative perspectives on matters like law, spirit, wildness and place. If Pachamama has rights, we cannot own her. We belong within the natural world, not above it. We are back to *buen vivir*, which, as John Borrows reveals, is part of the Anishinaabek legal tradition — and is therefore already embedded in the Canadian legal system.

"There's a concept in Anishinaabemowin called *Mino-bimaadiziwin*," he says, "which is an aspiration to live well in the world. And that is a *legal* principle."

Buen vivir. Completely at home on the shores of Georgian Bay.

Memo to My Callow Self

I want to say, in the end, how much I admire the people I've been privileged to meet through this project, how they infuse me with hope and happiness. Towards the end of our journey, Chris Beckett and I realized that we were documenting and experiencing the blossoming of a global citizenship. My primary community is located where I live, on an island off the coast of Cape Breton Island, and my broader communities are in Nova Scotia and Canada. But beyond that I have another community, a far-flung community of mind and heart and spirit, and it is exemplified by the people in this book.

So I would now say to my callow self, law could be a compelling, totally-fulfilling career choice, but you must shape yourself to make it so. Nurture your warrior nature, and choose your mentors with wisdom. But they are out there. I've now introduced you to a few of them, but there are many, many more. Think how marvellous it would be to study with these people, to article with them, to work as a colleague with them, to practice with them. Think how you could use the tools you'll acquire from them. Becoming a warrior lawyer would merge *buen vivir* with a professional career. What could be better than that?

What is that country that you dream of, that world you long to inhabit? Get out there, young Donald, and join with those who are creating it. That journey in itself will be *buen vivir*.

Meet the Warriors
The Interviews

The interviews are presented in chronological order, starting with David Boyd in 2012, and ending with a group of interviews conducted in France and the Netherlands in November 2015. The month of each interview is recorded at the top of the interview. The sequence and timing are sometimes important — for example, when someone talks about "the current government of Canada" or "the climate meetings in Paris next week."

Note: In the interests of clarity and brevity, I have edited these interview texts slightly from the versions on The Green Interview website. The changes have been approved by the interviewees.

DAVID BOYD
Your Right to a Healthy Environment
Recorded November 2012

In November 2012, David Boyd gave a lecture at the Dalhousie University law school in Nova Scotia that changed my life. I had never heard of such a thing as a human right to a healthy environment, but he reported that most countries in the world acknowledge such a right, and he thought Canada should too. That was the beginning of the GreenRights project of which this book is a part.

A leading environmental lawyer and legal scholar based in British Columbia, Dr Boyd had published two books on the subject in 2012. The first, *The Environmental Rights Revolution*, is a survey of the worldwide trend to entrench such rights in the legal system — often by including them in the national constitution. As the book demonstrated, the vast majority of nations now have environmental rights embedded in their legal systems.

Most common law countries, however, including Canada, have legal systems based on their British heritage, and they don't recognize these rights at all. So David Boyd's second book in 2012 was *The Right to a Healthy Environment: Revitalizing Canada's Constitution*. And that's where our conversation began.

David, why should the right to a healthy environment be a constitutional right?
A constitutional right means that it's the highest or supreme law of the land. It enjoys the highest level of legal protection possible in these legal systems. And it's also something deeper and more profound. It's a reflection of society's most cherished and deeply held values, so it reflects a real emergence of environmental consciousness over the past four decades.

A healthy environment is a core value, isn't it? Human beings can't get along without it. But it's been so overlooked.
Well, it's been a core concept in many Indigenous legal systems for millennia. Whether it's the Haida on Canada's west coast or the Mi'kmaq on Canada's east coast, environmental rights and responsibilities are a cornerstone of traditional Indigenous legal systems. But in the western world, it's a concept that really only

came to light 50 years ago when Rachel Carson wrote *Silent Spring* and talked about everyone's right to live in an environment free from chemical poisons.

Is there anything in common between those countries that have entrenched environmental rights?
Not really, no. They're found all around the world — in the North, in the South, in wealthy countries, in poor countries, in Christian countries, in Muslim countries. It's really not limited to a geographic or political culture. It's permeated the entire globe.

But there are common features among those countries that do not have entrenched constitutional rights, right?
Yeah, it's very interesting. The countries that are lagging behind are predominantly former British colonies, including the United Kingdom itself, which doesn't have a written constitution — so former British colonies who have a similar common law legal system — and then also about 25 small island states around the world. The irony there is that small island states are really at the forefront of the global movement to recognize the right to a healthy environment, and yet they don't recognize that right in their own constitutions. So that's something that I'm beginning to work [on] with people from the Alliance of Small Island States to move them forward both legally and morally in their efforts.

Why would they not have that?
Simply because they have constitutions that were brought in decades ago and they face often what they perceive to be more important economic, social and political crises that they're grappling with on a day-to-day basis. And for many of those small developing countries, the notion of constitutional reform seems like something of an abstraction compared to the day-to-day challenges that they face.

But in practice it doesn't seem to be an abstraction at all. It makes a real difference.
Very much so. The research I've done on 100 countries around the world whose constitutions explicitly mention the right to a healthy environment demonstrates that it has a transformative effect on their environmental laws and policies. It has a pervasive effect on the court systems in those countries in that people can go to court and actually enforce their right to a healthy environment when it's being violated. Most importantly, there's a clear correlation between environmental provisions in a national constitution and superior environmental performance. At the end of the day, that's what we're trying to achieve: cleaner air, universal access to safe drinking water, a nontoxic environment, and healthier ecosystems.

Tell me how this actually plays out in practice — in the Mendoza case in Argentina, for example.

One of the most compelling examples of how the constitutional right to a healthy environment can make a tangible difference in people's lives comes from Argentina. Argentina amended its Constitution in 1993 to include the right to a healthy environment.

There's a woman who's become a national heroine in Argentina by the name of Beatriz Mendoza, who moved to a very poor and polluted neighbourhood of Buenos Aires, the Argentine capital, about a decade ago. Within a couple of years of moving there, Beatriz Mendoza began to experience some serious health problems, so she actually went to visit her doctor and found through a series of tests that her blood contained extremely elevated levels of a chemical called "toluene," which is a by-product of petroleum refining. Of course, the area in which she was living is home to a number of petroleum refineries, other petrochemical facilities, and a lot of heavy industry. Toluene is a chemical that affects the central nervous system. It's a highly toxic substance.

Beatriz Mendoza, to her credit, didn't take this news sitting down. She gathered a group of neighbours together. They hired a lawyer, and they filed a lawsuit against the federal government, the provincial government, and the municipal government as well as 44 large corporations, arguing that the pollution in the Riachuelo watershed violated their constitutional right to live in a healthy environment. That lawsuit wound its way through the Argentine court system, and in 2008, the Supreme Court of Argentina, the highest court in the country, issued a sweeping and poetic judgment in which it imposed a whole list of obligations on the government to carry out specific activities on a very fixed and urgent timeline. For example, they ordered the government to create drinking water treatment plants, to build sewage treatment plants, to clean up the river and restore the riverbanks, to provide social housing for people who were living in riverside shanties, and to create a management plan for the entire watershed that would result in regular inspections of every business that was creating air or water pollution. Four years later, the progress in implementing that court order is nothing short of extraordinary. The government of Argentina, in collaboration with the provincial and municipal governments, set up a new watershed management agency to oversee implementation of the court's order, and they are spending over $1 billion a year in terms of building the infrastructure that the court ordered them to construct.

For example, they've built three new water treatment plants, which are serving millions of citizens. They've built or upgraded 11 sewage treatment plants, again, serving millions of citizens. They've created 139 monitoring stations to measure air quality, water quality, soil contamination. They've closed down and cleaned up 169 illegal landfills. They've hired 250 environmental inspectors to look at all the businesses and make sure that they're in compliance with the law. And just to put that number of 250 environmental enforcement officials in context, that's more than Environment Canada has for the entire country of Canada. They've also closed down completely 484 different businesses that were polluting the Riachuelo River, and they've planted thousands of trees along the banks of the river and created public parks.

One of the most touching parts of it is that the families who were formerly living in literally tin and cardboard shacks along the banks of the river — thousands of families — have been relocated into newly constructed social housing where children are living with running water and electricity for the first time in their lives. It's just a truly remarkable story of progress in a very short period of time, all of which can be traced back to the constitutional recognition of Beatriz Mendoza's right to live in a healthy environment.

Wow. One person!
One person working with a team of neighbours and a group of lawyers, assisted by non-government organizations. I have to give credit to the court, the judges who sit on the Supreme Court of Argentina.

The court also did a couple of really interesting things to make sure that the government followed up on the court order. They have the federal Minister of Environment in Argentina and the head of this new watershed management agency come and sit before the court every three months and provide a report to the court on their progress. The judges ask them very challenging, difficult questions about the progress or lack thereof. They also set up a system where politicians are fined on a daily basis if the court's timelines aren't met. Back in 2010, there were some timelines that weren't met, and the court followed through on its promise to fine politicians. I can tell you, that certainly jump-started the process.

That's an extraordinary role for a court to take, right?
Yes, that is somewhat extraordinary. But around the world, the role of courts is to make sure that governments obey the Constitution. So once a right to a healthy environment gains that constitutional status, then it provides an unprecedented level of accountability. Governments can't just make promises and violate them. In Argentina, for example, governments for decades had pledged to clean up and restore the Riachuelo River. It's been known for years as one of the most polluted watersheds in South America, but it wasn't until there was that constitutional commitment that a court could hold a government accountable and citizens could use the courts to demand that accountability.

You can contrast that situation with Canada, where we have extensive contamination of the Great Lakes, the water body that's really at the heart of our nation both culturally and ecologically. There have been government promises in Canada to clean up the Great Lakes dating back to the 1960s, and yet progress is painfully slow. Many people still suffer devastating health consequences because of the pollution in the Great Lakes, and there's just no way that Canadians are able to hold governments accountable for those broken promises.

You've said that in Canada this costs us 30,000 deaths annually from the environmental issues that could be solved if we had the right to sue over them.
Yes. The World Health Organization has conducted studies in every country on Earth estimating the proportion of deaths and illnesses that are caused by environmental pollution and other environmental hazards. For Canada, the World Health Organization's estimate is approximately 30,000 premature deaths a year. That's a very daunting figure, but as the World Health Organization points out, those are preventable problems because if we address the environmental pollution that's at the root of it, then we can actually prevent those illnesses and those premature deaths.

I think many Canadians will say, "That can't possibly be true." Who's dying and what are they dying of?
The single largest group is death caused by air pollution. What people don't realize is that there are air contaminants that you can't see or smell, that actually enter into your body when you breathe them in. Many people think, "Well, if there's dirty air, it must affect my breathing system." This is true, but these tiny particles also get into your bloodstream and contribute to cardiovascular disease. As you know, heart disease is one of the leading killers in Canada. A cardiologist in Montreal, Dr. François Reeves, said very clearly to me that he can tell he's going to have a busy day as a heart surgeon when there's an air quality advisory out. It's that clear — the correlation between poor air days and more people coming to the hospital and passing away because of cardiovascular disease. There are deaths from respiratory ailments as well that are attributable to air pollution. There are cases of cancer that are clearly linked to environmental hazards such as asbestos and second-hand smoke. The numbers that the World Health Organization has published are consistent with studies done, for example, by the Canadian Medical Association.

That's stunning. And you have other examples from other countries.
I could tell you stories from 95 different countries. You've got France, which has one of the world's oldest constitutions but was silent on the environment until the year 2005. They brought in a really powerful *Charter for the Environment*, added it to their constitution, and scholars in France say that the *Charter for the Environment* has had impacts wildly beyond expectation. For example, France last year became

the first country in the world to pass a law banning the practice of "fracking" or hydraulic fracturing for oil and gas, a problem which many people here in Canada and the United States are deeply concerned about.

In Finland, hydroelectric projects have been cancelled because of concerns that the impact on migratory bird habitat would violate the constitutional right to a healthy environment in Finland. In Brazil there was an oil spill off the coast by Chevron, and the Brazilian enforcement officials immediately fined Chevron $28 million, which is a sum greater than the total amount of fines levied under the *Canadian Environmental Protection Act* since it was passed in 1988. On top of that, the Brazilian officials are pursuing a civil lawsuit against Chevron in which they're seeking billions of dollars for damage to the environment. They've also filed a criminal prosecution against Chevron executives, seeking prison sentences of up to 30 years in jail.

I could really go on and on, whether it's protecting endangered sea turtles in Costa Rica, endangered salamanders in the Netherlands, cases requiring the clean-up of polluting facilities in India, cases in Thailand striking down approvals for new petrochemical and oil refineries — really cases from every corner of the world. Stronger laws and policies in all of these countries have had a systemic transformative effect.

The right would say, "What you're giving me are negative examples that interfere with economic growth." Who's going to go back and explore for oil off the Brazilian coast now? Who's going to build hydroelectric power in Finland?

Right, that's the natural response of big business. But the reality is, if you look at countries like Norway and Sweden and Finland that have these strong provisions in their constitutions, they also are world economic leaders. They come at the top of the international rankings for environmental performance and also for things like innovation and competitiveness. What the Scandinavian countries have done is shown that there's a myth about this trade-off between environmental protection and economic competitiveness. What really happens is that passing stronger environmental laws and policies stimulates innovation. It stimulates creativity, it stimulates ingenuity, and it creates a virtuous circle where those countries are then attracting more investment, attracting a higher calibre of people to their countries, and their health-care costs go down.

Sweden, which has had the strongest environmental laws in the world for decades, has the slowest rate of increase of health-care costs of any industrialized nation, which the Swedes themselves attribute to their strong environmental policies. So there's a virtuous circle that happens here, and it's a good news story that countries like Canada and the United States really need to understand and appreciate. Then you have countries like Brazil, one of the most rapidly developing countries in the world, which has much stronger environmental laws than Canada, including laws governing offshore oil and gas exploration. It's not that constitutional recognition of the right to a healthy environment will stop economic activity. It'll require that economic activity be done properly in a way that benefits people both today and into the future. There's a better way of doing business, that's the bottom line.

You trace a lot of this back to the incredible influence of the Stockholm Declaration 40 years ago. Tell me about the Stockholm Declaration.

Well, the Stockholm Declaration was a political statement that arose out of the very first Earth Summit, held in Sweden back in 1972. Canada actually played a major role in organizing and leading that conference. The Stockholm Declaration was the first formal statement that people have a right to live in a healthy environment and a corresponding responsibility to protect the environment. That Declaration wasn't a legally binding treaty and didn't have any enforceable provisions, but it's had a transformative impact on both environmental law and constitutional law around the world. It was just four years after that Stockholm Declaration that Portugal became the first country in the world to recognize the right to a healthy environment in its constitution, followed by Spain in 1978. Many of the countries who have incorporated the right to a healthy environment in their constitutions point to the Stockholm Declaration as the source or one of the inspirations for doing so. It really was a watershed moment in bringing together — for the first time, really — the concept of environmental protection on the one hand, and human rights on the other.

You mention responsibility there too, and you've also noted that Aboriginal or Indigenous traditions couple that very closely. You have a right to a healthy environment, but you also have a responsibility to provide one. That seems a very un-Anglo, un-common law perception.

Yes, that's right. If you look at Canada's *Charter of Rights and Freedoms*, it's all about rights and freedoms, and there's nothing in there at all about responsibilities. We act as though the only responsibility is an unwritten responsibility upon government to respect, protect, and fulfill our rights. But the reality is, given the global ecological crisis that we find ourselves in, all of us — individuals, governments, businesses, civil society — we all have a responsibility to do things in a different way to protect the environment upon which our health and well-being and the future of humanity depends.

Should that also be a piece of the law — that on the one hand, it gives you the right, but on the other hand, it imposes on you a duty?

Absolutely. There are actually almost 150 constitutions in the world that clearly state that the government has a responsibility to protect the environment, and there are 84 that also impose a corresponding responsibility on individuals. So it's becoming increasingly prevalent, and I think that's a very positive step — to make it clear that it's not just a right, but that we also have a corresponding responsibility.

In a way, it's a call to act as adults, isn't it?

It is — and I think that the fact that this has gained such global prominence in such a short period of time reflects a growing maturity of human consciousness. We've finally come to terms with the fact that this is a threat to our very health, our well-being, and our existence, and it's something that we have to give a level of credence to on par with the other fundamental human rights, such as the right to life, and the right to freedom of expression and freedom of religion.

This also raises the possibility that lawyers can be heroes! [LAUGHTER] Not the way we usually think.

Well, I was giving a talk in Wolfville last night, and I made a Freudian slip and I said "liars" instead of "lawyers." So you have to be careful — but yes, there's a role for lawyers to have a positive influence on society, certainly. I think of the right to a healthy environment and the responsibility to protect the environment as having the transformative capacity to bring us from an era of human destruction and environmental degradation into an era where we recognize our fundamental connection and dependence upon ecological systems.

We need to transform our legal systems because legal systems have such a pervasive influence on human behaviour. But we're so far from being sustainable at this point in history that we also need systemic transformations of our economic systems. We need systemic transformation of our education systems so that ecological literacy becomes on par with reading, writing and arithmetic. We need transformations of our health-care systems so that we actually prevent illnesses rather than simply treat people when they're sick. And we also need a systemic transformation of our democratic system so that everyone's vote and everyone's voice actually counts.

What you've just said there basically contains the outlines of a world and a society that's infinitely more desirable than the one in which we find ourselves. And yet we have such a hard time getting people to take seriously the whole philosophy about our relationship with the environment.

True — but another very interesting field of study that's just emerged in recent years is the study of human happiness. It's remarkable to learn that, for example, people's happiness increases with a certain degree of economic wealth, and then plateaus. Once you have the basic necessities of life, having more economic wealth doesn't increase your happiness. It's things like friendship and community and the social bonds that we develop. Countries like Sweden, Norway and Finland, in Scandinavia, and increasingly, countries throughout Latin America, have really grasped this concept and are shifting their cultures in ways that are profoundly hopeful and inspiring to the rest of the world. Ecuador has a new constitution that's based on an Indigenous concept called *sumak kawsay*, which translates roughly as "the good life." So Ecuador's vision, its road map for where it wants to go as a society, is the pursuit of the good life for all of its citizens. That's just such a beautiful way to frame a society's highest level of aspiration. It's something that we could all learn from.

And they were one of the first to pass legislation on the rights of Mother Earth.
Yes, and in fact, as a lawyer, I have to just correct you there. They were the first, along with Bolivia, to pass constitutional recognition of the rights of Nature and Mother Earth. So in Ecuador and Bolivia, the planet, ecosystems, mountains, rivers and species all have legally enforceable constitutional rights. In fact, the first court case in Ecuador was when a highway construction project damaged the Rio Vilcabamba or the Vilcabamba River. Some citizens went to court and an Ecuadorian court issued an extraordinary judgement that said the constitutional rights of the Rio Vilcabamba have been violated and according to the constitution, the river has a right of restoration. So the government has had to carry out a restoration project on the Rio Vilcabamba.

Similarly, Bolivia has a new law called the *Law on the Rights of Mother Earth*, which sets forth in great detail all of the various rights of Nature. It also clarifies that citizens, governments, businesses — everyone in Bolivian society — have a responsibility to protect Mother Earth. The law also establishes an ombudsperson to defend Mother Earth's interests. Bolivia has actually led the charge at a global level. There have been discussions at the United Nations General Assembly this past year about creating a Universal Declaration of the Rights of Mother Earth, which is a very powerful concept in highlighting the importance of changing our ways in a fundamental fashion.

I want to come back to that — but before I do, I want to go back to Ecuador, because one of the questions that occurs to people from the English Common Law tradition is, okay, you give the right to the river to have its well-being respected — how do you enforce that? Would a citizen in Ecuador have an obligation to take some kind of action? Is that how the question would get into the legal system?
Yes, a citizen would have a moral obligation, and also a legal right. In many countries where the constitutional right to a healthy environment is recognized,

citizens are able to bring cases before the courts in situations where their personal health isn't being directly harmed or their property is not being harmed but, for example, the habitat of sea turtles is being threatened or the well-being of sharks in the ocean is being threatened by the practice of shark-finning. Individuals are able to bring lawsuits that force governments to take actions to protect a healthy environment.

This goes back to our earlier conversation about, well, does that mean healthy for humans or healthy for nature? And as I said, those things are really inseparable. We have to have a healthy environment in order to have healthy humans, and so there are cases around the world where courts have upheld the constitutional right of an individual to a healthy environment in ways that have also created additional protection for the natural world.

That evokes the best in human beings, doesn't it? It rewards us for being responsible and thoughtful and considerate, and thinking long-term rather than short-term.
Yes, very much so. I think that's why the concept appeals to people of every stripe around the world. Polls in Canada show that over 90 percent of Canadians believe that government should recognize their right to a healthy environment. So certainly there's widespread public support for this concept.

The first time I ran across this idea was an essay by Christopher Stone called "Should Trees Have Standing? Towards Legal Rights for Natural Objects." One of the things that Stone imagined was groups of citizens applying for stewardship of certain natural features, like, "We are going to be the group that cares for this mountain," or "We're going to be the group that cares for this valley." Does that happen in countries where this right is recognized?
Yeah, absolutely. In all of these countries, there are literally thousands of citizen groups that focus on everything from a local creek or a particular species to national parks and large ecosystems. And so people are protecting their local environment, and they have a whole variety of motivations for doing so. Some people are doing it out of self-interest to protect the source of their drinking water. Others are doing it because they think they should protect the environment for their children. But the end result is the same: that empowering those people by recognizing their constitutional right to a healthy environment gives them the tools they need to get the job done.

Now let's go to the UN — because the prospect of a Universal Declaration would be a very powerful impetus for many countries to follow suit.
It would be, yeah. In much the way that the Stockholm Declaration spurred 100 countries to amend their constitutions to recognize the human right to a healthy

environment, a Universal Declaration of the Rights of Mother Earth could take us that next step in the evolution of our conception of rights.

You have to think about human rights as a subject that's not fixed in time. We all know that if you cast your mind back a hundred years or so, we didn't consider Aboriginal persons to be people who were worthy of human rights. African-Americans didn't have human rights. Even in the twentieth century, women didn't have the full range of human rights. So there are philosophers, such as Roderick Nash and Christopher Stone, who make the compelling argument that in the evolution of human consciousness, it's natural to take the next step and extend rights to Nature. In funny ways, our legal system already extends rights to things such as corporations, so there's precedent for extending rights beyond just the human species.

I think Stone calls those "jural persons" — legal persons which are not persons, like corporations, but also like universities and churches and ships. All of these have legal rights.
Yes, you're absolutely right. These are all legal persons.

Stone also makes the interesting point — reflecting what you said — that the history shows us the constant extension of rights to things that were not thought to be capable of possessing rights.
And it's a funny characteristic of humans that we often think that we're coming up with new ideas when, really, ideas have been around for centuries. In the course of my research on this subject, I came across a book that was written by a Muslim Sufi 1,000 years ago called *The Animals' Lawsuit Against Humanity*, where a group of animals banded together and brought a lawsuit against human beings for their mistreatment, for the violation of their rights. That's a story that not only is a part of Indigenous law dating back centuries, but is a part of Muslim Sufi culture that dates back an entire millennium.

That's phenomenal. I want to read the book.
It's a great story.

There's also a suggestion somewhere that the Canadian legal system is founded in part on Indigenous concepts, and that perhaps you could even tease out of the existing Charter a right to a healthy environment. I think there are people in Sarnia pursuing that.
That's right. Canada has three founding legal systems. We have the British common law, the French civil law, and we also have the neglected category of Indigenous law. As we've discussed, Indigenous law throughout First Nations in Canada includes environmental rights and responsibilities. There's a First Nation called the Aamjiwnaang First Nation whose reserve is on the outskirts of Sarnia in the most polluted place in Canada, a place that's home to over 60 major industrial facilities

such as oil refineries and petrochemical plants. In the Aamjiwnaang First Nation, people are suffering a devastating set of health problems because of those industrial facilities. They have elevated rates of childhood asthma, elevated rates of cancer, including leukemia and birth defects.

Two very courageous individuals from that community, Ada Lockridge and Ron Plain, have actually filed a lawsuit against the Ontario government and Suncor, one of Canada's largest oil companies, because of the approval of additional pollution on top of what they're already dealing with. Their legal argument is that Section 7 of the Canadian Charter of Rights and Freedoms, which is the right to life, liberty and security of the person, includes an implicit right to a healthy environment. From an ecological perspective, that makes complete sense. How can we have a right to life without a right to a healthy environment, given that we're dependent on ecosystems for the air we breathe, the water we drink, and the food we eat?

So they're currently before the courts in Ontario, and it's a David and Goliath battle, there's no question. They're facing defendants with deep pockets and far more resources than they have. But what's encouraging is that courts in 20 other countries around the world, from Argentina to Italy, have already reached the conclusion that the right to life includes the right to a healthy environment. So there are precedents that the Aamjiwnaang people can rely on from around the world as well as from their Indigenous legal system that make the case that both their right to life and their right to a healthy environment is being systematically violated by industrial pollution.

You would think that the Ontario government would be on their side.
You would hope that the Ontario government would be on their side, but in fact — and this is a very disturbing statement, but we've talked mostly about constitutional recognition of the right to a healthy environment — there are some countries who don't recognize it in their constitutions, but their environmental laws do. There are other countries who don't recognize it in their environmental laws or their constitutions but have signed international treaties that include it. And if you add up all of the countries in the world that have recognized the right to a healthy environment, you get 177 [2016: 180] out of the 193 members of the United Nations, which is truly extraordinary. It means there are only 16 [2016: 13] countries left in the world that have not yet recognized this fundamental human right: Canada, the United States, Australia, New Zealand, China, Japan, Laos, Cambodia, North Korea, Brunei Darussalam, Lebanon, Oman and Kuwait.

The United Kingdom?
The United Kingdom has actually signed an international agreement called the *Aarhus Convention*, which includes recognition of the right to a healthy

environment. But what's really striking about that is that you have over 90 percent of the countries of the world that recognize this right, a small number that don't, and Canada and the United States are the only countries in the world that actively oppose recognition of this fundamental human right.

Canada participated in the negotiations of the Aarhus Convention, which is an international agreement on the right to information about the environment, to participate in environmental decisions, and to have access to justice when your right to a healthy environment is being violated. And Canada opposed the inclusion of the right to a healthy environment in that treaty, and at the end of the day, everyone else said, "Canada, bugger off! We're going to include the right to a healthy environment." Canada, as a result, has neither signed nor ratified that treaty. Forty-five other countries in Europe and Asia went ahead and did so.

The United States is facing a case brought by citizens of Mossville, Louisiana, in the heart of the American oil industry. Those predominantly poor and black citizens fought their battle through the American court system, weren't successful, and have brought their case now to the Inter-American Commission on Human Rights. And the US government, under President Barack Obama, has argued that those people have no right to a healthy environment because there's no such thing. It's a truly extraordinary development for Canada and the United States to be the global renegades in terms of recognition of this most basic and fundamental human right.

That's astonishing, particularly given that Canadians think of themselves as being quite progressive people. But that's an illusion in the environmental sphere, because our environmental performance is much worse than most Canadians, I think, would believe. Yes, Canadians are surprised by how badly Canada ranks in international comparisons of environmental performance. For example, amongst the wealthiest OECD countries, Canada ranks 24th out of 25. When the highly respected Conference Board of Canada performs its comparisons, Canada ranks 15th out of 17. So there's a real disconnect between how Canadians view themselves and view their country, and our actual performance on these matters.

In terms of a right to a healthy environment, you get a similar disconnect because over 90 percent of Canadians think that government should recognize the right to a healthy environment. Over 50 percent of Canadians think it's already in the Charter. So there are these widespread misperceptions, and I think the challenge for those of us who wish to move forward on this issue is to somehow break down those Canadian myths because if the government really isn't reflecting and respecting the values that we cherish as Canadians, then we should throw the bastards out and get somebody in office who's going to do what the people want them to do.

Maybe what it tells us is that governments at both provincial and federal levels are largely captives of organizations who benefit from the absence of such a right.

That's right. I think that's a sign of a very unhealthy democracy. We live in a country, where about 26 percent of the voting population elected a majority government. Well, how does that work? We have a government in office, which the majority of Canadians not only don't like, but have very strong emotions against. And so, we need to reform our electoral...

And didn't vote for.

And didn't vote for. So we need electoral reform quite desperately in this country to reinvigorate and bring our democracy back into a healthy state.

How would we do this? We have a largely unwritten Constitution — not an entirely unwritten — but how do you go about doing constitutional recognition of the right to a healthy environment?

Well, in Canada, there are three pathways to constitutional recognition of the right to a healthy environment. One is through direct amendment of the Constitution, which requires Parliament's approval and the approval of seven of the 10 provincial governments. All of those approvals have to be secured in a three-year time frame, so it's a politically daunting thing to achieve. But as Nelson Mandela said, things always seem impossible until they're done. In fact, the Canadian Constitution has been amended 11 times since it was repatriated in 1982. So the challenge is daunting but not impossible.

The direct amendment of the Constitution is probably the most compelling approach because it has not only the powerful legal impacts, but it has a transformative cultural potential as well. So the *Charter*, of course, since 1982, has had a profound impact on issues such as the recognition of same-sex marriage in Canada and our values and cultural attitudes towards equality.

The second route towards recognition of the constitutional right to a healthy environment in Canada is through the courts — through lawsuits such as the Aamjiwnaang First Nation has going, arguing that there's an implicit right to a healthy environment in existing constitutional provisions, such as Section 7 of the *Charter*.

The third route is also a legal route, but it's slightly more obscure, and that's through a process called the "judicial reference." A judicial reference basically allows governments to ask the courts important legal questions. For example, there have been over 100 judicial references in the course of Canadian history on issues such as same-sex marriage, whether Quebec can legally secede from the country, and who owns offshore natural resources.

Many Canadians will remember the "Persons Case." Back in the 1920s, a group of very powerful women led by Nellie McClung and Emily Murphy started campaigning to have women recognized as eligible for appointment to the Canadian Senate. It's shocking today to think that women weren't eligible for the Senate, but back in the 1920s, the prevailing legal opinion was that women weren't "persons," as was required to be appointed to the Senate under the *British North America Act*. So they prevailed upon the federal government to initiate a judicial reference. The federal government asked the Supreme Court of Canada, "Are women 'persons' for purposes of Section 24 of the *British North America Act* and therefore eligible to be appointed to the Senate?" And the Supreme Court of Canada, in what must be its most infamous decision, said, "No, women are not persons for purposes of being appointed to the Senate."

Now, fortunately, at that time, there was an appeal process to the United Kingdom to the Judicial Committee of the Privy Council, where common sense prevailed. The Judicial Committee said, "For God's sake, of course women are persons!" And that decision in 1930 really marked a turning point in the evolution of women's rights in Canada. So I think there's potential for a similar kind of judicial reference to be brought here in the twenty-first century that would advance the cause of the right to a healthy environment in Canada.

Now, who can bring such a reference? Obviously, the feds can. They did it with the Clarity Act.

Well, interestingly enough, the federal government, any provincial government, or a territorial government can bring a judicial reference, so I'm particularly interested in the situation in Nunavut, where the Inuit are at the front lines of the impacts of global climate change. The Inuit have not been successful in trying to persuade Canada as a country to take strong action either at home or internationally on climate change.

But the government of the Nunavut territory could bring a judicial reference seeking to have the right to a healthy environment recognized in the *Canadian Constitution*, which could have a transformative effect on the legal system in Canada and eventually on our culture and our environmental performance. That's something I'm hoping to talk to politicians in Nunavut about in the coming months.

That sounds like the most lively possibility for moving this forward.

Well, in the short term yes, but in the long term, I think that we will have a new generation of political leaders for whom the environment is a core value. We have a federal New Democrat leader now, Thomas Mulcair, who, when he was the Environment Minister in Quebec, oversaw the inclusion of the right to a healthy environment in Quebec's provincial *Charter of Human Rights and Freedoms*.

The federal NDP has endorsed this concept. The federal Green Party has endorsed this concept. The Liberal Party certainly is the heir of Pierre Elliott Trudeau, who had such a profound influence in bringing the Charter of Rights to Canada. So I think there is actually potential — not in the immediate term, given our current federal government — but in the near-term future. I think that given the right political leadership and given the widespread public support for this issue, this is something that could come to pass.

If Quebec includes the right in their legal system, does that give leverage to the rest of the country? Could I go to court and say, "Look, we cannot have a legal system here which gives a fundamental right to the citizens of Quebec and doesn't give a fundamental right to me as a citizen of Nova Scotia"?
You could try that, Don, but you wouldn't get very far in the Canadian legal system.

[CHUCKLES] No?
No, it can be used as leverage in political context to say to the Government of Nova Scotia, "Why does Quebec recognize this right and not the Government of Nova Scotia?" but it doesn't carry any currency outside of Quebec. However at a national level, it is a powerful political argument to portray Quebec as an environmental and human rights leader because of the step they've taken. It opens the door to arguing that all Canadians should enjoy this right.

You'd think that the rights of a Canadian citizen should be consistent across the country.
I agree one hundred percent from a moral and political perspective, but the solution to that is not going to court in a different province. It's getting Canadians united behind the concept of the right to a healthy environment and making our political leaders do our bidding.

So in Canada, we have three routes that we could possibly get that right entrenched. What about the United States? They have a very complex amendment process for their constitution, right?
They do have a very complex amendment process, and in fact, back in the early 1970s, there were efforts to amend the US Constitution to include the right to a healthy environment. The same senator who came up with the idea of Earth Day, Senator Gaylord Nelson, introduced an amendment in Congress, which unfortunately didn't pass. There were also lawsuits in the 1970s arguing that there was an implicit right to a healthy environment in the US Constitution, none of which were successful. So in the United States, it will be a long and difficult struggle because of the challenges that are inherent in amending the US Constitution. There have been literally thousands of attempts to amend the US Constitution, and only a couple of dozen of those amendments have ever been successful.

Are there other routes there as there are in Canada? Like the judicial reference, for example?

They don't have anything similar to the judicial reference, but over time, as the legal system in the United States evolves, it's possible that lawsuits could be brought again arguing an implicit right in the right to life.

But that's been tried, and it hasn't been successful?
Yeah, it was tried forty years ago and hasn't really been tried since.

We just touched on municipal government, but that's been something you've been very, very interested in, and it's a place where you obviously see some real opportunities. Tell me about that.
The municipal level is where a lot of citizens have their closest interactions with government. That's where they breathe their air, that's where they get their drinking water, that's where their trash gets taken away, where their recycling gets taken away, and that's where they do their composting. So it's really the nexus for urban residents, which make up 80 percent of the population of countries like Canada and the US. It's the interface between human beings and the environment.

Municipal governments, in the absence of leadership from other levels of government in Canada, have stepped into the breach. Think of Vancouver, which is the greenest city in Canada and working towards being one of the greenest cities in the world. Montreal has passed a *Charter of Rights and Responsibilities* at the municipal level which includes environmental rights and responsibilities. Where there are political challenges to amending the Constitution, provinces are at different places and have different political parties running them at a point in time, I think we should be making efforts at every different political level to recognize the right to a healthy environment, and by doing so, building momentum piece by piece across the country towards the ultimate goal of changing our Constitution.

Now, if Montreal has that right within its municipal government, what does that actually mean in practice?
To be honest, it doesn't have a very direct practical impact, but it represents a recognition that the citizens endorse that right. It represents an aspiration. And the Montreal charter actually does have one very interesting innovative wrinkle: it allows any citizen to commence what's called an "initiative." So a citizen can draft up an idea for changing an environmental policy in the City of Montreal or for protecting a new part of Montreal or creating a new park, and they now have the right to formally bring that before the municipal government and have the government study it and create a public hearing process to evaluate it. I would say that's a real step forward in terms of direct democracy, giving people the right to actually put ideas on the table. And the results should be, given the creativity and ingenuity in our society, that we unleash that and harness it in ways that are currently not being done.

Will it give citizens the right to bring a suit against the municipal government for not performing?

Well, they can actually do that under the Quebec *Charter of Human Rights and Freedoms*. Cases have been brought since 2006, and Quebec is certainly ahead of any other jurisdiction in Canada in terms of implementing that human right.

Supposing a similar right were passed at the municipal level in Regina, say. Would that, in principle, give the citizens of Regina the right to sue the City to improve its performance environmentally?

Well, I have to resort to a kind of slippery legal answer there and say it would depend on the way that their right was recognized. If it was in a legally enforceable bylaw, then potentially it could do that.

Yeah, I recognize that you can't say what a hypothetical law in a place we don't even live in might mean to somebody. [CHUCKLES]

Yes, so hypothetically, the possibility may be yes.

I want to explore a broader matter that you bring up. Most of us tend to think of rights as being inherent, inalienable — just natural consequences of human society or something like that. But you make a very clear point that there is a whole evolution in time and in consciousness. Rights keep on evolving. Tell me about how rights happen, and tell me about what rights you see maybe beyond the ones we've been talking about.

Well, the classic statement is that rights emerge and evolve in response to wrongs, so the Universal Declaration of Human Rights really emerged out of the ashes of World War Two, when humans saw an unprecedented degree of rights violations. And the right to a healthy environment emerged in the 1960s and 1970s in response to an upsurge of global recognition of the damage that human beings were inflicting on the environment and, of course, on themselves.

The definition of a human right is something that's universal, meaning it's held by all human beings. It's got to be essential to human dignity, and it's also got this character, which you alluded to, that regardless of whether governments actually pass laws recognizing these rights, we have these basic rights, they're inalienable. So you and I and everyone watching this program has a moral human right to live in a healthy environment, but the catch is that in order for that human right to be enforceable, to make it really meaningful, it has to be enshrined in law. And once that happens, it's that legal alchemy that transforms moral rights into rights that are powerful in our contemporary legal systems and societies.

In terms of where we're headed, I think that the right to a healthy environment has spread globally over the last 40 years more rapidly, according to constitutional law scholars, than any other right in time. It's just been a remarkably rapid diffusion of this idea. And it still has a ways to go. There's no global treaty recognizing the human right to a healthy environment. There are regional human rights treaties ratified by 118 countries, but at the end of the day, every country in the world, every citizen in every country, should have their right to a healthy environment recognized.

In the emergence of the debate about the rights of Nature, we're seeing a very clear indication of where this should and probably will evolve in the decades ahead — that what starts out as a human right to a healthy environment will over time broaden out into widespread recognition of the rights of Nature in ways that are morally compelling and also socially beneficial. Recognizing the rights of Nature is not only the right thing to do morally, from my perspective, but will have salutary consequences for human well-being over the course of the long term. You have to remember that human beings are not built for sprinting. We're built for endurance running, and to achieve a sustainable society is like running an ultra-marathon. And yet we have kind of deluded ourselves into thinking we have to run as fast as we possibly can, we have to consume more resources, we have to become increasingly wealthier, when in fact, our whole physical evolution and our cultural evolution goes in terms of being ultra-marathoners and not sprinters.

Which is an encouraging thought — that we get there over the long term.
Yeah, look at some of the emerging science of human evolution and how humans were able to track down animals that are much faster runners than us simply because we developed a stamina for long-term pursuit and had the intelligence to be able to track different signs. On the African savannahs, there were creatures much faster than us, creatures much stronger than us, but we were able to carve out a living because we could, over a period of days, track down the animals that we needed to kill to survive.

You've alluded to the declining power of nation states within the context of proliferating trade treaties, which actually supersede the constitutions of nation states. Is this an instrument which gives citizens back some of that power?
That's a great point. I can give you an example from Costa Rica where a previous Costa Rican government, about 15 years ago, issued some licenses to an American company called Harken Energy to drill for oil off the coast of Costa Rica. That created a huge backlash amongst the Costa Rican people, who have a constitutional right to a healthy environment and also a deep-seated pride in the natural well-being of their country. So, during the next election in Costa Rica, that government was thrown out, a new government was brought in and the new government cancelled those licenses that had been granted to Harken Energy. Harken Energy said, "Well, under international trade law, you owe us over $50 billion for the profits that we

would have made if you hadn't cancelled the contract." And Costa Rica simply said, "We're not paying you a dime." The government said that the people were firmly behind their government in taking that stance, and Harken Energy, to this day, has never collected a dime from the government of Costa Rica.

There's a lot of talk about the declining power of nation states within these global investment regimes, but the reality is that they still have the legal power as sovereign states to do what they want to do as long as they're willing to stand up for themselves. And when a tiny country like Costa Rica stands up against a large oil company from the United States, that's a sign that there's a different way moving forward.

This has become very hot in the context of the Canada–China trade agreement. Presumably, if we had a constitutional right to a healthy environment, it would give us a real instrument as Canadians to say, "No, no, you cannot do that to our country. You cannot do that to our environment."

Yes. In fact, one of the things we haven't talked about is that in many of these countries where the constitutional right to healthy environment is recognized, those countries have determined that the current level of environmental laws and standards is a baseline which can never be reduced. It means that countries can only strengthen environmental laws over time, which if you look at the state of the world, makes complete sense. We have to have stronger laws, not weaker laws.

So a law like the one that was brought in in Canada earlier this year — which rolled back key provisions of the Fisheries Act, which totally destroyed the Canadian Environmental Assessment Act — that law would have been found unconstitutional at the very beginning, and we wouldn't have had to have the wrenching national debate about how ill-founded it was.

And it wouldn't necessarily have had to go to court, right?

No. It probably would have been reviewed by lawyers at the Department of Justice when it was initially drafted, and they would have told their elected superiors that this is unconstitutional, and governments generally don't bring forward uncon-stitutional laws.

I'm delighted by this conversation in part because ordinary Canadians don't tend to think of the law as having such creative potential. It's very exciting to think that this perception, which is so widespread in the rest of the world, may give us some leverage.

Yeah, I think it's tremendously inspiring for Canadians to be able to look around the world at these tremendous stories that are coming out of Latin America, Scandinavia, even other places in Europe and Asia, and to say, "Well, why couldn't that happen here?"

JOHN BORROWS
Profound Lessons from Indigenous Law

Recorded August 2013

In the British common-law tradition, which has shaped the legal systems of the English-speaking world, authority ultimately derives from the Crown. In the Indigenous legal system, authority ultimately derives from the Creator, from Nature. John Borrows moves between the two systems as easily as the birds move north and south with the seasons. Dr. Borrows is a celebrated legal scholar, a professor of law at the University of Minnesota [2016: the University of Victoria]. He's also Anishinaabe, a member of the Cape Croker First Nation on the Bruce Peninsula in Ontario, and thus the heir to a long, rich legal tradition written in stories rather than statutes. Because he belongs to both systems of law, John Borrows is uniquely positioned to reflect on the essential nature of law itself. He's written several books, most notably *Drawing Out Law* and *Canada's Indigenous Constitution*. And when we met in his stunning home territory, he brought a young Anishinaabe colleague with him — his daughter Lindsay, who is currently a student of law herself.

John and Lindsay, thank you so much for doing this. John, I wanted to start by asking, what is law? Because, you're deeply engaged with two, perhaps three, legal traditions that are very different from one another. So, how do they both get to be law?

JOHN BORROWS: I think of law as something that's authoritative, something that provides guidance for people in their lives. It's a set of standards, or principles, or criteria that people look to in making decisions and also regulating their everyday behaviours.

You don't think of it as something laid upon people. People in the European tradition often feel that the law is something "up there" that you'd better not offend.

JB: That's right. You know, all legal traditions are generated by people's interactions and then discussions and deliberations around those interactions. They might often have a higher level that they're recognized at through statute or in courts, but if they're not connected to some organic, living system of decision-making, regulation, they're not really guiding their lives. They're not really criteria, precedent, authoritative in the way that people want to pursue their ways of being.

These are very different assumptions. You've written about a professor named Noel Lyon who said that in the common-law tradition, everything derives from the Crown, but in the Anishinaabe and other Indigenous traditions, it derives from the Creator. And that produces a very different world, doesn't it?

JB: Yeah, it's where you look for your authority that makes a big difference in terms of what you regard as being directive or guiding in your life. So if you see the Crown as the source of all information — as the source of all authority — you have a view about what the decision-making criteria would be, what the responsibilities might be around regulation. But, if you see the Creator, or the trees, or the waters, or the animals, or people's own living interactions as being the source of authority — the criteria, the precedent — then you would obviously have another view of where you should look to find law.

In Anishinaabe, there's a different set of terms for thinking about law. One is called *Inaakinogewin*, which means "the great guided ways of decision-making." But another is *kinwezhiwewin*, and this word, *kinwezhiwewin*, means "to take guidance from the criteria that you find around you." And so, Anishinaabe people themselves have ideas about law that are more organic, that are more embedded in interactions and relationships.

If I go back to that "spirit versus power," "Creator versus Crown" division, that changes your relationship with the world, right? Because if it comes from the Crown and it's conveyed to individual people, then the world becomes property. But in the other tradition, no. Right?

JB: That's right, because in a non-Crown-based system you would find law in the things that deserve respect in the world. So, if you see a good set of behaviours from elders, you would find law emanating from those people because they are worthy of respect. They have demonstrated that through their actions, through the way they have talked and they've lived. If you see a bird, and the way that that bird takes care of its young and you recognize in that interaction there is something that you should be taking into your life, you would find law in that source as well. So you make a judgment about whether or not what you're seeing around you is worthy of emulating, is worthy of taking guidance from, is authority in how you should be living in your life today. It's on those bases that you start to generate legal obligations — legal relationships — and that's different from positing an all-time-and-all-places, Crown-centric view of what law might require.

Much more flexible, much more responsive to different circumstances, much less fixed ... ?
JB: Yeah, there is a certain sense that there are criteria that need to be followed, even in the flexibility of Anishinaabe law, but there is something about it that allows you to be a bit more responsive, more reactive. If you find that an elder is no longer behaving in a way that you once gave them respect, you would no longer see them as a source of authority, guidance, of law in that way. If you found what was going on in another relationship didn't comport with what the principles of good living were, you would no longer follow it. Whereas, if the Crown did something that was disrespectful, we'd still tend to follow its views. But, in Anishinaabe law, they would lose authority, the more disrespect they showed in the way that they're living with others.

I am a little bit surprised that First Nations have any regard for western law, given the fact that it's supposed to be the authoritative account of how one is going to behave in a certain situation — and the European tradition has never respected that. You make a treaty: that means that's the way you're going to relate to each other — but the treaties have never been followed.
JB: Yes. Well, a promise is a promise is a promise. There is something in all legal cultures — including Anishinaabe legal culture — that bestows great weight on affirmations of what people are going to do that are illustrated through ceremonies. When I think about western law, there's a term in Anishinaabemowin called *nindinawemaaganidog*, which is "all our relations." Whenever we create law and participate in law, it's a wholistic thing. It's not just Anishinaabe people with Anishinaabe people, or Anishinaabe people with other Indigenous peoples, or the rocks and the trees and the plants and the animals, it's those who live amongst us who are from many nations in the world. There were promises made when my great-great-great grandfather signed a treaty that were to be for as long as the sun shines, the river flows and the grass grows. Those promises were meant to be about all of us, in creating a place for all of us to live here. And so, we take seriously those obligations of *nindinawemaaganidog*, of all our relations. If we were only to think about law from our own smaller point of view that doesn't take account of the wider world that we live in, I don't think we would be as broad and as powerful as we might be.

It's implicit in what you're saying about Anishinaabe law that you have developed a profound moral sense somewhere along the line, so you can make a judgment as to which examples are worth following, which processes deserve respect, where you get leadership in your own way of living your life. Where does that come from? Western law is often understood as something that will force you to behave well, as opposed to something that you will give authority to because you already know how to behave well.

JB: You know, there's a concept, again, in Anishinaabemowin called *Mino-bimaadiziwin*, which is an aspiration to live well in the world, and that is a *legal* principle, *Mino-bimaadiziwin*. It's not formed by one singular set of teachings, but it's trying to understand the triangulated, intersecting relationship of traditions. So, if there is a moral sense that flows from the law, the sense is that there is a comparing and contrasting that's a part of this. It's not just taking what you learned as you were growing up — it's obviously respecting that — but then, seeing how that enters into conversations with other people's traditions, other ways of being. We talked at the beginning about "what is law." It flows from many sets of relationships that you find through time so that these, eventually, you hope, find some reinforcement from one another.

To the western mind, this seems hard to identify as law. Do you run into that in your work? That people just sort of say, "But, that's not really law," because it doesn't have that hammer of authority?

JB: Yeah. People, I think, often associate law with a court or with a legislature, with the force of the state that's behind it, and there's no doubt that that is an aspect of law — but I think it's the smallest aspect. Because, even in western, Canadian law, if all we relied upon was force and that ultimate imprimatur of authority from a parliament or a court, you'd probably find a huge disconnect between what's happening there and what's going on on the ground. There are many countries in the world where they have these high principles through parliaments or courts, and life is a mess on the ground. So it would be within Canadian traditions, so it would be within Anishinaabe traditions — that is, law isn't just force, law isn't just coercion. Law, at bottom, has to be about persuasion. It has to be about deliberation. It has to be about the heart and the mind and the spirit. Really, if we thought about that, it's not just an Anishinaabe thing. It really is more broadly the case, that law has to rest on a broader base of humans trying to work through a better understanding on how to regulate our behaviour, how to make decisions when we have conflicts with one another.

So if I take that back to European settler law in Canada, that seems to say that we have a whole range of legal activities — legal principles, legal understandings and so forth — that are completely outside the courts. Right? We don't recognize them as being forms of law, but they are.

JB: They are absolutely forms of law. We live in a world of customary law, in Canada, more generally. There is so much that occurs through patterns of behaviour that are replicated through time, that are implicit, but aren't necessarily identified in explicit ways as having the force of authority. And yet, we do it, because we know that our own selves would not get along as well in the world if we didn't follow some of these implicit norms of respect and understanding that we have. We know that our society, more generally, would have a great problem if, at some level, humans didn't co-operate in those customary, implicit ways of law. As it is in Canadian society more generally, so it is in Anishinaabe and other Indigenous societies. There's much of custom, there's much that's implicit, in trying to live in accordance with the law.

It's not traditional in western culture to regard that as law, and yet, you look at something like the golden rule, you say, "Well, the golden rule can be seen as selfish. I am treating you as I wish to be treated because I do wish to be treated that way on another occasion! [LAUGHTER] I am building up a little credit with that." The word rule is an interesting one there, isn't it? We wouldn't, in the European tradition, think of that as law; we would think of that as — I don't know — good behaviour? Maybe there's no difference, maybe that's the point.

JB: But then you see that around that so-called "golden rule" is a set of incentives to live in accordance with that. If you don't do that, then you don't then get to participate in those incentives. Or there's disincentives. If you violate the golden rule, you suddenly find yourself facing sanctions from your friends and your neighbours and your co-workers and your people that you're investing with. In other words, that golden rule has, surrounding it, aspects of law. It's not coercion, in the sense that we think of courts or parliaments, but there's nevertheless something that comes to have a binding effect because of the incentives and the disincentives that get thrown in if you don't fully subscribe to that. You find yourself in violation of the law and you find yourself diminished in your relationships and what you can accomplish in the world if you don't live by that so-called "golden rule." Not always — the world's not that simple — but often you find that there are then things that you can expand in your relationships.

Mm-hmm. And in a sense, that really is law. Now I don't want to be particularly political, but when you speak I think to myself, OK, in a way this is true of the British Constitution and the Canadian Constitution. It's implicit, it's understood — these are the ways that things are done. But we now face the Harper government, which repeatedly does things that affront those understandings. What do you do then?

JB: Mm-hmm. Well, one thing you have to do, is point out what the laws and the traditions are, of the people that are working in a mainstream. British constitutionalism is a system of conventions and customs and traditions that extend back through the ages through a long lineage. Part of the work ahead is pointing out that those rules of interaction *are* the rules. The British rules of constitutionalism are these informal laws, informal rules.

But, when you see them being broken by the ultimate authority in the country, it's hard to know what to do.

JB: Yeah.

Really, I am not trying to be political, but I think we're facing this kind of issue for a lot of people in this country. They're saying, "You can't do that!" But, there's actually nothing that says you can't do that, it's just that it normally wouldn't be considered decent behaviour. And there don't seem to be any sanctions you can bring to draw your own government back to acting the way that you think it should be acting.

JB: Yeah. You know, there's a Quaker tradition about "bearing witness." Within Anishinaabe world views, it's the perseverance of survival. I think there is a lot to be said, even as they are breaking the law, for holding them to the highest standards of their law — the highest standards of Canadian law, the highest standards of British constitutionalism. You asked the question earlier, "Why do Indigenous people sometimes put their faith in the law, when it seems to be violated like this?" Because law itself is so premised on respect that through time, if we give up on that hope, if we give up on that aspiration, if we give up on those sets of relationships that hold people to their highest points of view, we just lose the ground upon which we stand to build good societies. It's hard, right? Because there is no force there that you can necessarily go and just change the world in accordance with your own point of view.

LINDSAY BORROWS: Yeah, I was working for the United Nations this summer, for the Special Rapporteur on Indigenous Rights, and in international law, nothing is binding. So, people often ask themselves the question, "Why am I doing this work, if what I am doing isn't going to force anyone to change?" But, I think the way you need to see it, not only in an international setting, but in a national setting, a community setting, a family setting, is to recognize that you're like a gardener just scattering seeds. You'll scatter a lot of these little seeds and sometimes something bigger and beautiful grows from it. And I think that people like you, who are telling stories, or like Dad, who is working on Anishinaabekwe, it's just one seed. You may feel like you're doing something really small, but — have that faith that something bigger will come out of it.

So if you keep on saying, "No, that is not the way you behave. No, this is not the right way to do things," at some point the wrong way of doing things will bounce off that deeply-felt sense of the right way. The accountability will occur at some distance, and it will occur almost like a process of erosion.

JB: Yeah, there is that deeper sense of hope for the world and hope for people that, though we're in a mess, and though the world is deeply tragic, there's also an understanding that the world is amazingly beautiful, and that people have possibilities. It's keeping both of those things in mind, not being naive, but also not being naive about the fact that there is good in the world, that there is possibility, and that people can see things in other ways. When you keep both of those thoughts together, I think you have greater power, because there are more possibilities and options and recognitions of what can and cannot be accomplished.

You seem very comfortable with that complexity. You referred to law once as a "vicious, delightful thing." [LAUGHTER] Tell me about that.

JB: Well, you just know that people are complex. If we are going forward with law, law has to be very complex and has to take account of all the good and bad that humanity has as a part of it. I often say that law isn't just an idea, it's a practice. In other words, law isn't just a pre-formed, Platonic set of ideas that exist in the world in pure form in some way; it's worked out through custom, through relation, through practice. The idea that we can, *a priori*, go somewhere and find law and just pull it off the shelf and live in the real world with that, is probably going to miss the curves that human behaviours will throw at us. So I have taken to calling law, sometimes, a physical philosophy. Yes, there's aspects about it that are metaphysical, that are beyond our moments of understanding, but because law is a physical practice it has to deal with the harshest of what we can encounter along with the absolute reverence-inspiring awe that we find in the world and in our relations.

You seem very comfortable with, almost, shape-changing. In your writing, you refer to yourself as a politician, an otter and Nanabush. [LAUGHTER] There's a whole range of masks out of which the voice of John Borrows emerges. You seem very comfortable with the multiplicity of characters that are apparently inherent in you.

JB: Yes. I am a complex person. We all are complex people. I am trying to live my life in a way that's integral and that's kind and loving and helpful, but I know there's elements of my personality — and I see this in other personalities — where we try the best we can, but sometimes we're blind to the selfishness that we have. Sometimes we actually know we're being selfish, but we want that so bad that we allow that to override other values that we have.

The tradition of the trickster within Anishinaabe, and many other traditions, helps us contemplate the fact that at the same time we can be selfless and selfish, and charming and cunning, and kind and mean. If we can see that in another character like the trickster, it might cause us to be more self-reflective: Oh, there's something in here that's also like that. Maybe I am not always the measure of what the law should be, what the path forward should be. Therefore, I look to my daughter, I look to you, I look to the western legal ways of thinking and saying, "There might be something in there; there *is* something in there that could better shape how we regulate our behaviour, how we make decisions when we have conflicts."

So the trickster is all of us.

JB: The trickster is all of us.

It's a liberating thought. You probably know Edmund Metatawabin in Fort Albany, in Peetabeck?

JB: No ...

He's a lovely, lovely guy. We've just done a long interview with him, which for me, was transformative. He gave me a glimpse of the Cree tradition — the Muskego tradition — and its traditional way of life, which he remembers. He's written a book called Hanaway. *Hanaway is a legendary character that fights with windigos in the earlier part of the book and then later on in the book, Hanaway is the very human and somewhat autobiographical protagonist of the story. For a western reader, this is very confusing. You've got, in effect, a supernatural character over here and the next thing you know, he's in a residential school. It doesn't compute.*

But, as I read your work I thought to myself, maybe this is simply another way of looking at personality, that Nanabush really does live in you. Hanaway really does live in Edmund's character. I am not saying this very well, but I sense that this relates to the complexity that we've just been talking about, where there are many different characters inside an individual?

JB: That's right. And if you hear a lot of different stories and you participate in the tradition more broadly — and in other traditions — you start to see, by way of analogy, things that are going on. Say, in the windigo or the transformer characters you can say, by way of analogy, there's something here for me in my life, or there is something to distinguish here. I am not actually like this windigo. I am doing something that is better for my society, my family, my friends, because I am not going to follow that path that the windigo was taking in that setting. Reasoning by way of analogy and reasoning by way of distinction is something that happens when you're living in a world of stories, be they Nanabush stories or windigo stories. It just so happens that that is also the heart of the common law, legal-reasoning process as well.

There are cases out there of past disputes. You take them by way of analogy and say, "That past dispute might apply to this in this way," or you might say, "No, that past dispute, that case, is not like this case," and so you distinguish it. The difference, I think, is that the world of analogy in distinguishing the common law is controlled by a professional class of judges and lawyers. We, as Canadians, maybe feel somewhat removed from that everyday process of living in those stories. But when you bring this into an Anishinaabe context, or into other Indigenous contexts, it's not a professional class that's in charge of making the law and making those decisions. We as families, as communities, as nations, First Nations, have the responsibility of saying, "That Nanabush story? That applies to this moment when we see this nuclear power plant on our traditional territory that they're trying to deposit nuclear waste deep in the Earth." Or, when we see a burial site, just across the way here, and some developer wants to put cottages in, we can say, "Well, what are the stories that talk about this kind of behaviour? Where do we find the analogies for what *we* should do? We can't wait for Parliament. We can't wait for a court. We have responsibilities right now and we have authorities around us." The authorities are in the stories and the language and the teachings that are in the birds and the trees and the waters, the way that we talk with one another and the way that we interact through our customary behaviours. And through that, law can emerge.

This is fascinating. Indigenous law is about stories, and English common law is about statutes and cases — but you're saying that the cases are actually stories as well. I hadn't seen that connection.

JB: Yeah. Stories are the cases. You know, a statute is never self-enforcing. It's a set of words that will have ambiguity in it. A word can sometimes have two or three different meanings, depending on the context you put it in. Therefore you need a second layer of interpretation to make sense of a statute. That interpretation is sometimes easily linguistic, but sometimes it requires you to get a greater context and suddenly you're pulling on culture and stories and implicit understandings — even to do something as simple as interpreting a statute.

That happens in the Canadian legal system, and of course it happens in Anishinaabe legal systems. I was impressed when I was in New Zealand that they wrote their natural resources act by saying, "The meaning of what we want to do with conservation will be defined by these words," and then they put "Maori" on one side and "English" on the other side, and then the meaning is worked out between them. What an amazing context to try to think about law as inter-societal, as working in those moments of ambiguity and ambivalence, because it's inviting a conversation — a set of reactions to — instead of saying, "This is it. This is how we'll just do it for all time."

And the language has described two different realities, which brings me to a question for Lindsay. In Canada's Indigenous Constitution, John's quoted you as alluding to a specific Mi'kmaq way of looking at the world, and deriving the law, that is totally interwoven with their language. Can you talk about that a little bit? About the relationship between the language and the law in the Mi'kmaq?

LB: Yeah, when I was doing an Aninshinaabek legal project here at Cape, we were able to speak in English, but in very Anishinaabek ways of English, if that makes sense.

Yes, I think we've heard some. [LAUGHTER]

LB: Yeah, exactly. When I went with my friend to Eskasoni, a Mi'kmaq community in Nova Scotia, it was really different trying to speak English with them because I didn't have the English-Mi'kmaq vocabulary to negotiate those differences. I don't speak Mi'kmaq and the language is very strong in their community. So for the first couple of weeks we were wondering, well, here we are in Eskasoni, we're trying to figure out how we can learn about Mi'kmaq law, but we have this huge language barrier. Whenever we tried to share the stories — or that precedent that Dad was talking about — in English, it just went nowhere. So we had to just listen. We couldn't share anything with them; we couldn't share any stories that we had read in the books, because we didn't have the vocabulary to work with them. But they were kind enough to give us their Mi'kmaq ways of speaking English. And then we had someone with us who was a fluent Mi'kmaq speaker, so when people did switch into their language they could just go off, and then later, our friend helped us to translate it. So, it was really integral for them to be able to express certain concepts and to be able to put the stories into their own terms. We found out that the publications meant nothing to them. It was very much an oral tradition and had to come from their mouths and their living breath.

I remember Sakej Henderson, who lives in Eskasoni, saying that Mi'kmaq is very much a verb-oriented language. He said there was a word you would use for a chair, but it could also mean a stump in the forest, a stone on the beach. It meant "for sitting on." And what "for sitting on" was depended on the situation you were in.
LB: Mm-hmm.

It also sounds — and I think this is a really fascinating thing in Cape Breton — I gather that in Mi'kmaq, it's almost impossible to express ownership. It turns out in Gaelic, it's very difficult too. You can't say, "my wife, my pen, my dog." You say, "The pen which is with me, the woman who is at me." You can't say, "It's mine." And that changes the world. Did you see some of that? Some concepts that just wouldn't make sense except in Mi'kmaq?
LB: Well, I am not as well versed in Mi'kmaq, but I can definitely see that with Anishinaabemowin, the Anishinaabe language. I think it's very poetic, like it takes someone to really think about it. And then otherwise, I suppose if you grew up with it, it's more subconscious.
JB: You have an example of the verb-based idea of Anishinaabe in the word for blueberry pie...
LB: Oh yeah, the word for blueberry pie is: mitigozhiminibaashkiminisagan-ibiitosijiganizhegwaabikiniganibakwezhigan.

Easy for you to say! [LAUGHING]
LB: It means, "old-time Frenchman exploding blueberries, blueberry sauce layered

between things, bend-over and put it in the oven bread." [LAUGHTER] And so when you're speaking, you really do create images. Language isn't about efficiency. It's about your skill in being able to paint a picture for people, and to put people into a time and into a place and help them have a more sensory experience than just to get the point across.

JB: You can imagine the legal implications of having a language based in verbs as opposed to nouns, right? Nouns are persons, places or things, categories that you try to fix. Whereas, if you've got a language that's a verb, and then you build a legal tradition around it, it's about what are the relationships, what are the actions that are joined, how do we inflect those relationships that verbs often have at the heart of them. So, as you go into Mi'kmaq communities, which is also an Algonquin-speaking community, or Anishinaabe communities, where verbs lie at the heart, there is a different kind of poetry, there is a different sense of persuasion that's in operation, even if you might be speaking English, as you talked about earlier.

Yes, I noticed that. I lived in a French community much of my life, and a French-speaking person speaking in English carries a lot of French conceptual material with them. It's clearly the same thing in this situation. It must seem, sometimes, to First Nations people that the English language and the common-law system are incredibly rigid and inflexible, and don't reflect movement and change and development. In a sense, it would almost seem hard to grow in English if you have this other tradition at your disposal. Is that true?

JB: That's true at a general level. I think that when people generally think of the law, they think of it as being rigid and fixed and somewhat immovable. When law students come into law school, one of the hardest things that they then encounter is the fact that there's play within the tradition. There is not a right answer, but there is a process that you learn to start to generate answers that could make sense within that tradition. So, there is actually play within the common law tradition, but we don't often act as if that's the case. Then, it's important to note that there's traditions within the tradition, meaning that there's some people that will take up the common law and they'll view it very conservatively, and say, "There's very little room for movement within the tradition. We have to keep it pure, we have to have it stick more closely to what the original instructions are." There's other people within that tradition who say, "No, it's more fluid, it's open. There's moments for departure and creativity and innovation," and there will be people within the common law who will do that.

It should come as no surprise that within Aninshinaabe and other Indigenous legal traditions, the same thing occurs. Some people would be very conservative and say, "There's not a lot of room for play with this tradition, we have to be originalist in our conceptions, somewhat fundamentalist." Other people will say, "No, this tradition can speak to and be syncretic with other traditions and is more open in that way." I think that's an important insight, because it helps us to see that it's within our power. If it's not certain, if there's actually traditions within traditions, then there's a role for human agency there. There is a role for our own power, choices, opportunities, even our weaknesses, to think about what do we do, given the way that the tradition can be interpreted.

It's a very interesting perspective, isn't it? Because it's rooted in your respect for the tradition, but it's also finding a way for the tradition to adapt to changing circumstances and new challenges.

JB: Yeah, you know, tradition can be the dead faith of living people, or the living faith of dead people. [LAUGHTER] Right? And if we take our tradition and just freeze it in a pristine form because we want to preserve its initial authenticity, then that can make it difficult for it to speak to all of the new things and the new contexts and situations that we're interacting with all the time. The challenge is to be respectful of the tradition, to take wisdom and guidance from it, but also to be respectful enough of it to say, "You know what? The way we did that 20 years ago? It's not working for us, today. It would be disrespectful to keep trying to apply that when we are finding that these people are being harmed, or this is going wrong."

I think respect for tradition really does take us into the realm of being somewhat creative, and somewhat willing to question the way things have been done in the past, even as we value what we think has been done in the past.

Well, you know, there's another thing that I picked up out of your work that I really would like to make explicit. It's remarkable how I've never gone onto a reserve and been made to feel anything other than welcome — and, given the history, that's pretty amazing. But I pick up out of your writing this sense of the possibility of two nations living in the same territory. Almost like two layers or three layers of different people who have come from different places, brought different traditions, have different systems of law and so on. It would be a complex negotiation, but it's perfectly possible to live very happily together almost like different layers in the same place. Am I getting that right?

JB: Yeah, that's certainly what I think about law, not just as an idea, but as a practice. There's a lot of horrible things that happen between Indigenous and non-Indigenous peoples. There's a lot of tragedies that are writ large in Aboriginal communities across this country and must be acknowledged. At the same time, we must acknowledge there's a lot of successful interactions and negotiations and relationships that happen between Aboriginal and non-Aboriginal peoples. Fifty percent of Aboriginal peoples, Indigenous peoples marry non-Indigenous peoples and often those relationships are happy — often.

With the life that results.

JB: [LAUGHTER] With the life that results, exactly. If you look at that on-the-ground custom, the day-to-day kind of development, really, a full acknowledgment of what we're doing in this country has to take account of some of that goodness, some of that mutual benefit that happens every day. The problem is, we haven't been able to translate that into our larger, national institutional contexts. There is a lot that happens on the ground that can be helpful, but we've had a difficult time really moving that to the greater scene.

Below those differences — or within those layers — there are clearly two different views of what the world is, and how it's made up, and what has sentience and what doesn't. I was struck by a number of your phrases, "The Earth has a soul that animates its moods and activities." "The Earth is a living entity that has thoughts and feelings and is related to human beings at the deepest generative level of existence." Those ideas don't only exist in Aboriginal contexts. James Lovelock, with the Gaia theory, says pretty much the same thing. But, if we start to pay a little more attention to Aboriginal law, we have to pay a little more attention to Aboriginal views of who we are and where we are and what the world is.

JB: Yeah. Lindsay might have something to say with this too, but there's a concept in Anishinaabemowin called *akinomaagewin.* The word for "teach" in Anishinaabe is *gikinomaage*, which means to point in the direction of something and take guidance from it. So that's *gikinomaage. Akinomaagewin* is this word which means "we look to the Earth" because *"aki"* is Earth, *"nomaage"* is the direction that we take from it. *Akinomaagewin* means that we learn about what we should be doing by pointing to the Earth, by looking at the Earth, because the Earth is living. It has a soul, it has a breath, it has a life. That life talks to us. We learn.

There is a scientific method for learning through observation, which people interpret and take messages from the Earth, and that can be triangulated with and understood in context with some of the things the Anishinaabe and other Indigenous peoples are trying to say, which is, if you spend a time in a place observing, getting to know her personality in a certain setting, you start to know what Earth is telling you there, and what needs to be done in that place in order for it to be sustained and to be healthy. Or likewise, you see things that are going wrong and you can understand what the Earth is saying there about that. Now that's not just a singular thing, right? It has to then involve so many of these other factors — it has to be the stories, it has to be custom, it has to be language, it has to be deliberating with other people. But communicating with the Earth pulls all of those things together. When you listen to a cricket, you can tell when the seasons change. When you see a weather system arise, you can take guidance about how you might treat your neighbour in that moment. Lindsay, I don't know if you have ideas about the Earth and how we learn in that way?

LB: Well, yeah. I think one of the reasons why it's so important to take up this concept of *akinomaagewin* and learn from the Earth is because I found, learning it in the western law school, that the emphasis is very much on your mental intellect. They are always teaching to your mind. But when I learned Anishinaabekwe law, it was as equal to my mind as it was to my heart. I think that when you have that sense of your own place and your being becomes a part of the law, then you have a more positive view towards it, and you can pick up on these levels of richness that you just don't get when you're in this really competitive, indoor law school. It just makes all the difference to be out on the land and learning from it.

Somebody has defined a professor as being a person whose body exists primarily to carry his head between meetings! [LAUGHTER]

JB: And you often see that in schools, for sure.

In a sense, what you're talking about is a way of learning with all of you, not just your head.

LB: Yeah, and there's a word for that in our language too. If you walk out into the bush and someone says *"na,"* then you're all supposed to stop and you just listen. But it's more than just listening with your ears, you're supposed to really feel. The forests around here, and the water, are so special. My grandma always says that she feels like she's looking to another Earth or on the other side of the veil. And you can really feel the presence of our ancestors here, but it takes that understanding of *"na"* and how to just be and feel in a deeper way.

JB: It's really embodied as a set of learning experiences that includes the mind. We never want to give up on reason and interrogation and critique; that's always there. But there's other parts of us that can learn and as we triangulate those together, that helps us with the law project: regulating our behaviour, resolving disputes, finding what's authoritative.

At the heart of all this, it seems to me is, a deep sense of the value of mindfulness and respect. Those are two words that seem to me to come out again and again and again in various incarnations of this discussion.

JB: Yeah, respect always comes up as one of the …

Almost the great value?

JB: Almost the great value, that's right.

LB: One of my friends — who was learning Cree law — one of the women who was reviewing his work was saying, "I've heard these stories from those Cree elders up in northern Alberta about windigo, all my life, but they told them to this friend of mine in a different way." And so she went to talk to the elders and asked, "Why did you tell him these stories differently?" And they said, "Well, he was missing out a little bit on this characteristic in his life, so we needed to tailor the stories, so that we could help him."

I thought that was so thoughtful that these elders, who had only known this young man for maybe a week, and they were trying to teach him some Cree legal principles, they automatically tailored it right to him. I think so often, like in Canadian law, you really get just the story written in a book. But when you have people giving it to you, and elders who care, and there is a sense of accountability and "where there is rights, there is obligations" — then you get something deeper.

I think that's absolutely right. I think this conversation would strike a great many European Canadians as kind of touchy-feely, a little bit mushy-minded. But I think it's very tough-minded. I think it's the way forward for all of us. But there also are moments — and I'd like to touch on those too — when something has to be done. John, you tell a story about someone possessed by a windigo in the French River in the nineteenth century. It's analogous to criminal — it's not really criminal, because the guy is clearly not in his full possession of himself. Tell me that story, tell me how that works.

JB: This is a story about a man living in the 1830s who — the community became very aware that there was something wrong with his relationships, the way he was interacting with others. So they took him to live amongst them, I think from another community, as the snow season approached, so it was probably October or so. And then, from October, November, December, January, February, March, they kept observing this person and trying to extend aid and help to him. They really worked to see what was going on in his life. As this was happening, they were fact gathering. They were trying to understand what the needs were and what the situation was. They observe that he would cut his wrists and he would drink his blood. He would go out into the forest and he would put all these saplings over and he would build a big fire. When they fed him, he would just gorge himself on the food. And sometimes at two feasts, he would eat an entire deer.

It was quite clear that the way he was living was out of balance with those around him. Eventually, as this information was gathered — through quite a long period living with him — they decided they needed to talk with other people about what they should do with this person's behaviour. So, it was in a season, probably March, when the snow was a bit harder to walk upon, they went and they gathered with other villages to talk about what they should be doing with this person. In other words, they didn't want to take a decision on their own about what they should do regarding this person's behaviour and what they were seeing, because it was quite clear that he was not only a danger to himself, he was actually going to be a danger to the community he was living with.

So, they sought consensus. They sought the guidance, the counsel, of other people. They gathered together and at that council they did agree, in that instance, that he had to die in order to protect the community and to protect the other relations that they needed to have there — like the deer, because, you know, they're living on the edge of survival in the 1830s in the French River area. The decision was that he had to die, but who would do it? It would be the person's own best friend. That is, in taking this action, it wasn't to be vindictive or retributive; it was an attempt to recognize the harsh reality of sometimes decisions having to be made, but then trying to ensure that that harshness is attenuated, is diminished as much as possible. So once they did that, the person who took the life of the windigo, that person then became the son to the father of him who was no more, and so provided for and cared for that father. The rest of the community all made that old man presents so that that care would be a part of their relationships.

What's interesting about that story is many things. One is today, we would recognize mental illness, and we would see that we wouldn't apply capital punishment in those circumstances. But, we would also see that there was a process going on there that's very relevant for us: the fact-gathering period, that protective period, the talking with others to ensure that it's not just taking account of those who are harming, but also those that have been harmed, including those who are the victims, and the perpetrator's wider circle of relationships.

That's just one of a series of windigo stories in which death is really, often, the last step. There are so many things in the tradition that could be analogized to administrative law principles of notice and information gathering or constitutional principles of life and liberty and security. There's a balancing process going on here. That was in 1830, the way they were balancing. We would make different balances today, but the principles underlying it, they speak to us really strongly. They are hard-edged. And when decisions need to be made, they can be deployed in very concrete and real ways.

And that's the point I wanted to get at. In certain circumstances, the decisions do have to be very hard, and when they have to be, they can be. It sounds as though everybody has gone to great lengths to make sure that this is the last possible alternative — but if it has to be, it has to be. And then you do it in this very caring, mindful, sort of way.
JB: That's right, and you know, that is, I think, the aspiration of Anishinaabe law. It's to take account that the relationships be respectful, but act in the world, because law isn't just an idea, it is a practice. Custom is about living. It's not just about talking and being touchy-feely. It's actually taking all of that and having it move through a really complex life.

Yes. I have two other things I wanted to touch on, and one of them is treaties. One of the striking remarks — again, I think it's quoted by Professor Noel Lyon — I don't know who he is, but he seems like a very astute person. He quotes an elder named Crow saying, "The right of the white people to be on this land is founded in the treaty," and clearly that was a revelatory moment for Professor Lyon. I think it would be revelatory for a lot of people. But that also goes back to that whole business of acceptance that we were talking about earlier — the idea of layering? That you make this agreement and it's an agreement to live together. It's an agreement to inhabit the same territory respectfully side-by-side. And that agreement was not respected on the Crown's side.

JB: When my great-great grandfather signed a treaty dealing with 1.5 million acres of land, that we are sitting on here, it was an agreement that was made in accordance with how he viewed the world. When he came to the treaty council, he had understandings about what respect required. He had many stories that he brought to that place. He had linguistic understandings about what it takes to live this concept of *mino-bimaadiziwin*. He had seen settlers and other explorers come through the territory and his grandfather and grandmothers had as well. So he'd started to form some impressions about what was necessary to help us live better with one another, and so his treaties were signed. What he did is, he invited the Crown and people who were represented by the Crown to come and live in accordance with a set of relationships that tries to advance this idea of *mino-bimaadiziwin*, or respect.

And so, the right of people to live in this territory stems from the invitations like my grandfather and great-great grandfather and others made, which was, "We will live together in peace and friendship and respect. And here's the things that you can expect, settlers, as you come into this territory. You will be unmolested, you will be undisturbed. You will be able to take up the land for agriculture. We will be able to trade with one another. And we will be able to continue to hunt. You will assist us with education, you'll recognize that there are places like this reserve where we'll continue to replicate our ways of life." We see from that that we are all "treaty people." My grandfather and us today, as Anishinaabe people, are treaty people, but those who live on this land, who were extended the invitation to be here in accordance with his, and the Crown's aspirations, also live by the treaty.

There are other alternatives. The alternatives are not as palatable in our world. Because this is an amazing conception for us to think about as Canadians, that we actually live here, on this territory, through deliberation and consent and persuasion and blending of ways of understanding, as opposed to conquest, discovery, adverse possession, occupation. I mean what would you rather build a country on? [LAUGHS]

And that's the point of your book, isn't it? This can be a stronger and better and truer country if it's genuinely founded on that negotiation and those agreements.

JB: That's right. And those are historically real negotiations that continue to be talked about in this place. And, that others, Aboriginals and non-Aboriginals would love to be able to abide by, but we do have a choice. Like I was saying before, agency is involved. It's not just self-executing, self-evident that the world is going to be one way or the other. We can choose to found our country on force, on compulsion, on viewing some peoples as being less than others because they were discovered and had a more primitive life and therefore western law can override their law. We could choose that path. Or, we could say, We actually have alternatives that were here from the first moments, that were hospitable, and we can all consider ourselves a part of that relationship.

You've made huge contribution to this country in drawing those out so clearly and so persuasively and so generously. One final thing I wanted to touch on is the implication of the Earth being alive because, it seems to me, if your philosophy is mechanistic, and the Earth is all just dirt and stone and stuff like that, then you wind up basically fouling your own nest. We've now done 50 of these interviews, and I see it as a tragic situation. We've misunderstood who we are, we've misunderstood where we are and we are gradually making life — for ourselves, as well as everything else — impossible. If you see the world as sentient, as we discussed earlier, then this must be deeply offensive, this whole way of doing things.

JB: Lindsay might join this conversation as well, but one of the things that I —

[LAUGHS] I'm going on my way, sometime, but Lindsay, you're here for a while. [LAUGHTER]

JB: I talked about this concept earlier of *nindinawemaaganidog*, all our relations. Not only is the Earth alive, but the Earth — we are related to it. It's our mother; she's our mother. If our mother is not healthy and able to generate the generations of plants, animals and bugs and waters and human beings, there is going to be no life. It maybe sounds like too simplistic an analogy to make, but, it just happens to be true! [LAUGHS] We breathe because the Earth breathes. Water flows through our veins because water is flowing through this lake, here. If that stops, it's going to stop for us. We are not going to be able to breathe, we are not going to be able to have that blood go through our veins.

At first it might be just a diminished sense of life, so we still feel like we're living, but eventually there comes a point where you just can't live anymore. I don't think that's just an Anishinaabe perspective — we talked about others who have that — but it is certainly an Anishinaabe perspective. An important part of understanding who we are is understanding that we are related to the Earth in deeper ways than I can understand, and I'm grateful that we have these moments to be able to be explicit about that. Is it enough, then, to be explicit about that?

Probably not, because then there is a whole other set of traditions that we have to activate to try to get that. We have to put that understanding into our customs. We have to put that into guiding criteria for how we make decisions. That has to be the authority. If we think about it, what's authoritative? What's precedent-setting? What are the criteria? That outranks any Supreme Court of Canada case. However, there are strands of tradition within Supreme Court jurisprudence that you could pull out with that. There are scientific traditions, there are religious traditions, there are Indigenous traditions, there is our own creativity and feeling that we have. It doesn't just have to rest on one point. But they have to be joined together, because it's not just self-reinforcing to recognize that we are related. Lindsay, I don't know if you have thoughts about this?

LB: I agree with that. I think one thing that I was really impressed with this summer, because I got a snapshot for what's happening at an international level within Indigenous communities, is that everything had to do with the extractive industries, and Indigenous peoples standing up and trying to make sure that their land wasn't mined and that they didn't get relocated and there wasn't so much violence. Some of the signs in the video clips I watched were really powerful because people were basically saying, "You care more about power than you do about our ability to live, because if you choose power over food or power over water or power over the Earth, we are going to die." It was just so obvious how unsustainable it is to put money and put industry and so-called progress before caring for the Earth.

JB: I think that's a really interesting double-entendre there, right? You care for power more than you care for the waters. You care for power more than you care for the forests. Now, in that case, it was talked about as being hydroelectric power or oil and gas power — but you can see, right? There is another kind of power.

Absolutely, I took it to mean the broader sense of the word. We come back again and again to respect and mindfulness. The reason that Chris and I, and others, have become so caught up with the idea of environmental rights as something that should be part of the law, is that it moves us in that direction. If the environment, if Mother Nature has rights — or if we have the right to a healthy environment — that moves us much closer to the Indigenous perspective.

JB: Because we recognize that with all rights there are obligations. Rights come with constraints. Yet, the deep thing about constraints, properly lived by, it opens you up to further freedoms. If you can get that idea that living in accordance with a set of principles or living in a disciplined way actually empowers you to do other things that you couldn't do without that discipline. It's obvious that a piano player needs to exercise a lot of discipline. There's a lot of constraints that they go through.

JB: And, in some ways you'd say, "What a cramped life that person is leading," but then look at the beauty that can flow, that happens as a result of that discipline. If we could see living with the Earth in that way, that is, yes, there's constraints that come when we recognize that the Earth has rights, but those same constraints provide a discipline for us that allows the Earth to grow, but also us to grow in new ways, I think that there is so much that we can benefit from within that.

I think so too. For me, that looks like the most important single step we could take in this country to move ourselves forward in a sustainable way.

Mm-hmm, yep. Recognizing, being mindful, understanding that concept of *nah* or *amajise* that Lindsay talked about earlier.

Yeah. Stop and be there, that's what I took from that. Just really be there in that moment.

LB: It's like listening to understand, instead of listening to respond. The forest doesn't really care what you say to it, necessarily. But if you really understand, then you are going to change your life and how you live. Then you can live in harmony with what's around you.

CORMAC CULLINAN
Getting to the Wild Heart of Earth Rights

Recorded January 2014

Cormac Cullinan is a practicing environmental lawyer based in Cape Town, South Africa. He's the director of a leading environmental law firm and the author of the pioneering book *Wild Law: A Manifesto for Earth Justice* published in 2002. The book calls for what Cullinan describes as "Earth jurisprudence," which places human legal systems within the context of the laws of Nature, changing our relationship with the natural world from one of exploitation to a more democratic participation in a community of all life.

Cormac Cullinan is a member of the executive committee of the Global Alliance for the Rights of Nature and played an important role in drafting the Universal Declaration of the Rights of Mother Earth. He's a former anti-apartheid activist, and that's given him an understanding of just how fast and how completely social change can occur when the circumstances are right.

The recognition of the rights of Nature is part of a much bigger effort, because we humans are part of Nature. We share the same evolutionary history as every other thing that has come into being and that is part of this planet, and, as Thomas Berry said, despite the fact that we like convincing ourselves that we are separate from Nature or superior to Nature, we are so integral to Nature that we are more accurately described as an aspect of Earth, rather than anything different to it. We are part of Earth.

Now I think that if one looks at the significant crises of our time, most of which are characterized as environmental crises — climate change and so forth — they arise because of human behaviour. And that human behaviour is based on the false understanding — the delusion, if you like — that we are separate from Nature, and that our role on this planet is to subdue and dominate Nature, and that the best way to increase human well-being is through exploiting all the other beings on the planet.

Now in order to change that, it is necessary to shift the consciousness of the dominant industrial civilizations to the recognition, which has existed for most of human history, that our well-being depends on maintaining healthy relationships with the other members of the community, both human and other than human. And one of the ways of shifting that is by drawing attention to the way our societies have been structured. And law and legal systems are at the heart of that.

So the issue of the rights of Nature is important in shifting this consciousness and restructuring societies themselves. If you say that to a lawyer, it sounds absurd because we have been trained that the only possible holders of rights are human beings and what we call juristic persons, i.e., legal persons such as corporations. That means everything else on the planet, every other being — a mountain or river or species — which has come into being, which exists, is defined as property and/or a thing.

Now once something is property in the eyes of the law, it's incapable of holding rights. So when we defined people as slaves, they didn't have rights and they could be bought and sold. Now if you think about the relationship between the slave owner as a subject, with all his legal rights, and the slave as an object, as property, you can see that you've hard-wired an exploitative relationship between the two. The slave owner will always exploit the slave, and the slave is powerless to resist because without rights, you cannot use the machinery of the state, or social forces to protect yourself. And that is exactly the same relationship that we have hard-wired between humans and corporations on the one hand and the rest of the planet, the rest of this magnificent community of life that we're part of.

So by raising the issue of the rights of Nature one challenges, first of all, the assumption that we are the only subjects, because it means that Nature must be a subject — it must have volition of its own. And as soon as there are two subjects — humans and Nature, or different beings within Nature — we enter the language of relationship and relatedness, and so that shifts the paradigm.

The other important thing about rights of Nature is that it addresses the structural problems with society. For example, I am a white South African who grew up in apartheid South Africa and, interestingly, *apartheid* is the Afrikaans word for "separateness." It is the same thinking that we are talking about here. In that case the idea was that the best way for the white community — or a portion of the white community — to flourish was to deny rights to most of the community and to exploit them. And that's directly analogous to what we're talking about here. So the only way for South Africa to begin the road towards health was to recognize rights for all of the members of the community, so that the relationships can be negotiated — and also the possibility of the community healing is there.

That is directly analogous to what has to happen in this situation. Until we recognize that we need to change how we relate to Nature both personally and at the structural level, we'll have problems. Under apartheid, even if you weren't a racist person, the structure of society made it difficult for you to have black friends, for example, or white friends if you were black. You lived in separate areas, you were in separate schools, etc. So the structure of society is also important. So this is a long way of saying that rights of Nature is important for two very significant reasons: to change how we understand the world and our role as humans within it, and to change the structures of society to enable humans to heal their relation-ships with the natural world.

Why now?

It's a good question. The need for rights of Nature probably arose only in response to legal systems which imposed this property rights regime on Nature. If you look at Indigenous cultures around the world, most of them do not have a word for rights. They achieved these objectives in other ways. The concept of deeply respecting all beings was integral to their worldview, and so you didn't need this idea of rights. Once one introduces the idea of property rights and of humans and corporations being the only holders of rights, one creates a kind of an imbalance, which then creates, in my view, a need for a counterbalance, which is recognizing rights of Nature. Right now it's particularly critical because we find ourselves in a situation in which civilization is under threat from climate change, and many species are on the brink of extinction: we are in the early stages of the sixth period of mass extinction. We are really in a bad way and human society is driving the destruction of Earth and of other species at a terrifying rate.

But it's also important, I think, at this time, because we desperately need a new way forward, and environmental laws have helped, but ultimately it's clear that they're not enough. They are not achieving enough. We are still losing the battle. I'm very happy to say that there is a new consciousness arising, a new willingness to take on new ideas, to try things that are fundamentally different, which is arising all over the world. I'm not quite sure why. It may be because as the crises intensify people realize that they have to do something fundamentally different. I can't say. But whatever the reason is, in the last three to five years there's been a kind of an energy around these ideas which I haven't seen in fifteen or twenty years.

You've mentioned apartheid a couple of times here, and obviously that's got to be the dominant fact of a young South African's life in your growing-up period. You've said that once you realized how grossly unjust apartheid was you had to fight against it. Did you have a similar moment of illumination with respect to the natural world?

I certainly sometimes have the experience of déjà vu. When I was a student I was probably more interested in partying and having fun, but once I realized exactly what was happening — because of course information was controlled, and I got a lot more information once I got to university — I felt that I would be complicit if I didn't act. And now I berate myself — although I am acting — I berate myself for, you know, not giving up my job and doing this kind of work full time. I have the same conundrums. I can't identify a particular moment, but I was very fortunate to grow up on a large property in the hills outside a small town, and I spent a lot of my youth walking in the bush with dogs. And I've always loved nature. I was one of those kids who wanted to be a game ranger and ended up a lawyer. [LAUGHTER]

But that's never left me, and the connection with nature is probably the most meaningful connection in my life. If I am agitated, like this morning, I got up early and took a walk at dawn barefoot, listening to the dawn chorus of the birds. That centres and re-orientates me and grounds me. That's probably something which we all have, but get disconnected from. So this feeling, I suppose, has grown over the years as one sees the tragedy of this wanton destruction of this unbelievable community of life done in such a careless and meaningless way. So I can't say that I put it down to a particular moment, although I do remember, with a flash of insight, realizing that polluting a river is no different from slashing your arm. It's fundamentally self-defeating, self-harming and misguided.

If you haven't quit your job, you've done a second job on top of it by writing a wonderful book called Wild Law. I think you're the person that coined that term.
Yes.

How would you describe wild law? What is wild law?
Well, let's take a step back. I first started working on the idea of a new philosophy of law. Thomas Berry had first said that we need a new philosophy of law, which I called "Earth jurisprudence." That's a philosophy of law, but how do you implement it? For ordinary people, "jurisprudence" is a clunky word, so I first thought of using "wild law" as a catchier way of communicating the ideas. But once I started working with it, I realized it's much more profound than that.

"Wild," for me, is a synonym for the extraordinary creative energy which has produced this universe. I don't know what it is, but if one looks at the evolutionary history of the universe, we have gone from very few basic atoms to these extraordinary trees and plants and hummingbirds, and this amazing diversity — and there's something extraordinarily creative that drives us. For me, it's a wild energy. Wildness is that part which connects human nature with the larger nature. It's that creative streak that runs through us. It's the wild impulses of delight. Wildness is the juice that drives the universe. Wild law sounds strange, it sounds paradoxical, because our current conceptions of law are that it controls, homogenizes, dominates, etc. That reflects a controlling mindset — and I was saying, "Imagine if we had a legal system, laws that facilitated the flow of the fundamental juices, creative juices that run the universe. If we had a legal system specifically designed to enable us to participate and to contribute to the health and integrity of the whole. If our technologies were driven not just by the desire for profit, but the desire to contribute to the beauty, integrity, and health of the whole community, not just the human community. Wouldn't that be incredible?" So "wild law," for me, it's not just a catchy name: it's a way of showing people that we could fundamentally re-conceptualize our notion of law.

Most people think of law as being something that tells you not to do things, but you're talking about something that is not negative, not prohibitive. It's facilitative somehow, right? Yes. The broad thesis that I believe in is that if it's true that we are part of this larger system, the Earth community — and I believe that it's scientifically untenable to say that we're not part of it — then we need to be governed by the system, the larger system of order. So we may be like a cell in the body. We may have the power to self-regulate ourselves internally, but we also have to comply with the system of order of the whole. So the first thing is to identify what are the laws of Nature, as it were. What are the fundamentals of Nature? And if we look around us, we see Nature works on incredible diversity, but at the same time it maintains cohesion. The more an ecosystem diversifies, the more inter-relationships there are, and the more resilient that ecosystem becomes. So you have this paradoxical situation where diversity is matched with increased cohesion. We can observe these things, and, if you like, deduce rules of the universe from what we observe.

Now if we are going to take that as our starting point, our legal system should be informed by a desire to see how best we can regulate ourselves to be consistent with that. To me that is a much more interesting phenomenon. If you speak to Indigenous people, they all refer to the existence of immutable laws of Nature or laws of the Great Spirit. And a great part of the human endeavour is to identify what compliance with that law requires. Shamans are involved in that. You know, how does one fit in? How does one maintain those respectful relationships? And if we start thinking of law from that point of view it becomes not the fear-driven control impulse which is reflected in most of our law; it becomes driven by love, by the desire for connection. When I say "love," I mean the desire for connection in the broadest sense.

So one begins to look for situations which would encourage people, encourage diversification. So laws that would control people's sexuality, or any of those kind of things, to me seem contrary to the idea that there's natural diversification, and it's not a bad thing. So it's a different conception — it's a conception of law as a self-ordering of human societies, with the recognition that we are also members of a greater Earth community. Therefore anti-social behaviour is behaviour which is anti-social not just in relation to other human beings, but in relation to the wider society.

That's a little bit of an abstract explanation — but I think when one looks at a particular law, one can say, "Is this something that increases the integrity and beauty and health of the whole community, or not?" And if you apply those kind of tests, one can begin to see how it is possible to change the law to something which enhances our participation within the community, and enables us to be Earth citizens and not just good citizens of a town.

And it's quite a magnificent vision, because it starts at the cellular level, right?
Yes.

Everything relates both outward and also inward — self-organizing, but also organizing as part of a larger whole. And then it moves on out to the whole natural world and the whole human culture.
Exactly.

But there's also a tragic element here, and that is that we are trapped in what you call the homosphere.
Yes.

Tell me about that.
It's this mental construct that we've created which I think is extremely damaging to us. The construct is essentially that we humans live only within a human world, and are surrounded by a hostile, alien world of nature full of danger and full of potential threat, etc. And how that plays out is we attempt to control and dominate nature as much as we can, and also human society. In mediaeval times, there were these ideas that there was this crystal sphere over the Earth and that heaven was above, and that we were encapsulated within this crystal sphere, which was the sphere of humanity. I think that in our heads we have created something like that sphere, which is the idea that only human beings are subjects. We are the decision makers. We're in charge. All decisions are made relative to human considerations.

So the only law that exists is the law that comes from humans. It comes from the parliaments or a judge and the only thing that counts is the economic well-being of humans — and this creates a barrier; it creates a separateness. It creates an apartheid, if you like — a separateness between ourselves and the rest of the community.

And just as you had white South Africans who believed in apartheid feeling increasingly embattled, alienated, fearful and becoming more violent and vicious in response because they felt the otherness of the world around them, that's what's happening in our society. It's also driving things like consumerism, egotistical behaviour and narcissism, because the belief is that it's only us. But as soon as one lets go of that and says, "Instead of me feeling that I have to fight for my existence by resisting the otherness of Nature, this fearful world out there, I embrace the fact that I'm part of it," everything changes. I have this extraordinary right to be part of the most incredible community one has been able to find in the entire universe — and one looks at how to enhance connection. So breaking the homosphere is essential. It's that terrible self-defeating mind set which keeps us separated, which feeds alienation, which feeds the need for domination, which feeds the need to, quite frankly, stuff our faces and accumulate goods.

I'm fascinated that you use the word "fear" so prominently. So much of what we are looking at here is driven by fear. Outside the homosphere, you have this terrifying world of wild beasts and things that will harm you and bite you and give you diseases. But then we create within the homosphere the kind of society in which you're perfectly right to feel fearful. Our misconception of the natural world is transplanted into the way we behave towards one another.

Exactly. It's an interesting hypothesis that maybe this is part of the evolution of the human: we have to move from our reptilian brain, which is fear and impulse based, to our neocortex, where we can have these emotions of love and compassion. The great thing, though, is that we are hard wired to connect. E.O. Wilson talks about this idea of biophilia, the idea that we love other living creatures inherently. Certainly if you see a child in a room and there's an animal in the room, the child will make a beeline for the animal. I think we educate our children out of the natural sense of connectedness and love for other living creatures, into this fearful place. It's a terrible tragedy, and for that reason the exposure of all people, but particularly children, to nature in any form is extraordinarily important for the maintenance of healthy human psyches.

So once you've got that sort of understanding and you want to turn things around, people like Thomas Berry become very important to you, right? Tell me about Berry's conception of the Great Work. Because that leads to your conception of the Great Jurisprudence.

Yes. So when I first met Thomas [Berry] in America he was an old man and the first time I met him I was really struck with his sense of urgency. He spoke a lot about what he called 'ultimacy.' His idea was that we were in critical times as a planet and as a people, and that there was a moment of grace, a window period, in which it would be possible to avert disaster. He was an old man and he was wanting to pass the baton on. He was wanting to inspire future generations to carry on the work that he'd been doing. As a much younger man then — I wasn't a grey beard — I was very inspired by that and particularly by his idea of the Great Work. He said that at different times in civilization there have been great ideas driving the culture. It might have been an idea of empire, or something like that. But right now the task facing us is to reconceptualize our idea of the human and our role within this community of life, so that we can move from a destructive presence, as he called it, to a mutually enhancing presence, to play our role in the wider community of life — to fulfill ecological niches, if you like. Ways in which we can feed ourselves and make livelihoods for ourselves that also contribute to the whole.

So definitely meeting Thomas and understanding the urgency of the situation, and his idea of the Great Work, and that this is *the* challenge of our times was very important to me. I completely believe that. If you were an alien from another planet and you came to this planet you would in a short time conclude that the key issue was the relationship between the species that had populated all over the Earth — the humans — and their habitat, and that was the key issue of the day.

The Great Jurisprudence — Thomas pointed out different areas in society in which one needed change. And he said, the legal aspect is particularly important, because it's how societies structure themselves and how they perpetuate themselves. Thomas Linzey often refers to it as the DNA of society, and legal systems are quite like that. It's a good term. It's how they replicate and reproduce themselves. Thomas Berry called for a new jurisprudence. I thought somebody else would deal with this, but after a while, when nobody was, I sort of went where angels fear to tread and decided to just have a go myself. I coined the term "Great Jurisprudence" really to describe the situation where some of the rules of Nature, how the universe works, is already set. It predates us. It's beyond our control. I call that the Great Jurisprudence: the wisdom of the universe, if you like, the self-ordering structures of the universe, which are immutable as far as we are concerned.

In a sense, the great DNA of Nature?
Exactly. The DNA of the universe — that's a lovely way of putting it. What we then needed to do is develop human jurisprudence, human philosophies or theories of law and governance, which were consistent with that. I call those Earth jurisprudences, recognizing by using the plural that it's appropriate to have different variations in different places because cultures are different. But they would all share a consistency and a congruency with the Great Jurisprudence, and then one would have what I was calling wild law, broadly speaking, to implement that understanding of the rule of law.

One of the fundamental concepts there is the idea that we should behave in ways that enhance and enrich both us and the natural world of which we're a part. Can you give some examples of what that would look like?
Yes. I think Thomas Berry himself and Aldo Leopold and various other important

thinkers reached times in their lives when they recognized that the fundamental touchstone which you use to decide whether something is good or bad, whether it's a right action or not, concerns the health, integrity and beauty of the whole. Thomas Berry referred to the experience, when he was very young, of seeing a field of lilies and having that recognition. For Aldo Leopold, it was seeing the green light dying in the eyes of the wolf that he'd shot.

And I think that is fundamental. If one looks at the idea of an ecological niche — it's a situation in which some species has found a way of looking after themselves and which also benefits the whole. So you could think of perhaps a cleaner [fish], a little fish in a coral reef that picks the parasites off the gills of larger fish, the little fish gets its food and the larger fish benefits and because there is a mutually benefi- cial relationship it will persist, it's sustainable. The big fish will keep coming back and the little fish will be there to provide that service. What most humans, not all humans, have lost is the conception that we could fulfill our own well-being in a way which is conducive to the whole, rather than destructive. Now I don't mean by this a situation of "no harm," as it were. Ecosystems are held together, for example, by food chains, and it's really important that things eat other things. So it's not a situation where I would say nobody should hunt an animal to eat. Within limits, that isn't destructive of the system. But when humans slaughter vast numbers of animals or treat them terribly, cruelly, those cannot be ways of behaving which enhance the integrity, beauty, functioning and cohesion of the whole.

So a lot of what I'm speaking about is how we do things. This is where the concept of relatedness comes in. We need to negotiate our relationships. If one looks at how we've related to other animals, for example, our standard response when we come into conflict with another animal is to kill them and if possible exterminate them. But it becomes much more difficult — like in my home town, Cape Town, where the baboons in the national park in the centre of the city are protected and they come into the suburban areas often. It's easy if you can just kill them — which you can in most of the country — but if you can't, and you have to negotiate a relationship, it's much more difficult and much more complex. But that is exactly what we have to begin the process of engaging with, is how do we negotiate a live-and-let-live relationship with everything on the planet?

So in terms of mutually enhancing relationships, I would say, at a micro level, if one tries to adopt that approach — well, gardens are often areas where people try to exercise maximum control over Nature. But you could re-conceive your garden as a place of joy, not just to you but as a habitat for other creatures. We could start thinking of our cities as wild cities; as cities which are not just set up in opposition to the terrifying nature outside, and have a wall around them conceptually, but as homes not just for humans, but for other species, to allow that wildness to penetrate the city, to release the rivers from their concrete coffins and let them go wild. There are ways of relating which are mutually beneficial. We need to move away from ways relating to everything that is a one-way flow. If we have an exploitative relationship with any other person or being, it's not sustainable. It just either destroys the other person or ends the friendship, etc. So I think that the heart of moving towards this approach is to look at how we relate to everyone and everything, and say, "Could I reconfigure this relationship in a way that would be beneficial not just to myself but hopefully to the other participant, and if not the other participant at least to the whole?"

You'll be amused by this, but one of the things struck me as I read your book was how African you are. Your examples are very African examples. Your example of the animal in the city that you have to get rid of was an aardvark, [LAUGHTER] which most people like me have never seen, digging up fence posts that had been erected by farmers to keep jackals out — and I've never seen a jackal either. [BOTH LAUGH] That raises an important question, which is, how do we become Indigenous? Your background is Irish — your family grew up on this little green island far, far from where you are now. Mine was Scottish — just across the water — and now I'm thousands of kilometres away too. We don't belong to Scotland, we don't belong to Ireland. We clearly belong to South Africa or Canada, but we have no way of becoming co-indigenous with the people who were there first. But we can't go back: we somehow have to go forward to a state in which we really do belong where we are.

Yeah. Look, the most important thing to start feeling that you belong is to break out of the homosphere, and to recognize that it's your birthright to belong. You are an Earthling — each one of us is an Earthling — so we're all indigenous to the planet. Culturally, of course, it's a little bit different, as you point out. Although I was born in South Africa and my father was born in South Africa, my ancestry is Irish, as you say. But my consciousness has been shaped primarily by the environment that I grew up in. My sense of what a good day is, is informed by the fact I grew up in a sunny place. And I think how one indigenizes oneself, if you put it that way, is by relatedness, by connecting with place and with other beings in that place and accepting that the communities that we belong to are the ones we live in. The birds we hear when we wake up in the morning, the animals we see, the feel of the wind on our face, that is determined by the place that we love. And the more one loves and connects with a place, the more one is of that place, and the more one is a full and integral member of that place. But the point that you pointed to is significant: that the loss for many of us is the wisdom of the cultures that had accumulated knowledge of how to be part of that place over thousands of years, and could impart it directly to their children. Many of us have had our cultural libraries burnt. It's not that we can't be, or aren't, part of that ecosystem. It's that our human knowledge of how to do that well has been impoverished.

And we've also done, both in Canada and in South Africa, a terrible job of relating to the people who were there first. We've been deliberately burning not only our own libraries, but theirs.

Exactly. I mean it's absolutely heart-breaking when one looks at the wanton destruction of human cultures and languages and their conceptual understanding, because for me being exposed to Indigenous cultures around the world has been absolutely critical in expanding my idea of what's possible. When I first started working with these ideas people would say to me, "But if you're a lawyer, how can you be a lawyer for a mountain? You can't take instructions from your client, from a species for example." And it seemed to me to be quite a good point. And then you come across other cultures like in this part of the world, in Latin America, in the Amazon where shamans will go into a trance state and negotiate with the master of the animals about how many animals they can kill in a hunt and then they go off and hunt. Now whether one believes in a western sense that that's possible — it's not possible in a western conception of the world — the fact is that both societies have developed many mechanisms for communicating very directly with nature, to negotiate their relationships with nature. There are many different versions of it. So when you come across fundamentally different societies and particularly the societies that haven't fallen under the spell of the industrial, materialist, people-are-separate-from-nature way of thinking, it expands ones understanding of what's possible.

You begin to see that there's an extraordinary correlation between Indigenous cultures around the world — and to me that is very meaningful.

They all say it's really important that one identifies and follows the pre-existing laws of Nature. They all talk about that. They all talk about the fundamental importance of respect and maintaining respectful relationships. They all have rituals of thankfulness and recognizing reciprocity. If a shaman (*Sangoma*) in Southern Africa is collecting plants he or she will leave a pinch of snuff or tobacco as a symbolic giving for the taking, and to acknowledge the debt. And yesterday I heard Tom Goldtooth describing exactly the same thing in North America. So the Indigenous cultures that are left in the world are extraordinary repositories of knowledge, which our whole species desperately needs. People sometimes say, "Is this some noble savage argument or are you going back to some imagined past?" Not at all, this is a situation in which one is extraordinarily foolish if you're trying to find a way into the future and you don't draw on the existing knowledge of people who know how to deal with the problems you're facing.

Who have worked it out over evolutionary eons really.
Exactly, exactly.

And yeah, that's the library.
It's been tested in the laboratory of reality, of time.

Now if you look at the planet that we're on now, that's hurtling towards catastrophe, and someone comes along and says there is another way of doing it, it seems unbelievable that our species wouldn't just say "Oh thank God!" and go and look at that, right? Are you struck by a sense of unreality about the period in which we find ourselves?
I do. I periodically feel like that story "The Emperor's New Clothes" when only the child says the emperor's got no clothes on and everybody else pretends that they can see the clothes, because the fact is that if you look at most of society, we're collaborating in this incredible, collective delusion that we're in charge here; [LAUGHTER] that we run this planet; that we know; that we have a sufficient understanding of the complexities of how it works to manipulate it in a way that works in our favour; that we can have infinite growth on a finite planet. Our system is based on a vast number of delusions which — even by western scientific measures — are clearly untenable. It's completely untenable to say that we're not part of the system. It's completely untenable to say that in the long term the future of humanity is not dependent on the future of their habitat.

But we do also need to work with the internal levels. We have to recognize that, in the same way as telling an alcoholic that drinking is bad for them doesn't stop them drinking: they understand that, but there are other forces at work. We have to work at those deeper levels. We have to address issues like fear and we have to address these things both collectively and personally. One of the antidotes is to expose people to places where they can feel that connection — because once you've connected the wild creative forces of the universe flow through that connection. It's like plugging into a vein. Once you've got the connection and the wild energy flows through you and the connectedness increases, you have a sense of being part of the whole. And quite frankly the love, the biophilia also gets stronger — and that's the antidote to the separation. The separation I see is a kind of a constriction. When we separate ourselves from nature or people, it's a bit like we put a tourniquet around the vein or the artery. It starves that flow, and we are the plants that wither and die. So connection is extraordinarily important for mental health, and for who we are.

Now I hadn't heard that analogy before, but when you say that I think, Yes, if you close off the connection of a part to the whole what you create is gangrene, right?
Exactly, and the homosphere does that. It comes down and cuts off those connections. You know, the idea that everything out there is going to eat or kill you

if it has a chance. You know, all of those fears — they sever those connections or constrict them.

Yeah. But nevertheless, despite what I see as your tragic vision of where we are in the universe, you remain a very cheerful person. And a very hopeful one, I think, in a deep, deep way.

There are times when I feel despairing, when I hear about columns of methane gas bubbling up from the ocean bed and things like that. But I guess my working-model hypothesis is that if I go down into despair, I don't get out of bed on a Monday morning — and it would be terrible to give up and then to find out, at the last minute, that had we only taken some action, the situation would have been saved. But one of the things that is really important and useful in this — and I know that Vandana Shiva has talked about it — is letting go of the ends. In other words, saying that the reason why I'm participating in this work is not because I think we're going to win, but because I think it's the right thing to do.

In that regard I'm very encouraged by the generations of wonderful people, wonderful activists, people with huge hearts, who fought for the end of apartheid and never lived to see it. They went to their graves not knowing if it would ever end. But they acted through the deepest, best parts of humanity, through the conviction that it was the right action to stand up against what was wrong and to work for a better society. They had a faith that it may one day come about. All of us need to accept that despair is the enemy of action, and although one would have to say, if you were a betting person, that the odds are against us right now, and certainly success and transformation is by no means guaranteed, neither of those are reasons to stop doing what is right and to play a part in the whole. Thomas Berry had a faith that the universe and the Earth had a bias in favour of its continuing evolution and flourishing, and that because we're a part of that, there will be people who will arise — as we see now — to take forward that more hopeful vision. But the truth is, I don't know. It could end very badly for all of us. But I would rather go down having tried than having given up in despair.

One of the things that you've given to me is the example of apartheid as an apparently hopeless situation, just founded on brutality and injustice, and looking totally entrenched, and it collapses in no time at all. When the time comes, it just it goes away, and a person like Mandela, who's been considered a criminal, becomes one of the most admired people in the whole history of the human race. It's a wonderful story.

It's an extraordinary story and I'm particularly privileged to have lived through it. I think that's one of the things that I draw on, that I'm very lucky as a South African to have been a participant in a successful revolution. South Africa has its problems now, but it's nothing compared with where we were when I was growing up — and we live in it. I was at a concert in Cape Town recently celebrating Mandela's life, in the period of mourning before he was buried — after his death and before he was buried — and it was quite extraordinary because as a nation we were overwhelmed by the sorrow of losing this amazing man. He had been so influential all of our lives. But we also celebrated — and this occasion was mainly celebration — because to have had such an extraordinary human being at that point in our history was incredibly important. And for a man to come out of prison in his seventies and do what he did — and for that change that so many had dreamt of to actually happen, as you say, in an extraordinarily fast way, in a way which none of us could quite have imagined. I'd been to visit the ANC in exile in Lusaka beforehand and I didn't see it coming as quickly. I was in Europe when it happened, and it's taught me that it can happen; I've experienced it. It can happen and it can be unpredictable — but it would never have happened without those years of people working, working, working, working at it. You don't know when the tipping point is going to come. But it will never come unless you put in the work beforehand.

But certainly as an activist now in this much bigger, much more important struggle than the struggle against apartheid, I am able to draw on the experience of coming from a situation that looked completely hopeless — and triumph. It was wonderful standing in that stadium — there were little kids of all colours playing around with each other, little girls playing games, and no sense of colour. There were people singing and celebrating the new South Africa and Nelson Mandela's contribution. And I looked around at one point and I suddenly turned to my wife and I said, "Good Lord, we won! We won!"

Yeah!

You know, the vision of a post-apartheid South Africa happened. It's imperfect, but it's there.

Tell me again a bit about the Freedom Charter, because when you start to think about how that happened, things like the Freedom Charter become tremendously important, right?
I really believe that fundamental to how human beings work is, we have to have a vision of what's possible, whether it's a second where you believe you can get well again, or whether you believe you can change society. So, "the dream," as Thomas Berry would call it, and many Indigenous people would call it, is really important. If you can't conceive of a society beyond apartheid, you will never get there. So, in the 1950s the apartheid regime was extremely repressive, the civil society organizations were relatively weak, apartheid the ideology was in its ascendancy: there was lots of power behind it; there was force behind it. You had ordinary people in South Africa — the Indian Congress, the African National Congress, the Congress of Democrats — people got together and said, "We need a vision, a positive vision

that we can work towards, of a society that isn't like this." And they went around and they gathered submissions, and there were meetings all over the country.

It ended up in a conference in Kliptown which adopted the Freedom Charter, which is an aspirational document describing the society — the dream — the society that we aspire to. They had to make statements like "The doors of learning and culture shall be open"; "People shall have peace and security in their homes"; "It is a non-racial society of justice." And that vision that was articulated through a process that drew on many, many thousands of people — an articulation of the voice of the people that were suppressed by the official system — became an inspirational vision, which inspired and guided all kinds of actions. At protests for equal education, for example, you would see people holding up banners saying, "The doors of learning and culture shall be open."

That was one of the visions that took us into the new South Africa. That was a document that had no legal status. The government tried to suppress it as much as possible. But because it was authentic, because it had a legitimacy coming from the people — it was an expression of their dream — it came about and was extraordinarily influential. That's why, at this time, I think one of the things that we need to work on is, instead of only resisting the terrible things that are happening, we need to say what we're *for*. We need this vision of a better society — because as worthy as sustainability is, it's too boring. [LAUGHTER] Nobody's going to go to the barricades for it. People go to the barricades for liberty and freedom and justice, and for visceral things. And although I believe in ecological sustainability, what we need is something much deeper. We need to be motivated by a vision of a better society, a connected society where we feel part of this planet, where we can be more fully human beings.

So part of what I've been working on in South Africa is this People's Charter for Africa. We produced a draft just to start the conversation — but the challenge now is how to create a process which will pull as many people as possible into this conversation, because the mere fact of having the conversation is incredibly subversive to the existing system. As soon as people start talking about a different future the old starts being whittled away. So it's partially a way of getting people to think in a new way and to imagine a new future — but if you can pull it together into a cohesive vision that is shared by many people it sets in motion, I believe, a chain of actions, which are like a strange attraction towards a vortex. The dream pulls the action towards us.

That's a lovely vision, of the dream pulling the action. When you talked earlier about the un-channelling of the rivers by removing their coffins, I found myself thinking about my own city in a somewhat different way. That has been done in a number of places. Toronto now has a map of its original drainage basins, and people are slowly uncovering them and opening them up. And I thought what a difference that would make, just that one thing. You could start a river liberation movement.

A river liberation movement! [LAUGHS]

Liberate the river, let the wildness flow! Obviously one has to think about it. You don't want to get people killed in floods, but at the same time a liberated, living river that is determining its own course and has got wildlife associated with it is a thing of joy and inspiration in a way that a concrete canal isn't.

That's right, and that's perfect. You were also part of the group that drafted the Universal Declaration of the Rights of Mother Earth in 2010 in Cochabamba. When we've only got one life to spend, and only so much energy, it becomes really important to put your lever in where you can actually move something. Am I right that for you the whole environmental rights movement represents the point where your small amount of energy can be amplified to the greatest possible extent?

Yes. If one looks at an analogous document — the *Universal Declaration of Human Rights* — that also wasn't a legally binding document, but it shifted the norms of acceptable behaviour in society in a way that's been quite extraordinary, and it's now completely accepted. If a government is criticized or an organization is criticized on the basis that they're violating human rights, it really means something in the world. I think that this approach is also one of those leverage points because it addresses many things at once. You can't get your head around these ideas unless you shift to the understanding that we're not the only subjects and as soon as the world is full of subjects and it's not property, it's an animate universe we live in. It's a universe in which we establish relationships with the other beings and then re-enter the world of relatedness — but it's also simultaneously addressing the structures of society that impede that connection. So it works, I think, both at the internal level, at the cultural belief level, at the external level. In Ken Wilber's terms it addresses all four quadrants. So I think it's a good leverage point. It's got an energy behind it right now which I can't explain, but it's picked up steam in the last few years in quite an extraordinary way.

Chris and I got into this project through an extraordinary interview with David Boyd. David's book The Environmental Rights Revolution *really inspired us. I said to David afterwards, I think you have described, in a way, the unified field theory of environmentalism. This is the change which, if implemented, would resolve all kinds of other issues. One picks away at this specific and this specific and this specific. But this — environmental rights — addresses the whole thing.*

Exactly. The problems that we've got are systemic problems. Look at climate change:

climate change is not the problem; climate change is the symptom of much deeper problems. It's just one of those many symptoms of it and you can't really address climate change in my view at the symptomatic level. That's like mopping the brow of a person who's got a fever. The real issue is why they've got a fever, and there may be different causes. You've got to address the root cause. And this is one of the ways of addressing the root causes of all the problems, as you say. It gets to the heart of the problem and I think that that's one of the reasons why it's really important.

You refer to the Universal Declaration of the Rights of Mother Earth as containing the DNA of a new society, to come back to another theme.

Yes, exactly, because if one were to take what's in that universal declaration and implement it, it would change everything. The economic system would have to change. The legal system would have to change. Our conception of ourselves as being the only beings on the planet would have to change. Our internal ethics would have to change. Cultural values would have to change — and *would* change. Sometimes the values change first and the law follows and sometimes it's the other way around. In South Africa we have a great constitution, and one of the things in it, it prohibits discrimination on the basis of sexual preference. Now there are probably more people in South Africa who are homophobic than there are who are not. But that clause in the constitution is gradually changing South African society. Also the clauses which prohibit racial discrimination — the day that constitution came into force there were the same number of racists in the country as the day before, but it tipped the balance. Now the system works against racism and for non-racism. Before it worked the other way. It's a slow process, but gradually the society is tipping over. So sometimes society follows the legal norm and sometimes it's the other way around. But they are extraordinarily powerful ways of changing society and of dynamiting the homosphere. [LAUGHTER]

I want to end with a couple of quotes from Cormac Cullinan. "The day will come when the failure of our laws to recognize the right of a river to flow, to prohibit acts that destabilize earth's climate or to impose a duty to respect the intrinsic value and right to exist of all life will be as reprehensible as allowing people to be bought and sold." Now that strikes me as a highly inspirational statement of what the future should be like and it leads me to the observation that this is a book of great courage and integrity. I mean you start out as a lawyer but you wind up as being in a way a kind of an earth guru or a modern reincarnation of...

The crazy lawyer... [LAUGHTER]

No — it's a book, as I say, of great courage and integrity. I'm wondering how much flak you had from your own profession for heading out so far into the wilds.

Well, there's a point in the book where I suggest that if you're reading it at a law firm, you get a brown paper cover for it. [BOTH LAUGHING] I guess I did go out on a limb, and there are certainly people who think I'm on the crazy end of the spectrum. But the fact is that I'm a practicing attorney; I run a law firm which has done more environmental law than anybody else in South Africa. I'm very much in the mainstream in my day-to-day life and I went into environmental law because I thought I could fix it that way. I thought that we could deal with this within the system and I sadly concluded that we couldn't. So I believe that I have arrived at these viewpoints in a careful, considered way, and I've really examined my heart and mind in getting to them. Quite frankly, the first time I heard Thomas Berry suggest that maybe everything on the planet should have rights, I recoiled. I thought, the implications of that are immense.

To which he would have said, "Of course they are." [BOTH LAUGH]

Exactly. Animal rights is one thing, but everything having rights! And then I thought, just because something's big or hard or difficult to achieve doesn't mean it's wrong. This is a big thing that we're trying to do. But my heart and my mind tell me that it's the right thing to do, and I'm supported in that view by its consistency with wisdom cultures from all over the world which have existed for thousands of years. So in that sense I have got some flak, and I think that some people think "Nice guy, but a little bit loopy." But I'll take the flak if it makes a difference. I'm happy to take it.

Well, "happy" is maybe a relevant word here, because you do come across as a happy man doing what he feels he should do.

Thank you.

Which leads me to the last quotation from Cormac Cullinan, which is "much of what is best in us is contained in our wild hearts." That is a fabulous statement. In a way, it summarizes all of what we've been talking about.

Yes, and we must hold on to those wild hearts, because it's that wildness that connects our hearts with the whole, you know, and through that connection flows life.

MICHELLE MALONEY

Wild Law in Practice

Recorded January 2014

Michelle Maloney is National Convener of the Australian Laws Alliance. She's a lawyer who has been working on climate change, sustainability and social justice for nearly 20 years. She began at Australia's Sustainable Energy Development Authority, and then worked with non-profit organizations in England and California. She's done community building and sustainability projects with the governments of Australia and Queensland, and she spent five years managing an Indigenous not-for-profit community development organization in Queensland. A few months after our conversation, she obtained her PhD In law from Griffith University.

Since 2011, Michelle Maloney has been deeply involved with environmental rights and Earth jurisprudence or "wild law." The essence of wild law is to rethink and reorganize our legal systems so that they support the whole earth community — the interconnected web of life on earth — rather than exploiting and destroying it. She's co-editor of the book *Wild Law in Practice*. Michelle's particular focus is to prevent the construction of coal-shipping facilities in the already fragile Great Barrier Reef to support the vast new strip mines being developed in Queensland.

I like to think of the Australian Earth Laws Alliance as the Australian expression of this beautiful global movement of advocates who care for the earth and want to put the earth at the centre of all of our problem-solving and creative development of new ways into the future. AELA is only a couple of years old, and there's a number of really great people around Australia who work together just to create a space for other folks who are interested in this area and this work of wild law or Earth jurisprudence. It has been one of the great privileges of my life to be the coordinator of this really phenomenal group of people.

What kinds of issues do you take on?
The birth of AELA was the first conference in Australia. It was organized by Dr. Peter Burdon, who is one of our great writers and thinkers on Earth jurisprudence

and other social issues. But the organization itself, it's lovely how it grew. We had a conference in 2009 that brought people together who all stayed in touch for another gathering in 2010, and then by the time we organized another get-together in 2011, we realized there were a number of academics, people involved in government, a lot of activists, a lot of other people who wanted to continue the conversations. So what do we do? Because we are a fledgling organization that came about from the people who were already working in different environmental or other issues, we started out really focusing on education and raising awareness of these different ways of thinking about environmental governance and our stewardship of the earth.

But from our relationships with other folk around the world, and with other people and with other struggles, we're really getting very interested in the question of spaces for genuine grassroots advocacy. It's fine and good to have events to raise awareness, and to bring really great people together, but then you've got to take it somewhere else. The kind of work that we're interested in is not as easy as saying, "Save the whales. " We're actually saying, "Save the governance structures underneath [and] change them, and make the whole system better." System change can be difficult to communicate but we see the challenge of Earth jurisprudence as changing the entire underpinning structures that support modern industrial life — and turning them around so that every decision that individuals or collectives make supports the Earth first, and nurtures the world that nurtures us.

So this year we have got a strong focus on community-based economics, and collaborative sharing, and other alternative types of economic ideas that we can share with other folk. We're also very interested in the work that the CELDF folk in the US have done. That's the Community Environmental Legal Defense Fund. They work with communities who are really stressed and where everything they love is starting to be destroyed from fracking, from industrial agriculture, from any other issue — and they are actually turning the law around and making it work for communities. That kind of activism is really relevant in Australia because — well, think of any environmental issue and we're facing it at the moment in Australia.

Yes. Your situation sounds quite horrifying.
It's pretty scary for someone who's been trying to do good things, and working in the sustainability space for 25 years. In Australia what we're seeing, particularly in the last year or two, has been a significant regression of policy that supports social and environmental initiatives, and a significant rolling back of so many things that we've worked hard to create, both laws and policies.

Yes. Tell me about the phrase "Earth jurisprudence," which you used a moment ago, which I take it is more or less synonymous with "wild law," which is in the title of your upcoming book. What is wild law? What is Earth jurisprudence?

Earth jurisprudence is a term that was coined by Thomas Berry, who was one of the most wonderful and prolific and important writers and thinkers of the twentieth century. Earth jurisprudence is basically about a new law of the Earth. But he didn't just mean law, he was looking at the governance systems. So in his book *The Great Work: Our Way into the Future*, he critiques the current industrial system. He looks at the four main pillars that support the current industrial system, the big institutions — government, the economic system and corporations, education and universities, and religion. He said that all of these institutions are anthropocentric, human-centered, focused on growth and disconnected from the reality of the physical world that we live in. He coined the term "Earth jurisprudence," because he called for a change in the way that we look at governance of the Earth and of human societies. For lawyers, "jurisprudence" just means the theory of law. What's exciting for lawyers is that we finally have a really good, solid, broad and rich theory of Earth-centered law that also links to practice. And that segues nicely into our book, which is called *Wild Law in Practice*.

Back in 2011, myself and my colleagues in Australia worked together to create a conference looking at wild law in practice. We were very interested in how you take these broader ideas of Earth-centeredness and you turn it into some sort of practice on the ground. Think of Earth jurisprudence as the big picture, the broader underpinning theories of what we're looking at. Wild law is really based on the work of Cormac Cullinan, who wrote his book in 2002 — and it was equally delightful. It was a direct call to the legal profession to engage with these ideas and to bring some soul and earthiness back into the legal profession, which is about justice, and should be about human societies working together for the greater good. We often explain that a good law that is wild law is actually supporting or implementing the principles of Earth jurisprudence. But I think other people could explain it differently to you.

That's very exciting.
It is. We often joke that wild law brings many lawyers back into the fold, and I'm included in that. I was working on the periphery. I spent many years working on community development with some Indigenous friends in Queensland and for many reasons, including having a little girl, I had to stay at home a bit more and was starting to do a lot of the reading. That brought me back into the legal profession, or at least into work that thinks about the role of law.

Tell me about your experience with the Aboriginal people. Did that give you a sense that there's an alternative perspective?
Yes, I was very lucky. In my mid-20s I was working in London for a little while, but my brother was connected with the Gungaloo community, a wonderful, fantastic

group of people in central Queensland who were struggling against everything, from the introduction of native title laws, which in Australia are deeply complex and deeply divisive. This is the recognition of Aboriginal title of the land through the Mabo case. But the actual legislative implementation of these things got very complex and, to put it simply, Aboriginal communities were suddenly facing some of the most complex laws in the land, with some of the fewest resources.

But my personal journey — I feel very privileged, because I had always been really interested in Aboriginal culture, but had never had a lot of Aboriginal knowledge or access to that kind of information or communities that are involved in that work. That's even though I grew up in a town where all my mates were folks from different cultural backgrounds.

But when I met these ladies and they were all grappling with the very beginning of native title claims, they kept saying to me, "Michelle, you're a lawyer, come and help us with this." I'd say, "But I don't know anything about that law." But then I was slowly drawn into the sheer struggle they had in front of them, of trying to show the settler community the value of their culture, the rightful place of where they live, their land. In a lot of places in Queensland folks were forcibly moved onto reserves and taken away from their land. The Gungaloo story is a mixed one, because most of them stayed on country. So working with them suddenly opened up two new worlds: one was the worldview of these people and their amazing origin story in connection to Australia; and the other one is this strange place in Australia that exists between Aboriginal and non-Aboriginal people. I could talk about that for a long time but the shortest way to say it was that, as a person born into the privilege of a European background in a very rich country like Australia, I've never been exposed to some of those issues. It was definitely life-changing activity for me. I love those people all very dearly, and their struggles continue to shift and change.

Did that make me more open to wild law? I started out as someone passionate about the environment from a very young age, because my mom very much believed the same ideas, and as a child, helped me understand the importance of the earth. What wild law did though, was to provide a wonderful opportunity to bring European-style thinking about law and governance and open that up. Wild law invites you to think about the legal system differently. And suddenly all the work I had done with Indigenous people, enjoying people who have laws of the land as opposed to laws in the mind — I really enjoyed the fact that wild law invites mainstream, European-style law to open up its heart and soul to invite in the older knowledge systems, and the older peoples, and really rethink it and rejig it and get something new going. I hope that answered your question. [LAUGHTER]

It does. You know, the thing that struck me and Chris, when wild law really started

to emerge in our lives and work, was how it brought so much together, that it was so integrated.
Yes.

If you had a good set of laws based on Earth jurisprudence, you would resolve so many of the specific issues. Sometimes it feels like we face a shotgun blast of separate issues.
Yes, we do.

Wild law talks to all of those.
As a lawyer, that's what I find very exciting about Earth jurisprudence: it's the opportunity. One of my colleagues at university, who is a theorist, said, "It's been a long time since I have heard people talk about grand theory because post-modern thought is [that] there are no grand theories." But Earth jurisprudence returns us to this grand theory, this idea of a cohesive way of thinking about — well, anything, but in this case the Earth. I find it really exciting, because for someone like me who's got a lot of diverse interests, and who had wandered away from the law, it gives a bit of an umbrella for some of those interests, and it and brings amazing people together. People are interested in a lot of diverse issues, but in any society, from any time frame, humans have to organize themselves and work together, and manage themselves, and care for the earth. So jurisprudence is really the underpinning structures. If we can rearrange them without the top stuff falling off and breaking down, that would be nice, but that's a whole other story about how we create the change and how much we might lose on the journey to a healthier relationship with the Earth.

Let me take you off to another quote from Michelle Maloney, which was…
I've never been quoted before. I don't think I've ever been quoted by anyone.

Isn't it awful, to have that experience now? [LAUGHTER]
I'm very excited, what did I say?

I'm paraphrasing, but you said that you had seen an awful lot of good environmental laws that made absolutely not one whit of difference. I guess the question is, would Earth law address that? Or would Earth law be subject to that?
I think a bit of both. First of all, to clarify: I think there are a lot of environmental laws that have done amazing things, you know, laws that protect national parks, that created protected areas. In the industrial world, air and water pollution was really sorted out by a lot of old fashioned command and control laws that control pollutants, etc. But the argument within Earth jurisprudence is that these environmental laws are all embedded within a pro-growth system, and a human-centered system, and all environmental law is able to do is tacked on around the edges of a pro-growth, out-of-control industrial economy. Many environmental laws, and

all the environmental lawyers supporting them, are fantastic. What's happened, though, is you've got a culture that continues to believe that humans can just absorb, can use up the Earth in whatever way they want. Our classic economics tells us that there is no such thing as scarce resources, that everything can be replaced or that everything is possible, that there are no limits.

So the problem with our environmental law system is that it's part of a broader system that's got the wrong world-view about our earth. I guess the easiest thing about Earth jurisprudence and what all indigenous cultures know, is that if you put it around the other way, and look at the Earth first, understand what she needs, and live within those limits, then everybody, the Earth beings, humans, everyone fits together. But if you take that human project — and that's what's happened, the industrial economy has just blasted us out of the scale — then you've got a problem.

So back to your question. Many great environmental laws have been written by great environmental lawyers but they are trapped within a culture that doesn't want to implement them. And I don't mean the standard environmental response of, "Well the laws are good but we didn't enforce them properly." I mean we have an entire culture that won't accept limits. Ecologically sustainable development was all about weighing economics and social and environmental factors, and that's wrong! There's no weighing up to be done! You care for the Earth first, and you fit within it. You fit within that scale.

Thomas Berry has a great quote that western society is scared of limits, it hates limits, it sees them as a constraint rather than as a creative energy. So I think wild laws, or Earth jurisprudence, or rights of Nature, can easily fall into that same cultural reluctance, if not malicious design, to not implement them. This week, through the Summit on the Rights of Nature, we've heard heartbreaking stories from folks here in Ecuador who have the rights of Nature in their constitution, but current policy and decisions and the forces of large corporations are all working against the effective operation of the law. So again, that's another reason why Earth jurisprudence is so multi-faceted and why that's important. Because even the education work we do, and a lot of great folk around the world do, is sharing with people a different way to think. Changing culture, so that culture informs governance and law, and then changing laws. That can continue as a feedback system to support a different worldview and a healthier relationship.

There's definitely going to be difficulties getting an Earth-centered view of law into formal law. But there are many structures to try to do that. I believe it is the only way forward, and I think many of us do. We can continue to live in denial, but I liked Vandana Shiva's comment — we say the same thing in Australia — that the powers of the industrial society, even they know that fossil fuels, extractive economies, the economic system itself, it knows it's in trouble. It knows its days are coming to an end, because it's not working. In Australia the massive escalation of coal extraction and fracking [for] gas in the last 10 years just shows that these folks seem to be in an awful hurry to get it out of the ground and make their profits. To me, common sense would actually mean that you would string out the kinds of developments they're doing to make more money — but they seem to be in an awful rush, and I think that tells you an awful lot about what they think of their own future.

I've heard it suggested that the big rush is to assert their property rights over the resources that they're claiming, so that when the law does come down saying, no you can't take those resources out of the ground…
They can battle it.

Or they've got a claim for compensation. They may be mining for future compensation as much as for coal.
There are a lot of good investment reasons why they're doing what they're doing. In many countries like Australia the power of corporate interests, the influence they have over the policy makers is deeply disturbing, deeply destructive to democracy. To see these developments in a country as rich as Australia is, I've said it before, it's shameful. We are one of the richest nations on earth! We have our issues. We don't treat our Indigenous people in any way with the respect and the support that we should, but per head of population, we ain't starvin', we're going great. And yet, the greed of the government supporting these massive developments is unfathomable to some of us.

Do you think we can get a change in the paradigm here? Because really that's what you're talking about. The whole Earth jurisprudence, in a sense would mirror a different way of looking at the Earth and would perhaps help to create it. Maybe the two are interrelated. Can we get there without a massive catastrophe?
I think we can. I think we're on the way. I'm trying to finish my doctorate over the next few months — my PhD — and I'm looking at the role of consumption in industrial society and if law or regulation has a role, because everyone says the law is too blunt an instrument, it's all a socially embedded problem, and it certainly is. But I do believe we can change. I'll give you an example. We have had about 250 years, give or take a few decades, of the industrial, post-industrial revolution lifestyle. Cheap energy has fuelled this massive escalation of using up of the resources, in 250 years. Systems like our accounting systems, the early days of that are even older. But we've had hundreds of years of a mindset of governments and companies acting in certain ways.

In the western world we've only had maybe fifty years of response to that. I'm excited by that. Even if you start from 1972 with the Club of Rome report on *The Limits to Growth* — that stimulated a phenomenal multi-disciplinary response by the broader society. The development of ecological indicators, sustainability mechanisms, Herman Daly and the steady-state economy gave birth to permission to think about economics differently. And to bring it back to your question, "Can we make change without collapse?" It's already happening. All through those years we've seen these really exciting, community-based responses, particularly community-based, given the nature of the relationship between the large state structures and corporate wealth. Alternative economics. Even when I started at university, environmentalism didn't look so much at all of these wonderful, smaller ways of looking at the economy. I won't go into the details, but you know, there's a lot of great folk doing interesting work there.

So the revolution has started. It's happening in small places, and I think Earth jurisprudence is only one humble part of this broader, amazing group of people around the world working in ecological economics, working in collaborative sharing, de-growth, post-growth movements, Transition Towns, slow food, solar energy, community-based energy. We're seeing little groups, cooperatives, springing up in Australia, encouraging citizens to just band together and buy solar. We see alternative food systems trying to break away from this big industrial agri-food system. So the revolution is happening. Will it happen before collapse? Some folks are saying the collapse is happening. So I think there is a feedback system. The worse this crisis is getting — and there's no doubt about it, we are in a time of crisis — it's not *going* to happen, it's *happening*. But the positive stuff is already bubbling along, and movements like this one are exciting because they bring together folk who have been working on all these different things already — and the more we join together, that's the really cool stuff, when all the little dots start becoming big beautiful pictures. So, dot to dot. [LAUGHTER]

That's a lovely image! About the collapse, I'm not even sure what collapse would look like. I've actually read definitions of collapse.

Yes?
It actually says that it has to be at a scale — and I won't go into the details, because I can barely remember them, we're only crumbling. Collapse is much more dramatic — entire systems failing. But yes, there is crumbling and signs of collapse, and what people are seeing with the melting of the Arctic ice, and things like that — these are signs of a collapsing system. That's depressing. That's the challenge. That's the sadness. But many would argue that everything from the global financial crisis to the Occupy movement also indicate that the current system is collapsing.

What you've really described is that old Chinese symbol that means both danger and opportunity — that we're in a world that is literally at a pivotal point. So the kind of work that you're doing may be very, very important.

We hope so. I see the work that any of us is doing as just one small part. As individuals we have to live a life that fits within our ethics and our worldview, and then we have to join in collective action, whatever action that is. I work with a lot of volunteers, and give a lot of talks, and students come up and ask, "What should I work on?" And I say, "Well, what do you love? What are you most interested in? Think about what you love as an individual, and then think about all those other people who love it too and join the collectives."

You're a subversive law teacher. [LAUGHTER]

Yes, I often say that one of the reasons I'm doing my PhD is so that I can slip into academia and corrupt the youth, [LAUGHTER] because the law schools are full of people who really just want to make money, and work on business. But there are these lovely, delightful young people, phenomenal young people. I admire them so greatly. I know that in my early 20s I wasn't as amazing as those guys. But it gives me great heart and every now and then, in subjects I teach, which sometimes are completely unrelated, I'll still link it all back to some kind of social change or idea, or care for the environment!

It seems that it's become the lens through which Michelle Maloney sees the world.

I think I've always seen it that way. When I was seven I would sit there, and if Mom was watching TV she would cry if she saw foresters logging down giant trees, so I like to say that I was inculcated into the environmental worldview from my mom. And honestly, in Australia in the days when I was little, that was quite a wonderful treasure to have a mom who was already an environmentalist before there were a lot of them around.

What a gift.

Yes.

Before I let you go, I do want to talk about the river in Australia, the name of which neither one of us feels entirely comfortable ...

Ah! The river in New Zealand.

New Zealand, I'm sorry. Yes... that neither one of use feels entirely comfortable pronouncing. It's achieving some kind of special status.

Oh, it's wonderful. I think it is a really exciting development in just, good old-fashioned, western-style law. I can take a step back. The river you're talking about, when you look at it as an Australian or someone from North America you might say, "Wanger Newy." With an Australian accent, that's what you'd say. But I'm told with great authority by both Maori and other New Zealand colleagues that it's pronounced "Funger Newy" River. But I apologize if I got that terribly wrong and if New Zealand folk are laughing at me right now.

What happened is, at the end of 2012, the international press picked up that the Whanganui River had been given legal personhood — rights in law. Some of that coverage was a bit more enthusiastic, and perhaps a little inaccurate. So, when we made contact with some of the folks over there just to find out — because it sounded really exciting — some people were calling it a 'rights of Nature' development, but actually it comes from a different place. I'm not an expert, but I've looked into what these amazing developments are. In New Zealand, under the Treaty of Waitangi, there are compensation agreements. So really it's about negotiations between the Maori people and the government — the state. There's a lot of really intricate detail in there that I don't want to brush over with disrespect — but in a nutshell what has happened is that under some negotiations between the Maori people who are responsible or care for the Whanganui River, the beginning of an agreement is being reached. Apparently it hasn't been entered into law yet. But under this agreement — and I've read the documents — there is a record of understanding that starts to map out a lovely relationship. What it will do is — if it all goes through, and I really hope that it all does — it will recognize the river as having rights, legal personhood rights, the same rights as a person or a corporation. And it will be managed by, apparently, guardians: one, a representative from the Maori people and a representative from government.

Many of us are watching this space with great interest. It probably is a deep compromise for the Maori people, because it wouldn't be everything that they want — but what it does is, these people, these Maori people, have very effectively brought some of their custodial responsibilities and had them reflected in western-style law. Some of the lawyers who have been involved in the negotiations — one of them came to a conference in Australia last year — when they are asked, "What's it going to look like? How is this going to roll out?" He said, "Nobody knows. It's brand new, you know." I often say it's bubbling up from a slightly different source to some of the rights of Nature, and property lawyers will argue that it's very different to these other kinds of rights of Nature. What it's doing is supporting these ideas that natural systems need to be recognized in a more formal way in the legal system so that they can be greater protected. That's almost a patriarchal sort of word, but so that the humans that love them and are responsible for them can care for them, and have that relationship respected in law.

And that's very important because one thing I didn't mention is that the whole point of Earth jurisprudence is that it challenges the notion of the Earth as property. And so for the western system it's deeply radical. It's saying that there is an Earth community, not natural resources. So the relationship that we have with our Earth shouldn't be about the commoditization and the use of these things. Obviously humans need to use aspects of the world to live, but that should be a more respectful relationship, and within a scale that keeps our beautiful ecosystems alive and thriving and evolving.

Property is such an illusion when you start to think about. I bought a house, I loved it, I rebuilt it, and then I sold it. The house was there before I came along. It's older than I. It will be there after I'm gone. What does it mean for me to say that I own it? I mean I basically get the use of it for a while. Then that's just a house, that's not…
That's not even the land.

Not even the land.
All indigenous cultures had no belief that they owned land. Even in the cultures that did partition it up for households or larger groups, it was about caring for it and respecting it. Obviously that's a broad generalization, but the cultures of the Aboriginal peoples in Australia, the folks in North America and South America, they see the land as their mother. That's why it's Mother Earth. It supports them. It gave life to us, we will return to the Earth. Ownership in the middle? That's just a silly thing. [LAUGHTER]

It is silly.
The folks interested in the Earth jurisprudence movement aren't naïve. We don't think we're going to have some complete change of the property system overnight, and capitalism — I'm no economist, but you know, capitalism holds within it the deep need to continue to accumulate, so the system itself is problematic. And all of these things weave together: property rights, notions of personal freedoms, even lovely notions like liberty, have all been taken over by the machines that want to create wealth for a small sector of society. Property rights are embedded in that capacity to accumulate wealth, to trade and to continue the capitalist system. Someone recently asked the very important question, "Can we move towards a system that reflects an Earth jurisprudence structure if we have capitalism?" That's a really good question, because a lot of people say, "Not really."

But again, [there are] all these lovely little dots. The pictures that are forming, the groups that are bubbling up and doing amazing work, they are offering something different without being hugely conflict-oriented. We don't like what you are doing to our food, we don't like going into gigantic supermarkets and buying what you have stored for months on end. We are going to set up this cooperative over here and support the local farmers and buy our food directly. I love that. There is so much freedom. You can't always do it. For example, with extractive industries, you can't do it. You have to fight these guys, and stop them. But in other situations you can say, we don't like your system, I'm going to create something better over here, and that has caused shifts in the system. It hasn't caused the demise of some of these really big food systems, but they have really interestingly — in Australia at least — triggered a much greater interest in organic foods. So suddenly there are shelves full of stuff that you couldn't buy in a supermarket before. There are two ways of thought about that: either they have corrupted the system, or you're changing the system, but either way, lots of wonderful things going on.

And there are opportunities for you to choose things that weren't there before.
Yes. The biggest message that I've learned over the last few years of this journey into wild law, and learning from all these amazing people, has been that the disconnect not just of modern humans from nature, but the disconnect from all the systems that support us — and the longer the transaction chains towards our energy systems, our consumption of things we buy as food — the more difficult it is and often the less wholesome it is. If the food has been produced somewhere and then transported, and then shipped, and then stored, and then sold, it can take a very long time. But if you just buy it from the farmers or through a very short supply chain — both short geographically and short time-wise — it always seems to be a little more better for the Earth. If the source is better, the connections are better. You connect with the farmers; you support each other. It's a really simple idea, but I've learned that from a lot of my friends in collaborative economies and such, and from studying consumption.

Even just in narrow economic terms, you can pay more to the farmer than he could possibly get feeding it into this massive system.
Absolutely. And let's not even go into the complex world of subsidies and disadvantages...

No! Let's not go there. Let's go one more place, and that's your book. When it comes out in the fall, what am I going to find in it?
Well, it's actually a lovely mix of authors. Again, it came from our AELA conference. In 2011 we were looking at building theory and building practice. So Peter Burdon and I invited folk who came to the conference — and a few others — to write chapters that look at wild law in practice. It was really driven by our interest in what's going on at the grassroots level, and what's possible. So what you'll find in it is a collection of articles from people who give an update on how rights of Nature implementation is going in Ecuador; how rights of Nature — or the reflection of water rights in other systems — how it's actually being implemented, the

challenges on the ground. There are articles that reflect the challenges of thinking about things like, at the moment in the western world, we have animal protection laws, and animal welfare laws but a lot of the environmental laws and animal protection laws are very different. So are Earth jurisdiction laws a space to bring them together? What are the practical implications of that?

It's a really nice mix because sometimes in this space a lot of books that are published are very theoretical, but this one, by being in practice, brings together a mix of academics and grassroots activists. There are a few other theoretical pieces that are at least trying to piece together the big ideas and what we can do with them. So it's still a little bit of normative, idealistic — I'm actually thinking of my chapter in the book in particular… [LAUGHTER] My work looks at Earth jurisprudence and ecological limits and my own work with new concepts in science like planetary boundaries, so… I just gave a plug to my own chapter, in my own book! That's pretty sad, isn't it?

We hope that this book adds to the growing collection of folk who are writing about these really important issues. But I guess, me, because of the work I come from, I'm very interested in being, and I think this is maybe perhaps my final comment, the one thing I love about rights of Nature or Earth laws, is that it's rapidly becoming a hub for doing one of the toughest things around, which is linking really big theoretical ideas to absolutely grassroots change. And I think that's the really nice thing about this space and what we've seen this week at our summit here in Ecuador: the bringing together of very diverse worldviews, and very diverse people. So hopefully that's what our book will reflect a little bit.

That's a wonderful place to stop. Thank you so much. I know this was not easy for you to do but it was very important to us — and, I think, very important for those people who will get to see this interview.

I hope that it's helpful. Thanks for your time.

MUMTA ITO

Embedding Green Law in the European Union

Recorded January 2014

Mumta Ito began her career as a high-powered corporate lawyer, working in the heart of the City of London — Britain's equivalent to Wall Street. She was advising investment banks, multinational corporations and governments on large-scale, complex actions. She was very successful, until she found herself questioning the human value of her work.

During a leave of absence, she experienced a profound spiritual transformation and joined the entourage of Amma, one of India's foremost teachers, healers and humanitarians. Using her legal training to serve her reawakened spiritual consciousness, she set up a successful environmental organization in the Virgin Islands, which led her to challenge the whole relationship between human law and the laws of Nature.

She founded the International Centre for Wholistic Law in Scotland, and subsequently Rights of Nature Europe — a registered charity that is building a pan-European network of individuals and organizations from all walks of life to establish rights of Nature in law throughout Europe. She is now engaged in a European Citizens' Initiative designed to change the world by embedding the rights of Nature in the legal system of the 28-nation European Union.

In the EU, participatory democracy is a fairly new invention. It started in February 2011 with the European Citizens' Initiative. What the European Citizens' Initiative allows us to do is that seven citizens from seven member states can propose a law to the European Commission and, provided we raise at least a million signatures across at least seven member states, with the *de minimis* of about 0.01 percent of the population of at least seven countries, then the European Commission have to consider passing that law.

That's a big task — seven countries and several million signatures, right?
That's right. It will require a lot of awareness raising, education and building the network.

And there are 20 other countries, right? You can also take action in those, but separately.

Absolutely. We intend to run the Initiative for the rights of Nature across as many countries as possible involving all sectors of society because this is something that affects us all in a very fundamental way.

Now, that's "the Initiative." Tell me more about how environmental law is part of the problem.

Environmental law is failing — the evidence is all around us. If it was working well we wouldn't have an environmental crisis. In my career as a lawyer trying to protect Nature using the existing structures of law, I discovered that environmental law isn't designed to protect Nature, because it comes from the same paradigm that created the problem. Because environmental law is designed to support economic growth, its purpose is to manage the undesirable effects of business as usual, without challenging the economic system that causes the problem. This is why it has been ineffective in stopping the damage or reversing it. Even so, our governments are now deregulating to stimulate the economy, leaving the protection of Nature to market forces. Hence the Green Economy which puts Nature on the capital markets so corporations can profit.

Our current economic system needs Nature to be an object in order to keep exploiting it. So in law, Nature is property and this leads to practical problems that make it almost impossible to protect Nature. A good example is biodiversity. The endangered species listing system is failing spectacularly because it cannot keep pace with current extinction rates. It takes years of scientific study to list the species, and at the moment we are losing 150-200 species per day. In the time it takes to list the species, it's already too late. And it's a fragmented system. It's like saying in a human body we will protect the nose and finger but it's okay to stab you in the heart. With rights of Nature we protect the health of the whole body.

Also the current structure of law makes it almost impossible for people or NGOs to bring cases, because they are restricted to technical arguments about decision-making processes within legal structures that favour economic development above all else. And because Nature is an object in law, there is no duty of care. So the area of law that deals with obligations doesn't apply. After a disaster people can be compensated for their own economic loss, but there's no obligation to restore Nature. This is why, according to UNEP, we are now losing 150-200 species per day.

So how will rights of Nature change things?

Rights of Nature is the first step towards a wholistic framework of law that provides an ecological context for our existence. Ecosystems and other species would have legal personality, just like corporations, with the right to exist, thrive and play their role in the web of life. Which means redesigning our societal structures so that human needs are met in a way that protects the integrity of the earth and adds to its resilience.

Re-characterising Nature as a rights-bearing subject of the law is also a pow-erful counterbalance to corporate rights. It's a game changer, because it shatters the existing paradigm based on anthropocentrism and reductionism. It unravels the economic system that depends on Nature being an object. Rights of Nature is not just another law to add to the list of ineffective environmental laws. It's a fun-damental principle that changes everything. It provides a legal framework which will strengthen and support all complementary solutions that enable us to live in harmony with Nature.

Now, what would that actually mean in practice? Let's say I am a citizen in one of the countries in the European Union and I see some environmental outrage going on. What can I do about it?

Assuming that our initiative was successful, and that the EU adopted a directive on the rights of Nature, what that would mean is that the EU directive would become applicable in all 28 member states. So there will be a time period within which each member state will have to enact laws that give effect to the principles in the directive. Ordinary people will be able to bring cases invoking the rights of the ecosystems and species themselves rather than having to rely on technical arguments about whether the planning department followed the correct procedure, or proving that their property rights are affected.

There will also be an Ombudsman for Nature. We feel that whilst the adver-sarial system may be helpful in some circumstances, it is not well-equipped to co-create solutions to the complex interrelated problems that result in environ-mental issues. So we also recommend multi-stakeholder problem-solving forums that enable the co-creation of solutions and the healing of relationships.

However, the main transformative power is in the integration of these funda-mental principles into all areas of society and policy, particularly economic policy. Our draft directive provides that no subsidy will be given to any industry infringing the rights of Nature, and that subsidies will be diverted to solutions that enable us to meet our societal needs in harmony with nature.

Can you think of an example of something, which you can't now address, but would at least get its day in court if this were in place?

Yes. For example, something like fracking, which is currently very difficult to stop using the existing structures of law because the only conversation that can happen in court is whether the planners followed the correct decision-making procedure. At present there's no legal requirement for governments to formulate policies that prioritize the health of ecosystems, and to integrate this requirement across all levels and sectors of society. Accordingly environmental decisions are made exclusively at the micro-level under individual planning cases — with no regard to the cumulative effect of such decisions in eroding ecosystem and Earth system resilience. So a company can make multiple fracking applications across the country but each one is only assessed on a local level as if it's the only one which is dangerous. With rights of Nature in law, the ecosystem as a whole will have a right to its own integral health as well as all species, not just ones on the endangered species list. All people will have standing to defend Nature, not just people whose property rights are affected. This will give communities a much stronger basis to protect Nature using the law.

Another area is ecosystem restoration. Since the law now regards Nature as an object — as property — the law doesn't recognise a relationship between us and the rest of Nature. So there is no duty of care to restore Nature in a disaster because there is no legal "person" that can be harmed. With rights of Nature, ecosystems and other species will have legal personality just like corporations. So we will owe them a legal duty of care, which brings in obligations — including the obligation to restore.

So if I were a citizen and I wanted to take some action on, let's say, the pollution of the local river — if I go now, I have to show that that pollution affects me personally, directly, in order to have what they call standing, right?
Yes, exactly, usually this is the case. In Europe, NGOs have standing to bring cases in the public interest but it's still restricted to bringing technical arguments about decision-making processes within a framework that is already designed to prioritize development. This makes it extremely difficult.

But once you have that kind of legislation in place, then it becomes possible for me to go to court and say, "It doesn't directly affect me, but it does affect Nature."
Yes. Part of the mechanism that we look to build in is also to give community the right to defend the rights of ecosystems and of Nature and also the subordination of corporate rights. At the moment, rights of communities are not really recognized in our legal system, *per se*. There may be pockets where this exists, but it isn't really a given and it certainly doesn't enable them to speak up on behalf of ecosystems and biodiversity that is affected by human action.

In the [United] States, the approach they're taking is that the community itself seizes that jurisdiction, basically saying, "Within our city, within our town, Nature has rights." The hope is that this becomes a big enough movement that it eventually pushes the idea upward. But you're looking at almost the opposite direction, doing it across this large political structure.
Yes. In the United States, it's my understanding that municipalities are able to create their own ordinances. In Europe, citizens can propose laws via local and

regional citizens initiatives in around 18 European countries. However, in most countries laws made at the local level can be over-ridden at levels further up. Having pockets of protection at the local level isn't enough, but this is valuable in evolving the paradigm of law and setting precedents that show it's possible to make such laws. In the USA towns have successfully banned fracking on this basis. That also raises awareness by getting people involved in envisioning what they do want for their town, rather than just what they don't want. It also helps to build a grassroots movement rather than relying on a top-down approach.

Can you tell me something about your work with the International Centre for Wholistic Law?

The purpose of the International Centre for Wholistic Law is to realign our human laws with the universal laws that govern all life. Ancient wisdom from all around the world speaks of the "eternal law" — some fundamental principles that bring peace, harmony and balance to all of life. These principles ensure harmony with self, others and all of Nature and are a living, experiential embodying of law — very different to how law is used today primarily to protect economic interests with no regard to relationships. Wholistic law sees law in a paradigm of restoration, reparation and healing rather than the outdated paradigms that law is currently based on which stem from seventeenth-century science and philosophy — anthropocentrism, retribution and reductionism. If law is that which governs relationships, it makes sense that it governs all the relationships that we have. So bringing Nature into our legal system as a stakeholder in its own right, and putting law into an overarching ecological context is vitally important.

We train lawyers and law students by taking them through a transformative process so that they embody qualities that enable them to transform our legal system so that lawyers become healers of conflict and start actively influencing our legal structures and legal practice to take a more human and wholistic approach. This requires restructuring our laws as well as our methodologies.

So, the Centre for Wholistic Law will try to encourage an alignment between the existing legal system and the laws of Nature?

Yes, absolutely. Part of our work at the International Centre for Wholistic Law is looking at ways of resolving disputes that go beyond blame, that go beyond separation. We're looking at the wider issues that affect all of us. Legal issues cannot be separated from the societal problems that give rise to them — and looking at them in isolation produces injustice. So we're pioneering innovative methods of dispute resolution that allow the voices of all the stakeholders to be heard and taken into consideration as well as for trauma to be healed on an individual and collective level.

This sounds like a whole different legal process — not the adversarial process, but a process of finding solutions with many participants?

That's right. Our current legal system is based on a paradigm of retribution and as you know, when we look at relationships, if I'm having a dispute with my friend and I am seeking retribution, it's not really going to advance things in a positive way. So, in a similar vein, we have certain practices that take us towards war, and we have certain practices that take us towards peace; certain practices that unite us and certain practices that separate us. We're seeking to use law as a tool to unite us and to bring restoration, reparation and healing, rather than retribution because we cannot co-create solutions to complex problems simply by blaming each other and making people pay.

Let me take you back to the beginning of all of this because one of the things that I find fascinating about your story is that it begins in, of all places, the financial heart of London: the City of London, the very belly of the beast. [LAUGHS] How did you get from there to Findhorn and wholistic law?

It was an interesting journey. Yes, I did start out in the so-called "belly of the beast," or, as what some people may see as part of the problem. I was a structured finance lawyer. I worked in the City of London — London's equivalent of Wall Street. I used to represent investment banks, governments, large multinationals on very big transactions that involved several jurisdictions, etc — a lot of complex work.

And I found that my career was going very well on the outside, and I was making lots of money, but in my inner world something was not quite sitting right. One day I had a profound spiritual awakening and literally overnight, my world-view changed. And so, when I went back into the office, nothing there resonated with me anymore. Everything was back to front; it was inside out; nothing really made sense. I found that the work that I was doing was not really in alignment with what I really valued in this world. So I came out of there and I started to pursue a deeper inquiry. I started to pursue a path of healing and spiritual practice, and I trained with some of the most profound spiritual teachers of our time, mainly from the East which reconnected me with the yogic tradition I was brought up with as a child.

What was this spiritual experience that turned this over? This is a fascinating situation, where one day you're more or less aligned with what you're doing, and then suddenly it's gone completely out of harmony.

Well, I was raised in a fairly spiritual environment. I'd grown up practising yoga and meditation. I'd been brought up in the spiritual traditions of my ancestors. There came a time when I wanted to turn away from that and really experience what the mainstream of life was saying was the route to happiness, and this led to me pursuing the career path that I did. And I pursued it wholeheartedly. So, one day when my father wanted to go visit Mother Meera, who is an enlightened being, residing in Germany, he invited me and my husband to come with him. I was really not very interested. At that point I had convinced myself that there was nothing spiritual in this world; it's just a scientific material world, and that's pretty much what life is all about, and she's probably a fake and you know… it's nothing of interest to me. However, the reason that my father was going was because my sister was actually very ill at the time and he wanted to take her for healing. And my sister was refusing to go. So, my father pleaded with me and he said, "Well, if everybody comes at least I can say to your sister that it's a family holiday and you don't even need to come and see Mother Meera, you could just hang out." So, I thought, Okay, I'm not interested in going to see Mother Meera, but I am interested in helping my sister, so if it would be of help to her, then I'll come along. Of course, once I got there, I couldn't resist going to see Mother Meera.

And what happened then?
I walked into the hall. Mother Meera has two assistants and they balance the energies in the room by adjusting the seating between people so they would sometimes move people and ask people to sit in certain positions. So, as soon as I walked into the room, the assistant motioned to me and my husband and asked us to sit on a seat right in front of Mother. My initial thought at the time was, "Wow, they're very hospitable to skeptical people." And then, when my father and my mother and my sister walked in, they motioned for them to sit on the side and then I thought, "Oh, wait a minute, there might be something more to this because she's ill."

So, anyway, Mother Meera came into the room and I went into a deep meditation. All of my childhood upbringing and my deep reverence for the spiritual came back to me as soon as I was in the presence of this incredible being. I received Mother Meera's blessing, which she does in a very particular way. She works with a subtle energy channel — more subtle than the central energy channel referred to in most cultures, she says, where certain karmic codes are encoded and they appear in the form of knots. She looks directly for about six seconds into the eyes of each person and when she does that, she's un-knotting these knots within the central channel which enables that person to accelerate to the next level of their spiritual journey in life.

After the session that night I had the most incredible sleep and during that sleep I found that I was having these dreams where I was held by these beautiful swirling colours. I later found a book of paintings by Mother Meera where she was describing other dimensions of reality and in these paintings she had these beautiful swirling colours, a bit like I'd seen in my dream. So, anyway, I came out of there, and I came back to the office and it was like, the show was over! [LAUGHTER] "What am I doing here?" I thought.

And how did your colleagues react? Your body was there, but you had spiritually left the building.

Absolutely. One of the first changes that I made was that I turned my desk around because I had a beautiful view of the sky and I wanted to be a little bit more connected to nature and what was going on in the world. In my job, we used to work incredibly long hours, working all through the night through to the next day was quite common. Leaving the office at 3 a.m. was commonplace, so we never really got to go outside. So I turned my desk around to look at the sky and I started playing subliminal relaxing music in my room, and people used to come into the office and all of a sudden they would just forget what it was that they'd come to talk about and they would say, "Wow, I feel really nice in this room." [LAUGHS] And then they'd start talking about, you know, something personal. After a short time, my room became known as the "Love Room."

Coming to how I managed to come away from that period of work — the pain of being in that environment got more and more intense for me. One day when I was there late at night, working on a transaction, I ended up having a heart-to-heart with my boss, saying, "Why are we doing this? Why are we doing this to ourselves? What's the end result of what we do? Some corporation or some bank just ends up making a little bit more money and what are they doing with the money and — are they solving the problems of poverty and war in the world? No they're not! They're investing it in things that usually take us in the opposite direction! I don't really know why I am doing this!" So, my boss said, "Well, why don't you leave?" and I said, "Well, I can't leave, because I am in this situation where we're building a house ... I just don't know what to do." Something in him really heard me and he said, "Well, how about we structure it as a redundancy? Maybe I could give you say a year and half's pay, and that would give you an opportunity to finish building your house and by then you'd discover what it is that you really want to do. Personally, I think once you've gone out there and seen what it's like out there, you'll know how good it is here and you'll be back here. But, you know, how about it?" And I thought, "Wow. This is fabulous!" [LAUGHS] So I took it. And I haven't turned back!

Have you seen him since?

No, I haven't! [LAUGHTER]

I was curious to know what he would think about this.

Yeah, it would be very interesting actually. I'd like to see him one of these days. I got on fabulously with him. He was a great guy.

So that gave me the opportunity to really deepen my spiritual practice and I started travelling with my spiritual teacher Mata Amritanandamayi, or Amma, who's sometimes referred to as "the hugging saint," and embarked on a complete transformation of my being through rigorous experiential training. It was during that time that, at the back of my mind, even though the world of healing and the world of spirituality was absorbing me so completely and bringing me so much fulfillment, I really wondered why it was that I had been trained to the 'nth degree' in something that was now utterly irrelevant to me. I could see that the way law was structured was entrenching the victim–perpetrator paradigm in our society. I couldn't see how we could bring about peace through methods that are primarily based on war. For me law was a big part of the problem and I wanted nothing to do with it.

So, I asked Amma whether I should try to use the law in order to serve humanity or whether to just abandon that idea completely and focus on something else. What she said to me was very simple. She said, "Stay in law for now and when the opportunity comes to serve, just take it." So, about a week later, I found myself in the Virgin Islands and I was approached by somebody on the island saying that the government had recently given approval for a golf course and a five-star hotel in an area of international ecological importance — a protected area with a Ramsar code, internationally recognized as a protected area. Even though there had been debates for years and years, and lots of environmental studies, finally the government — the chief minister — had just unilaterally given his consent. So, the chief conservation officer was tearing his hair out because he wanted to bring a case, but no lawyers on the island would help him.

It was a small island; everybody knew each other, and so there were a lot of complex interrelationships between the people. Nobody would dare go against the government — and in this scenario, you'd have go against the chief minister personally, and the chief minister was the guy who personally would have to sign all the work permits and all the business permits of the lawyers. [LAUGHS] So, understandably, very few lawyers were interested in taking it up.

So, I thought to myself, okay, when the opportunity comes to serve, just take it, and so I went to go and see the chief conservation officer, and we had a discussion. We had three weeks to file a case. I had no knowledge of environmental law and I thought, "Okay! Let's do it!"

So, the first port of call for me was to start working on the energy with the spiritual practices and the healing practices that I had learned, and as soon as I had started to do that, I found that miracles started to happen. Within the time — three weeks — which is a very short time space to amass all of the evidence that would be necessary to bring a challenge, everything just came and we were in a position to file the case. At this point, it wasn't even clear whether citizens would even have standing, because no environmental cases had ever been brought in this particular jurisdiction.

So, we organized as an NGO. There was one Caribbean case where the citizens had gotten standing and that was only because it was brought by an organization with an international reputation and the scientific knowledge and all of that: it was Greenpeace that brought this case. So we thought, "Okay! We'll form the Virgin Islands Environmental Council." And we got hold of whatever scientific experts and prominent people that we could find in the community to come on board with this NGO. It was very difficult to get somebody prominent from the community to sign their name behind the case, and it had to be somebody personally bringing the case. Eventually, a prominent man in the community stepped forward and we filed.

What happened as a result of this? At that time, I was still volunteering and touring and studying with my spiritual teacher. As soon as we filed the case, I was off the island and I was on tour in Europe. I discovered a new way of doing law. We were in a new city every two to three days and I was working from morning until night in the organization of my spiritual teacher, running healing programs. So, I really didn't know where I was going to find the time or the space. I had no idea whether I would have Internet connection; how I would be able to get hold of people; when the hearings were going to be. I thought this would be very interesting.

What I found was that all I had to do was stand as a channel for grace — and I found that the case was doing itself. Miraculously, whenever anything needed to be responded to or any business needed to be transacted, I'd find that I would have Internet connection; all of the people that I needed to connect with would be online at that time; we'd transact our business in incredibly efficient time, and then I'd be back with my spiritual teacher.

This was a completely new experience to me because, working in a law firm, you would push and push and push and you know, be working on it, working on it, working on it — even though, in reality, things only move when they move. I started to notice that there was an orchestration and a timing that was beyond my control. All I had to do was be incredibly present to what was actually unfolding, and to be a conduit for the energy to facilitate the process.

The outcome of all of this, launching the case, was very useful. Even though, yes, it was engaging in the adversarial process, it was useful because it stopped work from starting. It stopped the diggers from going in. The first fortunate thing that happened in the chain was that the developer's funding got pulled as a result of the case. So that bought us time. However, we thought it was going to be a quick process, which is part of the reason that I was prompted to take it on. It was going to be a judicial review, and the legislation said you would get a result in three months. It took us three years [LAUGHS] because the developers joined the action and they kept stalling it. So they kept applying for the extensions and it kept getting pushed back and back and further back. By this time, we had a legal team, and the people on the island started to feel more empowered. Initially it was the kind of place where people felt very disempowered because the government ran the shots, and the people really didn't have a voice. But somehow, launching this case really kind of caught the imagination of the people. So we worked on many different levels. Because people were highly interrelated and they knew each other, we started working with dialogues, with building relationships, with rallying around the shared values. This is where we started working in a non-adversarial way, showing that actually, by preserving what we have in terms of our biodiversity and preserving nature, we're actually building a much richer future for our countries into future generations.

And the government started to change their view — so much so that by the time our court case came to be heard, in the government's national tourist brochure, they were actually bragging that they're such an environmentally friendly nation that we even have a local group that are challenging the government in court on environment grounds. [LAUGHTER]

So anyway, we won at first instance. Of course, because we were restricted to the planning and administrative courts, we had to find fault with the planning process, so we went for every single angle that we could get. What the judge found was that development couldn't happen, so we won purely on the basis that it was a protected area and it is prohibited by law for any development to happen there.

So, that was great. However, the developers did appeal and the appeal was carried out in St. Lucia. On appeal, we weren't so fortunate, because the St. Lucian judge decided to go with the developers. They were putting forward an argument that there was a technical drafting error in the way that the law had been created. Instead of calling it a "fisheries protected area," the law referred to it as a "marine protected area." In actual fact, the judge says, "Well, the area is not protected, even though there have been all these environmental studies." There was actually no dispute in the planning process about the protected status of this area, but the judge still ruled that actually it's not protected, and so the development can go ahead.

However — and this is the beauty of this case — the government had such a change of heart in the way they were perceiving the issue that they came forward and they said, "Okay, well, we'll just change the law." The planning permission had lapsed. "We'll change the law and we'll word it as the judge wants it, and on top of that, we'll declare the area a national park." So, anybody who has had any experience with trying to bring environmental cases in the public interest would know that this is an absolutely phenomenal result. Usually, if the government had still retained the same posture — say we'd have won at court — at the very best, all we would have won is that the decision would have gone back to the planners, the developers would make one or two changes to get round what the judge said and then usually the development goes ahead in some shape or form. So this was an absolutely astounding result.

After that, I came to the conclusion that, "Okay. I've got my learnings in law. I can see that this adversarial process just doesn't work. The law isn't designed to protect nature, and it certainly doesn't empower people to bring cases where real issues can be discussed — it's not for me. And that's great. If all changes happen fundamentally at the energy level, I will just continue focusing on that."

You know the most striking thing to me about that story is that because your vision is at a level above the adversarial process — the normal lawyer would take this on and would never question that framework, they'd just work within it in an adversarial way — but you're coming at it in a much more problem-solving way and a much more open kind of way. And then it sounds as though you — I don't know how much by design and how much by just evolution it was, but it sounds as though you basically had a whole educational process that went on that finally affected the government. It's really a fascinating story. What I'm hearing is, "So we bought a little time, and that gave people a chance to think. And then we got another little bit of time and that gave other people a chance to think. As they thought more about it, the people in the government started to think about it." It evolves in a very non-adversarial way, even though it's an adversarial process. It uses the law as a kind of learning process for the entire community.
Absolutely. Absolutely. Yeah, and this is the beauty of taking a wholistic approach.

Yeah. The other thing that strikes me in that story is the remarkable experience with Mother Meera in Germany. You go in there with no expectation of change. You've got the foundational understanding of the situation, but you've gone there, basically, to convenience your father and to do something for your sister. The idea that anything was going to change for Mumta is not on the agenda at all. And then you have this profound experience within you and you come out into a different world. But, the striking thing for me is, if you were ready for that, you didn't know it. Right? [LAUGHS]
Absolutely. In fact, the person who was leading the tour, taking people to see Mother Meera, she sat us down and she said, "You know, people sometimes undergo profound change. Sometimes their lives fall apart. If their relationships are not aligned, sometimes their relationships fall apart. If their work is not aligned, they find their work falls apart." And I thought, "There is absolutely no way on Earth that anything is going to fall apart in my life." [LAUGHTER]

And then it does.
Yeah, and then the whole thing fell apart! [LAUGHTER]

I think that's absolutely fascinating.
Fascinating. Mmm.

Let me come back to Europe — because I can see how you're thinking very differently, but you're also feeling very empowered, right? Because now you're starting a movement to change the legal system of 28 countries.
Absolutely. Again, there is a little bit of a story of how I came into that. It wasn't that one day I woke up and I thought, "You know what? We've got this problem and I'm going to do something about it." It was a little bit of an evolutionary process. After the Virgin Islands case, I thought, "Right! Well that's it! I don't need to do anything further with law. I'm clear. I'm just going to continue on my path of healing." I became a mom and our family — me, my husband and my daughter — we went up to live in the Findhorn community in Scotland. It was around that time when I had a minor physical issue, and I went to a kinesiology session. Kinesiology is a way of testing the muscles to see whether something is true or not true; it's a way of bypassing the mind and going into the body intelligence and usually, very usually they would test the muscles to see if you're allergic to certain foods and that sort of thing. But they can test a whole variety of issues.

So, I went for a kinesiology session about this minor physical issue and what came out of the session was that I need to put together a project that brings law and healing together, that shifts the whole paradigm of the legal profession from adversarial to a paradigm of healing, restoration and reparation, and that takes into account the rights of all beings. In order to know more fully what I should do, I should do a series of meditations — an extra two hours of meditation and I was already doing about three hours of meditation a day anyway! [LAUGHS] An extra two hours of meditation, and sending healing to the legal profession every day for a month, during which time I'd get more clarity.

I did that. At first, very disbelievingly [LAUGHS] and very much dismayed, thinking, "Oh, I thought maybe I could avoid certain foods and that would be all I'd need to do!" So I was a little bit skeptical when I went into these meditations about whether anything would come, but amazingly, a lot of information — a lot of clarity — came through. So, I would sit there each day with a note pad and jot down all the insights that came to me. That culminated in the creation of the International Centre for Wholistic Law. For our inaugural event, one of the things I was guided to pioneer is the use of systemic constellations in the context of legal disputes. Systemic constellations are a method that a man called Bert Hellinger, from Germany, developed in the context of families, which completely revolutionized the way psychology operates. It has been pretty much been incorporated into the mainstream in Germany. He got his insights when he was living in Africa and he observed how the tribal people dealt with their disputes and issues and how a lot of issues that people were carrying in the present had their origins with previous generations and unresolved energy from previous generations that continued to perpetuate itself.

You mean like, our parents were enemies so we're enemies? That kind of thing?
Yeah, that kind of thing. But it could be not even as specific as that. It could be something like, if our parents or our grandparents were enemies with a person because of a certain thing, we could be carrying an aspect of that and so we may be enemies with somebody completely unrelated to who our parents were enemies with, but the same dynamic is playing out that played out in a previous generation.

So Bert Hellinger devised this method of working with "representatives." He found that a phenomenon started to appear where representatives who had absolutely no idea or had never met the people whose issue it was, had no idea about their family system — when they were standing as a representative and asked just to be present to what was occurring in their body — would be downloading information relating to that system, information that ordinarily they would not know. So, somehow, people were tapping into this collective consciousness, and hidden dynamics would become immediately visible. He found that when things were acknowledged, this had a healing effect upon the whole system. So, things that were excluded, when they were included again, this then brought balance. He created something called the orders of love, which was an alignment of order that brought about peace and harmony, which, basically is in harmony with the natural laws that govern all of life.

So, at our inaugural event, we had a group come from Falkirk, who are a community that were facing fracking in their community, and we used systemic constellations to look at the issues related to that. We also did a constellation about the field of wholistic law, where a change agent would be most effective. For the fracking case, it was quite evident that the community group were quite burnt out and they really didn't know where to go next. They were feeling angry and they felt as if they were locked in this battle that they were not going to win with the energy company; they wanted some practical, pragmatic answers. At the end of the constellation, the man who brought the issue — who was one of the leaders of the campaign — said that he could see immediately how he'd become embroiled in this battle with the energy company, but the energy company were just part of a much wider systemic picture. That really, what we're up against is ourselves. He could also see how personally, how the energy company was bound to the people that it was serving and how he was also, by virtue of being a human being, also interconnected with that and he found it difficult to reconcile that on a personal level. He also found that during the constellation, the representative for energy had to leave the room three times to be sick... and she wasn't feeling sick before or after the constellation. So, there was a lot of energy that got moved during that.

At the end of that constellation it ended up with the position of the energy company becoming a lot more balanced, and the position of the citizen's group becoming reconnected with the original impulse that brought them to the work, and then being strengthened. After this constellation, the person who brought the issue said he felt that as a result of it that his consciousness has expanded and he can now see the need to work on multiple levels and multiple dimensions. It's not just a one dimensional battle against one company, but a much broader systemic issue. That's an incredible shift in insight and perspective to happen in just one hour.

They already had a signature campaign, but from that, they managed to get unprecedented number of signatures. That won them a public inquiry, and led to a moratorium on fracking in Scotland. So, somehow, the movement did get a new direction, new life through this process.

Well, it's another one of these events where you've got a very specific situation and somehow, if you step back, or look at it in a more rounded way, opportunities arise that you wouldn't have seen if you'd stayed in that locked-in battle.
Absolutely. And coming back to the European Citizens' Initiative, with wholistic law, what we found was that wholistic law didn't really have a place until all beings appeared on the scene. When a consideration of all beings were included in the framework, it was at that point that the mainstream adversarial system really didn't know how to deal with the situation, but wholistic law was there in its entirety to meet it.

From that I just got the clear insight that the rights of Nature is something that would really bring about the paradigm shift that we need to evolve our legal systems to really meet the challenges that we're all facing globally, today. Then I learned about the European Citizens' Initiative and I thought, "Well, it's obvious. We'll bring the European Citizens' Initiative to get the rights of Nature recognized in Europe."

If I can tease out one little thing there, when you mention "all beings" — that's what the rights of Nature does, isn't it? It expands your sense of the community that has standing, and whose interests legitimately need to be considered. It expands that from humans, and human structures, to the entire Earth community.
Absolutely.

And so that changes the definition of who the courts should be serving and what the community is — what the dimensions of the community are.

Absolutely. For me, it brings it to a more real construction of law. After all, Nature moves according to its own laws. We are also part of Nature, our bodies — we're made up of the five elements, just like everything else. So, Nature's laws bind us; our laws don't bind Nature. Nature carries on irrespective of what human beings decide is the truth. So, given that Nature's laws bind us, one would see that if Nature didn't exist and thrive, we wouldn't exist and thrive as well. In that sense, everything that we call a human right derives from the rights of Nature. If Nature doesn't have a right to exist and thrive, how can we have a right to exist and thrive? Because our very existence is dependent upon Nature.

So, all it's doing is just aligning, expanding and evolving our laws to recognize that when we talk about community, we exist within a much wider community. It's a community of all beings we share this planet with. That's the plants, that's the mountains, the rivers — we are intrinsically interdependent. It's just natural that if law is really going to meet the promise of the world that we would like to create for our children and our grandchildren, that it needs to expand its ambit and recognize all of the relationships that we have.

PABLO FAJARDO AND STEVEN DONZIGER

The Long Campaign for Justice in Ecuador's Amazon Rain Forest

Recorded January 2014

Lago Agrio is the centre of the oil industry in eastern Ecuador. It's also the epicentre of one of the biggest ecological crimes of all time: the massive contamination of perhaps two million hectares of the Amazon rain forest at the hands of Texaco, which is now part of Chevron. Pablo Fajardo grew up there in extreme poverty and, with the help of the Catholic Church, put himself through law school. His very first case as a lawyer was the one known throughout South America as "Chevron-Tóxico," a multi-billion-dollar action on behalf of thousands of Indigenous people. Fajardo became the lead Ecuadorian lawyer in a large team of Ecuadorian, American and international attorneys which ultimately won a $9.5 billion judgment against Chevron — only to discover that Chevron had exported its major assets and skipped the country. So the legal team is asking the courts of Argentina, Brazil and Canada to enforce the Ecuadorian judgment.

Meanwhile, back in the USA, Chevron sued Fajardo, community leader Luis Yanza and their American legal colleague, Steven Donziger, who has been advising the affected communities since the case began in 1993. Invoking the Racketeer Influenced and Corrupt Organizations Act, Chevron claimed that Donziger, Fajardo and Yanza are part of a criminal conspiracy to extort money from Chevron, and that the environmental case against Chevron was a "sham." Chevron won an initial judgment, but Donziger and his Ecuadorian colleagues are appealing, contending that the judge demonstrated clear bias against the villagers and had undisclosed investments in Chevron himself. While that matter remains before the US courts, Canadian lawyers acting for the villagers are trying to seize Chevron's Canadian assets to pay the Ecuadorian judgment. The Canadian courts have said they'll hear the case, but Chevron continues to fight.

We interviewed Pablo Fajardo in the very modest house in Lago Agrio which serves both as his home and his office. This was our first-ever Green Interview in

Spanish. By sheer coincidence, we ran into Steven Donziger at a hotel in Quito, so we interviewed him, too. First, here's Pablo Fajardo.

The greater Amazon Basin — including Brazil, Colombia, Venezuela, Peru and Ecuador — viewed from the air is like a giant broccoli of a forest that is so beautiful, so diverse, so full of life! It contains not only a diversity of plants and animals, but of people; human beings that have lived here their entire lives. For the native peoples who have always lived in the Amazon Basin, it's not just their land; it's their supermarket, their pharmacy, their home; the place where they exist in absolute freedom. They lived from and took from the forest only what they needed, because they didn't want more. They had everything. They had their entire lives. Of course, they had freedom, total freedom. Whenever one talks to the elders or any of the native peoples, whether Secoya, Cofán, they say that is the most serious thing that the oil industry took from them. They say, "Now we are not free. Before we could move freely through the forest across the rivers without any problems. Now we are not free."

The whole land was home; the whole terrain was home.
Yes, the entire terrain. For example, here, where this city is now had been ancestral Cofán territory. The Cofán lived in this territory and of course were able to hunt and fish and could travel freely. There are several different groups who occupied this area, but they knew their territories and their borders and they were free to interact with one another; to coexist.

And the hunting and fishing? That's all lost?
No, it has not been totally lost. There are a few places in the Amazon Basin, basically in protected areas, where that life has been somewhat preserved, but not in this zone where Texaco was active, along with other oil companies. Here it was all lost. It was lost because once the company came in, in addition to polluting the water, they organized the expulsion of the native peoples occupying the territory, forcing them to move to different areas.

And they also had health problems after that, right?
The Indigenous people, like the Cofán who lived here, enjoyed the freedom to move through the forest and rivers. it's important to understand that these peoples lived on what the forest provided. They didn't need to trade on the market because they obtained everything they needed from the forest. Their diet was based on fishing and hunting, and gathering fruit. When the oil industry arrived and began contaminating the rivers, the fish began to die off, which resulted in the elimination

---

The interview is translated by Judy Rein, and in the video, the translation is voiced by Chris Beckett.

of the principal food source for the native peoples. They were abruptly removed from their long-standing subsistence economy and were inserted into a violent market economy. So, when we talk about health-related problems, the impact has not just been on physical health, the health of community has been impaired: the disruption to the culture, the way of life, the food. These things affect overall health. When industry released toxic chemicals into the environment, new health problems emerged, that traditional Indigenous healers — shamen — were unable to treat. Shamen, in addition to being important local authorities, had knowledge that could treat common ailments. But when toxic pollution generated new diseases such as cancer, they were not able to respond. They began to feel increasingly powerless in the face of these new health problems and their inability to treat them.

It must also have been very strange that the people coming in thought they owned the land, as opposed to the land being a place that they lived in. I'm not saying that very well, but the thing about the change to property — all of a sudden, Texaco owns land, whereas people had previously just used it.

There are many interesting stories. For example, in one Cofán community that was near here, the last shaman, the last leader of that community — named Guillermo Quenamá — was very wise. When he saw that Texaco was dumping toxic waste into the river — they lived about three kilometres from here at the mouth of the Teteye River — Guillermo took his community away to another area to escape. He was very protective of the new territory, insisting that Texaco could not come into it. And he protected the land. Even though Texaco wanted to extract oil from it, he adamantly refused to allow the company in. So, the company sent in workers with alcohol to get him drunk. They forced him to drink a lot of alcohol to the point of poisoning and killing him. So, once he dies, the community is left without a leader, and the company entered the territory. To make the humiliation worse, the company took Guillermo's wife and forced her to work as a prostitute. She worked as a prostitute for 20 years.

An Indigenous people without a territory cannot exist, so they must protect their land.

But they didn't "exist" in the first place, legally, right? Because it was "undeveloped" land where nobody lived?

Well, the Cofán people were the first group to gain territorial recognition from the Ecuadorian state in 1974. Even though the state recognized the land as unclaimed territory — vacant and available — everybody understood that there were Indigenous peoples here; that they lived here. This was known. The company's operations were criminal and perverse, but the state was an accomplice in these violations of the Indigenous peoples' human rights.

These are not mistakes. These people know that they're doing something inhuman, unfair — and do it anyway.

Of course they knew. Of course they knew! The company knew what it was doing; it knew it was polluting. Moreover, in the 1960s, Texaco had filed patents in the United States, which were quite significant. In 1962, three years before Texaco came to extract oil in Ecuador, they published an industrial handbook that included a chapter on how to extract oil without contaminating water or the environment. It includes lovely illustrations of how to treat the water and re-inject it underground without contaminating and how to treat the gas by-product — truly, a very important guide of how to conduct oil operations without harming the environment. Notably, the book contained this special chapter on how to extract oil responsibly, which was written by Texaco technicians. Texaco technicians offer training around the world on responsible operations. Yet they never applied these techniques in the Ecuadorian Amazon.

Why? There are a number of reasons that I see. Three, basically. First, the company had financial incentives. The company was always seeking to earn maximum profit with the minimum investment possible. Second, because of the company's racism; Chevron — and before them, Texaco — considered, and continued to consider, that the Indigenous population of the Amazon Basin are worth less than any other population throughout the world. And third, the Ecuadorian State's inability to regulate or monitor the operations.

Working hand in hand, the state and the company?

There was state complicity in those years, but there was also complicity on Chevron's part. There are many documents that I can share with you. In the 1970s and 1980s, when Chevron took over Texaco, there was a report on bribes to Ecuadorian authorities. Chevron — as was typical of large multinationals at the time — was much more powerful than any state. They could set up or take down governments, or at least impose their chosen ministers and regulatory authorities. So, for example, the evidence shows that Chevron bribed regulatory authorities in the Ecuadorian state. There was complicity of the Ecuadorian state, but the company's bribes purchased that complicity.

Now, how did resistance begin, in this hopeless situation?

I think it is a process. My analysis, which is not at all technical, has always been that people unite out of necessity. For example, if you live in a city in a 50-storey building and you live on the thirtieth floor, and no one interacts with anyone else, you come and go to your apartment without engaging people above or below or next door to you. But if all of a sudden the electricity or heat or water is cut off in the building, then neighbours start knocking on each other's doors, saying, "Let's get together to make sure that there is water, services here." So people organize out of necessity.

In our case, people had many needs. There are health problems; there is extreme poverty in the population; there are human rights abuses. People suffered abuse and humiliation from Chevron, which had been Texaco, for 20 years, with the company and state together. People did not have any recourse, nowhere to seek assistance, nowhere to seek justice.

Faced with this situation, people began to join together and look for a way to demand their rights. In 1987, for example, in this area, along the highway where you came, there was a much rougher road. At that time, it took 12 hours to get here from Quito. There was an earthquake that destroyed the road and destroyed the pipeline, so people here were isolated — cut off from the rest of Ecuador. This made people join together even more to seek a solution to their problems. And, we had the support and solidarity of the Catholic Church, which had been working in the area for a long time. So we began to organize and look for solutions. A lot of people from outside the area began to arrive to work with us in those years, like students and doctors. The high incidence of cancer cases began to emerge at this time. There were also increases in miscarriages and childhood leukaemia. I became aware of it as well. It began to affect my life.

Getting off the bus, one could immediately see that the roads are all covered in oil because Texaco left the oil there. Everywhere you went there were hundreds of open wells, pools of crude oil; animals fallen into the open wells; gas combustion, creating an enormous curtain of smoke. It was a catastrophic landscape.

Working with the Catholic Church, I went with the priests and the missionaries to visit the communities and we saw that in every community we went to the problems were the same. People were sick: women were sick, children were sick; animals were falling into the oil pools. And everyone said the same thing, "I'm sick. There are these oil pools and no one has anywhere to go." At that point, we began to organize a small human rights committee in Shushufindi in 1988 to listen to the people. Then, we started meeting with groups in Lago Agrio, like organizations of women, Indigenous people, youth, rural workers, and after several years, in 1994, we established the Front to Defend the Amazon, to bring our case. So, it was a front. I was young, a high-school student and a little less crazy than I am now — but still a little crazy. [LAUGHTER] There were a lot of people like me back then, and we'd go together and do a lot of crazy stuff. This is a little of the origins of this social movement that sought respect for life, for Nature and justice.

But the company was resisting every way.

Of course they did — and still do. This isn't just about Texaco-Chevron, it's against an entire system of impunity for business that has existed, and still exists, through-out the world. What's this about? When we started our case, for example, many people told us that we were crazy, that this was impossible. We couldn't win against a big company like Chevron — that these companies dominated the [United] States. It would be impossible to succeed. And evidently, that this was believed around the world, since these large multinationals do what they want, wherever they want. This case of ours poses a serious threat to the systematic impunity for business around the world.

It's not that we were against the companies. They have a right to work, to produce. What we oppose is the crimes committed by businesses. If Chevron con-ducted its operations responsibly, respecting Nature and life, it would be different. We are not against these companies, just the way in which they act irresponsibly.

But you had to move from house to house? People were out to get you, right?
There were many problems, many problems with security and harassment. We still have these issues, and they keep getting worse, but what's at stake for Chevron is its reputation and a lot of money. For us, the stakes are about life — the lives of our people. When lives are at stake, you keep fighting for justice.

Your brother was killed, though.
Sí.

And they thought it was you.
This is what we assumed. It's difficult to talk about, because these are very upsetting memories. There were efforts and intelligence and an investigation, but in the end we were unable to determine for certain why he was killed. Yes, I was told that the victim was supposed to be me. I can't know for sure. The reality is that they killed him. It was a terrible death. He was cruelly tortured before he died.

I'm sorry. I am sorry to cause you pain again. But this is a very tough place, right? You really have to be both brave and desperate.
I live here. I live here. This is my home. I could leave, take my children and go somewhere else. But what happens to the rest of the people who live here? What happens to the Indigenous people who have been here all their lives? I try to do my duty to the extent possible by respecting nature, people, life and so that there is justice. I don't know if I am brave or cowardly, but I do what I must.

Your weapons are words and ideas.
Yes. When I took on the leadership of this case — I had been involved since the beginning, but took leadership in 2005 — I was the only lawyer on the case in Ecuador. The only lawyer. Chevron had 20 lawyers. I had one year of experience practising law. The youngest Chevron lawyer had 25 years' experience. Such a big

difference. They had 20 or 30 expert lawyers and I was barely out of law school. My advantage is that I don't have to lie. I don't have to figure out the truth, just how to communicate the truth. I am part of the story; the truth is in that story. It's difficult for Chevron: they have to figure out how to lie without making mistakes.

Tell me where the case is now.

There are a lot of different facets to the case. It's so big, but it's hard to explain. It's hard to explain, and it's hard for journalists to understand, so they also have a hard time explaining it to their audiences. The principal case in Ecuador, which we won, is in the judgement-enforcement phase. But, as you know, during the 20-year-long litigation, Chevron liquidated all its assets in Ecuador. So now, we have a very good judicial award, a very important legal victory, but Chevron has no assets in Ecuador, so we cannot collect on the judgment in Ecuador. So there are now three cases outside of Ecuador to try to collect on the judgment — in Canada, Brazil and Argentina. In the Canadian case, which we filed in May 2012, we sought a recognition, or approval of the Ecuadorian ruling. In the lower court, the judge did not rule in our favour — that was May 2013 — and of course we appealed that decision, because we believe that the judge misapplied the law. Last December 17 it was I believe, we received a decision from the appellate court in Ontario, it was a formidable decision — super bueno — for human justice, and for our case.

The case has not ended. It will never be over. But I believe that was an important step, an important blow to Chevron. We have another case in Brazil, filed on 27 July 2012. We believe that in this year, 2014, there will be a decision from Brazil's Supreme Court.

Good? Bad?

We can't know how the judges will rule, but we have a lot of confidence and hope because the law is very clear. And if the judges apply the laws as it should be, we will win this case. The third case in Argentina is taking a little longer. We had an injunction to seize Chevron's assets, which was overturned. But the underlying case continues. We had an order to freeze Chevron's assets in the Supreme Court of Argentina, but unfortunately, due to pressure from the company and the Argentine government, the Supreme Court withdrew it. But, the principal case is ongoing.

An important thing about this case is that our commitment and obligation is to pursue Chevron's assets all over the world until we collect the last cent of the judgment. This is my promise. We are not going to rest until Chevron pays the very last cent awarded in the judgment.

Yet the damage is so huge that even that large amount of money, it's still going to leave you with permanent problems.

Yes, but first there is another important aspect to the case, which is the RICO [Racketeer Influenced and Corrupt Organizations] case in the United States. This is critical to discuss, because of the magnitude, then I'll answer your question. The RICO case is important, it's important to our case, but it's also important for understanding what Chevron is and what it is capable of doing. It's important to understand that our claim was initiated in 1993 in New York. It was Chevron that fought and petitioned the New York court to move the case to Ecuador. And after nine years, they were successful. They affirmed in writing that they would be subject to, and respect the Ecuadorian legal process. Based on this commitment from Chevron, the New York judges decided to send the case to Ecuador. But then, when we started the case in Ecuador, with all this evidence, we were able to demonstrate that the evidence clearly supported our case that Chevron's damages were so real, so obvious, along with the scientific evidence that corroborated our case. Chevron started to attack the Ecuadorian state and attack the entire justice system of Ecuador to discredit the process, and supposedly demonstrate that in Ecuador, there is no justice. All their pressure on the Ecuadorian state — with the lobbying, the arbitrations — functioned as an unrelenting harassment against us, against the victims.

In addition to the physical intimidation — my brother's assassination — there was a real, brutal, legal terrorism. With the RICO case, for example, in 2012, Chevron actually stated that there was no environmental damage. They claimed that it was an illegal association of Indigenous and rural people and their lawyers to create false evidence and to extort money from the company: a conspiracy. But the damage is here. You can check for yourself. So they hire hundreds of lawyers, convince judges, bribe officials, lawyers. They are undertaking a huge amount of work, spending hundreds of millions of dollars trying to undermine this case. And even worse, they create a monster that doesn't exist.

According to Chevron's theory, my friend and colleague Steven Donziger was the mastermind in this case. According to Chevron, Steven was the one who managed the entire case and the rest of us were just a bunch of objects — puppets. Naturally, they had to do that, portray Steven as the centre of the case, since under the US RICO legislation if the principal accused — or criminal actor — isn't American, the law doesn't apply. Chevron thought that by destroying Steven, they could destroy the case. But they were wrong because Steven supports our case, works on the case and has done a good job. But he doesn't decide the case. He works for the victims, like us. The victims are the ones who direct the case; we make the decisions. Chevron has unleashed an enormous campaign against Steven with this RICO charge. It's a show. The important thing is that even when Chevron had

Steven corralled we kept getting favourable rulings. So, at the same time that the RICO action takes place, we get the Canadian decision. We are showing them that he does not manage the case; only the victims manage the case.

Even though we are sure that this judge, Lewis Kaplan, in the RICO case is going to rule against us — because the case can't go any other way — we are convinced first, that we will appeal the decision and second, that whatever that judge decides is not going to affect the principal case.

As I said, the important thing about the RICO case is that it reveals what Chevron is capable of doing to avoid justice, punishment for their crime. Chevron is trying to turn the victims into victimizers. According to Chevron, the company is a victim of our fraud, rather than us being the victims of their crimes in the Amazon. Another important front are the arbitrations. Chevron has an arbitration campaign, having brought three arbitrations against the Ecuadorian state in order to supposedly force the state to pay the bill for the crimes committed by Chevron. The RICO case, and the arbitrations are two shields made of ice that Chevron has to protect itself. In the summer heat, they will melt away.

But you are still not "people." You have no agency. You're being manipulated by lawyers. You're still not "people."

It is incredible. During the trial, Chevron's lawyer said to the judge that the Amazon region should be considered a zone for oil industry production, and that not a single person should be living in the area. This means that in Chevron's view, the Indigenous people who have lived here all their lives are not human beings. Those of us who have been here many more years than Chevron are not human beings. This is part of their racism.

The RICO case is another example. Under Chevron's theory, they are the only ones capable of bringing a case like this one. They can't believe that people outside of the United States have been able to bring a case and make a legitimate claim that can win. That's another aspect of Chevron's racism. Even Judge Kaplan, for example, in one of his decisions, refers to the "alleged plaintiffs," the "alleged victims." He doesn't recognize the existence of the victims in fact. I am sure that if the victims, or the plaintiffs in this case, against Chevron had been Spanish, French, German, English or Canadian, Chevron would have paid a while ago. But they're from Ecuador. I think that the most important achievement of this fight is the unity among the peoples. I have been here for 30 years. There are people who have been involved in this fight for 20 years.

People like the leaders at Chevron, and political leaders, often don't believe that a group of people can come together and take up a cause and not be shaken and not fall apart. They don't really believe in democracy.

If I may, this is extremely important. This action shows that when people get together, it is possible to defeat something that appears invincible. It also shows that no one — or no company — how ever large it is, is untouchable.

One last area, a question I started before: when this is settled and remediation starts, it's a huge task. I'm told that there is no drinking water in the entire area, that the water is contaminated everywhere. How do you deal with that? What do you do?

This is important. I believe that Chevron's worst crimes are irreparable. For example, the loss of indigenous cultures: according to our research, in the first five years of Texaco's operations, two separate Indigenous groups went extinct. There is no amount of money that can bring back those two cultures. Second, according to data from public health surveys, in recent years, at least 2,000 people died of cancers that could be attributed to toxins in the environment. This is human life; people who died. There is no way that they can be brought back with any amount of money. And when someone dies — suppose it's a woman — it's not just the victim. It's her children and her husband and the whole community that suffer the consequences. This pain can also not be addressed with all the money in the world. The third thing is Nature: ruined rivers, animals, forest. Everything that was destroyed is all impossible to restore. Even if they pay the entire judgment against them, it will fall short of the damage they caused.

Yet, despite that, we are working on plans for a restoration that is as comprehensive and wholistic as possible. The idea is our dream, actually. It's to fix everything that can be fixed in the best way possible, to show Chevron that Indigenous and rural people are capable of doing things the right way and are capable of recovering their lives.

This case is not about money for anyone. We are not asking for money for any particular person. We are seeking money to clean the soil, the water, the rivers; to fix the problems that the people in the Amazon have been living with for 40 years. Obviously, there is a lot of work, and unfortunately there is no experience of work in a case this big and complicated anywhere in the world. A case like this does not exist anywhere else. We've researched it, and there is nothing like it. We have to devise the remediation ourselves, and we need the support of the global scientific community to repair the damage and to show the world that this can be done properly.

We have been working on these plans for about four years. The plans are how to clean the soil; how to reconstitute the Indigenous communities, the culture, the food sources. There is still a lot to do, although a lot of planning has been done. On a weekly basis, we receive invitations from a lot of people from all over the world who want to learn about our case. We are happy to receive them. The big changes in the world will not come from big leaders; they will come from social movements.

Pablo Fajardo is still a young man, and clearly one of the most remarkable environmental lawyers of our day. With his colleague Luis Yanza, he's already won the prestigious Goldman Environmental Prize as well as a Hero's Award from the CNN television network.

Fajardo's US-based colleague, Steven Donziger, was a journalist before attending the Harvard Law School, where he played basketball with Barack Obama. He then became a public defender — a legal aid lawyer — and in 1993 he joined the legal team working on the Chevron-Tóxico case. In the intervening 20 years he has raised millions of dollars and enlisted the support of powerful law firms and international financiers, some of whom dropped out after Judge Kaplan condemned him. Donziger contends that Kaplan's finding was based on evidence fabricated by Chevron, and he is appealing that finding. *Business Week* summed up his achievement this way: "However the confrontation ends, it will have implications far beyond Latin  America because Donziger has rewritten the rules for how to sustain far-flung environmental litigation."

Here is Steven Donziger's account of this labyrinthine case.

The legal case against Chevron has, just this year, reached its twentieth anniversary and the reason it's taken so long, largely, is because Chevron's primary strategy is that the case never end. They don't want to pay for a clean up. Throughout the trial — and what I would call the "Ecuador Period" of the case, which was between 2003 and 2011 during the trial phase — they did everything they possibly could to sabotage our efforts to present proof. Chevron tried to manipulate evidence; they tried to deceive the court and drown the court in frivolous motions. There are just thousands and thousands of repetitive motions they filed. So, in the period from 2007 when the Vanity Fair article came out, to the time of the sentence being issued in 2011 was a brutal time. We had to fight through massive resistance from Chevron, just to get basic stuff done that lawyers take for granted in a typical situation.

Eventually the court decided the issues, despite Chevron's attempts to drown it in paper and paralyze it, and they ruled in favour of the Ecuadorian communities. Appropriately so, because there was massive and overwhelming scientific and other evidence that showed that Chevron and its predecessor company Texaco adopted a deliberate policy of dumping toxic waste into the Amazon lands and waterways where Indigenous groups were living, over a period of 25 years or so. People down there, as a result of that dumping, are suffering tremendously: lots of cancers, lots of deaths. This effort, this lawsuit is really nothing other than a movement by Indigenous and former communities in the affected area to hold this company accountable and get compensation so they can do a clean-up, and hopefully get justice.

Okay. So you win the case; you get the judgment — and Chevron has left the building, right?

Yeah. It's important to understand the history of this case. This case started in the United States in 1993. Chevron — or Texaco, I should say — then fought for 10 years in the United States to move it to Ecuador, all the time praising Ecuador's court system as being fair and independent and transparent. The Ecuadorians wanted the case in the United States because they wanted it before a jury and the decisions to pollute in Ecuador had been made in the United States, in the New York area, where Texaco's headquarters was.

Chevron then bought Texaco in 2001, and right after they bought Texaco, they appeared in the US court and said, "We want the case in Ecuador." So, we had to then shift gears, come down here, pull together a whole new legal team and get into a trial that Chevron did everything it possibly could to delay, sabotage and paralyze. The whole case took eight years, and as the evidence started to come in during the trial, Chevron realized that it was probably going to lose the trial, and they immediately tried to make it last for ever through sophisticated tricks and subterfuge. By the time the court finally ruled in the case, and ruled in favour of the communities — based on massive evidence — Chevron had fled the country. Chevron basically stripped all of its assets out of Ecuador, took off and said, "We're never gonna pay." As a result, there's now what I would call phase three of the Ecuador litigation — which is now in year 20 — which requires that the affected communities, which have suffered for decades, pursue Chevron like the fugitive from justice that it is, into other countries that have legal systems where they do have enough assets to pay what they owe in Ecuador, according to the judgment that was put into place in this country.

So, now there are lawsuits against Chevron in Canada, in Argentina, in Brazil and maybe some other countries to come, in an effort to force the company to pay what it owes, and to hold it accountable under the law. You know, the communities have won the case. It's over. At this point it's a matter of making sure Chevron pays what it owes, according to the law, and it's a bunch of collection actions that are really no different than any typical commercial lawsuit, where one party has to pay and they don't, and you have to go find their assets and get their money. What's a shame about it is that Chevron is, in theory, a reputable public corporation from the United States of America. It's the third largest company in the United States and it's running from the law, which is why the communities have gone to Canada and these other countries.

No point in taking it back to the States with the judgment in hand?
That's an option, but the communities have decided that they don't trust the court system in the United States.

Yeah, because there was an action recently, right? In which you were impugned?
The reason, thus far, the communities haven't gone to pursue Chevron's assets in the United States are several, but one is, Chevron gets 75 percent of its revenue from its subsidiaries outside the United States. Chevron is a global company. The Ecuadorians have decided that it is more effective to pursue Chevron's assets outside of the United States at this point. One of the reasons for that is Chevron doesn't play by the rules. They lobby in the United States; they put on political pressure on courts and governments; they've also launched a lawsuit against everyone involved in the case, including me, Pablo Fajardo, Luis Yanza — two key Ecuadorian leaders of the lawsuit. All 47 named rainforest villagers who brought the lawsuit are defendants, as well as our consultants, and pretty much anybody associated with those of us who have been working on the case for all these years. Chevron claims that all of us have been involved in what they consider to be a "sham litigation"; that the whole thing is a fraud in an attempt to extort money from them. The theory of the case is utterly absurd, yet with all their money — and I think they spent over a billion US dollars in this case, they have armies of lawyers and investigators and scientists and consultants who are trying to show that the Ecuador court system as a whole does not function properly; that is, that the court system where they wanted the trial to be held falls short of standards of international due process, and therefore, any effort to enforce the judgment in these other countries should not be upheld by courts of those countries. But there is simply no trust right now by the Ecuadorian communities in US courts. The judge that's handling the case has made derogatory comments about the Ecuadorians; has called them the "so-called plaintiffs," as if they don't exist; has said the whole case is not bona fide litigation; has called me a "field general," not a real lawyer. It's just been utterly insulting.

I just sat through a seven-week trial, and there's just nowhere to go. Chevron sued all of us for literally US$60 billion. I live in a two-bedroom apartment in Manhattan with my wife and son. I am not a man of great means and to be sued for $60 billion is, by the way, the largest potential personal liability in United States history. I just didn't know what to make of it. It was so much it was absurd. Two weeks before the trial was to begin they dropped all the damages claims against me and Pablo Fajardo and the Ecuadorians because they were scared of a jury. They knew they would lose the case and they wanted this judge, who we believe is biased against us, to rule alone. What that ended up doing is that it put them in a very difficult legal position where I don't think any decision this judge makes is going to hold up on appeal. I think, ultimately, not only are we going to win what is really a retaliatory lawsuit designed to chill our free-speech rights — not only are we going to win that, but it's not going to matter that much. The real cases that matter are the enforcement cases in other countries where judges are going to determine whether the system of justice in Ecuador is sufficient to hold this company accountable when it wanted the case to take place in Ecuador.

It doesn't sound like an enviable position for Chevron to argue.
I think Chevron is in an extremely difficult position right now. I think they're facing enormous risk and I would say their management is almost reckless in the way they're handling this case. You have a $9.5-billion judgement. It's been affirmed by Ecuador's supreme court in the forum where Chevron wanted the trial to be held. Chevron has fled the country, stripped its assets from the country, is acting like a fugitive from justice. Everyone who comes down here to see it — there's been dozens and dozens of journalists from all over the world — have confirmed the basic facts of the story, which is, the company deliberately dumped billions of gallons of toxic waste into the Amazon thinking they could get away with it, and as a result people are dying down here. Indigenous groups are decimated because of this contamination. I don't think Chevron at this point is in an enviable position at all. I think what Chevron should do is what any responsible company would do, which is, obey the law, respect the rule of law and pay the judgment. By comparison standards, $9.5 billion is obviously a significant amount of money, but compared to the magnitude of what has happened here in Ecuador, it's not. People in the region call this "the Amazon Chernobyl." We believe, based on our research, that it's probably the worst oil-related ecological catastrophe on the planet at the moment. By comparison, the BP spill in the Gulf of Mexico from 2010: BP's liability for that spill, which is offshore and has affected far fewer people, as bad as it was, is about $40 billion. In Ecuador, you have a spill that literally effects probably 200,000 people — not a spill, just contamination that was caused intentionally — that's lasted for almost 50 years. And the liability, according to the court, is $9.5 billion. Chevron makes $250 billion dollars a year. Okay? $30 billion in profit every year. This case has been going on 20 years. They've literally made hundreds of billions of dollars in profit over the course of this case and the court ordered them to pay $9.5 billion to clean up the mess they made. They can easily afford it.

I could keep going, but you probably want to ask me a question.

[LAUGHS] No, no, no. This is exactly what I want. It's a nice clear account of the situation. So now you've got a court in Ontario saying, "They can't run any more, we are going to hear the case." How do you expect that to unfold?
Well, I expect Chevron to do in Canada what it does in every other country where it's under attack by the Ecuadorian communities, which is, they're going to try and delay it as much as they can. They pay numerous lawyers in Canada to raise every possible issue, to slow down the process. For example, right now, they're trying to appeal to the Supreme Court on whether there's jurisdiction over them in Canada, which is utterly absurd, as I understand Canadian law, because the Supreme Court of Canada already has ruled that you can bring these enforcement actions in Canada.

The Supreme Court will presumably just say, "No, we're not going to hear that."
Well, right now Chevron is appealing to the Supreme Court on a preliminary issue, which is, whether or not the case can even happen. The Supreme Court of Canada may or may not take that narrow appeal on a technical issue. At some point soon, we hope, there will be legal action that will be somewhat of a trial for the Supreme Court of Canada to determine whether Chevron's defences, that the case was the result of a flawed judicial system, are valid. I don't think they're valid, and I think Chevron will do anything it can to delay that trial for as long as possible. And once we're in the trial, they'll try to make it as complicated and technical and as long as possible. When it ends, if they lose, they'll appeal and make that as long as possible. As a result, we're looking at two, three, even four years, just in Canada, to get to an end game, after 20 years — 10 in the United States and 10 in Ecuador. It's fundamentally not fair. It's a fundamental abuse of the legal system by a company that uses its superior resources, and I am talking billions of dollars, to try to throw sand into the gears of the judicial system so that it doesn't work properly, and so that they can just kick the can down the road.

It is cheaper for Chevron to pay hundreds of lawyers right now, in various countries, to try to delay this matter, than to pay for an actual clean up. That's the calculation that they have made. But, it's produced enormous risks for them because they're under enormous pressure from prominent institutional shareholders who believe the current management team has mismanaged the litigation in Ecuador. I believe they have. Chevron's chairman and CEO, a man named John Watson, is saying very aggressive things about the lawyers. He calls us criminals, for example. What CEO who has a confirmed $9.5-billion liability talks like that? How do you get off that limb? It doesn't make sense. It's not responsible management. I think the current management team of Chevron is on a crusade against lawyers and others they perceive as being a long-term threat to their interests, because the Ecuador case, ultimately, is not just about Ecuador, in Chevron's eyes. It's about, I believe, a threat to their business model, because Chevron — and this is not just true for Chevron, but for a lot of oil and extractive industry companies — has a lot of legacy and environmental issues around the world. I think they're very, very nervous about the precedent being set in this case, where Indigenous groups with very little resources were able to sustain, for all these years, a legal action that resulted in a victory. If the communities receive the money that they need to clean up this huge area — as they should — I think Chevron is extremely worried that they'll be hit with other legal actions by similarly situated peoples in other countries, such that their overall liability from these types of cases could be in the tens of billions of dollars, and even hundreds of billions of dollars. I think it makes them very nervous. As a result, in this particular case, they're investing massive sums of money to try to repress it, beat it back, kill it off politically.

Just stop the precedent.
Yeah. They've offered enormous payments to the government of Ecuador to kill off our case. And this is a private case — private citizens against a private company in a judicial system where Chevron wanted the case to be held. Once the case started, they've been working actively with the US Embassy in Ecuador to undermine the case. It came out in Wikileaks — in the Wiki cables. They've offered the Ecuadorian government a sum of $700 million to settle the case without consulting with the communities. The Ecuadorian government has rejected these offers as completely inappropriate and, really, illegal. Chevron has hired 25 or 30 lobbyists in Washington to pressure the United States government to pressure Ecuador's government to kill off the case by cutting trade preferences for Ecuador that could cost hundreds of thousands of jobs in Ecuador. They play across all platforms. To Chevron, the legal system is just one little area where a conflict might play out. But what they try to do is then pressure the legal system through governments and investing money in oil fields and gaining power and influence, so that judges and courts ultimately feel like they can't rule against them. I think that's what they're going to try to do in all the enforcement countries. They've done it in the United States; they've done it in Ecuador. It didn't work. They're doing it in Argentina, Brazil and I believe there's activity in Canada that suggests they're doing it. But I think at the end of the day it's not going to work. I think judges are going to do their duty and be independent and make sure this company doesn't get away with this abusive litigation strategy.

One further layer that seems really vile — correct me if I'm wrong — but it's my understanding that they've gone to one of these horrible trade tribunals outside to get a

ruling that says if Chevron ever does have to pay, Ecuador will then have to compensate
Chevron — basically to nullify the judgment if the judgment is upheld.

Chevron is engaged in an impressive amount of forum shopping. They keep looking for different courts to try to rule in their favour. They almost never seem to win, but it drags out the litigation. So one of the things they've done is file an international arbitration claim against Ecuador's government, trying to shift the entire cost of the clean up to Ecuadorian taxpayers. They want a taxpayer-funded bail-out of their liability to clean up Ecuador, from Ecuadorian tax payers. That is, they want the very victims of their pollution to pay for the clean up.

It's subterfuge, in my opinion. Basically, the whole international commercial arbitration system is stacked against people who don't have means and don't have resources. The trade arbitration is a litigation between Ecuador and Chevron. The Ecuadorian communities who are the real partied interests — the most affected, the people who are suffering and dying — do not have a right to appear before the arbitration panel. The panel meets in private; by rule, everything is secret and closed off to the public, including closed off to the media. The public almost never knows the results of their decisions. We cannot appear. It is a completely unfair process that is structured to favour private corporations over governments and citizens. Beyond that, in this instance, there's really no case because those international arbitration panels are supposed to rule on legitimate disputes between companies and governments. They're not supposed to rule on private disputes between private citizens and private companies that just happen to go into a civil court.

The implications of the private arbitration panel are profound in this sense. If one was to accept Chevron's theory that Ecuador's government is responsible to clean up their mess, then the people of Ecuador who have been affected by the pollution will have no place to go. There's no rule of law; there's no court they can go to. They tried in the United States; Chevron wanted it in Ecuador. So they tried in Ecuador and they started to win. Then Chevron said, "Uh-uh, we don't like Ecuador now. We're going to an international arbitration panel where you can't show up, by rule. And they're going to be the ones to decide your case that we wanted to take place in Ecuador!" The whole thing is preposterous. It's absurd. And it really has very little legitimacy and credibility. No matter what they rule, I don't think it's going to matter that much, because I'm confident that Ecuador's government will not really succumb to what is essentially a form of legal blackmail to just pay Chevron what Chevron really owes. They're not going to do it. It would violate their own laws; their own constitution and international laws, not to mention their national dignity. And I think this investment arbitration panel does not have a lot of credibility. I don't think it's really going to matter to the judges in the enforcement courts in Canada, Brazil and Argentina. I don't think a private panel of secret arbitrators is going to impact the case much at all.

That's what those panels are set up to do.
Of course, but I just don't think it's going to work in this case for all the reasons I've outlined. This is what we call in the law a sui generis situation. There's never been a situation where a private arbitration panel thinks it can rule on a dispute between private citizens and a private company. These are state-party investor arbitration panels. So, Chevron is just trying to make up a dispute with Ecuador's government as if that's the real dispute, when the real dispute has already been resolved by Ecuador's courts. I don't think it's going to work.

I hope you're right. Those things scare the hell out of me.
They did me at first, but I've studied that panel through and through. I think they don't have a leg to stand on, legally speaking.

I don't mean in this case, but I mean in general, that whole investor-state dispute…
Look, I've written about it and I should send you an article I wrote. But it's a private system of justice for the wealthy to avoid being held accountable by regular public court systems. It's very dangerous.

Yeah, it really is. And for reaping money from governments for profits that are entirely theoretical.
Exactly, yeah. It's extraordinary.

And yet, all the governments seem to get sucked into it. Here is Obama this morning talking about how he's going to do the Trans-Pacific deal, which strikes me as abominable.
Well, yeah. It's a private system of justice — these trade pacts, for the wealthy, for corporations. There's a huge movement in the United States to block that treaty. But, you know, the corporate class always seems to prevail with these trade treaties. Sometimes they're hard to understand. In the host countries — Ecuador is an example — I don't think many of the people in government pushing the treaty understood its negative implications. There's now an effort by the current government of Ecuador to revoke the treaties.

Good. Glad to hear it! There should be some of that. And apparently Australia has said that they won't sign any treaty that has investor-state arbitration in it.
I didn't know that.

So I'm told. Mind you, I'm told lots of things. Some are true. One last thing, and then we're going to go down and meet Pablo Fajardo and he's going to give us a little tour of some of the affected area — which I am both looking forward to and horrified at. Is

there anything that you would particularly want to note that I should ask Pablo? And are there any particular scenes there that you think I should see?
Sure. I'd say a couple of things. One is, it's important to emphasize — and you'll see this when you talk to Pablo — that this is an Ecuadorian case. It's not an American case. It's not my case. I am one of the lawyers on the team. It so happens I've been working on it for 20 years. I don't know whether to laugh or cry when I say that, but I've been working on it a very, very long time. It is a case of Ecuadorians, and Pablo Fajardo is the lead lawyer of this case, and he is an extraordinary young man. Courageous …

Was and is? The lead lawyer?
Yeah. He was and is, since probably 2005.

He sounds extraordinary.
He grew up in the area. He grew up in poverty. He worked in the oil fields for maybe $50 a month when he was a young adult, to get money for his family. He also taught an adult literacy class at night through the local church, and some priests noticed his talent and paid for him to take a correspondence course, to become a lawyer, which required him to study very hard and come to Quito one week a semester to take exams. So over several years he became a lawyer, and started working on the case when it came to Ecuador in the early 2000s. Little by little, it showed that he was the smartest guy in the room, who knew the people, knew the issues. And he became the lead lawyer in 2005. But for him, I don't think the case would be in the good position that it's in today. He's an extraordinary man. Chevron has done everything it possibly can to undermine him, attack him, get in the way of the work he's doing, drown him in paper, threaten him — and he just holds steadfast and is great. There's also a huge community base out there in the Amazon, about 80 Indigenous and farming communities that meet on a regular basis in an assembly, to give their lawyers direction and to be informed by their lawyers. I've had the privilege of attending some of these meetings; they're extraordinary. This is a grassroots movement of which the lawsuit is a component piece. There's a lot going on and it's just an extraordinary accomplishment historically, what the communities have done through this lawsuit.

The other thing I'd say is, when you go out there, you'll likely be horrified. I first went there in 1993, if you can believe it. I've been there dozens and dozens, if not a couple of hundred times. And every time I go — I was most recently there yesterday — I am equally, if not more horrified. It's just sitting out there, this massive pollution that's visible to the naked eye. It stinks, you can smell it, there's vapours coming off these pits and it will be there for centuries unless it's cleaned up. And while Chevron left Ecuador in 1992, the pollution they created while they operated here is still there, and it's still polluting; it's still leaching into the soils and ground water. It's still causing harm. It's causing even more harm today than it did when they were here because it has a cumulative effect on people in terms of their exposures to the toxins. So it's horrifying and I haven't met a single person who has come down and seen it that hasn't left thinking that they had some responsibility to try to help the communities down there who are living in this area. It's extraordinary.

Everything I've read about Pablo Fajardo describes exactly the man you're describing.
Yeah, he's an inspiration. I've worked closely with Pablo for almost ten years, now. We're colleagues; we're collaborators. I've learned a lot from him. That's part of what's interesting about this case. The real genius of the people who were affected comes from them. It's the understanding of Nature, and the forest and what's at stake, and how they will settle for nothing less than a full clean up. And how their lawyers come from the communities. And how they've aligned themselves with people in other countries — like myself — to broaden this into other areas of the world because that's the only way you can hold Chevron accountable; it's a global company and it won't pay for the Ecuador judgment. What's ended up happening is the creation of an extraordinary global network of lawyers and supporters who are trying to help these communities gain control of their own destiny. You know, Chevron dumped and they thought the people couldn't fight back. They tried to consign them to what literally was the trash-heap of history. They thought this would never happen. They thought they could get away with it! They planned to dump! This was not an accident. They planned this to save money. And here we are now, almost 50 years after those decisions to dump were made and look at the world, how it's changed. You know, the people of Ecuador who were affected by this have obtained the largest environmental judgment in the history of the civil judgment system, out of a court, from a trial. These are people, for the most part who historically have no money — not that they were poor, because they were very rich living in the forest — but they had no money! How do you do this with no money? When Chevron is spending hundreds of millions of dollars a year? That takes imagination and intelligence and heart ... and they have it. So do a lot of other people working on this. As a result, we are where we are: we won. We now need to get the clean up.

Yeah. The other thing that's in the back of my mind is, even with $9.5 billion, can you really clean it up?
Well, you probably need more. But you can do a whole lot of good clean-up for that amount of money. It's going to take a lot of years. And actually, the process of cleaning up — there's no blueprint to cleaning up a delicate ecosystem that is affected by this much oil. There's no precedent for it. So it's going to take a lot of

smart people to come together and figure out how best to spend the resources that are going to be available to clean this area up in the quickest possible way.

Chevron has never tried to blame Texaco. This was something done by Texaco, but Chevron bought Texaco in 2001 and had been warned by many people about this potential liability and in the excitement of a merger, pretty much ignored it. They never did due diligence, and they probably concluded that the people of Ecuador from the Amazon rainforest were just like a little nuisance, and would never get to the point where they've gotten. So, Chevron's problem is, in buying Texaco, they own the liability. They own all the benefits, they own all the assets they got from Texaco; they also own all the liabilities. So, right now, Chevron is full in, doesn't blame Texaco because they own 100 percent of Texaco. It's Chevron at this point. And Chevron's strategy to avoid paying for the harm that Texaco caused has caused enormous additional harm to the people of Ecuador. Chevron is full in, in our opinion it is now their fault because they absorbed Texaco and they're litigating this case, we believe, in an abusive manner — not respecting the rule of law, not respecting court judgments. So, there's no effort by Chevron to blame Texaco at this point, it's all one entity. And Chevron knows that ultimately it's going to have to either take responsibility or be the entity to keep kicking the can down the road.

I will say this, though. Chevron has a lot of trademarks in Ecuador and we have achieved an embargo from an Ecuadorian court to own their trademarks from which we could potentially generate some money to start a clean up. So, it's not true that they have no assets here. They do have some, but they're very minor compared to their assets around the world and they're not nearly enough to pay for a clean up. But, they at least allow the communities to get potentially some level of assets that they could start using to try and make an impact on the Amazon and clean up the damage.

I'd never thought of trademarks as being an asset that you can't take out of the country. It's complicated. The trademarks generate a certain amount of money a year, as they licence them to local entities who market their lubricants and Havoline and all their products. There's a way to get that revenue. It's not a lot but it's better than nothing. And also, the precedent to show that the communities are starting to collect on the judgment is important.

[2016: As noted in the "Buen Vivir" essay above, the Ecuadorians won in the Supreme Court of Canada in 2015, whereupon Chevron launched yet another action challenging Canadian jurisdiction in the case. As several commentators have noted, the matter has now come before 18 appellate courts in Canada and Ecuador, and the Ecuadorians have won every time, supporting Donziger's belief that Chevron's strategy is to prolong the legal actions indefinitely.]

DANIEL SALLABERRY
Putting Argentina's Right to a Healthy Environment to the Test

Recorded January 2014

Buenos Aires, Argentina, is one of the most beautiful cities in the world. It's often called the Paris of South America. But for hundreds of years Buenos Aires has had a dirty little secret. The Riachuelo River, which forms the boundary between the City of Buenos Aires and the province of Buenos Aires, is the estuary of the Riachuelo-Matanza Basin. The Basin is 80 km long, and it's home to nearly five million people. For more than 200 years it has been horribly polluted, carrying the run-off from tanneries, oil refineries, chemical industries, shanty-towns and farmlands. In 2004, however, a little band of residents from an impoverished riverside neighbourhood brought a lawsuit against the city, the province, the national government, fourteen upstream municipalities and 44 private companies, alleging that these organizations had damaged their health and infringed their right to a healthy environment — and the Supreme Court of Argentina agreed to hear what's become known as "the Mendoza case."

Their lawyer was Daniel Sallaberry, who was frustrated that Argentina's admirable environmental rights statutes had never had a solid, real-world test. On July 8, 2008, after four years of hearings the Supreme Court handed down a landmark decision, not just for Argentina but for the world. In a judgment that David Boyd called "sweeping and poetic," the court ruled that government and industry had indeed infringed the residents' right to a healthy environment, and were obliged to repair the damage. Furthermore, the work would be supervised by a citizens' group and by a judge. But then the court found that although the companies involved had indeed infringed the plaintiffs' right to a healthy environment, the plaintiffs should nevertheless pay their own whopping legal costs. That finding will be appealed to the Inter-American Commission on Human Rights.

The interview is translated by Judy Rein, and in the video, the translation is voiced by Chris Beckett.

Tell me where the case came from, and tell me about your clients. You had 70 clients?
Yes, 70 clients.

And how did that come about?
Its implications — it has two implications, a legal one and a sociological or social one. The legal implication is related to the incorporation into Latin American law, in this case, Argentine law, of third and fourth generation rights, which include environmental rights, the rights of Nature. This legal regime was incorporated into the national constitution in 1994, in three articles. Article 41 incorporates these rights by establishing that all inhabitants have the right to enjoy a healthy environment.

That's in the constitution, right?
Yes. Article 41, which guarantees citizens' right to enjoy a healthy, stable environment able to support human development and productive activities that satisfy current needs and the needs of future generations, at the same time incorporates the obligation to conserve this environment. It incorporates the rights to bring class actions, and it establishes in subsequent provisions the legal procedures for defending those rights.

Subsequently, laws were passed, like the general law of the environment that provides how these rights will be implemented. This was in 1994; then, from 1994 to 2004, when we brought the lawsuit, 10 years passed in which these laws were never applied. The big problem in a country like Argentina is the effectiveness of law. The law can be declared in the constitution, but if it is not properly practised, it is just dead letters.

Then, in 2000, after six years had passed since these rights were established, the newspaper *La Nación* published an editorial noting that in the Riachuelo River, 500,000 barrels each containing 200 liters of toxic waste were dumped in the river on a daily basis, and that the Secretary for the Environment — the agency charged with enforcing the law, monitoring industrial pollution and protecting natural resources — was well aware of this, and permitted companies to dump the toxic effluent.

At the same time, the newspapers began reporting on victims who were affected by the pollution. There were people who had lead in their blood as a result of being poisoned like the case of Dock Sud, and the case of Beatriz Mendoza, and another group of families who formed the basis of the suit. There were seventeen families, a total of 120 individuals, in which evidently they suffered health effects. And the question arose, how many cases could I bring?

I had read somewhere that Beatriz Mendoza cut herself and couldn't feel it. Is that true?
That's one of the pathologies that the pollution caused in this charming case. In

Dock Sud there are 18 gases. These components mixed together affect health in different ways. In Beatriz Mendoza's case, the pathologies were loss of sensation, general malaise, and problems with concentration. In the case of Villa Inflammable, the children suffer from lead poisoning; the levels of lead in their blood are significantly higher than that of workers in the industry.

This is the sociological aspect: there were no efforts to deal with the problems. There were no claims, just a very superficial investigation. So I got in touch with these people and I began to develop the groundwork for filing a suit. In this sense there was a legal process and a sociological process, in that it was necessary to make the law work in practice, since in Argentina there is a disconnect between what the law says and how it works in practice. And since this work cannot be done by one person — it is too much work — we brought together a team of very prestigious lawyers, very capable people with diverse knowledge, to draft the complaint. This was a team effort with other lawyers, colleagues. Finally, we signed off on it after two years, because when I explained the idea, everyone said it was crazy that we were going to sue the national government, the provincial government and the municipalities, as well as 44 companies that were among the most powerful in Argentina. Nevertheless, I was able to convince them, and they contributed a tremendous effort. We were able to submit the complaint in July of 2007 to the Supreme Court.

May I ask about money? That's a lot of lawyers — and lawyers aren't cheap. How was this financed?

At this time the country was beginning to change politically, and new members were appointed to the Supreme Court. With new members that had an open perspective, the court permitted this type of class action to be brought. Since the law provided for it, they recognized that they had to follow the law. Article 41 states that public agencies have an obligation to conserve the environment. It imposes on public authorities the responsibility to go beyond the minimal mandate and commit to caring for the environment, because they are part of the environment and will be affected.

The economic issue is a different process. In environmental cases, in this case, when we started to work on the environmental case with the legal teams in the year 2000, we knew that we would have to invest our own resources to bring these cases since the victims in environmental cases are the most dispossessed, most marginal, poor people. Thus, we have invested our own money to develop the case. Perhaps, once the case is over and the parties who are responsible for the pollution have a judgment against them, the court will award damages and we will be able to recover our costs and fees. There is a law that sets the rate for attorney fees in Argentina. So, once the process is over — the national, provincial and 14 municipal governments already have a judgment against them going back to 2008 — when the court reaches a final ruling on the 44 companies, if they are found liable they will pay the attorney fees. For the moment, we lawyers have invested our own resources. I'll conclude: the lawyers defending the companies are legal corporations; they are very big firms. They have received their fees from the defendant polluters at international rates, and it is estimated they have billed around $400,000 from each defendant company over the course of these years. We haven't billed anything; we have only put in our own money.

This is the challenge for environmental cases. The fact that the people affected do not have resources, and to go up against a powerful company, or the government, and the time required to go through the entire process to the end, makes it very prejudicial toward such plaintiffs, even if they get a favorable ruling and remedy at the end of the process. Because a lot of time has passed since we initiated the case in 2004. Now it is 2014, ten years, and we are really in the beginning of the case. Despite the fact that the case itself has been seen as a fantastic thing and we have made progress in the adoption of environmental rights, we are only just beginning; we haven't won anything. The victims still need to survive while waiting for a judicial remedy. None of the victims have received anything yet.

So the system is still tilted, right?
Yes. There are two realities. Even though within the judiciary, and the Supreme Court in particular, there are very worthy people who know the law well, it does not acknowledge these realities. There are two realities, one is what is said, and the other is what is done. Today, there may be 200 years of pollution, but in 10 years they could have done a lot more than what they have accomplished. The court does not have the components, neither the human nor the economic resources, to manage the problem. The government can be ordered to put together a plan to clean up the pollution, but the administration may not have the capacity to follow the order. It is moving along in an improvised manner. In addition to the pollution, execution of the court's order to the administration is undermined by corruption.

It's my understanding that the court did some very unusual things: it held hearings for many people to participate in, it wasn't just a narrow legal proceeding — and then afterwards it imposed some legal requirements that other people had to take care of.
I believe that the important thing about the court's judgment was the incorporation of a more transparent process — how they handled the cases. In public hearings they asked each of the 44 defendant companies to respond to the complaints and present environmental studies, giving them the right to be heard and offer explanations. And of course every one of them stated that they had never polluted. Subsequently, the

court did not make them responsible for providing environmental remediation or clean-up of the river and its natural resources; as I noted earlier, this is the government's responsibility. But there was not a lot of confidence that the public agencies had the capacity to carry out the clean-up, so they made a plan, called the Comprehensive Plan for Environmental Remediation, and they established benchmarks to monitor the progress of fulfilling the requirements of the plan. The court even imposed fines on public officials who failed to carry out the Plan's mandate and missed the required benchmarks. As it turned out, the targets were not met. The supervising judge in charge of monitoring the implementation of the plan has been charged with corruption, along with public officials, and the companies handling the clean-up. And the NGOs that also participated in the citizen clean-up — this was another of the court's objectives, to involve non-governmental groups in monitoring the remediation process — were not heard. There were a number of groups involved, like Greenpeace, the Neighborhood Association of La Boca, the Center for Rural and Social Studies. Significantly, human rights and environmental organizations did monitor the process, but their reports and conclusions were not taken into account.

It seems to me that everybody is impressed with the idea that there is a plan, but there are different ideas about how well it's going.

Yes, this is the contradiction between what is said and what is done. For example, the General Environmental Law has a provision covering whoever is responsible for pollution, specifically, causing environmental damages, which are understood as relevant disturbances to any aspects of the environment, natural resources, ecosystems, environmental values and products. The law requires, and the Constitution does as well, that the first obligation of the polluter is repairing the damage, and the companies in this case, and the government, are responsible for their actions and omissions. The government is liable for omission: allowing the companies to pollute and failing to exercise proper monitoring. And the companies are responsible as the direct agents of polluting the river. This liability is presumed to be objective, according to the law. They are jointly liable: those who act by omission, and those who directly pollute. Even if it can't be determined which of the companies are most responsible, they are all held liable.

Up until now, all the court has done, after 10 years of litigation, is to enter judgment against the government for its failure to monitor the companies. The companies, despite the suit's allegations, have never been judged liable. Eighty percent of the contamination in the Matanza River Basin, which is the extension of the Riachuelo in its last leg, is the result of liquid waste from 30 companies — 30 companies that have nonetheless yet to be found liable, which — after 10 years! — is incomprehensible to us.

Going back to the original case, there were two parts: there was the environmental and the health case. The health part was taken out, what happened to that?

That's correct. When the court took the case, it divided the allegations of the victims, the affected plaintiffs, into two parts. One part involved individual damages, the specific health effects suffered by individual victims. This other part was sent to lower courts to adjudicate each individual case separately, since the health impacts were different for the individual plaintiffs. The court agreed to hear the part that related to "collective rights" that are guaranteed by the Constitution. The Supreme Court has jurisdiction over what in Argentina are called "collective rights," and the collective, or class action was severed from the individual health claims. In our opinion this decision was incorrect, although there is the argument that the court would be burdened with too many trials at the level of the first instance if it agreed to hear those cases individually. However, in this case, it would have been correct to try all the cases together, because there is a procedure that would allow for anticipation of damages, especially in an environmental case, thus providing the victims with some anticipatory relief: awards for treatment, hospitals, and other assistance, which with the passage of 10 years have not been met. Health cannot wait for this period of time.

Is that case finished now, or is that still going on?

We are not even halfway there. We have done a lot, but there is a lot more to be done. Now after 10 years we are bogged down with our own life vest.

Has it made a difference in the lives of your clients?

No, this division that was made between collective damages and individual damages made the victims' situation worse. They are hurt since the collective environmental case is under the Supreme Court's jurisdiction, and the lower courts that are adjudicating the individual claims have no knowledge of environmental law, which underlies the individual claims. The lower courts are afraid of taking on this large case, because they are accustomed to handling the classical work of common disputes, like commercial law, and the simple disputes that emerge from daily life. Environmental law is uncomfortable for them to take on because it is not like traditional law. It is a new vision of law that modifies and decodes all traditional legal reasoning, since the environment does not adjust to law; it has its own law. So, procedurally, it is hard for the lawyers and judges who are involved in the case; they didn't study the subject, nor did I. When I became a lawyer 30 years ago it did not exist. It has only emerged in the last 20 years or so, since 1994, as a subject to study and an idea to consider.

We have a philosophical view. We have had 2,000 years of culture in which humans are the owners of Nature and the laws were established as a function of natural resources existing for the use and enjoyment of human beings, of the human species. By placing humans at the centre, law adhered to this cultural concept. Now we are beginning to think that Nature, animals, other peoples, have rights, and we are beginning to recognize this change in perspective, especially in the countries of South America.

Does the law include legal rights for natural objects? For animals? For trees?
Not exactly, but yes, they are recognized as subjects of rights, including the generation of cultures, something which had not existed. Implicitly. It does not say so specifically. But it is recognized in practice, since any inhabitant has the third-party right to bring an action against an attack on Nature, natural resources or ecology.

Seen more from the human perspective, something I find remarkable is that the Matanza–Riachuelo River seems like it always has been there and it always has been this way. Yet it is not a river since there is no water, fish or animals, just an open cesspool. Nevertheless, there has never been a single demonstration of people who live there and see this state of affairs that have always been this way, who rise up and seek change. So this has been a big advance. Before the court's ruling in this case, there were 39 agencies that had some responsibility for water issues, for at least the last 50 years. None of them fought to improve it, they just defended their own interests. It's always been this way. It was very well established. It is remarkable.

Let me come back to the clients. So the clients, in terms of the health issues, have been just hanging for ten years?
Each one has done what they can in terms of treatment; they have not been recognized. Because the complaints for health damages were sent to the lower courts, the victims face logistical hurdles due to technical procedural issues relating to jurisdiction. Each victim has to file separate claims against all the companies in different jurisdictions. So, people who live on the other side of the river have to file claims in Buenos Aires Province and those on this side of the river have to sue in different courts. Since they are lower courts, and every case is handled by a different judge, the outcomes may not be consistent. This is why I said that in this case the Supreme Court erred in separating the individual health claims from the collective action. It is practically impossible for the lower courts to make any decisions until the Supreme Court rules on the liability of the companies.

It's striking that in the environmental case the court has basically said, the Basin is one thing — but in these health cases, the Basin is not one thing.
The concept and the practice are different. For example, this court, which favoured the adoption of environmental rights and rights for Nature in practice by taking this case, is the same court that last year changed long-standing precedent in its

Chevron decision. Chevron Ecuador was a magnificent judgment in that it succeeded in attaching assets in Argentina and in other parts of the world to pay for the remediation. But this same court vacated the attachment. It completely changed its own posture, overturning the decisions in the trial court and the appellate court that upheld the precedent attaching Chevron's assets. In essence, in nine days the court erased its own jurisprudence, which it had been developing over years. These are the contradictions that persist.

One last thing. You were actually making law, you and your colleagues have been making law, which is quite a wonderful thing.

Yes, 10 years to initiate rule development. In my own case I am motivated. Once we have gone through the academic review and we have the knowledge and tools to act in the face of reality like the Riachuelo case, transgenic crops, and fracking — hydraulic fracturing is the case I'm working on now, we have it in Argentina with Chevron — once you know the reality, you can't not do something. There is an ethical-natural obligation, if you like, that you must take action. What we can't do is keep our arms crossed and be indifferent.

ANTONIO OPOSA JR.
The Wizard of the Catalytic Intervention

Recorded October 2014

Antonio Oposa Jr. is known to the public in the Philippines as "Attorney Oposa," and to his friends as "Tony." He's not a big man — but he's a giant. He's the lawyer who sued the Philippine government on behalf of future generations to stop logging in old growth forests, and won — the first time anywhere in the world that the rights of future generations were recognized in court. The principle is called intergenerational equity, and it's known around the world as the Oposa Doctrine. Then he launched a legal battle to force government and industry to clean up the desperately polluted Manila Bay — and he won that too. Tony later organized an enforcement squadron to stop poachers from fishing on coral reefs with dynamite and cyanide, and went after the poachers personally. The poachers put a price on his head, and one of his closest associates was assassinated, but the incidence of poaching plummeted. Currently he's fighting to have fifty percent of all the country's highways reserved for bicycles, pedestrians and public transit, arguing that although only two percent of Filipinos own motor vehicles, all Filipinos pay for the highways. I'm betting he'll win that one, too.

Tony, you've brought some of the most important and inspiring legal actions of our time, and we'll get to those, but I think you've been able to do this because you have a remarkable conception of the law. For example, you think of a legal action as a story-telling activity. Tell me about that.

The nice thing about the legal action are four things. One is that it tells a story in a manner that is organized, orderly, logical and backed up by evidence. Number two is that it brings the issue on the table of discussion. Otherwise it's just going to be in the media, or in symposia that nobody listens to; in these cases we just talk to each other. But in a legal action the person who you would like to listen

---

This interview took place at Pace University in White Plains, NY, where Oposa was a visiting professor. The previous evening we had attended one of his public lectures, to which he makes some references.

to your story will have to listen to that story. Number three, it spurs action. And number four, it may take five years, it may take 10 years, it may take forever, but there is going to be a resolution.

Now, going back to the story. There is a line I read once that says, "He who tells the story of a nation need not care who its leaders are." From one of my early cases — the children's case — it told a story. It told a story of how there was only 800,000 hectares left of virgin forest in the Philippines; the government had granted logging concessions to more than 4 million hectares, and we were cutting it down at the rate of 120,000 hectares per year. And the story is: the children who were the plaintiffs, the petitioners, in the next five, seven, eight years they would not have any forest left. So the story is there, it's just that it became more significant when the Supreme Court understood what the story was all about and expanded the idea of this story. It has been five presidents since and the story lives on.

In a sense you've forced the issue to a resolution, but the story doesn't go away. It's now part of the national story, right?
Yes, it is part of a national story — and even as you heard last night, it's studied by all those law schools all around the world. The message of that story is really very simple: that we have a responsibility. It's pretty obvious that we have a responsibility to make sure that our children and our grandchildren, and their grandchildren are going to have water to drink. I mean how simple can that be? We send our kids to school, we take care of them, we don't even want to have a fly land on their bodies. But why will we not take care of the water that they drink?

It seems terribly obvious but it wasn't part of the law, was it?
Yes. There is a line that I read once, "What is the difference between the obscure and the obvious? The obscure is figured out sooner or later. It is the obvious that takes a lot longer." (LAUGHTER)

And this is so obvious. This is so common sense that actually I'm surprised that it never made headlines in the Philippines. Nobody heard about that case in the Philippines when it was rendered. Even I did not bother to read the decision. I just read the positive post at the end and I said, "Never mind, it doesn't solve anything." So, I just forgot about it. The magic of Internet was not yet as wide as it is now, and it seems to have caught fire. It was just so simple an idea that it caught fire. Why did it catch fire? Because it was such a simple idea.

And it's the heart of the Oposa Doctrine, as it has now become.
The heart of the case — I don't even want to call it after my name — the heart of the message is that we have our children who will come after us.

And we have a responsibility to them, which we always knew — but it wasn't a legal principle.
Yes. We always knew that.

I want to talk a little bit about the Philippine legal system. I think you have some tools that Canadians don't have. For example, the Constitution says that "The state shall protect and advance the right of the people to a balanced and healthful ecology and in accord with the rhythm and balance of nature."
"Rhythm and harmony of nature."

"Rhythm and harmony of nature"?
Yes, very beautiful language.

It is very beautiful. Is that the foundational piece of the cases you've been able to bring?
Yes. I found that nobody of course, read that. It was not even in the Bill of Rights. It was not listed under the rights of the people. It was a motherhood statement under the policies and principles. But if one were to dissect that provision, which I did, you saw that the state has a duty to protect — and then the people have the right. So there is a duty, there is a right, and if you violate that there is what we call in law a cause of action. There is a reason to take action.

Yes, so it really is foundational, isn't it?
It is foundational, and all constitutions have this — not that specific word, but all constitutions have the right to life.

Well, we haven't been able to find it in the Canadian Constitution quite yet (LAUGHS), but that is David Suzuki's current preoccupation, getting that right into the Canadian Constitution.
Rights of the environment, you mean.

The right to a healthy environment.
Yes, the right to a healthy environment. But all constitutions contain the right to life.

Yes, and that may be the way that this is in there already.
Yes, this is what our good friend M.C. Mehta was able to do in India. And that is what the first topic of my talk was yesterday. When we use the word "environment" — you know, if you are an environmentalist people look at you as if you're different. You're a hippie, you're something marginal. But if you really frame the word "environment" to redefine it as life and the life sources — I don't even want to call it life elements because that's more difficult to understand — but the sources of life, the fountains that make life possible: land, air and water. How simple can that be? Without land we cannot eat, without water we cannot live for three days, without air we cannot live for three minutes. Then, if you reframe that, then everything else

becomes easy because who wants to dirty the air? Do we want to go into the back of the exhaust pipe of a car and then breathe that thing (LAUGHTER), snort that thing for one minute? No, we don't want to do that. But that's what we're doing.

And "the environment" also suggests that there is something out there separate from us. Yes, exactly. It's outside of us and you just have to take care of it. No. You have to take care of it because it's part of us. When I breathe I take in and I humanize the air. I take in the air because it becomes part of me. When I eat it becomes part of me. When I drink water it becomes part of the 70 percent of my body. So — again — I tell that story about the paintings and the cave walls because those brushes, we need to use new paint brushes. The words "paint brushes" — what I call the paint brushes — they are a new way of thinking of the environment. And I said you know we can't understand the word environment because it's not even in English, it's a French word!

Yes, yes. You have some legal instruments I think in the Philippines that I'm not familiar with. For example, the writ of "kalikasan." What is that?
That's very new. It's a legal tool, a procedural tool, that was passed only in 2010. It says where a damage to the environment extends to two or more cities, or two or more provinces, where the damage is of such magnitude, an ordinary citizen can file directly in the Supreme Court for immediate relief.

Without going through the lower courts.
Without going through the lower courts. It was just used recently. There is a news article now where a mountain, a watershed of a city, was being damaged by roads by different people. In fact the flash point of that was when a certain congressman bought land within that watershed, was building a facility, and just bulldozed a road. So the people there initiated a legal action in the Supreme Court. You can find it in the news today. The court just issued a blanket order saying, no development. They call it a temporary protection order, environment protection order.

So no development can occur in that area.
Yes, no development in that area.

Interrogatory letters. Tell me about those because I'm not familiar with those either.
It's very simple actually, but we don't use that. The United States used that more. That is contained in practically all jurisdictions. When I sue someone, for example, or when I'm sued, or we have a case, there are what is known as modes of discovery, because the idea of a legal case is to put everything on the table and sort out the evidence. So if Mr. A were to sue Mr. B for a collection of a sum of money, and then Mr. B says in his answer, "I have already paid," Mr. A can send him a letter without waiting for the trial itself, which is going to take a long time, and can say,

"Okay Mr. B, you said that you paid, where is your receipt? Where is your evidence that you paid?" Then Mr. B will have to reply under oath. Here they even call it depositions. There are different kinds. There are motion to produce documents, physical examination, depositions and interrogatories and interrogatory is just a simple letter that Mr. A can send to Mr. B and Mr. B will have ten or fifteen days to answer under oath.

The "under oath" is just part of the process.
Yes, because then if Mr. B were to say something false then he can be sued for perjury. I used that in the Manila Bay case. Remember, I sued eleven government agencies, and I was all alone. I didn't want to have to wait for the trial because, you know, you're one against eleven. That's not going to be very cost efficient. And I don't have any funding, I don't have any resources, I'm just an ordinary lawyer. I don't even have a proper income. I gave up my commercial law practice in 1998. So I said, "How can we use this to shorten the process of trial?" Because if we went through the process of trial it would take at least 10 years to get all the evidence. Our trial, by the way, in the Philippines, is not like the U.S. or in Canada, probably, where when you sit down you have to finish it in one or two weeks. Here, when you begin the trial it goes on and on and on and on. There, you have a hearing now, and then you present evidence, you present one witness — and then the calendar is so crowded that the lawyer of the opposite side says, "Can we do our cross-examination next sitting?" So the next sitting will be scheduled maybe two months from now, and then at that next sitting the witness has to come back, and then he will have to be cross examined — and then after the cross examination the plaintiff will say, "Ok, your honour I have another engagement," or the court says, "Well, are you done? Okay, we'll have another witness, so can we reset it?" So another two or three months, and then the same process, and the same process. The whole trial takes between three to five years. It's ridiculous. They are trying to do something about it now, but —

But the interrogatory letters let you get to the heart of the thing right off the top.
Right off the top. There is a 1977 provision that Marcos wrote, which said that where a body of water is polluted, it is the duty of the government agencies concerned, quote, unquote, to clean it up. Then you have concerned government agencies and I said, "Who are the concerned government agencies? They are the department of the environment, the department of public works, the department of health, the department of education. Are you concerned?" Yes. Then you have to be included in the petition.

So, ask them a question. Do you know about this law? Yes. Of course they will say yes. Do you know that Manila Bay is polluted? Yes. Question number three. Do you know that you are one of the concerned government agencies that is referred to by this provision of the law? Yes. So question number four is the clincher. What have you done? Then they get stuck. Then you just narrow the issue.

So by the time we got to pre-trial all I said was, "Your honour, there are two main issues. One is an issue of fact. We all admit that Manila Bay is polluted. The only fact that needs to be proven is how polluted is it. And number two is the issue of law, which is, are they required to do something about it? Are they the concerned government agencies that must clean it up?" So you abbreviate. It could have taken 50, 100 trials, 100 sittings, but we finished in four or five sittings.

Because you'd already cut through to the heart of it with the letters.
Yes.

And then what does the court do? You've established that these are the concerned government agencies, the bay is polluted, and it is their responsibility to do something about it. Now the court says — what?
My prayer to the court was for them to prepare a detailed plan of action complete with tasking, complete with timetable, with what to do, when to do it, and who is going to do it. I already suggested that the department of education conduct educational activities to raise awareness on the bay, and the department of public works should identify where are the encroachments, and the easements of the river and the waterways that lead to Manila Bay, and the department of the environment identify this and that, and the sewerage authority must identify where are these sewage sources, etc., etc. So I already prepared a prescription on what the court can do. So I'm not saying you must do it, I'm saying this is how to go about it. And fortunately the trial court adopted it and said, "Okay, prepare a plan of action and submit it to the court." And then the government appealed the case to the court of appeals, so that took another three and a half years. And then we won, and then it took another three and a half years in the Supreme Court until there was an oral argument and then about five months later we had a decision. It took a long time.

And at the end of it you have a plan, which you basically laid out at the beginning.
Yes.

And the court says, "Okay, you now have to do this."
Right.

And if they don't do it, what — ?
Well, if they don't do it, technically you can sue them for contempt (LAUGHS). I did, I sued them for contempt. The decision was December 18, 2008. And then, by August, no one had yet filed a report. I said, they must think I'm joking. So (LAUGHS), just being naughty, I knew some of the cabinet secretaries, so I filed

a case against them for contempt of court, for not complying. That shook them up, and from then on, they have been submitting quarterly reports. Every 90 days they submit, so I have a bundle of reports now.

And what has happened on the ground? What has changed at the actual bay?
You know, there have been things that are unpleasant; there have been things that are pleasant. A few months ago for example, I received a text message from someone who said, "You know your efforts have not been in vain because the news just showed that they were catching different kinds of fish there now. Thank you very much." I mean it's a good thing. They are catching crabs; they are catching different species of fish, shrimps etc., etc. That means life is coming back. Whether or not this is actually getting cleaner I really don't know. I mean we can only do so much. If I were president of the Philippines, that would be clean tomorrow.

Well, some of this you can see. On the shorelines, for example, all that garbage has been taken away. The shorelines look like shorelines now.
Yes. The most important thing I think was that number one, it heightened the awareness of the condition of the bay. Number two, the government agencies that really wanted to do something but could not do anything — for example, getting away squatters, informal settlers from the riverbanks. It's is a very difficult thing in the Philippines because, remember, they're voters, and remember that you have to go through the mayor. You just can't come in — national government agencies can't just come in and bulldoze them away. You have to talk to the mayors and the mayors will always say, "Oh, no…" They will always drag their feet because you know these are voters.

The beauty of that decision, as I belatedly found out — well, you know when I got the decision, I just forgot about it. Just like the children's case. When I saw the decision I didn't even bother to read it. I said, "I've done my share, I've told my story, and that's all I can do." Using the law to tell the story is as much as I can do. Nobody pays me to tell my story. But I was very surprised recently that one city sent me a letter and they said that they were going to give me, on their foundation day, on their charter day, they were going to give me an award. I said, "Why are they giving me an award when I am not even a resident there?" They gave me a very nice plaque, which said, 'You have made a contribution, because it was your decision, it was that Manila Bay decision, that strengthened their hand, to say, hey, I don't want to do this, but look, there is a Supreme Court decision that we have to clean this up.'

Now that's an important point, because the same thing happened with the children's case, didn't it? Your actions tell public officials that they must do what they know they should do, and probably want to do, but they've had all these constraints. In a sense, you've said, "Blame me!" (LAUGHTER)

Yes! Blame me! I don't care, nobody's going to sue me anyway (LAUGHTER) because they are all afraid, you know, they can be hit with harassment suits very quickly. They will have to defend themselves, they will have to hire their own lawyers, and when they are no longer in positions of power, the cases will still be there and it's going to get really messy, and they will have to pay the legal fees themselves. But with this piece of paper, if they get sued, they can say, "I have no choice."

I have no choice. It's a court order.

Here's the decision, yes, there is a court order. I did this with great effect fairly recently with encroachments in the Island of Bantayan. There were foreigners who started buying beachfront properties and started fencing off the beachfront. This is part of the thing that I told the story about, that people from other lands come in and they take over as if they bought the sea. So what I did — I said if I sued all of them it's going to get messy. Each one will have a lawyer, and I'll be fighting so many battles. So what I did was I talked to the department of the environment and I said, "This is your job. Under the law you have to destroy all of them, you have to demolish, remove all of these structures." And then they pleaded with me, they said, "We know this is the law, but if we did that we'd be slapped with twenty cases in one afternoon. And we are just ordinary civil servants. We cannot afford a lawyer." So I said, "Okay, we'll do this. I'll sue you. I'll sue you technically, as an institution, and then it's up to you to either agree or disagree. If you agree then we can enter into a compromise judgment, which will now give you the legal shield of a court order to remove those structures."

And that's exactly what happened. When they got the court order, they started removing all these structures and nobody could sue them. I was in touch with the lawyers of these resorts and they said, "You know we've been going crazy, trying to figure out what cases are we going to file against these government officials because it's easy to file a case against a government official. But what cases are we going to file against them? They have a court order. So what happens if we file against them? They will just show, here's a piece of paper that says we have to do it!" So it's really helping them. It's providing them the wind beneath their wings, in a sense.

That's a lovely analogy, because it's not really an adversarial situation, is it? You're saying, "This is what the law says," and you're basically giving them a shield that allows them to apply the law

Right. And that's exactly what I'm doing now with the road-sharing cases.

Tell me about the road-sharing cases.

I showed last night how messy the traffic is now in Manila — and I'm not just talking about Manila. The other picture I showed was Los Angeles and New York. You go to New York now, and it's just crazy. And why is that so? Because we're all crazy about having cars, about individual mobility at the expense of [the] collective. A nice line I read says that our insistence on individual mobility has resulted in serious collective immobility. We are so enamoured with individual mobility, with our cars, that if everybody were to have cars, then nobody's going to move. And that's what's happening now in the Philippines. I showed you the pictures yesterday that it's not moving anymore. It's a terrible thing to come to Manila. And it's not just Manila. All the urban areas are getting there, all because of movies.

What is happening to the urban areas is the same thing that happened in the sea as far as the shark is concerned. One movie about the shark — *Jaws* — led to the massive slaughter of sharks all over the world. In the same manner, the movies showing how beautiful having a car is, how barrelling down a road at 80 miles per hour — why don't they show, for example, that a Ferrari can get stuck in traffic, or a Lamborghini can get stuck in traffic. I wish that they would do that. Then my little bicycle here would be faster than them. (LAUGHTER)

This is all madness for cars, for motor vehicles, for the internal combustion engine that powers the motor vehicles. I have a car too, but I would rather not have a car. Chris was just saying he was in Amsterdam recently. I was also in Amsterdam last June, and I have been also to Denmark. These are the two places in the world that don't have traffic jams. Why? Because people ride bicycles, people walk even in winter, and they have trams. They have collective transportation systems so they don't have traffic. Two, three miles, four miles, five miles they can take a bicycle. It's healthier, and the car runs on hydrocarbons, but walking runs on carbohydrates. We'd be a lot healthier if we took a bicycle or if we walked more.

Okay, so we agree with all of that. Now what do we do?
What is the solution? We make more cars? We're stuck again with something that is so obvious. Are we going to make more cars? Are we going to widen the roads? Where will we get the space? Lose our own houses already? No — so what is the solution? I read it somewhere: it's called the road diet. You just narrow the road so that people won't bring their cars anymore. People will walk, people will take a bike, or people will be encouraged to move their minds from individual mobility via a car to collective mobility — and cheaper mobility too. You can just pay a few dollars, a few pesos to ride a bus. For me to go to the city, for example, in the Philippines — I live south of Manila — just to come to the city, I spend maybe $35 to $40. That's a lot of money. That's about the equivalent of about four daily wages of an ordinary citizen. Imagine this. Throwing — not even throwing — burning

that money! Burning your money just to get from one point to another! I mean, how much is it going to cost me if I took a car to go to New York from here in White Plains? Tremendous amount of money. But if I took a train it's only $8.

Now how do you use the law to deal with that?
Oh! First, two grounds that are powerful. One is less than about one percent of the population in the Philippines of 100 million people own cars. But all of the roads are given to cars. What's that? That's unequal protection of the law, that's a violation of a basic human right. You are favouring the one percent and discriminating against the 99 percent. So that's a noble argument that I came up with. (LAUGHTER) They haven't answered that. Government cannot answer that. How can you provide so much resources for one percent of the population, and you don't even provide a sidewalk for people who want to walk?

Number two: I was able to find a law in the Philippines, which precisely said this: "That the new paradigm in the movement of men and things must follow a simple principle. Those who have less in wheels must have more in roads." Section nine, executive order 774, dated December 26, 2008. And it continues for this purpose: "The new system of transportation must favour non-motorized transportation systems, including biking, walking, cycling," and the one I showed you yesterday, "man-powered mini-train."

Yes, you showed some marvelous inventions of mass transport that were not actually driven by internal combustion engines.
Yes! It's so simple! I showed you the picture. I invented those things. I didn't fabricate it with my hands, but it was my design. We have to move following the principle of the ant. I call it the principle of the ant. Follow in single file. The ant, numerous as they are — I begin my road-sharing talk with asking them who is more intelligent, the ant or human beings? And they say, "Of course, human beings." Then I show a picture that says the ants are billions and billions and trillions, but they don't have traffic jams. Whereas human beings, we're only a few thousands and we have traffic jams. Why? Because they follow a simple principle, the principle of the ant. They follow in single file.

So, we just follow the simple principle of the ant. Follow in single file, do not take up more space than necessary for walking, for example. I did not have the time yesterday but part of my presentation is I ask somebody to stand up. Okay, so (TO CAMERON), please stand up, extend your arm. One. Just one. Okay. Standing up you only occupy about one eighth of a square metre. Sitting down you occupy only one fourth. Make it one half of one square metre. But taking a car you will occupy at least 15 square metres, not even moving. What's that? That's a waste of space! And what is the most valuable resource of an urban area? Space!

And we're wasting space! This is part of the paradigm of waste that human beings are so accustomed to now.

And Chris was just showing that, you know, all these plastic things that we just throw away after one use, one single use. These all came from oil — took 200 million years to become what they are. Then we eat it and then we throw it away. And so, my demand on that petition is divide all the roads by half. Half for non-motorized transportation, meaning walking, cycling, you can even make a vegetable garden, and then half for motor vehicle transportation — collective preferably — collective transportation: and if that happens, then the world will be a better place. That is going to be the game changer, what I call the catalytic intervention.

Now tell me about that because that is a phrase you talk about — catalytic, and catalytic interventions. What you do over and over again is use the law to force a catalytic intervention. I just developed that theory three days ago.

I know that! (LAUGHTER) I know that, but it's a great name for what's already there. Yes! I did it, it's a more simple way of saying that's it's probably game-changing. It will be the game changer. Catalytic means it's an intervention, an action, which is going to spark a series of other actions that will lead to a massive change. I showed an example of the negative side. You have a forest [and] you build a road right in to the middle of the forest. Before the end of the year, or two years, it will become a parking lot.

In Africa roads like that have allowed the hunters for bush meat to go in and slaughter all the animals. But if you don't have the road, they can't get in there. The road has those kinds of consequences.
Yes. Exactly. This is an example of a catalytic intervention. And then I showed that the re-introduction of the wolf in the Yellowstone National Park — you've probably seen the little film that they...

That George Monbiot narrates...
Yes, Monbiot narrates it. The re-introduction of the wolf led to the reduction of the population of the deer and the grass started to regrow. Vegetation started to regrow and everything else followed. This is catalytic intervention. In the road-sharing case, if you just change the road system — number one — people are going to be healthier because they will walk. They will want to walk. And then they say, it's hot. Of course! You just put the trees so people will walk. You put trees in. What's the best air-conditioning? Is it LG, is it Daikin, is it Carrier? No, it's that tree. It's for free, and it's the best air conditioning because it releases pure oxygen! (LAUGHTER) And the air conditioning that we have doesn't release pure oxygen. It just releases cold air.

So the idea is, okay, divide the road. People will say this is probably the craziest thing that I am doing. But notice the benefits. I showed yesterday that this transportation system — if you took in all the carbon footprint of the life-cycle of the car, of the motor vehicle, from the mining and refining of ore and oil to the making of steel, to the making of the car, to the making of aggregated cement, to the making of rubber, to wiping out real forests, just to plant rubber trees — if you take it into account, the carbon footprint of that is about half of all the climate-forcing gases, the heat-trapping gases. Imagine what — people talk about the UN framework on climate change. They cannot even agree on one percent! And just by a simple catalytic intervention, we can achieve 50 percent!

The other benefit that we'll have is people will be walking, and if I see you on the street, "Oh, hi Don! I haven't seen you for a long time!" So you restore connection between people, which is totally lost when we're in cars. I can't even see you if you're in a car. And if we get to bump each other, we may even be quarrelling instead of being friends. We're suffering from floods in the Philippines. Why are there floods? I showed yesterday that this is the reality of the map. We will have more rain and we will have more snow, because that is a meteorological fact and if that is so, what is our solution? Will we pave over everything in concrete? (LAUGHTER) So, no. We take out some of the concrete, and restore it into wetlands.

Let me just make it clear for those who haven't followed your actions as I have that when we talk about giving up 50 percent of the road, you're saying, split them right down the centre line, all of them. Don't take the roads away, don't change the roads, don't make new roads. Just say that the left-hand side is for people, bicycles, walking, and the other side is for motorized transportation. And of course the reason it becomes collective is because...
You'd be forced!

Yes. If it was difficult to get down that road before when both lanes were for motor cars; it will be impossible when only one lane is... right?
Exactly! (LAUGHTER)

So let's work out some way that 40 of us can go together...
Exactly! Then you ride a bus!

Yes! And that also is a social activity.
Exactly. When I get into the bus, and then I see Donald. "Oh!" We sit down together, "Oh! How are you!" And then you see other friends, and you can even have a little concert in the bus. I mean it restores connections!

It's a virtuous circle.
Yes! It's a virtuous cycle. Not a vicious but a virtuous cycle. If you divide the road then, without many cars, parking lots will be opened up. I'll show you, you should

take a look. How much space? Probably I measured about one or two hectares. You use hectares?

Uh-huh.

Hectares! Just for parking of motor vehicles! One other benefit: number one, you can just take out half a hectare, you can get all the hobos there who are homeless, who have nothing to eat. "You, Mr. So-and-so, here this twenty square meters, you plant vegetables there. You Mr. So-and-so, you plant vegetables. You, you don't have a home, okay we'll use 3,000 square meters, 5,000, we'll just put up a rough building there. We have the space. Remember that in urban areas the space is the most expensive. Somebody was just telling me that a studio in Manhattan now is costing something like anywhere between $3,000 and $5,000 a month, depending on the location. For one year you can buy a house in the Philippines for that! (LAUGHTER)

And in eastern Canada too. In our part of the country it would go a long way. What would that be, $60,000? Yes, you can get a house. Not in the city, but you can get a house in the country for that.

Exactly. This is all the paradigm of waste. By the way, the synonym of waste is the very core and foundation of the economy of the world. Consumption. Everyone wants to consume. The synonym of consumption is waste. Look at the dictionary, it says waste. It says also tuberculosis. (LAUGHTER)

So, disease and waste.

Yes, disease and waste!

Well, that's true. Somebody said to me during one of these conversations that the economy is actually a device for turning the planet into junk.

Exactly, that's a nice way of putting it. We're trashing the planet and we call it progress. And this for me — this road sharing thing — is probably, one would say, the craziest thing that I have ever thought of, that I am trying, that I may not see in my lifetime happen, but as you saw yesterday the seed has been planted and people are beginning to wake up. We just need to succeed in one city. If people are listening to this, just get me one city who will implement this.

Well, you just tried it in part of one city for a brief time.

Yes, for four hours.

And it seemed to work pretty well.

It seemed to work pretty well, except for the car owners who were inconvenienced. If you go to the newspaper now, they are all attacking the group that made this happen. So they are receiving so much flak. Fortunately the mayor was supportive, but he is also receiving so much flak for agreeing to it. But it worked! For four hours people were so happy, they were biking. But the car owners who are more influential I guess because they are the car owners...

They are the wealthy.
They are the wealthy, and they make up less than one percent of the population. And out of probably one hundred ... two hundred kilometers of road, this was just about five kilometers of road that was being used. It's not about changing roads. It's about changing minds.

And it's partly getting people to see where their own best interests lie. The flak from one percent wouldn't count if you had solid support from the 99 percent, right? But they don't necessarily...
Speak!

... see where their best interests lie. Well, they may not speak, but they also may not even see it.
Right!

And that may be a bit of an issue too.
Yes. It needs a lot of education. That is why I'm moving in a different direction now and instead of just filing the case, I can just forget about that case. Let it go. Dismissed? I'll file again. And dismissed, I'll file again! Who cares, if you're going to take another 10 years, or 20 years? And even if I get an order from the court, it's like Manila Bay, is it going to be clean tomorrow? No!

It's going to be a process, so I'm using what we call the sandwich theory of social change. Where the top meets the bottom and the bottom meets the top. The bottom being us, the people, talking with the mayor and the city officials. Let's try this! I just sent the road-sharing organization an email now that said please don't be discouraged. I talked to the students yesterday and I'm organizing a little party here tomorrow. It's going to be a fun party. I will get them all to sing. But more importantly, I'll get somebody to sit down here and compose letters, and send the letters to people concerned so that they don't get discouraged, because the worst thing is to lose morale. We can fight wars without guns, but not without morale.

So now you have another use of the law, as public education, right? You're doing the storytelling, you're giving strength to public officials to do the right thing, you're using the law for educational purposes. This is a very broad and innovative and imaginative way of using the law.
You know, Don, it's funny that you say that, but I have never thought of myself as a lawyer. Even now, I don't look at myself as a lawyer. I say I am just a storyteller. I use the law as my medium for telling a story. And maybe because I have no respect

for the law, no reverence for the law as a sacred text that came down from Moses — it is probably that kind of attitude that makes me able to play with the law. You met my research assistant — she's very bright — at Pace Law School? So at our first interview when she signed up, she was expecting some mumbo jumbo from a lawyer, a legal scholar, quote, unquote — and the first thing I tell her is, Forget about the law. (LAUGHTER) She raised her eyebrow. What?! Forget about the law? Yes! We will do more interesting things.

Speaking of interesting things, tell me about your work in the Visayan Sea. This is where you grew up, where your heart is, right?

Yes. I grew up in Cebu City, but we had a place in Bantayan Island. My grandfather had a place in Bantayan Island and, I say, you know, whatever degrees I have doesn't really matter. My real degree is what I call the CBB: the Certified Beach Bum. I just love being by the sea, and unfortunately not too many people in my country love being by the sea. They love going to the malls, probably because — again, this is all western influence — we don't have open spaces there. We don't have parks, and our beaches have been either dirty or almost all, 99.9 percent have all been just taken over by private enterprise, or private companies, and so they block off ordinary citizens, ordinary people.

So it was there that, you know, I learned. I started adopting that place. It was just a little beach house of my grandfather and I started adopting that place when I was 20 years old. I saw how beautiful it was. I didn't know the science of it, but I saw how beautiful the sea was. Then I became a scuba diver, and then I really saw how beautiful the underwater was, and how badly damaged it has been. This is about the time that I filed my Manila Bay case, when I redirected my energies to the sea, having done my work on the forest. It is just so sad that our own people do not appreciate the wealth that we have. We are the centre of the centre of marine biodiversity on Earth. On Earth! I hope people just understood that.

Now the beauty is, you know, if you say something often enough, somebody is bound to listen. And fortunately, the gentleman who was responsible for that Sagay Marine Reserve I was talking about, he started off as a mayor, then he became congressman, now the governor, Governor Freddie Maranon. He is like my adoptive father. He is about 80-something now, still very healthy, still very visionary. So we are really very, very close friends and when he became governor we together convened all the governors of the Visayan Sea. Now we have a group — we have a working group of the Visayan Sea governors and he has also infected the other governors having seen his work in that Sagay Marine Reserve. You wouldn't believe the crabs! Remember this was the centre of dynamite fishing before, but because of the change, cyanide, all kinds of crazy fishing...

The most destructive possible fishing.
Yes. But because they took care of their mangroves, they replanted their mangroves, you know they were protected from (Typhoon) Hayan, because of these mangroves. You can Google them: Sagay and mangroves. He was a very, very visionary governor. You should meet him. This is a forty-year work, this is not work you do overnight. As any respectable, any good piece of work, it always happens over decades. You should see the crabs. Their crabs — they grow crabs as big as this. The body of their crabs are bigger than this plate (LAUGHTER) and I am not exaggerating. You should see it!

Recently we had a Visayan Sea governors' meeting. There was a new governor who won recently. So the daughter of the governor was there, and I asked Freddie, Governor Freddie Maranon, to bring a sample so he could give it away. As he was talking I said, "Excuse me, can you get the sample please?" Okay, we got the crab — tied, of course, the crab, so the crab doesn't bite us. I asked the daughter of the new governor — she was my student in environmental law — I said, "Come here, come here," I said, "Put your arm here, and put the claw of the crab here. So which is bigger?" (LAUGHTER) Wow! Can you imagine! I mean it is the most graphic thing you can see!

So they were all laughing, and then — very humbly, this man is very humble, this governor Freddie. I call him *mano, mano* Freddie. "*Mano*" means a very respected elder brother. He says, "But you know, truth to tell, this is only medium. (LAUGHTER) This is only the medium size of our crabs." (LAUGHTER) Because they've taken care of it! I mean how difficult can that be? You don't kill the goose that lays the golden egg; you fatten it so it will bring more!

But in fact they were killing the goose that laid the golden egg. And you took very direct action there — at some risk to your own welfare.
Oh yes, plenty. Plenty. I am a little more behaved now, because they've already taken over. That governor was pretty inspired and he launched a task force against illegal fishing so they've been cracking down — and then the other governor, who we already contacted before and was part of the governor's group, he has also been very seriously cracking down on illegal fishing. I just received an email two days ago from one of my friends in that other island province saying that the marine sanctuary that they put up there — it was inspired by my work, and people dive there now — is now so teeming with fish that the bureau of fisheries is asking for a small piece of land because they want to build a small marine station to feature it.

So, the tide has changed. *Mano* Freddie and I met in 1999, just about the time when I decided to go back into the sea and started to do serious work on the sea. On or about that time, he was still — no he was not mayor anymore, he was congressman, and he was ending his term as congressman — and we became very, very good friends. When we started working on this, we were just voices in the wilderness. Nobody listened to us. They said, "Who cares about the Visayan Sea? It's too far away." You know who did this? The two of us talking to each other! (LAUGHS) And now people are listening, and the beauty is, the tide is turning. That's all we can do. In the same manner, the tide is turning for our forest. There are still abuses, there are still illegal activities here and there, but it's no longer the massive and legalized destruction that it was before.

You used the same basic approach with the Visayan Sea that you used with so many of these other ones too. There is the law; there is what you're supposed to do; this is illegal; you're poaching. But then you went out with your own task force and did your own arrests —
Yes. Because the government does not enforce the law, then I decided to enforce it myself.

Now how do you get away with that? If I go out to the Visayan Sea and say to a poacher, "I'm arresting you," he gives me a clout on the side of the head and walks away.
Yes, he beheads you. (LAUGHTER) But I was very strategic. You see, I coined this line: abundance breeds waste, scarcity breeds efficiency. I am a very efficient user of money because I use my own money. So, my one dollar, my ROI for my one dollar must be at least 100 times. Not even 100 percent, because one dollar will only get you two dollars. But my one dollar must get a return on investment of at least 100 times. That is my mental calculation, because I don't receive any funding. Nobody is going to fund me for the crazy things that I do. It is too far out on the horizon.

So what I did is I got to talk to the NBI, our local FBI, the National Bureau of Investigation. They are pretty honest; they are pretty good. I was able to get allies there who believed in my cause. Then I would just pay for their transportation, because they would not have funding for gasoline and food. So I just pay for their transportation, for food, and then we did strategic enforcement work. Like, for dynamite fishing, I got a policeman who would accompany me because he has the uniform and the gun. So we would do the arrests. As far as the NBI is concerned, we went after the syndicates that were selling blasting powder and blasting caps. That's the catalytic intervention in a sense, because if you hit them, then — it's like drugs. If you hit the sources of the drugs, then there would be no user. Of course it's more difficult with drugs, because it needs a lot of money...

And the end user of the drug wants to have the drug. The end user of the dynamite isn't addicted to the dynamite.
Yes, he just doesn't know any better. So I am an ordinary citizen, I have no power, I

have no position. I say that I only have one position: a sitting position or a standing position. But that's about all. I guess the lesson is that if you have the real determination to do something, then just go ahead and go do it. Just go do it. Be strategic. Then, you can make a dent — and we've made a dent, a little bit. It's still far from over, but at least the tide is turning. There is more awareness, there is more effort. And then I got them involved in making fish condominiums, and even my former adversaries are now making fish condominiums.

Because you didn't say, "Punish these guys." You said, "Release these guys into my care." And then you've turned them around.

That is my achievement! It's not the arrest. Any policeman can do an arrest, but for me, something that you don't find in the newspapers or you don't find in the Google about my work, is that my former adversaries have become not only my allies, but have become my fellow advocates. That is for me the highest achievement. It also springs from a belief that life is about redemption. We all commit mistakes. We committed 100,000... I have committed 100,000 mistakes, but if you get me an opportunity to correct myself, then you restore my dignity and I will try to do better. I am so tough in court against them. But after they are convicted, I tell this court, please — I talk to them in advance. I say, "Do you want to go to jail or do you want to help me? Are you going to help our cause?" Of course they say they'll help your cause. Then I give them an offer they cannot refuse, in a very positive way. Do you want to go to jail? That is going to take you at least 10 years. You have your wife here, you have your children there, and by the time you come home your wife is going to have another husband. (LAUGHS) And of course that gets them! And this is true!

Of course it is. (LAUGHS)

Of course it's true, because the wife is going to find somebody who will support them! Anyway, what do you want? You want this or that? Oh, we want to support you. Okay, when we go to court now, you plead guilty and then I will talk to the judge that you'll be released on probation, on a suspended sentence for 5 years, whatever, 6 years. But as a condition of the probation you will serve to protect the sea, and to restore the sea you will have to report to my Sea Camp every so often, and you will protect the sea. And that's what they're doing. It's something I'm really proud of.

Absolutely! You're making that same suggestion basically at a national level with the confrontation over what you call the West Philippine Sea, and what the Chinese call the South China Sea.

Oh, you know about that?

Well, I read your suggestion that the Philippines should declare the entire area an international marine reserve and national park complete with an international marine station, much like the international space station —
Rather than fighting over it?

Yes! And it's a very tough thing for the Chinese to resist. They'll be ready for you if you're going to use force, but if you're going to use this kind of approach...
That's what I suggest, but nobody listens to me. (LAUGHS) If we only had a president who'd say, "Go, we will support you," I can mobilize the whole world. I know a lot of people around the world. I can mobilize the UN General Assembly, for example, to pass a resolution. Instead of fighting over it, let's make it a park. Let's make it a marine park. We now elevate ourselves: instead of fighting it with guns and fists, we will be fighting on the level of moral authority. We want that sea to remain as beautiful as it is, so that future Chinese, future Filipinos will still benefit from that. There is a lot of sea there, but sadly, not only is the Philippines not listening to that, it is trying to exploit it.

So we don't have moral authority. If they say, okay, we will do this, then the rest of the world — IUCN is going to help up, the scientists will help us. Even the beauty of the suggestion — I've thought this through — the beauty of the suggestion is that we can even get the marine scientists — and we can use their gun boat, we can use our gun boats — we will load it with our best marine researchers. They can load it with their best, and then we can have a drink there, we can have a party there, we can have singing there. Then we restore amity between peoples.

Governments are crazy. But people are good people. The Chinese are good people. It's their government that wants it. I just talked to some Chinese over dinner just last Friday — less than a week ago — and I said, "Your country and mine, our governments are, they do not have a good understanding." And she said, "Yes, let our government have it, but we're friends." Your country — we're of course in good relations, Canada and the Philippines — but your country and my country can go to hell. Their governments can go to hell, but we as people are friends!

What strikes me about that approach to the disputed sea is that just ignores the premises of conflict and adopts a premise of cooperation. You're very good at this, at framing it in such a way that it's very hard to resist. It's like your adversaries-to-allies project. You're right, the guy is going to be crazy if he says, "Oh, I'd rather go to jail." (LAUGHTER)
You want to go to jail? You want your kids to die of hunger? But this thing is still far away and maybe it's never going to happen in my lifetime. We'll go on a shooting war and nobody's going to win. But if we just had a little more sense, especially with the climate crisis happening, we will need fish and if we do not take care of that, if we just compete — and then we want to drill it for oil. We don't even know

if there is oil there! We're actually quarrelling over an egg that has not even been hatched! (LAUGHTER) How ridiculous can that be!

Your next battle — and I know very little about it, but tell me about it. This is a really colossal one. You want to do global legal action on climate change using the United Nations. How does that work?

Um, I try not to talk about things that I am not yet going to do. I only talk about things that I've done. Yesterday, that was just a sneak preview of the necessity to use the law again to trigger a massive change for greater consciousness and greater action throughout the world. This is in your words, "colossal." All my earlier work is going to be like a walk in the park and this road-sharing thing is just one of the aspects of that. You want the entire world for this one. There is already consensus that the crisis is happening. We just had a climate summit here last week.

But very little action.

Yes. And hopefully this global legal action is going to be a little catalytic intervention. Maybe. It's going to be a very long process, but I'd like to be as healthy as you when I'm your age, and it's going to be a long walk. But I like the line I read once, it is, "Perhaps it is the destiny of people who follow the path of their ideas to realize that the path is endless, and that in walking it, we do not find the end of the path, nor the fulfillment of our ideas. Rather we only find the joy of walking." So, enjoy the journey. (LAUGHTER) The destination is six feet under the ground! (LAUGHTER) So why am I in a hurry to get there? (LAUGHTER)

THOMAS LINZEY AND MARI MARGIL
Fighting for a Community's Legal Right to Say No
Recorded October 2014

The Community Environmental Legal Defense Fund (CELDF) is a non-profit, public-interest law firm providing free and affordable legal services for communities facing threats to their local environment. Its technique is to help individual communities to assert their right to local self-government, and to recognize the rights of Nature. This may sound dry, but it involves organizing, educating and nurturing local groups in scores of municipalities — groups made up of ordinary citizens who have discovered, to their shock and horror, that their democratic communities are the playthings of corporations, which have rights that mere citizens don't have. CELDF has assisted more than 110 local governments, not to mention the governments of Nepal, India and Ecuador. CELDF was a founding member of the Global Alliance for the Rights of Nature, and a co-author of the *Universal Declaration for the Rights of Mother Earth*.

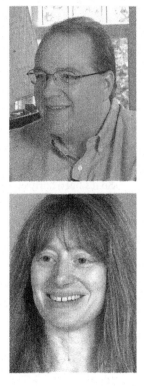

Thomas Linzey is the organization's visionary co-founder and Executive Director, and Mari Margil is its incisive Associate Director.

Your work seems to come down to the legal right of a community to say no. Is that fair?
THOMAS LINZEY: It's where we started. We had communities that were faced with toxic waste incinerators and factory farms, sludge dumping and fracking and thousands of different single issues that communities face every day. What we found about the U.S. system of law — and now over the past 10 years, what we've found about other systems of law, like the Australian and Canadian and even in some ways the Nepalese system of law — is that communities have been cut out of having any authority over whether corporate projects come into their communities or not. They've been under a structure of law in which they can't say no. And the reason they can't say no can be tracked back to certain corporate legal doctrines which have

emerged and been transformed over the past 150 to 200 years, in the U.S. at least.

It's basically put communities in a box. They have these legal doctrines on each side of the box that if they attempt to say no — say, fracking has come into your community — if they attempt to say no, then the corporation that is affected by that fracking project actually has recourse to a system of law that allows them to punish the municipality for even attempting to say "no." And so, as strange as it may sound in a country where people talk about democracy, no democracy exists in our municipal communities today, because communities can't say no to these things. And if you can't say no to a big box store coming into the community, you can't say yes to a viable downtown. If you can't say no to Smithfield Foods Corporation coming in to put a 20,000 head hog factory farm in the middle of your community, you can't say yes to sustainable agriculture. If you can't stop fracking, you can't say yes to a sustainable energy future. If you can't stop the bad things from coming in that are interfering with your vision of what sustainability should be, then you can't define the future of your community.

So it's been fairly controversial work in the United States, and fairly confrontational. But at this point in the U.S. and these other countries, sustainability is illegal. Even to move in the direction of sustainability is stopped by the law.

How does that work? How can there be such a blanket prevention?
TL: Well, we have doctrines like preemption in the [United] States, and to other extents in these other countries. The way that preemption operates is that the corporation, in a given area like energy, goes to the state government or the federal government and puts a law in place that forbids municipalities from adopting anything different than what the state or federal government has put into place in terms of a regulatory framework.

In addition to preemption you have something called corporate rights. It always sounds strange to people but corporations have certain constitutional rights in the United States and elsewhere that corporations can sue municipalities for violating their corporate constitutional rights. We're used to people having constitutional rights. We have free speech rights and due process, equal protection and other rights — but starting in the 1800s, and going back into the 1600s in England, courts and systems of government have recognized corporations as having the same constitutional rights as persons. Among those rights are what are called Fifth Amendment rights in the United States, which allow corporations to sue communities for taking corporate property.

So, if the state has issued a permit to say you can frack here, and the community says, "No you can't," then the corporation has a cause of action against the municipality for damages. The state has created a constitutional right to frack on behalf of the corporation, so they have a constitutionally embedded right to frack, or to put in a factory farm or to do all the bad things.

When we say sustainability is illegal, it's because there are these reinforcing doctrines in place that basically put the community in a cage. As activists, we've heard that it's time to rattle the cage. Well, it's not time to rattle the cage; it's time to break the cage open. Rattling the cage is actually trying to ask others to fix your situation for you. We're in a cage; we want more food or more rations or more water or whatever. But in this case the cage has been carefully built so that we have no control over big issues like energy and agriculture and transportation, even.

The work that the Legal Defense Fund does is really about busting open that cage, to say that we have a right to local community self-government. That includes making decisions about agriculture and energy and transportation, or whatever. In our opinion, we can't get to sustainability by changing light bulbs and taking shorter showers and composting. Those are all good things but in some ways they validate the fact that we have no lawmaking power in our own communities. And if that remains the situation we're pretty much cooked.

MARI MARGIL: Our communities ask us, why is the structure this way? It doesn't seem logical; it certainly doesn't seem to be "We the People." And communities, I think, come to an understanding, as we have, that the structure of law is set up this way to aid interests other than our own. Those interests are a constant, endless expansion of development, of growth, of extraction. The structure has been designed to make sure that that "progress," as many choose to define it — endless growth and development — continues unimpeded, that communities cannot interrupt that flow of development and extraction. The structure of governance and law has been to make sure that communities and activists can't interfere with the flow of commerce. So communities have been subordinated to the point where they really can't decide anything.

The structure is actually designed to ensure what Richard Grossman, the historian that helped to develop our Democracy Schools and our theory, described as the endless production of more. Just more. What? More stuff, more everything. If we understand the structure of law to be designed to ensure endless production of more, then it makes sense that it would be designed to keep everything else out of the way.

TL: So the question is, can we build sustainability by leaving those doctrines on the table? For the past 50 years, environmental activists, and labour activists have said, Yes, you can leave that basic structure on the table and then try to work around it. The past 50 years of environmental activism has been working around it, to do things like permit appeals. You know, the state issues a permit for fracking, so we go and try to appeal the permit. But we're operating under rules that were written by the corporations that the regulatory system was supposed to regulate.

The whole premise of our organizing is that we have to get rid of those doctrines. We have to liberate or free our communities — because until decisions are made by those impacted by the decisions, then we will never have sustainability. There is no interest in Royal Dutch Shell, or Smithfield Foods, or Monsanto in sustainable communities. Their job is to come in and extract. Their job is to take.

Whereas the community's job is to keep, preserve and conserve. There are two different value systems there, and the law supports the corporate value system, not the community value system. So the question is how do you occupy the law to actually change its operation to support the communities rather than the extractive interests.

It's interesting that you use the word "occupy" because it occurs to me that this is the Occupy movement in a legal framework, almost. Just before we move on to other things, there is something quite bizarre about this because the fundamental principle is that the corporation gets compensated for purely imaginary profits, right? For profits that they weren't allowed to make because of the unreasonable objections of the community? It seems to me that the international free-trade deals have now extended that principle so that even our nations are not allowed to interfere with corporate activity.
TL: Yes.

And it's the same doctrine, isn't it? This imaginary profits?
TL: Yes, except the law doesn't treat them as imaginary. I mean the fact that...

No, but we're talking about real life. [LAUGHTER]
TL: The corporation has a lease to extract within a community, and they can calculate how much gas they are going to be able to extract through that lease. Then the community says "You can't," and bans the fracking. A corporation then says, "Well, hey, we have the lease. It's a property interest and the fracked gas is our property — and we would have pulled out $2 million worth of gas from that deposit." Then the lawsuit comes against the municipality for that amount.

So the law treats the gas as a very real interest, not imaginary, even though the community says that we want to leave it in the ground. That doesn't matter, because the law doesn't see the community's interest at all. With the trade agreements, it's the same deal. The MTBE [methyl tert-butyl ether] stuff or the other issues that have come before trade tribunals, NAFTA and GATT, and the new trade agreements that are now being negotiated — all of those see commerce as the overriding value, and community protection as a lesser value. Not surprisingly, perhaps, that's the same structure that the U.S. Constitution puts into place. We have a constitutional structure that was adopted in the 1780s, and that constitutional structure was about putting the rights of commerce and property above the rights of communities, people and Nature. That's how it's written and when you read it, it's hard to see anything but that.

You know, the founding fathers didn't understand deforestation, didn't understand acidification of the oceans, wouldn't have understood climate change. They saw an endless bounty of natural resources on the horizon and they saw their job as helping to exploit that natural bounty because that's how you became a major power, so you didn't have to worry about getting invaded anymore. Liberty and progress all flowed from that property transformation, from the exploitation of resources and making them into useful products. That was their mindset in the 1780s.

So we have an archaic constitutional structure that places property and commerce rights above everybody else's — and we can either try to live with that structure, which we have in the past 60 years of activism, or we can change it. That's the option. The communities we work with have begun to understand that constitutional change is necessary — that community change has to inform and enforce constitutional change higher up. I think we're seeing nothing less in the United States than a push towards major constitutional change that actually seeks to put sustainability as the overriding value, rather than protection of property and commerce.

Given the malfunction of federal governments in a number of countries, certainly Canada, the United States and Australia at this point, it's not a very promising environment for constitutional change. Mari, when we last met, you were talking about doing it from the bottom up. That was a very fruitful thought.

MM: Well, two things are happening in our communities. One is that our communities are finding that they are being threatened by fracking and mining and what have you, and that they don't have they authority to say no. Through our organizing, our communities have bumped up into a lot of walls, their walls being their elected officials at the state legislatures. In New Hampshire, we've worked with a lot of communities that are facing the privatization of their water by corporations that want to stick a giant straw into their aquifers and siphon off millions of gallons of water a day to bottle and sell. And communities call up — in New Hampshire it's the department of environmental services — and say, "Hello, our state environmental agency, can you help us protect our water?" But what they find is that their own government, instead of helping to protect their water, is authorizing the corporations to take it.

It's the same way across the United States: the communities are looking to their state elected officials and their state environmental agencies for help to protect their water and their communities and instead they're finding that their state governments are working for interests other than their own. They bump their heads into their state government, and very similarly they bump their heads into the United States Congress, which has been basically stuck in a no-go zone for years on protecting the environment.

So communities are coming to the conclusion — and we've come to the conclusion with them — that the only place right now where we can make change is at the grassroots level. That comes from a lot of lessons that we've drawn from past people's movements. We teach something called Democracy Schools, weekend trainings that communities host. We've held close to 300 now across the United States — and we've had some in Canada as well — in which we've looked at these past movements. How have people really driven fundamental change? How did the abolitionists end slavery and recognize rights of the freed slaves? How did the women's rights movement, which built up in the 1800s, how did they ultimately drive amendments to the U.S. Constitution? That all built up from the grassroots. And we see the civil rights movements built up from the grassroots, and it involved law making, and using the law, going into courts. It involved using the law to reveal how the existing structure of law worked, why it was illegitimate and unjust, and why it needed to change and how it needed to change. These movements built the power up from the grassroots to drive change at the state level and ultimately at the federal level in the United States.

When we look back at these other movements, like the abolitionists, the U.S. Congress was not leading the charge to end slavery. Our state legislators were not leading the charge to recognize the right of women to vote. They had to be forced in that direction. That means we need cultural change, and we need legal change to make that cultural shift binding. So we're beginning to make change in the only place where communities can, which is at the local grassroots, in their local municipalities.

We're beginning to now look at bringing communities together. In a number of states, like Pennsylvania and Ohio and Colorado, we're beginning to form state-wide community rights networks, in which communities which have dealt with different issues — like fracking or factory farming or GMOs — are joining together, because they understand that the common denominator is a structure of governance that doesn't allow them to decide what happens in their own communities.

They're now coming together to drive change upward to the state level. In some states which have citizens' initiative power, communities and people can come together to directly write laws and bring them to the ballot for a state-wide vote. In 2014, we worked with our Colorado community rights network to draft a state-wide constitutional amendment to constitutionalize the right to local self-governance and bring that to a state-wide ballot. Driving that kind of change from the local level to the state level is much like what past people's movements have done.

We've also been in other countries. We've done Democracy Schools in Montréal, and in the Yukon, and we see a very similar conversation unfolding. We have to begin at the municipal level, and join together to drive change up to our territorial level, our provincial level. In Australia, in the fall of 2013, we saw a very similar conversation; they're seeing an extraction of fossil fuels just increasing exponentially across that country. One author described Australia now as "Asia's quarry." And they see a very similar structure of law in place, a structure of governance which is making extraction a central piece of the economy, in which communities don't have the local authority to say "no." Their state governments are authorizing corporations to frack, so when they look to their state agencies — just like in the United States — for help to protect them from shale gas drilling, they find out that their governments are actually legalizing that, no matter the environmental consequences.

So we're talking with folks in Australia about building a very similar organizing pathway, to begin at the municipal level, then join communities together to drive change at the state level and ultimately at the federal level. We're working in the European Union now, with people that are seeing the need to build up from the grassroots. Whatever their starting issue is, whether it be fracking or water privatization or otherwise, that change has to build upwards. We need to mobilize enough people to force that kind of change.

TL: Yes. We need an offense. For so many years we haven't had an offense. Our environmental activism is constantly on the defense, trying to keep things from getting worse. There hasn't been an offense in this country, dealing with corporate power and corporate rights, since the 1890s and the populist movement. But listen, if you asked the abolitionists or the people in the 1830s, what's the chance of Congress abolishing slavery, they would say the chances are less than zero. And this movement…

MM: And beyond that, the U.S. Congress gagged itself from even having a discussion about abolition. They didn't want the debate to occur on the floor of the House of the Senate, because they understood that even having a conversation about ending slavery in the U.S. Congress would actually open up the idea that maybe we shouldn't be enslaving other people. So to look to our Congress to end slavery was out of the question. It had to be forced there. Similarly, to look to the United States Congress to do something about climate change, that's not going to happen until it's forced.

TL: And forced in a certain way. So the Ted Wells, and the William Lloyd Garrisons and the abolitionist movement leaders… they didn't set out to create a Slave Protection Agency.

MM: Right.

TL: They didn't seek to create a regulatory structure to regulate how many lashes slaves could get. That's pretty much where our environmental movement is stuck today — on the defensive, attempting to make the harms a little less worse. In fact most of the institutional groups don't even think about going on the offense. They don't even know what that means. And so we need a plan. And the plan is a grassroots revolt. A community revolt that begins to redefine communities as not just the people who live there but also the nature and ecosystems within those communities, and then builds a structure of law that actually elevates those rights above the rights of corporations and commerce. It's pretty simple when you lay it out on paper. It's just the fact that most people believe they live in a system that they don't live in. And they believe that some of those things are already there. Our job, in many ways, over the past 10 years, has been to prove that they're not there. That system of law doesn't exist. It has to be created.

What Marx used to call false consciousness, right? You think this is all working for you — and it's not.

MM: Maybe it's human nature, but it's not until a threat really comes into a community that people can see clearly, in stark relief, how the structure of law works. You have to see it play out. We had to see it play out. We had to wrestle within it to understand just how it worked, and then why did it work that way? Our communities have to go through a similar learning process. I think people are coming to a place where they can take big leaps forward because things are becoming so blatant and so bad. People are able to say, "I understand how this is working." We help them understand the history of how it got to where we are today. Then they're able to say, "This cannot continue; we refuse to accept this in our community." And they are beginning to take real action.

TL: Part of that is about picking fights. You don't change existing systems of law unless you pick fights with them. A lot of this is about communities putting into place systems of law that will be the systems of law in 60 or 70 years, but aren't yet, and then they're saying, "C'mon in. We're ready for you now. We've written the script. This is the law. And now we're going to prove the difference between the existing system of law, and what that new system of law needs to be." It's that cognitive dissonance between the two, which is beginning to build a movement. But it's that fight, it's that confrontation, that struggle, that produces eventually that new system of law.

MM: It helps in some ways when government becomes more transparent about what it's trying to do. In Colorado, Governor Hickenlooper has publicly stated that he is going to sue any community that tries to interfere, ban fracking — and he's made good on that promise, bringing to bear the state government against its own communities to overturn their democratically-enacted prohibitions on fracking. When your own governor is saying that he's going to sue his constituencies, his communities, the people who put him into office, when they're trying to protect themselves from something that is a very real threat — that makes things very clear to people. That opens up a window of opportunity, which is why in Colorado people were ready to move forward with a constitutional amendment to say, we need to take this decision-making into our own hands.

And certainly not in the Governor's. That was successful, wasn't it? The Colorado initiative?

MM: The initiative was introduced — and then, like any initiative, it has to go through a state approval process before you can bring it to voters to collect a certain number of signatures. I think it's 85,000 plus in Colorado to qualify it for the ballot. The oil and gas industry, not surprisingly, challenged that the initiative was even being proposed. They sued to keep it from ever reaching the ballot, let alone having people sign it. They were able to successfully delay it a number of months, and that didn't give enough of a window of time for the Colorado Community Rights Network to collect enough signatures to qualify for the November 2014 ballot. The group is going to reintroduce it shortly so they can qualify it for the November 2016 ballot. But they understand that the oil and gas industry will do everything they can to prevent it from moving forward, both from collecting signatures to qualify it for the ballot, and then once it is qualified, they will run a very intensive campaign to make sure that nobody votes for it. Their goal is to prevent any kind of blade of grass from growing.

TL: But these folks in Colorado beat the oil and gas companies in the Colorado Supreme Court, which issued a ruling in favour of the Colorado Community Rights Network that this was a legitimate, valid initiative to be placed on the ballot. That's the hurdle that everybody goes through in Colorado when they try to put initiatives on the ballot. Now it's been validated to move forward, which is a huge deal in Colorado, especially when we're dealing with an initiative that would, for the first time in the United States, return real power to the municipal communities to defend the rights of communities as well as the rights of Nature within those communities.

You said November 2014 or November 2016?

MM: The next time they can bring it to the ballot is November 2016. So that's what they're aiming at now.

In Canada the municipality is a creature of the province. I don't know if that's the case in the states as well?
MM: Very much so.

So presumably the state is consistently saying — and the province would be consistently saying — this is ultra vires, this is beyond your powers. What happens then? When you said return the power to the municipalities — they never had it in the first place, did they?
TL: That's correct. It's about returning the power to the people within those municipal communities. In Canada and the United States, you open any conventional law book and it says municipalities are creatures of the state, with powers wholly controlled by the state. So the state chooses to create, the state can abolish. If the state chooses to get rid of the City of Philadelphia tomorrow as a municipal corporation, the State of Pennsylvania could do so with a stroke of a pen. It may not be the best political decision that people ever made, but there's nothing constitutional or illegal that stops them from doing so. This work is about taking municipalities and the people within those municipalities out from under that structure. In a lot of ways that structure makes no sense.

We had cities and municipalities before we had states. They predated states. So to say that municipalities are merely creatures of the state is just plain wrong from a historical perspective. There were, in the late 1800s, two battling theories of law in the United States. There was Judge Cooley, from the Michigan Supreme Court, and there was Judge Dillon, from the Iowa Supreme Court. Judge Cooley said people have a right to local self-government in their communities, which means that states can't abolish the municipality and that their municipal government has certain rights and powers that they can exercise against the state — so they're not a creature of the state. Dillon, on the other hand, said of course municipalities are creatures of the state, and in fact it's not even necessary that people elect their representatives within their municipalities, because since they are just an administrative arm of the state, the state could appoint the officials. There's no need to elect them, because it's not a democratic entity.

So both theories climbed up, both had about 20 state court converts, so 20 states in one camp, 20 states in the other camp. The issue went up to the U.S. Supreme Court, which picked a winner, and the winner was Dillon. Dillon's rule says that municipal corporations are merely creatures of the state. They only have the powers that the state gives them, and if they try to operate outside of those, they automatically become *ultra vires*. That's what happened in the United States.

What's fascinating today is how the state mechanism responds when municipalities begin colouring outside the lines. So people in Pittsburgh, for example, the first major municipality in the United States to ban fracking, also stripped corporations of certain constitutional rights within the city of Pittsburgh. It also recognized that the rivers within the city have certain rights of their own, as ecosystems within the city. They passed all of those things.

Well, the Pennsylvania legislature passed a law that says, "Okay, if you pass something like that, you're going to have to go through the special scrutiny of a state agency, and we're going to give a state agency — not even the legislature — the power to overturn or nullify whatever is passed within the locality." Earlier than that, other municipalities in Pennsylvania had passed factory farm laws saying, "No, we're not going to allow corporate farming in our municipalities." In response, the state legislature steps in and now puts the state attorney general's office under the control of the agribusiness corporations. So no longer is the corporation running around trying to sue these individual places; now it's state taxpayer money that is being used to sue these municipal communities — in the name of the state, not the corporation. But all the corporation does is pick up the phone and call the attorney general's office, and they assign an assistant attorney general to come in and sue the municipality.

So, the problem in many ways is not the corporation. It's the structure of law. It's the governmental system that enables the corporation to do what it does within our communities. There's a phrase that we use, which is "the corporate state." We have a corporate state that enables the corporation to do what it does within the communities.

What we've developed in response to all that is a theory of law that people within U.S. communities have a right to local community self-government. It's a constitutional right, and that right is violated by corporate rights that are used to try to overturn it, and also by pre-emptive rights when states attempt to set a ceiling so that they regulate fracking, and communities can't ban it. Under our theory, they could. Our job, as complex as it sounds, is to give birth to that right. Because once you birth that right, the other doctrines have to change accordingly. The doctrines in that box have to be removed — and this is how communities are beginning to remove them.

MM: You asked the question of what happens when a community confronts that structure. There's the substantive overrides that occur, as in Pennsylvania, where industry went into the state legislature to get them to pass laws saying that communities can't ban fracking, or ban factory farming. So there's issue-based law making that occurs.

In addition, the procedures of law that are available to us also get shut down.

For example, the first place that we developed a community bill of rights framework was Spokane, Washington. There's a citizen's initiative process in Spokane, so communities can draft a law, then bring it to the voters to sign and qualify it for the ballot, and then it goes to a city-wide ballot. That's happened now several times in the city of Spokane. But each time that it's happened, there's been a response by the city. So you have communities coming together within Spokane saying we want to establish rights of the Spokane River. We want to establish rights of workers. We want to establish the rights of neighbourhoods to make decisions about major development projects that are coming into their neighbourhood. And you see the city government itself coming out in opposition, not only verbally, but also beginning to change how that initiative process works, trying to make it more difficult for people in the community to use what many call their direct democracy authority.

We see that coming in other states as well. Communities are moving forward with initiatives, and you see their own government trying to restrict their ability to do that. You also see pre-election challenges being brought by industries that don't want to see a community in Oregon, for example, bring a question to the voters about banning GMOs. Agricultural interests say, we don't even want that question to come forward.

If we think about what that means, we see that corporations are able to direct what we actually get to vote on. They're able to restrict our democratic powers. It's not only that they get to interfere with what agriculture policy looks like, they get to interfere with our own democratic processes within our communities. We were recently in the Yukon Territory, where communities also have a binding referendum power at the municipal level, which is not used very frequently. We've been talking to people about what it might look like if, for example, they were to ban fracking and establish a right to sustainable energy and self-governance in their communities. Well, a territorial legislator told us that even though that process is used very infrequently — that binding referendum power — even now the territory government is thinking about restricting it. That's the response that comes from industry and higher levels of government.

TL: And to do the work we do means reviewing all of these state laws and federal laws that have been put in place, and to recognize certain powers that municipalities have. It is to our amazement that in the Yukon they have a municipalities act that allows corporations to vote on initiatives that have been advanced by citizens. So if citizens put a ballot initiative onto the ballot, there is actually a line item that gives corporations a vote on the initiatives within the municipality. We haven't seen anything like that before. In the U.S. people joke about it. "Oh, well if the corporations had a vote"... Well, in the Yukon Territory, the corporations do vote.

That's breathtaking. Do they get one vote, or do they get votes in proportion to their — ?
[LAUGHTER]
TL: Proportionate votes may be coming down the road, I don't know. But you know, if the corporation is a person, as in the United States, that leads logically to, hey, corporations should have involvement in elections as well. We've joked in the U.S. about it. "Oh what if corporations had a vote?" But here we tripped across a place where the corporation does have a vote, and people there didn't even know about that provision.

Well, corporations spending money are now considered to be exercising free speech in the States, right? As a result of the Citizens United decision?
TL: It's the result of a case called Bellotti back in the 1970s. Citizens United took it one step further, and used it to knock down campaign-finance laws in the United States, to say that if corporations have free speech rights, you can't have campaign finance laws that restrict how and how much corporations can spend in elections. The Supreme Court struck that down. But we have a long history of cases in the United States. The State of Vermont required labelling for BGH in dairy products — that's artificial Bovine Growth Hormone, which Europe has banned. And the grocer-manufacturers association brought suit against the State of Vermont contending that the labeling requirement violated the corporation's right not to be compelled to speak, under the First Amendment. So, corporations have free speech rights, but they also can't be compelled to speak under the First Amendment. The court ruled in their favour, and the labelling law was struck down.

Do you, yourself, have the right not to speak?
TL: Yes.

Do you? Okay. I guess under the Fifth Amendment, you can't be forced to incriminate yourself, but you cannot be forced to speak, more broadly than that.
TL: That's correct. And people sometimes say, "Well, yes, corporations have the same rights as persons." Corporations are just accumulations of persons. But the problem is that under this system of law, the more wealth you have, the more rights you have. And so, when you take the corporate rights, and combine them with wealth, a Walmart or a Monsanto has more rights than the people in the communities in which they're operating. It's that combination of the two that weaponizes the corporate rights.

What you're describing here is a corporate–governmental grip on communities and on individuals that's quite breathtaking. So how do you attack that? You guys are agitating at the grassroots to change all of that, but it sounds to me as though the more successful you are, the more the avenues are being closed down, and are likely to be closed down.

How do you get around that?

TL: Well, we think that we're in a pre-movement phase. A lot of people like to say, well there's a movement against corporate power in the United States. There really isn't. It's just the beginning stuff right now, pre-movement stuff. With 95 percent of the American public, if you go into a room and tell them they don't have a democracy, they think you're nuts. They think you're crazy. So there's no way to build a movement until you have enough people who understand the system. Richard Grossman, a predecessor of ours, used to say, "Fish are the last to discover water."

So part of our organizing is picking these very controlled confrontations between communities and the corporations so that when that lawmaking gets done, the two systems — sort of like matter and anti-matter — come into conflict. People can actually see and learn from what's happening, and understand how the system operates. The organizing is done in the faith that once people understand that they operate under a corporate state — that it's not a democracy — they will actually begin to put energy and resources into creating one. But until you get past that stage, you don't have a constituency that can actually begin to build a national movement.

So we think that the ordinance–making that communities are doing now is crucial. We've worked with over 500 communities over the last 10 years. Two hundred of those have passed and adopted local laws that put forward a new system of law in contravention to the existing one. The more those are challenged, the more judges that say, "Of course you don't have a right to local self-government," the more state attorney generals who file briefs that say, "You don't have a right to local self-government" — the more that that's reinforced, in some ways, the better, because more people will begin to understand the system under which they live. They won't listen to Tom Linzey or Mari Margil, they won't listen to the Sierra Club, they won't listen to a group — but once the system itself explains it to them, that they don't live under a system that recognizes their right to self govern, then people begin to come to grips with that fact.

Then there's, like, a mourning period. "Oh my God, something has passed here and we need to build something new." And that building of something new then begins to evidence itself in concrete ways, like the Colorado constitutional rights amendment. The folks in Colorado that are beginning to run for office would override the courts, so if the courts in Colorado are saying of course you don't have a right to self government, then people begin to override the courts with those constitutional amendments. And eventually they'll begin to change the federal constitution to override all the courts and all the legislatures.

But that's an arc that has to build, and it can only build if enough people understand the system in which they live. And right now very few people understand the system, because it's all been camouflaged. They only see it when they hit it, and they only hit it when they want something different than what's being delivered to them by the system. So we operate in that confrontation zone where we talk with communities to say, "It's not about getting just what you can get under the existing system; it's about getting what you really want, and what you need." And with climate change and species extinction, and deforestation and all these other problems on the table, people are beginning to see the difference. We actually help them to build law based on what they want and need.

That cognitive dissonance between the two is beginning to build the energy and space for a movement to arise. That movement is going to be something that we haven't seen in the United States in the past 100 years, 150 years, possibly back to the American Revolution. It's about taking the archaic system of law that we have, and tossing it to the side, and then building a whole new system of government in its place. That's a huge task, but to us, that's the only fight worth fighting right now.

That's a phrase to linger on: "That's the only fight worth fighting right now." Now: once you've got the constitutional amendment in place, the courts cannot rule in favour of the corporations over the communities, right?
TL: Well, they can always try to find a way.

I don't mean that it's easy, but that's the essence of the matter, isn't it? That it's no longer at the discretion even of the court system.
TL: There will be courts that try to say something means something that it doesn't. But you can't rely just on the text. Once that constitutional amendment is written, it's more than just ink on a page. It's actually backed by people in communities. The magic is not the ink on the page. The magic is not the constitutional amendment going into place. It takes eternal vigilance after that, and in fact we think it probably takes another round of constitutional change after that.

So, what's happening in Colorado right now is what I would call "liberation amendment," which is to say, okay, these places that are making these ordinances at the local level, we now need to seize the state to legalize them, to say you're now okay to make more of these and to enforce them. That's what the state amendment level is about now. But eventually, you need 300 communities, 400, 500 communities in the state who then begin to drive those community bills of rights up, to actually embed those in the state constitutions as well, so that the state constitution says, People have a right to a sustainable energy future, and ecosystems have certain rights to exist and flourish within the state. There's a procedural amendment, and then I think there's a substantive amendment as well. It's going to be a constant cauldron of bubbling matter. You need a movement of constant confrontations between the corporations and the communities to produce people who begin to move up to the state level and eventually the federal level.

It's going to take 30, 40 years, probably, for much of this to go. Of course things can move faster than that as we saw with the Berlin Wall. A perfect storm sometimes happens. But it has to happen. If people had been doing this 30 years ago, we would be in a much better position than we are now. But having said that, we have to do it.

MM: And I will say that what's happened in Colorado, even though they've only just introduced this initiative, other states are looking to Colorado, essentially seeing it as a model. Communities learn that even when you better regulate Shell gas drilling, you're still getting fracked. It's not enough for us to try to regulate bad things a little bit better. That still leads to ecosystem destruction. It may delay it a little bit, but it still means we're getting fracked, and we're getting factory farmed and so on. Communities are beginning to see the re-framing — that we don't just have a fracking problem, we have a democracy problem; we don't have a factory farm problem, we have a democracy problem.

And that's why people in Colorado who are concerned about different things have come together. We need to actually establish our right to self governance in our own state constitution, so we can make decisions at the local level. That's re-framing. It's creating a discourse in the state of Colorado that's spreading outside of Colorado as well. That's why our state community rights networks in places like New Hampshire are beginning to take that language of Colorado and say, What would that look like here in New Hampshire? Our issues may be a bit different, but we have the same structure of law and governance that's preventing us from deciding what happens in our own communities. It's not enough for us just to try to make changes at the local level, we must join forces to drive that change upward and establish our right to local self governance within the New Hampshire constitution, and within the Pennsylvania constitution, and so on.

So it's taking the energy that's come out of Colorado, which has been so important, and actually seeing what it looks in other states as well. What people in Colorado have done is essentially revealed the structure for what it is, which is anti-democratic, and now people in other states are saying it's helping them to see, too, the kind of change that's needed. It's a pathway that's being drawn for us. And I think that's been very, very important. Some people say, "What's the point? You never got it on the ballot, you never even got a chance to sign it and qualify it there, let alone lose at the ballot when the oil and gas industry mounts a No campaign." What's important is that people can begin to see the kind of change that's needed, and that creates the cultural change that is going to drive the legal change.

TL: We get two types of pushback. One is people saying, "Well, we don't want to have to deal with the corporate rights stuff, or the pre-emption stuff. It's all Greek to us. We just want to ban fracking." To which we say, well you can pass a one-paragraph ordinance that says we ban fracking here. But that sucker is going to get struck down quicker than a judge can sign the order striking it, because it goes against all of these other doctrines. You've got to deal with the doctrines. They are the structural stuff that actually has put into place your inability to say no at the local level.

We have a lot of environmental groups who running around saying ban fracking here, ban fracking here, but they're not getting into the structural stuff — and to us, that's a disservice because what happens is that people mobilize, they pass the fracking ban, they go into courts, the courts strike you down, then everybody goes home. They say, "Oh, I guess we can't."

The other pushback we get is "What's the point of passing this thing that nullifies corporate rights and pre-emption and the Dillon's rules stuff, and recognizes the right to local self government if you're just going to go into the courts, and the courts are likely to strike it down on the same grounds, which is that the U.S. Supreme Court has said that corporations are persons. You can't say they're not persons in the municipality."

To which we say, "Well that's what civil disobedience is all about." Civil disobedience is all about recognizing unjust laws and calling them out. Our work is just more structured than laying down in front of the bulldozers but it's the same thing. It's the community saying, we don't want it here, and we're going to seize our municipal structure of law to stop it. It's almost like saying to the four African-American kids that sat down at the lunch counters at Woolworth's, what's the point? You're going to go and sit down, and you're going to get arrested, and nothing's going to change. Well the kids that sat down at the lunch counter said to themselves, number one, it's the moral and ethical thing to do. The earth is being destroyed, so let's talk about morals and ethics and about how our activism has to line up with that. But second of all, they thought, if they did it somebody else would do it. And if somebody else did it, there would be 10 more, and then 100 more and it turns out within three weeks there were 200 sit-ins! But nobody knew. Nobody knew when it was going to start. Nobody knew how it was going to start. But these kids said, "Okay we're going to do it." And everybody opposed them. You know the elder reverend church community said, it's too soon, it's too fast, it's too radical.

MM: We hear that all the time, and I think that to your point, one of the things that we as activists need to become much better at is recognizing that this is very much a long-term generational kind of change. You look at the suffragettes. It took 80 years in the United States to actually recognize the right of women to vote. The abolitionist movement took generations to end slavery. This is definitely going to be a long-term movement. We have this immediacy in our culture — it's not just in our activism, it's our culture of immediacy — that we want instant gratification. But that's not how real movements grow. They grow over time and they recognize that they're long-term, and that we're going to have fits and starts. But it's all about making a significant cultural shift that will allow a significant legal shift. It took us a long time to get where we are today. It's going to take us some time to get out of it as well.

I think people who are not directly involved with the law often think of it as a cut and dried thing. You go into court and I sue for this, and you resist, and we come to a decision, and whatever we were fighting about is resolved. Everybody goes home. But Tony Oposa says the law is telling stories, which is a wonderful concept. It's a way of telling stories where there is a record — and even if you lose, the story is still out there. What you're doing has the same character. It's education, it's consciousness-raising. You're not expecting to win big in the short term, but you keep chipping away at it, and you keep growing the circle, as you said about the kids at the sit-in. That's the perspective that it has to be, isn't it?

Yes. And in some ways, work along these lines is having a side effect of beginning to influence some conventional court decisions. In earlier 2014 we had a court in western Pennsylvania rule that corporations were not persons for purposes of certain sections of the Pennsylvania constitution. That hasn't happened in — well, forever. She wrote a 20-page opinion, going back to 1776 and looking at the intent of some of the drafters, and holding that corporations were not entitled to certain state constitutional rights. That was ground-breaking in itself.

Then we have a decision dealing with the state legislature telling communities that they couldn't do anything about fracking or oil and gas extraction. Some municipal communities stood up and sued the state. And the Pennsylvania Supreme Court came out with the decision that municipalities have duties that are independent of the state, which is something we haven't seen in a hundred years in courts. So here's the highest court in Pennsylvania saying that there are some municipal powers that the state can't tinker with, that the state can't change, the state can't abolish, that the municipality has separate duties. That's completely foreign to the U.S. legal structure. What's also fun is that in both of those cases, the lawyers didn't even really brief those issues because they were such a long shot. These are judges stepping in, picking up one fragment, one small thing within those briefs, and making that the decision. I think that's a lesson for the lawyers: that we need to begin to be more confrontational in the briefing. We need to reach farther, not just taking the established law and arguing from that, but also reaching to bring the new stuff in.

MM: Private corporations don't see the law as static. In fact they are constantly changing the law. In the Citizens United decision in 2010, they were able to overthrow existing law. Existing law restricted how much they could give to influence elections, and how they could it. To them that was a barrier, and instead of trying to work around it, they just smashed right through. They know that they can change law because they do it constantly. We have a tendency to see law as something static and immovable — and if we continue to hold that, we're not going to be making the change that we need. We need to adopt a very proactive, offensive strategy. We have to be able to change law.

Even as kids we're told that the thing to do with law is to obey it. The idea that the law is malleable — that idea is a foreign concept, I think, for most citizens.

MM: We have to do a lot of myth busting in our work. Myth busting about the United States Constitution. There is a mythology about the Constitution. In our Democracy Schools, we talk a lot about what that mythology looks like, about why people thought that the Constitution was such a democratic document, and that we have the best democracy in the world — perhaps the only one, as many people believe. But the abolitionists looked at the Constitution and saw it as a slave document because it codified slavery. Women looked to the Constitution and saw nothing there. They weren't even recognized within the Constitution as having rights, let alone the right to vote, or to own property, or divorce their husbands. There was nothing in there for women. In fact, William Lloyd Garrison, who Thomas mentioned, one of the leading abolitionists, used to burn the Constitution at rallies because, he said, "This is a slave document." He would look to other things like the Declaration of Independence, which said, "All men are created equal," and would plant his feet there, not in the U.S. Constitution. The U.S. Constitution, he understood, needed to be gotten rid of. That, of course, was blasphemous to say, and continues to be blasphemous to say.

I was going to say, This is heresy.
MM: That's where this is heading.

TL: If you listen closely you can hear the tremors of what's coming. In mid-September of this year, in Colorado, the curriculum board for the state said that they needed to rewrite the history textbooks to eliminate civil disobedience. To actually stress obedience to the law, that's how the curriculum board said it. A thousand high-school students walked out in protest of the curriculum changes, which would be pretty abstract to some people. We're talking about textbook changes, and a thousand high-school students walked out in protest. So there is something still there in our collective memory. It's very small, and it has been pushed to the back. But it's still there, and this work is about triggering that.

What emerges has some of the energy of a jilted lover. Here I thought I was living in a democratic country and now I find that I'm not. I'm good and mad. Right?

MM: That's very true. When we meet with communities, and particularly in Democracy Schools, which are really intensive — 10 or 12 hours in a community where people are coming together to really examine how the structure of law works, and why does it work this way, and how are other communities beginning to change it? You know, people can end up in tears because they are discovering that their country isn't what they thought it was — and it does feel like a betrayal. People in other countries often say to us that for them it's very clear how the United States works. The United States doesn't just betray it's own citizens, it's also going outward into the outside world and doing similar things. Our corporations are going into other countries and stripping them of their environmental protections and so forth. So in some places it's easier to see it than here in the United States, where it is very well camouflaged. But more and more people are able to see it clearly as the structures of government are coming down on them and telling them very, very blatantly that they don't have the power to protect themselves.

TL: There are some funny moments. We've done some Democracy Schools in Indigenous communities, and we'll have some white people, Caucasians sit in with the Indigenous people in the school. And in one of the schools the Caucasian folks from the municipalities were having real trouble with all of this. "My God, we actually live under that structure?" There was this mourning period, where people get pissed off and sad and all of those things. So they were going through this fuss, and we were trying to answer them — and then the Indigenous person stood up and said, "Wow, that's really bad that the white people don't even know the system of law that they work under." She goes, "At least we know we live on a reservation." [LAUGHTER]

But in some ways it's the same thing. We're not free. It sounds strange to say that, but we're not a free people. You're not a free people when you're harnessed to fracking whether you want it or not. Or resource extraction, or forced pooling, these laws that the fracking and extraction companies can come in and take your resource from under your land even if you don't sign a lease. They can force you into those agreements. Those are not the laws of a free people. We are not free in our communities. Our communities are not free communities. They are enslaved in many ways. Until we are able to dismantle that structure of law that's over top of them, we are always going to be in that position.

Tell me about a Democracy School. If I go to a Democracy School what am I going to see? Or if you guys bring one to my community and I go, what will I experience?
MM: First we'll hand you a 350-page curriculum. (LAUGHS] And of course there is a pop quiz…

And now that the first 40 percent have left the room… [LAUGHTER]
MM: We struggle in the Democracy Schools, because you have to draw some sort of balance. We begin by talking about, How does the existing structure of law work today? Generally we talk about it within the environmental context. What happens when a community is facing a factory farm? How does that structure work — not only the legal side of it, but the cultural side of it? So for example, you can have a factory farm come in, with 10,000, 20,000 hogs, and it produces all sorts of problems. Not only just for the hogs themselves who are in very unpleasant conditions. But also, what do you do with all those tremendous amounts of manure? And what do you do about the air quality, and the water quality and all of the other impacts that come with a factory farm? Not to mention the fact that it throws small farmers, family farmers, out of business. We've lost hundreds of thousands of farms and farmers over the last 30 years because of the industrialization of agriculture.

So how does the structure of law work? The community calls up their state agency, and the state government says that if you want to get involved, we've got a permitting process to permit a corporation to site a factory farm. They get people involved in that permitting process. But under that permitting process, which we examine in the Democracy School, communities can't say no, because the state government is literally permitting a corporation to come in and site that factory farm. So in the Democracy School everybody gains a similar understanding of how the structure of law works — and then the question is how did we get here?

That's where we have to define a bit of a balance. How much history do we go into? Because it is a lot of history. How did we end up with the American Revolution, our first major rights movement in this country? We stood up to the existing structure of governance in England, the king and the Parliament, saying we refuse to accept this any longer. It took a war, but we broke away from England and defined our own country. That was our first major civil disobedience movement, you could say. So how did we get to that place? And what were the forces that actually brought it along? It was continued action, like the Stamp Acts, and other acts that interfered with the ability of the people in the colonies to self-govern. We look at those past movements to learn the best lessons out of them. How did they actually make the change that they were seeking? And what did it take, not only in terms of time but the actions? The suffragists, for example, drove 400 different referendums forward to try to recognize the right of women to vote.

We look at how the structure of law works today. How did that history end us at a point today where we can't say no and protect ourselves in our own communities? And then, the juicy stuff, what are communities doing now? What does that change look like in our communities today? It's a deep examination, very intensive. It can feel like a betrayal once we go through the Constitution and the curriculum and say, "Wow, codified slavery!" People don't know that. People don't realize that in our U.S. Constitution the Supreme Court could be made up of one person. One person could have that power to make those kinds of decisions. We don't know that. We don't realize that our president is indirectly elected, that the U.S. senate used to be indirectly elected, appointed by others instead of We, the People. We have so much that we have to reveal in a Democracy School. People say, "I didn't realize that my structure of law worked this way. I didn't realize the government worked that way."

Democracy school is a launching pad for communities to say, "We understand now that we're talking about systemic, structural change. It's not enough for us just to try to do a single-issue ban on fracking for example. We actually have to take on the system of the law itself to protect that ban on fracking." The Democracy Schools are really intense. They take a lot out of people. Then the question is do they want to move in a different direction with their own activism?

TL: The linkage that we find in the Democracy Schools in other countries is the English common law system, because we started out as an English colony. England's early colonies were corporations controlled by English common law. That's our link to Australia, to Canada, because they all have similar legal systems based on that English common law system. Including Nepal.

And England.

TL: Yes. And to some extent to Ireland and Northern Ireland. There's a common linkage, so it's not like starting the language from scratch when we've gone into these other places. In Canada, for example, where we were recently, about 80 percent of the law is the same in terms of corporate rights stuff. It's slightly better in Canada because Canada doesn't have a commerce clause. In the U.S. we have a commerce clause, which corporations use to actually stop communities from interfering with interstate commerce. Since oil and gas extraction is interstate commerce, sometimes that's used by the corporations to strike down municipal laws. Canada doesn't have that, but Canada has been adopting some of the U.S. jurisprudence on commerce into other parts of their law. So everything bleeds over.

So now let's say that my community has been confronting a hog farm or something, and you've run a Democracy School. I come out of the Democracy School — and what happens now?

MM: We don't target communities to work in; they contact us. If they want to move forward with a Democracy School, we hold a Democracy School. Often what happens after a school is that a core group of folks say, We want to move this rights-based organizing forward in our own community. The Community Environmental Legal Defense Fund will work with them on that process, which means helping them to draft a local community bill of rights for the municipality, helping them to navigate what their own structure of lawmaking looks like. Do they have to go to their municipal board of supervisors? Do they have a direct democracy, a citizen's initiative process? We help them to understand and to educate their own friends and neighbours and family members. You have to do that so that people understand why we're addressing corporate rights, for example, when all we want to do is stop fracking. That need for systemic change has to be a community wide education effort. Then we help them to draft a local law. Then people begin to move into campaign mode, in which they develop their campaigns through their municipal elected officials, or through their initiative process. The Legal Defense Fund has both the public interest law side of our organization and our grassroots organizers, both working directly with communities to help them make this shift.

Tell me about your use of film. Will your We the People 2.0 film provide another major tool that you'll be using in the Democracy School — but perhaps more broadly, too?

MM: Yes. *We the People 2.0* — we've been working with Tree Media for the past couple of years to tell the story of this organizing, the stories from communities, to show how and why it's evolved. I know they spent some time in Pennsylvania talking with communities where our work first began, to talk about why communities are on this journey and essentially all that we've been talking about with you. The film is really to share that story and we do think it will be very powerful to be able to share that. We've talked about taking snippets of it to show in Democracy School and public talks and public forums. Communities themselves can watch the film, and other films like this one, and really hold a discourse in their community. It moves them from getting so deeply involved in the environmental regulatory processes, to really wrestling with this idea of democracy and what does it look like to change their own community.

TL: This work is so different that the media is only helpful if it actually gets people to do a different kind of organizing. Unfortunately most of the one-off media — like the articles that we get in the newspapers, the national press — they don't do that. They tell the story in a conventional way, and then people don't understand what it means. It's worthwhile in some ways, because it publicizes the work, which is good, and people find us, which is good — but it rarely ever leads to new communities going through this kind of organizing process. That's the work we do, and it's one-on-one stuff. It doesn't come from media pieces or Twitter or Facebook stuff or whatever. It's always good to get a piece in the New York Times or the L.A. Times — that's great — but it doesn't necessarily lead to more organizing. In fact, it draws a bull's eye on the communities that we're working with. Then the corporate boys know what's happening in those communities. It's a double-edged sword for us. But the more intensive stuff that can help people understand why they need to move in a different direction and do a different kind of activism is very valuable.

My thought was that a film that tells people what the hell this is all about would seem to be a very useful thing. I call you up, and I'm an isolated individual in some corner of the country, and you say, "Well, there are a few things you can do. Here are some books you can read. Here is a film you can watch." It would be a nice way to fan the flame.

MM: Yes. We continue to develop those tools. I think film can be really valuable in that sense. People can watch it on their own computers, so it's an easy way for people to engage. We have PowerPoints, and we had a book that Thomas co-authored called *Be the Change*, which shares these stories. But what we have found the most important piece of our work is the one-on-one interaction with people in a community. That is the absolute most valuable thing. That's why our staff is largely made up of community organizers who spend all of their time in communities. Past movements had circuit riders, people who would go out to the countryside and give lectures, and stay overnight, and go into the next community and so on. We think the most important work gets done in person, which is difficult, time consuming and very resource and time-intensive. The films are a way for people to begin to engage in the conversation, but ultimately we need to have those direct conversations with people. That's the primary way people truly engage.

TL: Right. It's very rare for someone to pick up the book *Be the Change*, and then all of a sudden move into being an activist. One of the reasons it's so difficult to move in that direction is because it's so easy to stop the organizing from happening. So somebody picks up the book, or sees the movie or whatever and says, "Hey, I want to do this," and they go to their elected official and they say, "Hey Jerry, we need to move one of these ordinances here" and Jerry says, "Well that's crazy. [LAUGHTER] We can't do that because we're a municipality and we're a creature of the state. We don't have the power to do that. You need to go talk to your congressman or to your state legislator." And that stops the person, because they say, "Oh, he's right, we are a creature of the state." And there's nobody engaging him to override that concept.

THOMAS LINZEY AND MARI MARGIL   209

Or Jerry will say, "That's a really good idea I'd like to do that with you," and he turns to the municipal lawyer and says, "Hey we want to do something about this," and the municipal lawyer says, "You can't do that. That's unconstitutional, that's illegal." Right? And the base is not there yet for the individual activist to then go to the lawyer and say, "Well let me talk to you about that. Let me discuss that with you, about whether that's right." Generally that concept never enters the lawyer's brain, about whether to try it or not. It's just the law, right? And then how do we get the city council to override the lawyer? That takes a lot. The lawyer says you can't do that, you're going to get sued. The elected officials have to say, we don't care; we need to stand up for what we need and we're not getting what we need — and they have to override the lawyer.

So, how does all that stuff happen? Well, it happens by confident, self-confident, aggressive people. And you don't get that from reading a book or picking up a newspaper article. You need that constant engagement by our community organizers. Here's a book that deepens your understanding on how the abolitionists did it, or here is a book on the populists, or let's have an hour phone call with the core group, and talk about what challenges you're going to meet. We can predict them because we've been doing the work for so long. You're going to hit this first, you're going to hit this second, you're going to hit this third. How do you get ready for it? Not only get ready for it, but understand it's predictable?

And when the lawsuit comes under the door, here's how the lawsuit will be drafted, because it's boilerplate: it's one, you can't do it; two, it's unconstitutional, it's illegal. We have expert lawyers now who have seen all of that before. They know it. It's not an emergency. It's not "Oh my God, head for the carpets! Hide yourself! We're scared of all of this, it's terrifying." It is — it's terrifying and horrifying. But we know what it looks like now, and here is how you respond to it. We know that stuff. But if you're not working with us in a very close capacity it's very, very difficult to do it alone. You've got to do it with other people — maybe other communities next to you that are doing it — which is something that's worked — or directly with us. But it's more than just, "Here's the tools."

MM: We take both hope and lessons from other movements, like the abolitionists. Ted Weld became a leading abolitionist and a circuit rider. He went out and met with people in different communities to talk about the need to end slavery — and he was by himself. Talk about isolated! He traveled on his own for a long time, but ultimately he trained 12 people to essentially replicate himself. They were able to hold these kinds of conversations in communities. Then they replicated themselves, training other people. For a long time the women's rights movements — you had Susan B. Anthony and Lucy Stone and Elizabeth Caddy Stanton, and they would go out into the world and have these conversations — and they were by themselves. It starts very, very small. One of our challenges in this work — because it's so people-to-people oriented — is training other people to have these difficult and complex conversations, deepening their understanding, enabling them to share the story of why they even got off their couch to do this work at all.

It becomes not just a passion, but a way of life, building the universe of people who are not only willing to have the conversation but are willing to take it to others. I draw hope from Ted Weld, one person going out into the world to talk about ending slavery and changing the Constitution. That's a really important lesson for us and one to take to heart: it can start with one person. That's why I think we are at the very beginning, just like they were at the very beginning. But it is beginning to spread as more and more people say that they want to participate in it, and not only participate in their own communities but take it into other communities, and take it to the state level and beyond.

Isn't it true that you're also rowing upstream in terms of the fragmentation of attention? This is not something that you can do on Facebook and Twitter. A friend of mine says that there is research that shows the average attention span of a first-year university student is five minutes.

TL and **MM** (TOGETHER): Babylon! (LAUGHTER)

This is stuff that you really have to pay attention to.

MM: Yes, that's a really key challenge, that fragmentation not only of our attention spans but also our issues. Jane Anne Morris has written a lot about this, and we use one of her pieces in the Democracy School called "Help, I've Been Colonized and I Can't Get Up." She talks about how we, within the environmental movement, fracture ourselves by — I think she says — "one species, one tree, one toxin." We're all working on this particular toxin today, and other people are working on this tree and that stand of trees, and what have you. Anyway, the point is that we fail to see the common denominator that connects us all, which is that we don't actually have the power to protect that stand of trees, or to stop that toxin from being dumped into a frack well. The structure of law is set up to make sure we don't have it, and we fail to see that connection.

Once we're able to overcome that, people understand not only in their own community, but in other communities and even in other states. We understand that we all share the same common problem and that it's systemic change that's needed. Reframing the problem helps to broaden people's way of thinking about it. Their attention span becomes broader and longer, and their willingness to engage becomes deeper because it it's not just about the problem that we face today, it's about the problem that we're facing throughout our lives.

TL: I think generally we have two constituencies coming in the door. One is first-time activists, people who have never done this work before, whose attention span is longer than five minutes because it has to be. They have to understand this stuff because they have looked at their other options, and none of those are actually going to stop what they want to stop in the community. When they come to us, it's a different dynamic. We become relevant. They're saying, "We need you, and we're willing to listen and we want to figure out if our community can use what's happening in these other communities. We need what you can provide — and so our attention span is longer than five minutes."

The other constituency is refugees from the existing environmental, progressive, liberal organizations. Every once in a while, we'll get someone who has worked for 20 years in the regulatory environmental system, who has burned out in that system, and understands that it is intended to burn you out. That is its intent. Those people will come straggling in the door every once in a while. When they come in, you have a person whose attention span isn't five minutes, who has a wealth of information, who can serve as a testimonial to the existing system not working. They come with a treasure trove of different skills and resources and assets and we put them on our board or our board of advisers. We actually try to integrate them into the work. We call them the "refugees" who have tried to make the system work. Many would argue — I would argue — that the system will be worse now without them on the front lines actually trying to make the system work. But now they are coming to a self-realization — like we did after doing 10 years of conventional traditional environmental law — that the system has nothing to do with environmental protection. It has to do with something different, which is about legalizing harm. That's what the permit system is about. And so when those refugees come in the door, they're a big boon because they bring with them constituencies and information and resources and skills, all things that the new activists don't have. So we hope to join those two together. That's how we get around the five-minute attention span issue.

That's quite fascinating. Would you repeat — I'm not sure of the phrase, was it "the existing system is there to legalize harm?" That's really a crucial insight.
TL: Yes. If you want to dump mercury into a stream, but you don't have a permit to do so, it's an illegal activity. You can't. But if you have a permit, that legalizes it. So you can put certain parts per million of mercury into the stream.

They're not called permits for nothing. They permit a certain activity to occur. And even when there is a problem, it's the right of the corporation versus the right of a property owner downstream or someone else that's affected. But the stream doesn't have any rights and the ecosystem has no rights. So when you go to court, those things aren't even on the table. Those entities, they don't even show up. It's like being in the 1830s and being a slave. When there was a conflict, or your slave got beaten by the slave owner down the road it was treated as a property damage crime. Murder of a slave was not a crime; it was a property damage action. So you brought a property damage action against the person who beat the slave for loss of use. Rape for women wasn't a crime in the 1890s. It was not a crime. It was a property damage action, because the woman was never seen in the court. Just like ecosystems are not seen in the court. It becomes a dispute over property only. So in much the same way, people within their own municipal communities are not seen by the courts because they have no power independent from the state or federal government. So they're not on the playing board either. So a lot of this work is about revealing them and making them seen by the court when those disputes arise.

LARRY KOWALCHUK
The Hidden Powers of Canada's Charter
Recorded April 2015

Larry Kowalchuk is a Saskatchewan lawyer with a deep commitment to environmental and Aboriginal rights, which, he argues, are intimately connected. The resources that the fossil fuel economy requires are widely distributed in Canada, mainly in Aboriginal territory. Getting unfettered access to those resources requires the destruction of Native title, Native values, Native cultures. In short: genocide.

Conversely, if life on Earth is to have a future — and climate change driven by the fossil fuel economy threatens that future — then both the exploitation and the genocide must stop. For Kowalchuk, though, law is not a set of rules, but a place to hold a discourse on the kind of society we want to create. And that's what Larry Kowalchuk is all about. That's why a lawyer from the Prairies finds himself representing two citizen groups in New Brunswick that have launched dramatic legal challenges against the New Brunswick and federal governments and the petroleum industry.

I was in-house counsel for a union for several years and then I went into private practice. It was almost the next day that I started working with people in northern Saskatchewan through a group called the Committee for Future Generations, who you should meet. It's a committee of people who are premised on the fact that we need to change the way we relate to our environment for present and future generations. That's why they call themselves the Committee for Future Generations. So there were at that time people who identify as Métis, people who identify as First Nations, people who identify as Aboriginal, people who were cottage owners, settlers, environmentalists — and they all came together to work on one concept and that is, we're all treaty people. In northern Saskatchewan it's "treaties," but we're all treaty people. Our responsibility is mutual. We signed a deal or contract — whatever you want to call it — and both sides have a responsibility to enforce it, and should.

They went to try to stop uranium mining in court, so I got to meet people and they met people here. Then I got a call, I suspect through Willie Nolan [*a leading anti-fracking activist — ed.]*, and they asked me to come to New Brunswick. I went to a gathering of people to talk about the concepts of stopping climate change, or protecting the environment, and dealing with what I'll call genocide of Aboriginal people. We met at a coffee shop and things went from there.

Willie Nolan told me that you had said to them, "I am humbled to be able to work with you," and she said, I never thought I'd ever hear that from a lawyer.
Oh, that's an understatement. I have the privilege of meeting people who — every part of their life has been a struggle for justice, concretely, in their words and more importantly in their actions. Their commitment to — you know, in some cultures it's called Mother Earth; in others, it's called Gaia; and in others, it's just simply the land and the air and the water. It's not humbling in the sense of me/them; it's just how incredible the learning curve I'm getting from meeting and talking to people, and becoming part of something that really is quite beautiful to see. That's what it is — and while she might not expect to hear it from a lawyer, there are lawyers and doctors and scientists and politicians and people — that's who we are — who are easily capable of appreciating moments of beauty when you see them.

Let me take you back to that early meeting. You're meeting all these new people, and you're asked to be involved with several cases. Give me a thumbnail of what those cases are about.
Well, there are two. Because I'm from Saskatchewan, I don't have the right to just practice law wherever I want, so I have permission to act in two cases at this point. One is — I guess the simplest way of putting it is — it's a pure science-based argument. It's NBASGA — New Brunswick Anti-Shale Gas Alliance — they are one of the plaintiffs and then there are some individuals who are part of NBASGA who are plaintiffs as well.

That lawsuit is premised on two things: one is that we're in the middle of climate change — and by that I mean we are in the middle of a situation where what's going on, on the surface of the planet could lead to the extinction of life on the surface. It's a serious threat to humanity — but more than just humanity, to the four kingdoms of water, air, plant and animal. So this lawsuit says that climate change, which has that kind of consequence, violates the Canadian Constitution — in particular, Section 7 of the *Charter*. Section 7 of the *Charter* says that we have the right to life, liberty and security of the person. This lawsuit says well, "If you have the right to life, liberty and security of the person guaranteed" — it guarantees these things, in fact it requires government to promote the rights that are contained in it and the freedoms and it overrides all laws and policies which might interfere with those. So quite simply, Do we need water in order to live? Do we need air in order to live? Do we need food in order to live? And do we need land as human species? Do we need those things? If we do, then if we lose one of them, does that prejudice our right to life and security of the person? That legal argument is part of that particular lawsuit.

The second thing is that — in that context of a legal position, which is what's in this Statement of Claim — these rights are not guaranteed only to existing Canadians. If you look at the *Charter*, it doesn't say, we guarantee the right to life, liberty and security of the person for those citizens who are living today. It's a forever guarantee. And if it's a forever guarantee that we have the right to life, which includes air, water etcetera then we don't have the right to do anything which is going to prejudice the right to life, liberty and security of the person of future generations. It's a forever right, and therefore it's a forever responsibility. So you can't denigrate the water, you can't denigrate the air, you can't denigrate the land, which could cost not just life on the surface but that clean air and water, like if you go home — you live in Cape Breton, is it?

Well, my heart's in Cape Breton but my body is mostly in Halifax.
Okay, if I could use the example of a rural family, you go home, and you drink that nice clean water or you use the water to clean, to cook, to nurture your livestock, your crop, your garden, your plants, your flowers, your pets. That's not a right that you own today only. It's a right that we have, and your children and your grandchildren also have. A hundred years from now they have the same legal right, they have the right to drink that water and have it for those purposes. Same thing with the air. So that's an aspect of the legal challenge, which is that these are not temporary rights. If all the premiers in Canada get together with the federal government and unanimously agree to amend the Constitution and take it away, they could do that, but that's not what it says right now. So that's a main aspect of it.

Another aspect of it is directly dealing with fracking and shale gas and unconventional gas and oil development — UNGOD is the short acronym for that. Unconventional gas and oil development is ungodly. So that lawsuit, amongst a number of its remedies, argues that unconventional oil and gas development — and particularly using fracking or hydraulic fracturing as a process — scientifically, it is going to harm the air, the water and the land, and violates the right to life, liberty and security of the person as well. So they're seeking a moratorium.

So that's the main remedy? Just stop doing it for some period of time? Or forever?
Well, in their pleadings in front of the court they sort of leave that open. It goes this way: nothing is forever in terms of even the *Charter of Rights and Freedoms*. We evolve as a society. So their lawsuit pleads that until you can prove, beyond a reasonable doubt — which is the criminal standard of proof, because we're talking about life — with scientific certainty, that what you're doing in your laws or

policies won't contribute to climate change, you can't do it. So, it's sort of like a moratorium until they meet that test.

So this is the precautionary principle. This is the essence of it, isn't it?
Yes.

You don't do things unless you can be sure.
And when you're talking about human life and animals and the survival of the surface of the planet, the test would probably be as high as just about anything else, you know? So that's what that lawsuit does. The second one is similar, but it goes broader. It alleges — well, both of them allege — that it's a violation of international law to do these things, to engage in government activity through action or inaction, in funding or not funding, taxation, policies, laws, like permitting, licensing and so on. You can't engage in activity which is going to prejudice life. That violates international law.

The other lawsuit — which is, I think, in the court documents going to be referred to as *"Nolan et al."* — is a group of individuals who are Aboriginal people and non-Aboriginal people, most of whom are part of the traditional territory known as the Wabanaki Confederacy. The lawsuit says that, based on the fact that this land was never ceded — I mean there's a Peace and Friendship Treaty but that was to work in harmony with each other, it didn't surrender any land or rights to the Crown — because of that you can't come in to this territory and do things without our consent. In particular, you can't do things like resource development and extraction processes or even industries that are going to contribute to climate change, because if one honours those original cultural laws, that's not part of the law. You're supposed to live sustainably with each other, the land, the animals, the water, the air, in a way that's respectful. And fracking and shale gas and unconventional oil and gas, which contributes to a fossil fuel economy, which contributes to climate change, isn't that. So it's incompatible with original law, and it's not allowed to be done without the consent of the people — and that means their actual consent.

And the other aspect is — which is supported by international law — they plead in their pleadings the United Nations Declaration of the Rights of Indigenous People, and a number of international covenants, saying, "Look, when you're interpreting the *Charter*, like Section 7, you should be interpreting it in a way that is consistent with international law, at a minimum." The other aspect is protecting freedom of expression and freedom of religion, in exercising your right to stop activities which are going to prejudice the air, the water and the land and your rights as Aboriginal people and as citizens. So those are added dimensions in that lawsuit, which are in addition to the first one.

As I listen to you describe this, I think, if these cases are won, or if they're lost — but particularly if they're won — they change fundamentally a lot of things about the way we understand the law, the country, the relationships between the various peoples who are now living here. These are really profound lawsuits.

Well, the pleadings can be viewed as that. I'm not — it's probably not proper to use the word "pessimistic" — but one of the beautiful things about the legal process, the court process and the *Charter* and international law in particular, is that it provides a place for discourse. There's a writer named Amartya Sen, and his book is called *The Idea of Justice* and it's a beautiful approach to the concept of law and the rule of law. Lawsuits like this and others give us a chance, as citizens, to have a discussion about what kind of society we want. The *Charter* guarantees these freedoms and rights, they can only be limited by Section 1, which at the end of it says, "that promote a free and democratic society." There's no definition of those words. There's no definition of them, and so I think that in New Brunswick, all across Canada and probably most of the world now, people want to have this discussion. Who knows what the discussion will lead to? The government is going to be there, if we end up in court, with its positions on those kinds of things. And citizens will have a chance to participate in the discussion about what kind of New Brunswick we're going to have, or what kind of Canada we're going to have. That's starting to happen more and more in all kinds of forums, and in the courts, and it's a way for us to resolve — not resolve differences, but to arrive at an understanding of where we want to go, without violence.

Canada's *Charter* is unique in the history of the world in the sense that it gives the court system — which is not elected — authority to say to government — which is elected — you can't do this, because there's a higher purpose here, a higher moral and ethical concept of how we want to live that you've crossed here, and that's unique. And we're learning how to deal with that. Most judges — in fact a lot of lawyers — we weren't brought up in a legal system where we could go to court and say to our government... I mean, can you imagine in 1981, one citizen saying, "I don't like what the federal government and Prime Minister are doing, I'm going to take you to court, and the court has authority to order you to stop it." So I'm hopeful that this discourse is going to be valuable. Are people going to appeal it? We'll see. We have a chance — I mean, the Premier, and I want to say this, the Premier of New Brunswick, just gave people a moratorium. They identified five principles — duty to consult, environmental harm, water and so on — to determine whether it's good for the citizens, but they also included a concept called "social license." So I think that we should give this government as much nurturing as we can to make that successful.

New Brunswick is a beautiful province. Part of the reason why I'm here is because I love it. My dad was in the military so we were stationed all across the country and this is one of the places — the people here, because they're so close to the land — wherever you live in New Brunswick, you are really close to the land and that includes the water and the air. There's a friendliness. People use the term that people here are friendlier here than they are elsewhere. I'm not going to say that because I don't want to insult people where I live — but you hear people say the closer you are to nature, the closer you are to each other, and that's true here. This is a beautiful, natural place and it has a great potential for developing a way to nurture the beauty of New Brunswick. You've got the Bay of Fundy, tidal energy, solar, water; it could become a world leader, a Canadian leader in those things. So there's a possibility that this discourse, which more and more people are engaged in, could lead to good things.

I understand what you said from a more narrowly legal perspective — and you're the lawyer, I'm not — but I think I hear you saying that it may very well be that if these cases are won, the New Brunswick government might not choose to appeal. It might just say, "Okay, that's consistent with who we are and who we want to be, and it's a statement of the relationships involved that we find quite congenial, so there's no need to pursue it any further."

And there may not even be a need to pursue it all the way to a decision in the courts, you know? There are stages in the legal process.

Wouldn't you want to have it at some point on the record so that —?
There's a precedent?

Yeah. I'm thinking of the time that I won a little case about the possession of liquor and it challenged the procedures that the police had been using to prosecute people for open liquor. The judge found in my favour, but he did not write a decision, because it was going to upset the whole way that things were done. So you'd want to get it on the record in some official way, wouldn't you?

Well, I take instructions. My role here is to do what I'm asked, and give advice. If people here come to a resolution without having a court decision, that's a beautiful thing. It's still a precedent — maybe not in the justice system but it's still a precedent in the human system — and that's where things matter more. So I'll get instructions on it if we ever get to that stage, but in the way I practice, it's not really about the precedent on the record, in the books. It's more about whether or not you accomplish what you want, and for the people you're acting for — and if they're happy, then you should be happy. Other jurisdictions can voluntarily do what you do here, or other people can file lawsuits, too. I do know that across Canada and the

United States and generally now in the world climate change lawsuits are becoming quite popular, so this discourse that's going to take place — that has been taking place here — is happening all over.

Again — on another more narrowly legal matter — we've been doing a lot of work on the whole idea of environmental rights, both the human right to a healthy environment and also Mother Nature's right to be protected and respected. When you lay out the reasons for thinking that those rights are inherent in the right to life, as guaranteed in the Charter, *that seems to me just an irresistible train of logic. There are other cases that are trying to tease out essentially the same thing. Ecojustice's case in Sarnia with the Aamjiwnaang First Nation is similar. Has that ever actually been tested? Are we now getting to the first time that anybody's ever said, "Okay, if you have the right [to life], you've got to have the right to breathe and drink?"*

The *Charter* is — some people, some academics, and the courts have agreed to call it a living tree. It's only been planted since 1982, and it's still in its early childhood in the concept of law. So we're trying to define it. Formally, I'm not aware that there's a lawsuit like this. The New Brunswick ones might be the first that are actually asserting that is what the *Charter* and international law support — formally — but there are a growing number that are actually taking that view.

The other thing is that, because it's an evolution, people need to appreciate what it's like to be a judge now in Canada. One day, through the proclamation of the *Charter*, you now have all this authority and responsibility, and we're trying to struggle with the words. It's a wide open book. What does "freedom" mean? We as lawyers, we look at a statute, we read a word and then we try to figure out what it might mean. The word "freedom" — there's no dictionary or regulation attached to the *Charter* saying, "Here's what 'freedom' means." Lawyers are no more qualified than you, or any citizen, to give an opinion about what that word might mean.

So Section 7 — originally we looked at it and we go, well, right to life, liberty and security of the person and it goes on with rights not to be denied except in accordance with the principles of fundamental justice... Well, that just deals with the legal system. So the development of that section of the *Charter* took place mostly around DWI *[Driving While Intoxicated — ed.]* charges. Can you be arrested? Because if you're arrested and you go to jail, then your freedom is gone, so that clearly covers liberty and security of the person. So the law went through all of that and then some people did try — well, I was part of a group through the Court Challenges Program that tried to argue that the right to life included social assistance. If you weren't able to provide for food, clothing and shelter on your own, then the state had an obligation because otherwise you wouldn't have any life, liberty or security of the person. And the courts were reluctant to go there, but in the last four years, again as a society, as lawyers and as judges, people have come forward and said, "How about this?"

And so there are two big decisions. There's the "Incite [Human Services]" decision that you might be familiar with, from British Columbia, where there was an attempt to shut down methadone clinics, and it went all the way to the Supreme Court. And the Supreme Court said, "Well, the consequences to the people, if we don't provide those clinics, could prejudice their health and safety." So Section 7 got to be viewed as something that would protect citizens outside the criminal justice system from serious harm that might threaten their life.

And then there's the — I'll call it the prostitution case. Again, that went to the Supreme Court and there was a discussion about criminalizing and putting mostly women in jail for being on the street. There was an argument — it had been made several times, but finally it was accepted by the Supreme Court of Canada — that the prejudice to the health of those women by criminalizing them didn't warrant that kind of treatment in the criminal justice system.

So the court has sort of opened up the door to, what does "health" mean? If you have the right to health under life, liberty and security of the person, does that include other things? So now we're going to have a discussion about, does it include water and air — and to what extent can we count on the state to protect water and air, which is part of health?

It's a fascinating development, and your view of the law is also quite fascinating. You clearly do see it as an evolving living tree that changes and grows and adapts, and not as a lot of people see it, as a very rigid thing. "That's the law!"

A mentor of mine, a professor at the university where I took law, says that human rights documents, like the *Charter*, like international law, covenants, declarations, the American Constitution, right to life, liberty and the pursuit of happiness — those are guidelines for society; they're not rules. How can you make a rule that — well, even rationally — "You have freedom of expression, sir." Well, what does that mean? Inherently it's about human rights and if you accept the theory of evolution, which I happen to, we need to evolve. So you can go online and watch some of the techniques at Harvard Law School, for example — but in a lot of law schools now, the discourse is what's important. Today we might not agree that this is what we want to do, because we've never talked about it before in an honest way — like gay rights for example. People have honest beliefs about that. Now are they beliefs that we agree with? Some won't, some don't — so what we look at in the discussion is, Well, I want to hear your honest view, What do these words mean? What kind of society do we want?

And then it gets to, okay, can we at least agree that our differences shouldn't result in harm? Our differences as human beings shouldn't result in harm. We shouldn't as a result of our beliefs be allowed to kill, assault, or hurt people because we have a difference of opinion. And when you get to that stage then, okay, how do we prevent that harm? Well, we need to protect those who are suffering it — and that leads to a discussion about, How do we protect those who are suffering it? Well, let's ban that behaviour. That is the basis of human rights. You can't hurt somebody because they are Aboriginal, black, female, gay, disabled, etcetera. And as we grow we may not need that any more. What we need to do in terms of remedies, solutions — I mean in the judicial system we call them remedies — but when we get to the stage of, okay what do we need now to stop the harm that's going on — that's going to change, and we want to keep room for that discussion. We don't want to say, It means this forever. We want to say that, for now, we are going to use this law to stop this harm in this way. We may not do it that way tomorrow.

It's a fascinating process when you look at it in this thoughtful way.
It's a privilege to be in the courtroom having that discussion. Something even more important came from a decision, again around Section 7 and 10 and 11, which is around DWIs in the Court of Appeal in Saskatchewan in a leading case called *Therens*. It was a criminal justice case, and they were asked the question — and they asked themselves the question — "Well, we've got these words in this very short document called the *Charter*." We end up with some laws that are a hundred, two hundred, three hundred pages long, and then a set of regulations. The *Charter* is essentially 15 sections. And the court said, "Since this is written for the people, shouldn't we give it a meaning that the people think it has?" Well, who figures that out? The people do. You can go to court on your own — you don't need a lawyer if you're defending yourself on the *Charter* — or you can have a lawyer go to court and argue your words for you, but that's the general view of the living tree doctrine. It's nothing to do with what I think; I just got to be part of the process of that evolution. I graduated from law school just as the Section 15 of the *Charter* was being proclaimed.

You feel quite strongly that something very beautiful has happened in New Brunswick over the events with which you now find yourself engaged. Tell me about that.
I would say there are three parts to it. I'm not from here, but I'm judging from what I've learned and heard people say, and what I've watched. One is there seems to be a fear about questioning government and holding it accountable. There have been some victories in the NB Power issue, but there's a general sort of "Can we really do anything about this, using the law?" Secondly, around fracking and the environment — in New Brunswick, but it's also happening elsewhere — what is beautiful is that people now, through the work of NBASGA and those people

associated with it, people in New Brunswick are now participating in a discussion about how they want life to be here. There's nothing more beautiful than when somebody says, "I want to have a voice." I see you nodding your head because you know what I'm talking about. When someone says, "I want to have a say about my life," that's a beautiful moment to be part of, and to be present to hear. Nothing but beautiful things can come from that discussion, if everybody feels safe and entitled to have a voice on a topic. In New Brunswick citizens ended up having that in an incredible way in an election. It became a topic in an election against a government that was very strong. I will avoid using words other than that, but it was a very strong government, it had a lot of authority and support from powerful structures in New Brunswick society and this topic about "I want to have a say about my environment. I want to have a say about the quality of the life I get to live in my province" became the topic of the election.

The moratorium against fracking became a symbol of that sort of notion: "Do I have a right to say what kind of water, what kind of quality of life me and my future generations are going to live?" And they defeated a very strong government that way. Well, that's a beautiful moment. And the government has listened. They declared a moratorium. The corporations, the oil and gas industry — they're not insignificant in Canada or in New Brunswick in terms of their ability to influence everyone, and shale gas in particular is something that everyone's looking at as the next big fossil fuel energy source. But the Premier listened and the government listened and declared a moratorium on that. And now the consequence of that is they want more discourse, so it appears that this government is taking the lead in involving its citizens in a real discussion, an honest discussion about the impact of unconventional oil and gas, fracking, shale, maybe in the context of climate change.

The option in the discussion from the government includes looking at sustainable energy, and involving citizens in that. Who wouldn't want to be part of a society that's doing that? So this is quite a powerful moment and it could provide leadership and direction to — I personally think — almost everyone else who wants some guidance about how do we get out of the mess we're in when it comes to the environment? And how do we stop doing the harm — I use the word genocide, intentionally so, how do we end the genocide of the original people in this territory? How do we end that? It's got to stop. And the convergence of that is climate change.

If you look at all original cultures, sun is honoured. Water is fundamental, and in some cultures a goddess. In all original cultures water is sacred. Well, guess what? We now know the reason for that — because the alternative to fossil fuel is what — the sun, solar, water, hydro or tidal or ocean, air, wind energy. It's there for us, and New Brunswick's in a position to have a discussion about that too. So that's why what's happened here is beautiful: the engagement that's taking place on having that kind of relationship. It has an inevitability about it. Most of my original culture is from the land, in the Ukraine and then here. Farmers, rural people know this. We all do. When you live in harmony with the land, you have a tendency to live in harmony with each other. It just flows. So there's the discussion that's happening here in New Brunswick where people who never used to talk to each other are now talking to each other.

You have a quote that's a very powerful one, about the importance of getting things right between the Indigenous people and the settlers in this country, and the future of the planet. Tell me about that.

When I began looking at all this — and I can tell you the reason, I think it's important to hear why I started this area of law. My son, who's 21, came home one day — or came over, he's living out — and said voluntarily while we were watching a show that he's not going to have children. And I freaked out at that. I'm a kind of over-protective dad, and I'm going, "Well, what do I not know? What's going on? Why are you telling me this?" That was all in my head. I just kept it there. So, on commercial break I said, "What do you mean? Why did you say that?" He says, "Climate change. I understand that I'm probably not going to be alive for more than 20 to 25 years. Why would I want to have children?" And that shocked me because he's not your radical — you know, he's a typical — I still call him a teen. He partied, he worked, he goes to school. Then I started hearing that more and more from a lot of other parents and young people that there's this sort of belief that we don't have much time left to live. I don't know if you were alive in the 1960s but the threat of nuclear war — we were worried about that, but that was a worry. There seems to be a growing acceptance that [climate change] is just a fact. I don't know how you can live like that. I don't want anyone I love to be living like that. And so that led to me getting involved and then I started listening to people talk about the original ways, the natural laws, the way we used to be, our original culture, our original laws. We used to have our own system. I started listening to what that was, and paying attention to what everyone was saying about that, as much as I could using social media and research.

And it became clear that Canada is where a substantive portion, if not a majority of the remaining scarce fossil fuels exist, like the tar sands, the oil sands. If there's going to be any expansion, people have to come here, companies and corporations and countries like China need to get it out of the ground here. And turns out that most of that, if not all of it, is on land where Aboriginal people live. So eventually I saw a quote on Facebook from *The Guardian* in the United Kingdom. It was fascinating. It's important to remember that [*The Guardian*] is not a Canadian publication. The quote goes something like this: "The human rights of Indigenous people in Canada, and our support for them will determine the fate of the planet."

And when I first read that I was going, "It has to have some meaning that I don't get, and if they can see it all the way from the United Kingdom, in Britain, then there must be something to it" — and there is. They see that unless we stop the genocide — and genocide does include the end of a culture, the end of a way of life and everything that went with it: the customs, the beliefs, the rules, the laws, all of that. Genocide destroys that, removes it from existence. Well, if we want to stop climate change, we have to shift away from the fossil fuel economy and move towards sustainability. [The fossil fuel economy] wants to remove that culture and prevent Indigenous people from having any self-governance, any basis for living their own way of life, all in order to get to that fossil fuel. The original cultures lived in harmony with the earth, with the animals, with the water, with the air and the land in a way that preserved their societies for tens of thousands of years.

The fossil fuel economy has only been in existence for a little over a hundred years, and in that short period of time, in a little over a hundred years out of the hundreds of thousands of years we've been on the surface of the planet, we've brought it to the brink. Whether you think it's man-made or not, we are threatening the whole existence of life. So if we destroy that culture, then we'll never know those ways. We won't learn them, and that's what that quote seems to say to people: we need to pay attention to what's going on here with original culture, original people. Why is the government, why is everyone looking at taking away their rights? There's more to it. At this moment in time in New Brunswick — which is another aspect of what's beautiful here — there is that discussion. People who are farmers or settlers or non-Aboriginal or whatever term you want to use, and those who are Aboriginal or original culture are sitting down and talking to each other and hearing each other's stories and learning about the solutions to the problem that we are all facing. And the solution is to learn, understand, respect and honour the way of living that survived all these centuries, you know?

To me that's one of the most striking things about this whole anti-fracking movement. There are two or three things that really strike me. One of them is the courage, that ordinary people are willing to go out there day after day, saying, "Thou shalt not pass" — and they get arrested, and go to jail, and have broken limbs coming out of that — and nevertheless, they just don't stop. The courage of those people strikes me as being a really profound inspiration. The second thing is the coalition, the reaching out to each other and finding each other over all the divides that have been holding us apart, and finding that we can do these things together. To me those are perhaps even more important than the fracking itself.

I would agree with you and even go further. It's fundamentally what's necessary, and it's happening and that's powerful. When we start breaking the walls down between us as humans, walls that have been created for all kinds of reasons — genocide, racism, sexism, homophobia — when we start realizing at the end of the day we're actually all human, we all love the same things, we all feel sadness and joy and happiness and despair. We all want to live in a way where we accept that we're all different. We don't eliminate the differences between us. We just don't want to have those differences to be the basis upon which we hurt each other. And when people start talking and acting like that, well …

And maybe the next step is that we don't want to eliminate those differences, because we recognize them as a form of wealth. They provide a series of choices that are all available to all of us — provided they still exist, and are honoured.
Yes.

Tell me about CSIS.
Bill C-51 was brought forward, and if you follow social media and even the mainstream media, people were really scared about the fact that it was going to expand the powers of CSIS. It would have the effect of making protesters and people who just disagree with government policy potentially arrested without warrant, monitored as if they are terrorists. I hate that term. You are either a person who kills people without reason, and therefore a criminal, or you're not. But there was a lot of fear going on in this country — a lot of opposition but also this sort of, "Oh, my God." The people in New Brunswick that you were talking about were feeling, "If I stand up, I can be arrested even more than I was before. The possibility of me being punished for having a voice is going to be dramatically increased." And people saw that, you could read people. In fact there are suggestions in media stories and stuff that there's proof in articles that they were going to target environmentalists and Aboriginal activists, and that was the purpose of C-51. So CSIS having all of that power, watching your every move, and being able to share the information they gathered on you with every other government agency was building an awful lot of fear in people, in terms of jobs, employment possibilities, grants, you name it. If I'm on the wrong side and I get flagged, it's going to cost me.

So I was at a gathering in Saskatoon of Aboriginal activists, mostly women, some elders, some grandmothers and some environmentalists and some farmers, and they were learning about what was happening with each other and telling their stories. Then it became a time to talk about "Well, what are we going to do about this?" And out of one workshop there was a discussion, "We need to be united, we need to send a message to the government and everybody that we, Indigenous people and settlers, are united. You're not going to divide us. It's going to have the opposite effect." So somebody said, "Well why don't we just form CSIS?" And so it's the Canadian Settler and Indigenous Solidarity is the name they came up with and immediately, I mean I felt myself going, oh my, that's so beautiful, and it's so correct, which is such a horrible term. But it's just so right, that in the face of what appears to be a law which is to promote fear and keep us from talking to each other like we were talking about before, to "We're going to talk to each other even more than we used to. In fact we're going to build solidarity with each other like we've never done before." That flips everything! It removes the fear. It can be fun — we can have a lot of fun, you know? I won't go into all those ideas, because everybody can play with them themselves. I mean, you were coming up with ideas too. For example, do we want to have CSIS training in Canada? Do we want to have CSIS training in the schools? Yeah, let's have Indigenous and settler solidarity training, let's learn how to talk to each other, let's learn how to support each other. So that was just a cute, beautiful…

But it wonderfully muddies the waters too. If somebody comes up to you and says I'm a member of CSIS, what does that phrase mean? All of a sudden you've turned it upside down. You've confused it. You've taken a lot of the sting out of it.

That and more. I'm a fan of the concept of dialectics. It's a political theory it's becoming established. It's like, some people don't like dark, some people don't like light — but this concept says, "You have to have dark; otherwise you'll never know what light is." We need that kind of relationship. And CSIS, these four words that form that acronym, turn the light on to the darkness that people perceive CSIS to be. That's kind of cool. There's nothing new about this concept, if you look at how we have evolved on the surface of this planet as people, as humans. Every time we stop being scared of each other, and learn to talk to each other and respect each other, we move forward and incredible things happen.

JAN VAN DE VENIS
The Shadow Ombudsperson
for Future Generations

Recorded November 2015

Jan van de Venis is an extraordinary Dutch lawyer who lives at the intersection of human rights and sustainable development. He's deeply concerned about the human right to drinkable water, for instance. Industrial developments often use vast quantities of water and leave it totally contaminated, but sustainable development requires respect for the human right to water. And so, in addition to running his own law firm JustLaw in Utrecht, Jan van de Venis is also Director of the Legal Desk at the Swiss water conservation group WaterLex. In addition, he's the co-founder of a public service organization called Stand Up For Your

Rights, and the President of TheCrowdversus.com, which uses crowdfunding to support and protect environmental defenders around the world. He's a member of the influential network of Dutch leaders called Worldconnectors, and within Worldconnectors he leads the effort to create a new position within governments called the Ombudsperson for Future Generations. Indeed, he's sometimes described as the Netherlands' own shadow Ombudsperson for Future Generations.

Finishing law school, starting to work, I had already my doubts whether I could really go into this hard, focused business law society and work for big firms, big cases mostly dealing with money. But when I was doing an internship, during the last few weeks of my studies, I actually thought and saw that I can be a lawyer if I just maintain my own ethics. So as long as I keep to my ethics and my morals, I can do this — and I actually have done so from the minute that I started. I started as a corporate lawyer. However, after six or seven years I did get the feeling that my future would only be about making more money, and not getting more interesting cases, because only the monetary thing would change in the cases, not the content.

As I realized that, I also thought, "Is this really what I want?" I saw that I have certain talents. Do I just want to use them for others to either make profit or bypass their responsibilities — because often lawyers do that, or they make contracts that are in the interest of one party. Often I saw the bigger picture — and I started thinking, "Is it the UN, or is it environmental, or is it human rights?" I saw the link between human rights and sustainable development already, linking environmental issues to human rights issues and law issues. The emerging sustainability development agenda was not really taking law into consideration. I was also looking at mechanisms, through corporate law, enabling and stimulating companies to be more sustainable.

And through this process I ended up at a vacancy at Greenpeace International to become their in-house corporate lawyer. So I did for Greenpeace the legal matters on ships, planes, offices, mortgages — Greenpeace is obviously a big organization globally. Having done that for two or three years, and having gotten even more contaminated with the human rights and sustainability virus — which I call it — and also seeing that people needed to do more with that, also the NGOs, I started sort of an internal campaign at Greenpeace to do more with human rights. I said, if people take down a forest in Brazil, they don't just do something that's very negative to the Earth and to Nature, but they also directly violate human rights, for example, those of Indigenous people, and maybe even my rights here in the Netherlands — because I can no longer visit that forest, and who owns that piece of forest?

And then, as we will discuss later, I also thought, "But what about future generations? Don't they have a voice?" They're not recognized in all laws. They are for instance in the Constitution of Brazil, where the Constitution says there are human rights to a healthy, clean environment for present and future generations. And that also got me thinking. I was thinking, "I'm a lawyer, and I actually have a whole lot of clients that do not exist yet. Who is calling out for them? Who is their lawyer? Who is invoking their interests? Who is sometimes stopping us from just living today and not thinking about the world that we actually are going to leave behind?" Because we are leaving that world behind, and it will be a heritage that our future generations cannot refuse; they will be stuck with it.

Having done that within Greenpeace, I found it was not yet the time at those big NGOs to make the link between both environment and human rights because, on the other side, I also went to NGOs like Amnesty International, and they also acknowledged that the work that I was doing was very good, and was a good vision with climate change and environmental issues growing. This was almost 10 years ago and Amnesty also saw that this will be a topic — but not yet. They also said, "How do we tell the people that are backing us, how do we explain that we've suddenly become environmental and are not just human rights?" And I already said then, there is no distinction between human rights and environment, if it comes to that, because in fact a rights-based approach to sustainability and environmental issues really goes to the core. It's humans that impact the environment, it's humans that enjoy the environment, so it's also a human rights and a human needs issue. For me the link was very clear, and that, actually, with the support of several others, led to me setting up Stand Up For Your Rights, an NGO that actually is a bridge builder between human rights development and environmental NGOs. We were not planning the next big new NGO, but really using our networks that we had build up between those NGOs to have them start working on joint issues. That's about nine years ago that I started that.

At the same time I set up my law firm JustLaw. I always had the idea that if I do 50 percent of my time paid work through JustLaw , then I can spend about 50 percent of my time unpaid, working for Stand Up For Your Rights or any other work on sustainable development and human rights. I have on average been working in that manner for the last seven to eight years.

About half of your time basically paying for the rent and the mortgage and the food, and the other half working on what you believe are the most important issues in the world? And the nice thing is for me, as an individual, is that whereas there was not that much work on human rights and sustainable development when I started eight or nine years ago — I really had to also make my living advising NGOs on corporate law and contracts — it's really shifting. And sometimes also the work that I used to do unpaid is now paid. This shows me that now we are starting to see the value of this work, including the monetary value of it. I've been advising institutions on how they can work on human rights, advising existing human rights institutions how they can work on sustainable development goals with a rights-based approach, training human rights institutions over the world to work on sustainable development, water issues, climate issues, all in relation to human rights. Which for many of them is a very new world, because many of the national human rights institutions globally really focus on the more traditional civil and political rights: racism, discrimination at work, other sorts of discrimination. That's definitely very good, but we should not forget the economic, cultural and social rights, which are the rights actually connecting humanity as a whole and connecting it to the planet as well.

You're telling me about a theme that we've seen in other areas, but that I hadn't seen in organizational issues, and that's reductionism. One of the things that has gotten us into trouble is our habit of breaking things down intellectually into compartments — so we only work on developing an energy system that serves a particular purpose, but we don't see it in the context of our whole environment. And this is the same thing isn't it? Traditionally, human rights and sustainability have been separate concerns, but you're saying, "No, no, no they're all connected. It's all one big thing."
It is — and it's for many people a paradigm shift as well. You can probably

understand — if you understand this principle and this paradigm shift that we are going through — that mostly I have to combat or reason with the human rights professors. They used to say, "Sustainable development and human rights — no, no, no, that's not a human rights issue." And now actually they are becoming, instead of a rare species, more of a common species.

I think it's also because the issues are becoming more realistic in today's world. It's not just predictions any more. We see sea level rising, we see climate change and climate litigation, we see the human rights to water and sanitation being accepted by both the UN General Assembly and Human Rights Council. Now, human rights institutions, ministers, government officials suddenly need to work on themes like water. That used to be mainly a technical issue for the Dutch, for instance. How do we solve water issues? And now it suddenly becomes a human rights issue. So is it affordable? Is it acceptable? How do we ensure that in the long-term it's sustainable? How do we keep our sources protected? How do we clean up the mess that we've made in the past? Who do we hold responsible for that? All those issues were non-issues in the past and indeed now really are connected with human rights.

An additional element that really helped is development in the international law realm of human rights and business. Professor Ruggie, who was the UN Special Rapporteur on Human Rights and Business a year or five ago, really presented a strong framework on guiding principles for business and human rights. Since then this has really gotten the attention also of the UN, and it's created a responsibility of business to respect human rights. And this responsibility's often called upon toward governments, towards business — and all these little elements are really telling me that this was a right vision already eight years ago and that we're actually moving in that direction.

It's the perceptions of young people coming to these issues that are often the genesis of change, right? Here you're a young lawyer, and you see it suddenly differently from the older lawyers.

That's absolutely true. And this is also why I really like this, because it keeps me fresh as well. I've been doing this since about 10 years ago. I'm in my early 40s and still feel young, but young people don't see me as young any more. And they bring a whole new vision to the table. Things are moving so fast. They are actually bringing "What if we talk about human rights and what if we talk about a bigger picture — can't we then say that Nature itself has rights? Can we not say that forests, rivers or Mother Nature as a being, as an existence, as a living organism has rights? The Nature which we are all connected to has rights as well. Who can then defend such rights?" I mean that concept has been only a few years old and it's already popping up everywhere.

I really see things speeding up on that. I had to plead for a human right to a healthy environment. Now we see this emergence of even more new rights. People are saying, It's just not humans that have rights. The next step to me — from a human rights based approach — is that also future generations that have rights and needs, so we have to respect and safeguard those in our lives today. But a whole new movement says, "Yes, and we could say that Mother Earth is a subject and thereby has rights too."

You must be familiar with Christopher Stone's work.
Not directly but…

He wrote an essay many years ago called "Should Trees Have Standing? Towards Legal Rights For Natural Objects." I ran across this when I was working on a book called The Living Beach. The beach acts like a living thing — and I thought does it have the right to be respected, to pursue its own processes?
I always say, "Law becomes law after ethics are being put on paper." So the ethical element of it is popping up. We are looking differently at how we use our planet, how we enjoy nature, how we are a part of nature. It would be almost ridiculous 10 years ago to say, as a human rights lawyer, "I feel a part of nature." Now I don't just say that I feel a part of nature, which I do — but let's be honest: I *am* nature. I drink water, I need air, I need food, I need to sustain my body, I refresh by contact with nature. My body is nature.

So if I am nature and part of nature, if we progressively show and prove as well that nature has a health benefit on our lives — more and more recent academic studies have proven that people are more healthy and happy as they are more in contact with nature — and if you then say, "What is the meaning of life?" you can link that to all sorts of religion. But if you keep it small and you say, "Let's try to be happy now, today, let's focus on well-being. That's worth more to us than welfare or income or prosperity," then connecting to nature makes you a happier being and creates more well-being.

Is there a growing tension between the abstract and over-simplified view of the world which exists for business, and the broader view of the world that we're looking at here? I'm thinking particularly of the whole conflict over water in Cochabamba, Bolivia. You and I would take water to be a human right, but it becomes a corporate asset and there are profits being made from it — and people are in the streets, furious about it. Corporate property rights are running straight up against this new perception that we've been talking about, right?
Yes, I think that we can acknowledge from the last decades that in many cases business took over from government. Business was quicker to adapt, to jump into

new technical means, actually even jump into areas that used to be governmental. For instance, providing water. In many cases governments have said, "Then we privatize or then we sell the licenses." In almost all cases where this has happened, especially to the elements that are truly human needs, there have been violations of the needs of people, because the interests of the company is just to make profit for the shareholders. Thankfully we are seeing more social business emerge every day where the interest of the company is to contribute socially — to make a good living, but not just work for the profit of the shareholders. And every time that that profit for the shareholder is stressed too much, we lose track of, what is the bigger picture?

I sometimes call it a schizophrenic or dissociated way of working. I know people that work at major oil companies like Shell, and during the day they, through their work, are actually destroying our planet. A good example is the tar sands industry, for instance, in Canada, taking away pristine forest and nature, destroying the habitat of so many living beings, scraping up tar sand, which costs one gallon of oil to create two gallons of oil that we can use. So it's amazingly energy intensive as well. But those same people that do this in their 'box in their office' in the morning walk with their dog in this beautiful Dutch forest and say, "I love nature, and I really enjoy nature." Often they even support or are members of nature conservation groups. So how come as a person you can love this nature, and you step in to the office and you lose this? I'm very happy to see that more of the younger generations somehow refuse to do this. They say, "I can't live that dissociated life where what I do in my job actually goes against what I stand for as a person." And I think it's a very honest message as well, that we should stop doing that. We should stop saying, "What I do at work is work, and what I do at home is home." You cannot with one hand pat the Earth, love the Earth, and with the other destroy it through your work.

And that's the same integrating pattern that we've already talked about. People are saying, "I can't be disintegrated in that kind a fashion."
Yes, and it's also difficult because as a lawyer I feel most confident on legal matters, but I suddenly have to know not just something about climate change; I have to know a lot about climate change because I want to talk about climate change. And I have to know a lot about water. It's difficult as well because water people now need to know about human rights.

And some subjects like water really do flow literally right across the spectrum. Water has been a major, major factor in your life, hasn't it?
Yes. Like water, many things flow in the path of least resistance. Water has been a very crucial element in all the work that I've done. I also work for a Swiss NGO,

WaterLex, where actually this human rights-based approach to water governance is key. We assess laws of countries, we train human rights institutions and judges and politicians on what it means to have a right to water and sanitation. This will be a crucial element for the years to come. There are many issues — from environmental degradations to the going-extinct of species — but water will touch us more than anything else, I think.

We have really, through over the last decades, taken so much from our natural resources. We've already pumped away one third of the global sub-terrain water reserves that are accessible to us, and we're not filling them up again. We're taking away forests that are keeping the water down, and we are creating desertification. We are using water in an unsustainable way. We're just often just saying, okay who needs water? Ah, business calls first? Then business gets first. So 70 to 75 percent of all water goes to agriculture — which, yes, we need for our food but not that much — and if we use it more smartly, we first direct it to people, and then we can use that water, which has more nutrients in it, for agriculture. But in this case now, we use water for agriculture and it comes up polluted, and we cannot drink it without treatment.

Also, scientific proof is coming forward to prove that more and more global conflicts are actually sparked by water. There's a big link with the first start of the Syrian conflict that started with water. There are several Sudan conflicts that — yes, there were interreligious or intercultural, inter-tribe issues but water was the drop, as we say in Dutch, the drop that made the bucket spill. It's the English expression, it's the straw that broke the camel's back. We have a similar expression where we say the bucket is full, and this drop was max and now the bucket is overflowing. Which is a very nice link to water and maybe we can introduce that in the English language as well. But it's a crucial issue and a crucial matter.

You could say this is the drop that broke the dam — and now we're back to Holland in a big way.

And talking about that, we just recently had a big dam break in Brazil, creating an enormous spill of chemicals. I think the number now is 250,000 people that do not have access to clean drinking water because of the bad governance of a company in charge of a mine project. As a society, we are putting such great risks into the hands of corporations that are actually just there for profit. That's a risk we just cannot take — because what happens if they fail? You would see the bankruptcy of the company, but what happens to the people that failed? Well, in most law, in most situations, they would be untouchable because they were just the directors. And we give the rights to the legal entity.

So who cleans up? Government. So we all pay for the negative impact, and the profit, the short-term profit that was made, just goes into the hand of a few. Many corporate people will say I would be exaggerating. When I was a lawyer for the corporations back then, I would also say that, but it's not so. I've really seen that. Water cannot be traded as a commodity. It is truly a common good not just for now, but for our children and for future generations — and we should treat it as such, as a treasure.

We treat it as a free good, though and as an infinite good.
But it is a public good. With limited sources. And limited in quantity if we are to serve the needs of all, including future generations.

Are we now facing a situation where we may literally not have enough water for the most important purposes?
Yes. Every year there is an issue in California on drought and availability of water. Recently we've seen even more alarming reports that the Sequoia forests were going dead in certain places, and it was thought that it was a bug due to climate change or softer winters; the bug was actually killing the trees. But now they actually see that many of the trees are also just drying out. There's no water. We're sucking out ground water at such a speed that these big trees — thousands of years old — are running out of water.

In all kinds of places there's a cause and there's an effect, but we don't make the connection. We don't say, for example, that X number of people in Amsterdam are dying of air pollution. We say they're dying of heart disease, they're dying of pulmonary disease, they're dying of many different kinds of things. But those are symptoms. The real cause, back upstream, is that they're not breathing good air.
Yes — and the bigger picture of the real cause is humanity not living in balance with nature. Also, any new development that we make, we jump on it and we start doing something — and we often do not use a precautionary principle. Our planet is showing many systems of a disease, which is called humanity. We had a hole in the ozone layer. We had acid rain. Now we have climate change — and climate change is becoming so big that I'm not sure whether we actually will be effective in combating this. But if we just do this based on CO2 emissions, and we don't change as a species, we will have a next issue. It will be either water related or will show that we've taken away too many forests, or we went in so deep that we opened a virus to come out of the forest that has never been in contact with humans, etcetera, etcetera.

And we're just not taking that in consideration. I fully agree. An example of that is that in the Netherlands we have 15,000 people that die every year due to air pollution. Fifteen thousand, and hundreds of thousands hospitalized for asthma, from bronchitis etcetera. And we only have a thousand people that die in traffic — or less. But we always try to reduce those people who die in traffic. Why? I think one element is because we see them bent around a tree or crushed against another; this creates fear, true fear. But 50 times more times more people die because we emit particulate matter — and it's a nasty death, it's a long cancer death. We take a year off our lives, also scientifically proven in the Netherlands, and we just accept this.

Why do we just accept this? Why don't we see this big link? For me the hopeful thing is that every new program on renewable energy — for instance, there's an EU program for 2030 on renewable energy. So now the official government bureaus or institutions that have to calculate what actually happens if we do that, are also calculating the positive impacts on health. They are actually saying if we meet this 2030 objective, that is actually going to save us millions, maybe billions, on healthcare, because people don't go to the hospital. They don't need their asthma medicine.

And this brings us to the other side. You also addressed this when we briefly spoke before on true pricing. I always say, "Now that we see that we're getting so many negative impacts of working with fossil fuels, it's time to start charging a realistic fee at the gas station." All these negative impacts — the oil company's not paying for that; the taxpayer is, though not directly. But if we would directly pay for that at the gas station, electrical cars would be booming already! They are emerging now, but they would be booming! Driving an electrical car on your own solar energy — which I've been doing for the last four years — is dirt cheap already. It is! And it's positive. There's nothing coming out of the car. There are many reports by World Bank and others that prove that governments are still subsidizing fossil fuels four times to five times more than renewable energy. There are many people that say: renewable energy, it's a subsidized fuel. No, fossil fuel is subsidized four times more. So we are creating economic incentives that are not realistic. So charge what fossil really costs to people that need to buy fossil, but on the other hand make sure that you stop subsidizing a fuel that we need to say, "bye" to anyway, because the future is renewables.

Worldconnectors, of which you're a part, has a whole foundation working on pricing. How is the foundation addressing that issue?
The foundation is called the True Price Initiative, and this is actually one of the main issues that we focus on with Worldconnectors. We're working with future generations, and we're working with energy. How do we look at energy? What is a true price? Many of the Worldconnectors have either been former ministers or government, NGO executives but we also have business, former CEOs of the biggest banks, biggest businesses in the Netherlands. They like this business approach, and they've also said, Why is it that we are not paying a true price? And they've

actually worked out a scientific model that, per product, could really calculate the price. So what does it cost, for instance, if I eat organic grapes that have to be flown in from South Africa? It's not possible to sell those for one dollar or for one euro per kilo, because with the impact on CO_2 emissions alone, the whole trip should cost much, much more.

Buying your phone charger from China off the web for $3 is not calculating the environmental costs, the labour costs, the travel of the product, the waste that will be left with the product. We are not calculating these costs to the person that buys the product. We're not calculating it to the producer of the product. Then who are we calculating it to? Well, to the bigger us, which now, today, we don't care about. We'll either throw it away or burn it. We take things from the environment, precious metals and rare metals, but we don't give this to our future generations. And this is also behind this calculating model. How can we, for each product, calculate as well as we can, a true price and a realistic price?

And if we had that, how do you get that to be the price that's actually charged? We know what it is, but we're not charging it. How do we make that jump from what we know to what we do?

The nice thing is, it's two ways. One, I would say, it requires a government that does so. I mean, why is the government there? I'm not a socialist that says we just need to have a government because of the fact that we need a government. No, but there are issues that you cannot leave in the hands of people and companies with short-term interests. They just don't look at that bigger or longer-term picture. We need government to do that.

This is also why we need an Ombudsperson for Future Generations, to show the impact and to show those elements of long-termism. But the other side of things is, if we do this, if we create this true price, it actually supports companies that are already doing this, who are more working in an organic way or are looking at how do I make my supply chain efficient — not just in a monetary perspective, but, for instance, how can I use as many local products as I can? Support the local economy, produce locally, so that I do not create these costs for the environment. This actually makes the whole process more efficient. And I think, in the end, this is also what business is about — being as efficient as we can.

Lord Stern, in the Stern Review said that climate change was the biggest market failure in history. Given the climate case here in the Netherlands I wonder if there's a way of using the courts?

Well, this is what I've been pleading for, for many years. There are for me, four ways to use the law. One, law is actually writing on paper what is the ethics and what needs to happen. In many countries, ethics have gone beyond what is currently the law, and then you get case law by judges — and then suddenly this case law is also put into law, and that becomes the law. Why is that necessary? Because that's the second step, law is a tool to be used. Law can be used to set the boundaries of what we actually can and cannot do. And, stepping into the next point, when it's a tool to be used, it's also the rules to be respected. Business is a law subject; they are a corporate legal person and they can act as a person. But when they die — when they go bankrupt, or when they mess up — we don't have people or real things to chase after. So then they're gone, and then, like you said, the government is there to take care of that. And that's a system that doesn't work.

You want to create a system that supports individual capacity like capitalism in some way does. It creates. There's a lot of energy in it. If you think about something new, you can do it, you can put it in the market. It's the American dream, you can make a change. But in many cases the law doesn't give you these moral or legal restrictions, saying, But if you do this, you do have to take care about other people, about the environment, about future generations. You just cannot take out and not put in. And I've also pleaded for many new laws on that. For instance there is a law in the Netherlands — and in many countries — that if you are as a director or board member of a company responsible in some way for the bankruptcy of a company, then the curator, as it's called here, can go after you and your private money to recollect some of the money that you messed up through letting the company go bankrupt. For all those businessmen, this is clear. They learn this in their education, so they know this law.

But why don't we extend that to violating human rights and violating the environment? Because then it's not only a moral that people need to abide by, but it's their business books and it's in the books of the corporate lawyers. They will learn that you can't just let a company go mess up with the environment. Why not? Because it's ethics, and it's put in the laws. I think it's very important. We still have a lot of ground to cover to create better laws to actually safeguard our planet for the longer run. I see morals coming up, and business is changing, but we need to institutionalize these limitations to business as well, because often businesses say, "We're not doing anything against the law, we're abiding by the rules. And as soon as we have to change because of a new law, we will, because we're not doing anything against the law."

But now I've put three of the elements on the table. The fourth element is, if we don't manage we have to be able to go to court. Even before the climate case here in the Netherlands, I was part of a working group that actually was working with several NGOs to plan such a case. Why? Because I knew that based on human rights and based on law and based on ethics that need to become law, the way we are dealing with the economy and the way we are dealing with climate change is not just. It's not right. And judges will say this, and judges will create this new law if government doesn't do so.

In a good country, politicians create the laws that we need to abide by, and so I would appeal to politicians to do so. But I also know that politicians have short-term interests. They are there as long as they are there, and if they're re-elected, part of their big interest is to become re-elected again. So this is also why we need, for instance, those ombudsmen and guardians for future generations that do not have this political term but have a longer term to sit and to work.

But we also need, definitely, judges. We need these cases. Going to court is not a bad thing. I often hear, "If you sue someone that's so negative." No. I say A, you say B, we don't agree — let's ask the judge, what does the law say? In this climate case as well, let's ask the judge, what does the law say? All the political parties and the government that now have said we will appeal this ruling, not many of them have really read what the judges have written. The verdict for me as a lawyer is very well reasoned. It's very well balanced and it's actually doing what I've always felt that needed to be done. The judges say, "You know this is the law and if you don't abide by this as a government, then I will correct you, and this is why I'm there."

I actually like this new pillar because many, many people in government say, "If we want to change, so if people want to become more sustainable why don't people buy more sustainable products?" And that's just not the way society functions today. I know that 75 to 80 percent of all people want more renewable energy — but if you see how many have solar panels on their roof or buy from a green energy company, that's much less. Why? Because the incentives they have are also short term. They're marketized: it's cheaper if you go to me, so the short-term incentives are triggered with people through advertisement. But thankfully there's a growing group that's actually appealing against that, and there's a growing group that also says, we cannot do this any longer. People are becoming more active, standing up for their rights and actually also seeing the bigger picture, seeing how they are connected. If I buy a T-shirt here in the Netherlands that creates water use of 3,500 litres in India or Uzbekistan to grow the cotton, I am actually using water in Uzbekistan. Then that T-shirt can never be three euros or three US dollars, that's too cheap. And thankfully more and more people are seeing this, are actually saying we have to object against a system like this. This system is bankrupt, and before we all fall over we have to make changes to this.

Which brings us to the whole issue of future generations. Tell me about the idea of an ombudsperson for future generations. How would that work?
I should first explain a bit on why an ombudsperson? I'm part of an international

network of ombudsmen commissioners, parliamentary commissioners on future generations. It's called the Roundtable for Institutions for a Sustainable Future. Let's call it the guardians, guardians for future generations. Why? Because for many people the institution of ombudsmen has a whole different meaning. An ombudsperson is a complaint mechanism against governmental laws and regulations and acts that violate the rights of people. In the Netherlands we have an ombudsperson for veterans, and we have a children's ombudsperson and we have a general ombudsperson who deals with complaints against the government — for instance, if you're incarcerated or if the government is ill-behaving towards its citizens.

But part of the elements of the ombudsperson in the Netherlands, and in many other countries, is that they can do research. They can monitor. They can advise. They can be requested to advise on new rules and regulations and on intended steps that governments want to take. And this ombudsperson has a period of five to six years, which is not connected to the political re-election period. And the job of an ombudsperson of future generations, which for instance Hungary also has, is to look beyond that spectrum, to advise the government on new laws and regulations. So for instance if the Dutch government would want to privatize water, then the ombudsperson could either, requested or non-requested, give feedback on that, and say, "Look, if you do this, this is the impact in five to 10 years — but it has this and this impact on future generations. Have you enough taken that into consideration?"

Moving towards renewable energy will clean up the air, will create healthier, happier lives for people. Have you taken that into consideration when you just signed a new deal to make a gas cylinder for us to store gas and put 10 billion euros in that to enable Russian gas to go through our country and to go abroad? This is a fossil fuel subsidy. Around the globe we see more and more guardians for future generations. A nice example is that recently a law has been adopted in Wales, which is called the Act on the Well-Being of Future Generations. It doesn't do only the environmental side of things, but it also looks at economy, cultural values and natural heritage. What do we have in our country that is so precious that we want to protect it for now and for the longer run, for future generations? And the guardian that they've created in Wales is a Commissioner for Future Generations. So every country can have its own wording or name. For the Netherlands this would really fit well within the Dutch system.

And the commissioner or the ombudsperson has primarily a persuasive role?
That depends on the country. There is an example of an Israeli parliamentary commissioner who had to safeguard the rights of future generations and he has stopped several laws. He had the right to stop the law if it was not taking into consideration the rights and needs of future generations. He did that several times.

So this is an existing position in some countries.
Yes, but the example just mentioned is no longer there. So you need sufficient democratic legitimacy as well. Obviously the ombudsperson needs to be morally very clear, but on what he can do and what he does, he needs to have diplomatic skills as well. If you would have the right to block a law, and you would block the first five laws that you see, then politicians will definitely look at a way to get rid of you, and this is already what we've seen internationally. So yes, this ombudsperson needs to have high moral and high standing, a high level of appreciated feedback. The question is, do you want this ombudsperson in fact to block laws? Even Obama has the right to veto laws, but in many cases when you do that, it's also the last law you veto. This is also a long-term interest that needs to be balanced as well.

And you said Hungary has such a person?
Yes.

How does it work in Hungary?
The Hungarian Ombudsman for Future Generations has a strong mandate, based on a constitutionally recognized human right to a healthy environment. Based on that mandate, he can look at developments. He's been involved in the privatization of water. He's been involved in taking away protected environmental areas for development, which he stopped. He's just a constant reminder of taking into consideration the longer term. So we would say, This is a protected area, but we need to now build a parking lot or a space for business to emerge — but did we really think about, "Do we still need that business in 10 years? Or by then will we have destroyed this piece of land and have empty offices, so it's a lose, lose situation? Do we really need it here and now?" I think this element, this really long-term thinking, is crucial.

This is also very nice because as humans we've always been connected to history through tales, myths, religion, history, and we are connected to living people because we interact. But it's the first time I think that consciously, in western society, we feel connected to future generations. That's partly because we do studies into what will happen in the future, and we're actually seeing that we are, by the ways that we are living today, restricting their future and their development. Old and ancient and Indigenous people have this reasoning, and have institutionalized thinking about future generations. There's this seventh generation principle in several Indigenous tribes and groups around the world where you do not do something if it can impact in a negative way seven generations to come. So you take this into your system. We just never have, and it's time that we do.

That's a fascinating perspective. In many of our interviews, we've encountered the wisdom of the Indigenous peoples, who do understand things that are just not on the radar of western industrial countries.

Yes, it's like they are connected not just to nature, but to a bigger planet in time as well. So they see what they do to the land; they see what they need from the land; they see what their impact will be on the land.

It seems they're doing the same thing that you've just described with the studies: they've looked back at history and they see what has come from certain actions far in the past, and they look forward and say, well those are the kinds of things that will happen from actions in the present. So you see yourself as a temporary piece of a very long process — and I don't think that's been the western outlook at all.

No, not at all, no. Peaches come from a can and chicken is from the supermarket, right? We don't know where our products come from. We really don't know. We just go to our office in the morning, do our work, like I said, with sort of a blindness for all the impact that we have. And we go back home, we buy our food and we live. We don't see the impact. Paying the true price could be a start for that. In an Indigenous society, you cannot live separated from nature and from this long-term thinking, because every day you are reminded. But we have designed our lives to be disconnected from the longer term, and that really needs to be re-implemented again.

It's a huge mental shift that we're talking about here.

Yes, and it's just very hard to change people because they, no matter whether they're one hundred percent happy in their lives, it does create their security. They're stuck in a system where they have mortgages and houses and gardens, and where there's pressure to leave money for your children, and to drive a bigger car than your neighbour. To step out from that, and step into this world of interconnectedness and taking into account your effect on this whole is a major shift. Young people can do it more easily. People over 50, or even above 40, have difficulty because they've really learned to work in settings that were created to maintain this old system. It's tough for many people to come out of this. But it's time to knock on the door and say, "How long can we still wait?"

It's tough but it's very exciting.

Definitely. I can tell everyone that as soon as you step into this world and into the world of sustainability, it's just exciting. There's so much positive energy and reconnecting to others, to other cultures, to nature. It's a beautiful thing, and it does make you a happier person. It has not made me a richer person in my bank account, but it has made me tremendously richer as a person.

It hasn't made you a richer person in your bank account, but I think that the European social democratic tradition is a form of wealth that's often not recognized as wealth. I think it's a good deal, you know?

It's a very good deal. The happiest people of this planet live in these countries, the Netherlands, Denmark, Norway. Even the richest people in those countries are the happiest, whereas they pay most tax relative to others around the world. And why is it? It is that you are part of a society. When you need health care you have health care. Your children will have proper education. The whole system around the economy is also protecting you, so you are part of this bigger system, and this is what is making you happy.

And this is real wealth, isn't it? This is a lot more than money in your own bank account.
Definitely. You can be very wealthy and very unhappy.

And lonely, and still exposed and vulnerable to all the misfortunes that are taken care of in a more deeply democratic and caring, compassionate society.
Yeah. There was a recent article that said, of all those countries the Dutch are not the most happiest in the world — we're in the fourth or the fifth place — but our children have been the happiest children on this ranking for many, many years. There's an additional element in the Netherlands where many mothers, and even fathers, can work part time. Many countries would say, "That's ridiculous! You have to work because then you make more money." But children become more happy when moms or fathers are around more. I've done the same when my children were smaller, and still I'm flexible in my work, and I try to be part of their lives as well. It makes me happy to see my kids grow up and not be in an office — and have children for what? To realize when I'm 60 that I have grandchildren? No. These are my children, and I'm really enjoying life with them. Sometimes we put a burden on ourselves that we have to work, we have to be productive, and maybe that is so, and I'm wrong, but my way does make me happy.

Well, what is the purpose of work? It isn't production for some abstract, mindless reason. The purpose is to provide yourself with a rich and fulfilling and satisfactory life, right?
Hear, hear to that! And I'm very happy that I can add to that for myself and others from a legal perspective.

Now one other element in your really creative life that we haven't talked about and that's TheCrowdversus. Tell me about TheCrowdversus and how that came about.
I will. TheCrowdversus is a very exciting thing as well. What TheCrowdversus does is, it uses modern technology to enable people to stand up for their rights. We started TheCrowdversus as a crowd-funding platform for legal cases around this planet, typically cases of Davids against Goliaths. So we have a case of Mexican organic farmers against the big company of Monsanto. We have a case of a small

group of people living near a natural reserve in South Africa, which is one of the last strongholds for rhinoceros, against a big coal company who wants to dig out coal in that area. And we have a tar sands case at this point. I've already addressed a bit the tar sands and how this is destroying our planet.

We judge the cases before we put them online. I'm not saying that we are the judge over the cases, and I'm not saying that we guarantee that all our cases will be won, but we do make a judgment on the cases. We see so many violations of human rights — environmental, economical and social — that cannot lead to court cases because people do not have the money to go to court. We've said, It's time to empower those people with modern technology, so put those cases online on TheCrowdversus.com and ask for support. If we have 20,000 people that give US$5 to this case or 5 euros, then we can do this case. If we win it, we might even get some of the money back that we can put into another case.

We've made a small change recently with TheCrowdversus, because we saw that crowdfunding itself is really time limited. Normally you would say, "I need to raise funds to make a product. Fund me, and then you'll get your product for this price, and the rest will pay more." But in a court case is more difficult to do that. And it's difficult to share the message to others because you would say, "I just gave US$5 to rhinos against a coal mine in South Africa." That's not something too sexy to share on Facebook — maybe on Twitter — and we really saw that as something that was blocking us. So from the people that ended up on our website, we got, one, a relatively high amount of people donating money and, two, relatively high amounts of money — but somehow the people were not visiting our sites.

And then we said, "Why don't we make this different" and this is also really the voice of today. "Why don't we get people involved in our campaigns?" So yes, you can give money — but there's also an element of participating. So we are now moving into the realm of creating arts around those cases. So now if you look at the website TheCrowdversus.com, you would see new elements — new cartoons that can also be printed on T-shirts and new videos, and music videos, songs and videos that we will actually launch and people can support that song and support that cartoon. And the best cartoon wins a prize, but by sharing the cartoon and the song you also share the message of the case that we crowd-fund for, and we get money in for that. So we now create participation, so we create more consciousness in a bigger group of people and we create, we get the money for the lawsuit. And this is very exciting because it's new and I think it's something that we need.

Like you said, I've been working with environmental human rights defenders for many years. I know I can speak out on this video, but I also know that when I went to Rio+20 in Rio de Janeiro, I returned safe and sound. Two fishermen from a village near Rio de Janeiro never got back home. They were not that loud, but they protested against a violation and interference in their fishing grounds by Petrobras, a big Brazilian oil company — and they were found killed, one tortured, one tied up on the bottom of his fisherman boat. They never got home.

It's for people like them that I think we need to empower the law, to work for people like that. I feel protected, I'm part of the network of the Worldconnectors. People won't just tie me on the bottom of that boat. TheCrowdversus is for the people that do not have a law degree, but that see these human rights violations and need to be protected. Hundreds of people die — I think it's averaging two environmental human rights defenders that die every week, globally. Many are threatened, raped, incarcerated, treated as villains, because they stand up for human rights. We want to empower those people via TheCrowdversus.

And this is, I think a very great way to have to public participation through that. The only thing we say is that we enable this case to go to court, and the judge will rule. We feel confident that the ruling will be good but if it's not, it's not. But if you believe in this case, support it. We're very happy that many celebrities are already behind our scheme as well. Everywhere that we've explained this, they've said, "Wow, this is really a good thing!" The only thing that we have some issues with is traditional media picking this up and actually helping us to get more people, more traffic to the website.

It hasn't been covered much?
No. Somehow the traditional media does not really support us yet. They often say that crowd-funding itself is not new. But crowd-funding for cases based on funda-mental rights is. Some have said, "As soon as you have the first case that can go to court than we will do something on that." So it's the chicken and the egg. How do we get this to be covered? More and more, I think, with our new approach where we want donors to actually feel part of the solution, we are getting there. I'm very proud to be the Board Chair of TheCrowdversus. Many of the things that we're address-ing today are still for some people experimental, or some people would say, "Do we really need this?" Even the right to a healthy environment is still under debate in some countries, where it is a no-brainer and a constitutional right in others.

What do I think will happen in the future? Five years from now we're sitting at this same desk, and I think this element, which is going so fast, of Mother Earth having rights will be much further. Animals having rights will be much further developed. There will be more guardians or ombudspersons for future generations. There's another big campaign — you may have interviewed her as well — with Polly Higgins, the ecocide movement. Ecocide, if it's not there in five years, it will be there in five to ten years. It takes time for these things to change, but it will be in our conscience that intentionally or maliciously destroying nature is a crime, a crime against Nature and against humanity. Those elements will spark up and will grow.

For me there are two scenarios. We either live on this planet in 2100 — so this will be in what is it? Eighty-five years? If I'm still alive by then — probably I will be because technology will change, so maybe we can even have this conversation again. Let's hope so. By that time I see two scenarios: we either live on this planet in a sustainable way, probably with a few billion less than we envisage right now, so we create also this consciousness that we just cannot live on this planet with 20 billion people in the way that we do right now. So ideally we get a little less people, which is an automatic process, which we don't interfere with, and we are on a more sustainable plan.

Or I see scenario B, which is a realistic scenario — we will have gone through many, many global wars, many disasters, climate change disasters, people get killed, refugees come knocking on the doors of the United States and Canada and Europe, people that need water, that need food. That will actually create wars, and we will have a lot less people then.

I opt for option A, which is the positive outcome, and I think we can do this. If we use technology for the benefit of all, and not just for the rich few in the top of the pyramid, we can re-create this planet. If you look at self-driving cars today, there will be self-driving agriculture machines in the future so we can do the planting, the harvesting, everything automated. People will have to work less and we will have food and natural areas because we together say that we need this. So this will be the more social democratic element. If we stay in neo-liberalism or uncontrolled capitalism we're lost, we're doomed as humanity, I really think and feel so. And I think we can have this talk in five years and we can have a positive talk in fifty years. If we really use the enormous energy and positive development in technology on renewables and your own energy storage, on water, on waste water reuse, on desalinization with solar panels and membranes — there are so many promising new technological developments that can and should benefit all of us. Not just the rich or people in more developed countries. No, really, all of us. All members of humanity, including future generations. I could talk about that for hours as well. There's so many that if we really come to the understanding that we are one humanity, with one global common future, and we use knowledge in that way, we can create a prosperous happy future for all.

FEMKE WIJDEKOP
Defender of Those Who Defend the Earth

Recorded November 2015

The Peace Palace in The Hague, in the Netherlands, houses the highest court in the world, the International Court of Justice, also known as the World Court. Across the street is the Institute for Environmental Security. One of the associates of the institute is a remarkable woman named Femke Wijdekop. Femke is a lawyer, an author and a Senior Expert, Environmental Justice, at the International Union for Conservation of Nature, Netherlands. She's a dedicated worker in the movement to have ecocide brought within the jurisdiction of the International Criminal Court — which is also in The Hague — along with such other heinous offences as genocide, war crimes and crimes against humanity. But her particular passion is the defense of environmental defenders, the citizen activists around the world who resist the onslaught of mega corporations bent on destroying established communities, both human and non human, in the naked pursuit of profit. Every week she says, many such environmental defenders are tortured, raped and beaten — and every week, three are murdered.

Femke, is it fair to say that law, up until now, really has been in the service of exploiting the natural world, not protecting it?
Absolutely. The protection is at the margins of the system, you know. But the logic of thinking is still one of seeing the Earth as an object. Our relationship to the Earth is one of ownership. We can exploit unless there are rules that say, this piece of land is protected. But the basic rule is that the Earth is an object and we are the owner. That is the base line.

Which, when you think about it is a very, very odd thing, isn't it? The Earth was here before we were, the Earth will be here after we're gone. How can we be said to own it, when we are actually its creations, and we're temporary?

Femke and I began talking while the camera was being set up, not having formally begun the interview.

Exactly. It's a very recent way of thinking too. The roots can be traced before the industrial revolution, before the age of enlightenment — some people even trace it to Christianity and some Greek philosophers — but I think the worst came with the industrial revolution, when we got the means to actually have this mindset but also put it to use in the world. Actually, it had some feet to it.

I think we've already started our interview.
Yeah, I'm just dabbling you know, warming up.

Let me take you back to a couple of points that you already raised. One of them is that you started out as a lawyer, and then you stopped being a lawyer, and then you became a lawyer again. Tell me about that evolution.
I studied law at the University of Amsterdam, and from law school I went straight to the academic world. I started a PhD on constitutional international law. It was a subject that had my intellectual interest, and it was handed to me. I thought it was interesting and I was quite eager to learn, I love to study. I was 23. But at one point in my life I had some inner changes. The way I looked at the world was changing, and I was wondering what I was really doing with that subject. It was a very specific study subject, as PhD proposals often are, and I didn't see how it would really help to make the world a better place, or what would be its value to society. So in that point of my life, I felt no inner drive to do it. I tried to still do it and add a little bit more of my new thinking into it, but it didn't work because I was still in this narrow research paradigm and that way of thinking, and at that point it didn't have any soul for me. So I decided to stop with it, because I felt I couldn't really defend it and own it.

As a student, I had worked at the American Book Center for some years. That was a lovely place, a big store in the center of Amsterdam. So all of a sudden there was a position free to become the buyer of books on consciousness and spirituality. At that moment it was perfect for me, because I was very much interested in those subjects — about how our own consciousness influences how we act with others and how we engage with the world, the power of our own beliefs etcetera. So I took that position and I spent five happy years there. I also started to host a spiritual book club, to host events and to discuss with others the materials we read. I started to organize book signings with authors and doing interviews also with authors. It was quite easy to have access to national and international authors because we were in touch with the big publishers from the US. And I started to see myself as a communication channel, to communicate information from America and England to mainland Europe, and do that in the field of consciousness and spirituality.

And then, I was doing this radio show called "Samen," which means "together," and we were illuminating all sorts of initiatives in Amsterdam that were contributing to society — initiatives where people felt more connected to each other, that focused more on what we have in common, that focused more on how can we build each other up, how can we realize that we are citizens in one country and in one city. So focus was really on trying to be an agent for good in society and in the world, and we interviewed lots of authors, people who did all sorts of positive things to generate a lot of positive energy. It was great.

At one point a friend of mine told me she had been in London at the Hub — this was the sort of place where you can rent a desk for a small amount of money, and you can work with other entrepreneurs and they will have inspiring speakers or events. And this friend said, I saw Polly Higgins there; she was there with Charles Eisenstein, who was also a very interesting author who writes about sharing economy, sacred economics. My friend said, you should check out this Polly Higgins, because she talks about law in a very new way and she talks about making ecocide a crime against peace, and she says we owe a duty of care towards the Earth. And at first I thought, Wow that sounds really interesting, but also a little bit utopian, even though I was really immersed in all this quite idealistic stuff. But part of me felt maybe a little bit skeptical that something like that could be possible in law.

I checked out Polly's TED talk, and I was like, "Wow, this is really very interesting and it's really rooted in law." It's really making a connection between a more wholistic world view, a world view where we are in relationship with the Earth instead of owning the Earth, a world view where we recognize the Earth has intrinsic value, to how can we do that within the current system? It was really bridging the more ideal world with, how can we get there from where we are right now? It was also showing that this way of thinking is not something new, that actually already in 1970 there were people talking about making ecocide a crime against peace.

It was like something in me shifted, it was as if something in me woke up. I felt excited. I said, If this is what law looks like, I want to be part of the world of law again. I read Polly's book, and then I contacted her team because I wanted to interview her for the radio. We did an interview and she noticed that I was also understanding the legal background. It was a great conversation, and I said, "We've got to invite you to Amsterdam and you should give a workshop here" — because I was also involved in hosting workshops — "and it should be Earth guardian training." I felt, "You have this information that I want to spread it" — but also, what can individual people do? How can individuals become an Earth guardian?

Then I heard about a European team called End Ecocide in Europe. It was started by a German woman called Prisca Merz who once heard Polly Higgins speak about this subject, and she was also triggered and inspired. She was really into the European student movement organization, and connecting European students for certain goals and aspirations. So she said, "We can now organize a European Citizen's Initiative under European Union law." With the Treaty of Lisbon, there was a new provision which said that European citizens can, if they gather one million signatures, they can propose legislation to the European Commission. So Prisca decided to have such an initiative on the subject of ecocide. This office, the Institute for Environmental Security, was the headquarters in the Netherlands for that effort. So that's how I became active with the End Ecocide movement. We had the workshop with Polly Higgins, and then I got connected to this place and I started to do research into this subject of ecocide law and also into the right to a healthy environment and how we could give that hands and feet in law. That's how I got involved in law again.

That's a fascinating mechanism, that the citizens are able to come up with an idea they want to have included ...

It's meant to introduce more direct democracy into the European mechanism. But at the same time the thresholds are quite high, the requirements for people signing up and supporting it quite technical, so with End Ecocide we didn't reach the million votes unfortunately. Out of every five visitors to the petition website, only one signed the petition because, for many countries, you had to fill in your passport number, your ID, and you had to fill in a code to make sure you're not a computer but a human, and people would get error notifications. So the EU wanted more direct democracy, but they didn't make it very easy. That was one of the reasons that the initiative didn't make it to the one million, but at least it was discussed at a commission of the European Parliament, and so European parliamentarians have heard of it.

End Ecocide in Europe later fused into the End Ecocide on Earth movement, with academics and lawyers and doctors and everyone who wanted to join from other countries as well. These people were willing to take this further and to really help raise awareness about the need to make Ecocide a crime — and to lobby politicians, or write academic publications, or do whatever the person, him or herself feels is within his or her reach. People resonate with this idea that the massive damage and destruction of ecosystems should be considered an international crime. The Earth is worth being protected and defended, but right now we cannot do that in the right way because the punishment for destroying ecosystems is not severe enough for the perpetrators — which are often companies, multinationals — to really change their model of making money.

And at this stage it's mostly national too, right? It's not an international crime. It's a national crime, if it's a crime at all.

That's right. Within Europe there is some regulation of environmental crimes

— for wildlife trafficking amongst others, and for some pollution crimes — but that is only a small part of environmental crimes. Ecocide looks at the destruction of ecosystems on a massive scale. But there is no international prohibition of ecocide — and even if you would make a law on the national level, we live in an international, globalized world. So perhaps other foreign companies could still do it on your territory, or your own companies — which is more the case in western Europe — actually cause ecocides in the non-western world. It's an international phenomenon, which needs international regulation.

We should talk about what ecocide is and what it isn't. When I first heard the phrase, I thought, this is the whole thrust of our period, of our time on the Earth. We're committing a massive elimination of life forms globally, and that's what the word must mean. But that's not what you mean when you talk about it in terms of law. You're talking about something that's pretty large, but it's definable right?

An ecocide is massive damage and destruction of an ecosystem which lasts for at least one season — for at least three months — and that has grave impact, and the territory of the ecocide is several hundred miles. Those are the thresholds of the 1976 Environmental Modification Convention, an international treaty prohibiting the military or other hostile use of environmental modification techniques. So what Polly Higgins has done is, she has looked at existing law already outlawing environment damage, and she has used that as an example of the thresholds that needs to be there. You've got to have that in law. Otherwise it creates a situation of legal uncertainty. As a principle of legality you've got to know what conduct is permissible and what is prohibited. Examples of ecocides are the Chevron oil spill in Ecuador or the Deep Horizon oil spill in the Gulf of Mexico or the Niger Delta oil spill in Nigeria or many people would say that fracking, which causes pollution of the ground and groundwater and the atmosphere on massive scales, are examples of ecocide. Or the Fukushima nuclear disaster, or overfishing of the oceans, where the fish stock is completely gone. So you have to really think of major environmental disasters.

We have one of those in our part of Canada and that's the virtual destruction of the cod stocks. One of the great fisheries of the world is now basically gone, and nothing has happened. Forty thousand people have lost their jobs, entire communities have closed down, and nobody has been held responsible — but that was done all by human agency and under human supervision.

Right, that's the problem with the legal system as it is. It doesn't offer real protection for massive infringement of the natural world. Those infringements also affect human rights — the human right to employment, for example. Often these ecocides affect the human right to health, the human right to life, and people have to be displaced because their territory is gone. There is a real connection between destruction of the environment and us destroying our own health and our own well-being. And the interests of the people, especially the people who are the first to face those kinds of disasters, are often Indigenous peoples. The interests of the Earth and the animals are not represented in law as they should be. They don't have enough voice, and ecocide law is a proposal which aims to give a voice to those interests. And there are other proposals too, like the wild law movement, like the movement to give rights to Mother Earth as the Global Alliance for the Rights of Nature does.

So I see these as expressions of a consciousness that understands that Nature has intrinsic worth and value, and that law is an instrument to give expression to interests that are worth protecting, that should have a voice in our political system and in our society. Now you see people standing up, lawyers standing up, that want to give voice to those interests. That's what Roger Cox did when he started the climate case, saying that the Dutch state had a duty of care to lower CO_2 emissions in relation to climate change. He was representing the interests of the Dutch — and, of course, the global citizens, because this affects all of us — but also thinking about future generations. What are we leaving to our children's children? What are we leaving for future generations? So it's coming from a broader view of what are we doing, who is it affecting, and who needs guardians. The Earth needs a guardian, and future generations need guardians. So in my view this is all very connected, all these different lawyers speaking up in different ways.

We've seen the globalization of the economy. Are we now seeing a matching globalization of conscience and awareness?
Yeah, I see it that way, for sure. My own interest in consciousness, spirituality — that was all, for me, about realization. We are interconnected beings, you know? We are part of one organism, which is the Earth, and this is reflected back in this initiative to make ecocide a crime, and this initiative to give rights to Nature. These ideas sprout everywhere around the world. I was just talking to a recent member of our End Ecocide team and he said, You know, years ago me and a friend of mine, we discussed this. And we said, Mother Earth should have rights too; we should not only have a Universal Declaration of the Rights of Man, but also of the Rights of the Earth. And I said, "Wow! And at the same time Cormac Cullinan in South Africa was thinking the same, and Mumta Ito was also realizing the same." Ideas whose time have come, they sprout into minds that are receptive, that are open for inspiration and willing to be a solution to the problems we see.

That's a theme in your life too — you're really interested in how ideas like this spread.
Absolutely.

What's the process? You have a good example at the moment with a television show,
right? Tell me about that.

I'd love to. When I joined the End Ecocide in Europe team, another Dutch
woman whose name is [Katie Olivia], joined us too. She immediately resonated
with the whole idea, and we became friends and colleagues. She was there at the
Earth Guardians workshop with Polly Higgins, and quite quickly she thought,
this subject has to be the topic of a show of the TV program *Tegenlicht*, which
means "Backlight." It's a TV show that really gives the stage to progressive ideas,
that presents solutions to the problems in the world — the economic problems,
the environmental problems. It's a very high quality program that reaches a lot of
people, and it combines good research with a creative outlook, and also focuses
on solutions. Katie accidentally met a director of this show, and she pitched the
idea. She said to him, "Isn't that a great idea if you would follow Polly Higgins work
to get ecocide on the international agenda?" At first he had to think about it, but
after some effort — and she can insist quite a lot — he actually said, "Well, this is
interesting; let me look in to it."

Then he says, "Yes I want to do it. This is really a topic of these times. How
does that work? One woman got a great idea, people feel that she's right but yet the
system seems to be so opposite of all the values she's promoting. How does that
work with contacting politicians? How does a movement like that happen? What
does it take for heads of state to say, I want to take it further?"

After she pitched him the idea, the researcher of this program contacted me,
and I gave him a lot of background information. And last week, one week ago, they
broadcast that television show, and it was very well received. It was beautifully done;
it really captured the essence of this idea. We have a Green Party in Parliament —
it's called the Animal Party, but it's a party that looks at environmental issues in
the broadest sense and also at human issues — and I'm sure they have seen the
program. They've heard of ecocide law before, but at that moment they felt ready
to actually address this in Parliament. There is a new member from that party who
had his maiden speech in Parliament last week. They were talking to the Minister
of Foreign Affairs, and he addressed this topic, "What does the Minister think
of ecocide law? Does the Minister think it should be prohibited that states and
companies destroy the environment on a massive scale?" He said that we think it
should, and we would like an answer — and if the Minister doesn't answer or agree,
we might raise this as a topic for official voting in Parliament.

This is only one example of how this TV broadcast contributed to this topic
being put on the political agenda. It was a topic of discussion in an audience of
public opinion, but also in that atmosphere the politician felt there was enough

momentum for it to be put on the political agenda. This would not have happened, if you trace back the events, if my friend had never felt brave enough to talk to the director and to insist, because she believed in it. Then the program wouldn't be there, and 200,000 or 300,000 people wouldn't have learned about it.

Maybe it would have come in another way, but it just demonstrates that when you feel so alive, when you learn a new idea, when you feel so taken by it, it makes your heart open and also it makes sense to your mind — if you act upon it, things can happen that go beyond your expectations. Things can happen that can affect change in a bigger way. I really believe in that. I've seen it happen with my life, with Polly's life, with a lot of the people who are involved in this.

Well, if you start with Polly and start tracing the chain of events from there, there's a direct line right from her to this discussion in the Parliament of the Netherlands, isn't there?
This is just the example of the Netherlands, but this is happening in Sweden too. The Green Party now has officially adopted a motion supporting the prohibition of ecocide. The End Ecocide on Earth group also presented an ecocide proposal to the French President, Hollande, discussed it with him, and to the UN Secretary General Ban Ki-moon, and with other politicians. Also the Austrian Green Party has proposed a motion to the Austrian parliament to support a law of ecocide. All these things are contributing to increasing the gravity for this topic to be taken seriously, if we're waiting for governments to take the step to publicly internationally support it.

One national government somewhere needs to take this up? Is that the next step?
Yes, because the aim of this campaign is to make ecocide a crime against humanity under the *Rome Statute*, which is the Treaty of the International Criminal Court, which is located here in The Hague. For that to happen one state has to propose this as an amendment to the *Rome Statute* and then two-thirds of the parties have to agree for it to become an amendment. But the first step is to really officially have it presented. This week, the yearly assembly of the member states of the International Criminal Court is taking place in The Hague — so this is quite an exciting time for us, because we're trying to make that happen.

So the process would be that a state proposes this as an amendment; it becomes a subject of discussion and debate, and finally perhaps it gets adopted. Then it's part of the constitution of the European Union?
No, because the International Criminal Court is an international body. It's not just European, it's international. Canada is part of the ICC too. I think 123 countries are member states of the International Criminal Court.

So it's a global thing. Some states are not party to it but most are.
Yes. Of course, some states that you would want to have on board are not party to it,

but at the same time we think this is a good start. The crimes that the International Criminal Court can prosecute are the worst crimes that exist — genocide, war crimes, crimes of aggression, crimes against humanity. Ecocide was actually meant to be part of the *Rome Statute,* but it was removed from the draft Treaty text in the 1990s. We have a provision that environmental damage and destruction is prohibited under war crimes — but the thresholds are very high, and it's only in war times, and it's only directed at states. It doesn't cover ecocides caused by multinationals, for example. In reality ecocide is more often caused by companies than it is by states. But states can also be perpetrators, and also complicit, because they allow for it to happen or they profit by economic activities that make a lot of money, but at the expense of the environment.

What state is going to bring it forward under the Rome Statute?
Well, there are several options, and of course I don't know. The Small Island Developing States are the ones that are faced with the imminent effects of climate change, the rising sea levels, the risk of losing their territory entirely by climate change. So they would have a lot to gain if ecocide — and large scale climate crime is also ecocide — if that becomes prohibited, and if states would have an international obligation to assist them when they are faced with such ecocides. When they are confronted with losing their territory, they need assistance for immigration actually to other countries. That's part of the idea of ecocide as a climate crime — that states would have a duty of care to assist other territories who need to take emergency measures because of ecocides. Another possible candidate to propose the ecocide amendment is the DRC — Democratic Republic of Congo.

It's a concrete embodiment of the idea that we are a single human family.
Exactly. You often have these pictures of forests where you see trees and they all are separate trees — but underneath the roots are entwined. Ecocide thinking is the same kind of thinking. We are all affected by what we do to our planet, and we will all feel the consequences. The long-term consequences of human behaviour particularly affect those who have done little to contribute to pollution, who actually often live more in harmony with the Earth than many of us. It means taking responsibility for the effects of a world view — the world view I think is the main problem, that we are disconnected from Nature in our thinking and acting. Ecocide says we are connected to Nature, we are part of Nature, we are a huge part of the problem, and we can be part of the solution.

People who get this want to be part of the solution. I want to be part of the solution! I love that I can use my legal skills and communication experience to play my part. The story of that TV program and the effect it had on people and on lawyers and intellectuals and artists and on politicians is a great example, because

I think maybe the biggest problem is that we feel we have no power. We feel disempowered and hopeless in the face of those big injustices, but we have influence, and if we combine our thinking, we can make a big thing happen. That's the good side of how we are connected. We are part of a bigger whole that does make a difference. Today I just read, "I cannot do all the good that the Earth needs but the Earth needs all the good I can do." I really love that because that just says it all. It's not an excuse to say I cannot do it all so I will do nothing. No. You have to do what you have to do.

And that brings us back to the Urgenda case. Wasn't that exactly the position that the government took? "Look we're a tiny piece of the problem, and there's no point in us trying to take that level of responsibility," and the court saying, "You may be a small piece, but you are a piece."

Exactly, that's right. The court said, "You have a responsibility to address your own contribution to the big problem." In building that case, Roger Cox, the Urgenda attorney, was also quoting jurisprudence from the United States. I think the case was EPA vs. Massachusetts, in which the American courts said that you have a partial responsibility for your part in polluting the environment. So even in preparing that case Roger Cox was using information from other parts of the globe. The fact that we could become co-litigants in that case — I became a co-litigant — this case was set up in a very inclusive way. It had to be a case of the people. They also used social media in a great way. They said, "We'll do this through crowd-funding, but we will also want to crowd-litigate. If you have good arguments, if you have information, please share it with us. It can help us build the case."

Using the collective intelligence of the people to present this case on behalf of the collective — I really loved it. And I really love it that they translated everything in English, the summons and all their paperwork — a thousand pages of preparation, in English — and they just give it for free to other organizations in the world who want to start similar cases. If we have that on our side, that kind of thinking, that kind of collaboration and creativity, that intelligence is bigger than the greedy intelligence it wants to destroy

I have the impression that the people involved with that case were quite aware that, if they won, it would make a worldwide ripple.

Yeah I think so. For me it was something that I thought, "Wow! Okay, I will join that." It was very wonderful, I was proud that they were doing it, but I didn't dare to think beyond the verdict. Even though I so much believe in the reasoning behind it, I was very surprised that we won. It was a big break in the usual thinking of the courts that they dare to interpret the duty of care in such an extensive way. I was there that day in court and you know, maybe there were 150 people, and there were some camera crews, like yours. We didn't realize that it would be broadcast on BBC and on Al Jazeera and everywhere around the world! That was an amazing moment — and I read yesterday that in American a group of kids also won a climate case.

They won? I knew they were bringing a case, but I didn't know...
They won! It was in a Washington court, and the judge said that the state has a public trust obligation and a constitutional obligation to make sure that we have a right to a clean and healthy environment and that the atmosphere is protected. It was public-trust reasoning and constitutional duty of the state to think longer-term on behalf of future generations. It just happened the day before yesterday.

That's huge! I knew about the case, but I didn't realize that there was a decision yet.
My friend from the US just texted me and she told me. Of course you can always look at the instances in which they lose. There are many politicians who don't want to endorse this, but I feel that it's so important to pay attention to what works — and to really learn from what doesn't work — but especially to build on what does work, and to also tell others. So I told Jan van de Venis, who you just interviewed as well, and many others. They got really excited and they are sharing it — because this just gives hope to everyone you know? And for us, as part of Urgenda case, it's very endearing that people really got hopeful after what we did.

You made the comment about the ineffectiveness of the political process. That's maybe one of the most exciting things about all of this, is that the legal process basically goes back beyond today's politics to the principles on which the society is founded, and says "According to those root documents, according to that understanding of who we are as a people, you have to do something about this issue, even though it may be politically unpopular." And that is a huge change in consciousness.
I would say so. You never know why it happened. I do think that the more climate case victories there are, and the more people who talk from this more integrated perspective, the more it affects the collective thinking of the people, and this is part of our times. Law is also a body that is embedded in society. It's not separated from the consciousness, it is an expression of the consciousness. It can regulate the consciousness, but it is embodied in it, it has its roots in it, and in the end it has to reflect changes in thinking in society. It always has.

I've heard it described as the DNA of society, the embedded instructions for how things unfold.
It's a very important framework for connection, and for what do we value. Criminal law really shows which values we hold so dear that they have to be protected by criminal enforcement. But sometimes the crimes that make it into the criminal code are not the ones that are the worst attacks on society. Certain lobby groups

have a lot of power. They can make their own interests heard, and protected, and represented. A lot of this is about, How can we make the voices heard of those who still have less power, or who cannot speak for themselves? The whole idea of the Alliance for the Rights of Nature is that we have to be the guardians for the natural world because the natural world can not speak for itself. But we are embedded in it; it's impossible to have a legal system disconnected from the natural laws and still function and still be sustainable. It's impossible because we are totally dependent on the natural world. So we're all trying to harmonize, in our own specific way.

You've just touched on another of your great passions, which is the defense of the defenders, the environmental defenders. Tell me about your work in that area.
Those people that are standing up and are defending the Earth, that are defending the integrity of ecosystems — we call them environmental defenders. A British-based NGO called Global Witness has done a lot to put their work on the international agenda. Unfortunately it is very dangerous for environmental defenders — especially in countries that are rich in natural resources — to do their work. By protecting the right to a clean and healthy environment, and the right to life, and the right to family life, they are often coming against the interests of big extractive corporations that want to use those resources for profit. So these environmental defenders, they are facing a Goliath kind of opponent and they are the little Davids.

They are speaking out on behalf of other people too. Often they are the ones who first notice the effects of this extractive system, because they often belong to communities that are small-scale farmers and fishers and that live in a more harmonious way with the Earth. Those people are the first to feel the effects of our system that treats the Earth as property, as a commodity — but when they speak up they are faced with these forces that really don't want to stop these operations. So what we see is a very dangerous activity. It's really crazy that the people who are actually A+ citizens of a country , because they actually stand up to protect the environment — which the state should do, as a duty to take care of its inhabitants and its territory — environmental defenders are the ones who take that state function. But the effect of their work is, they get intimidated, they get harassed, they get killed.

According to the latest report of Global Witness, "On Dangerous Ground," three environmental defenders every week are killed. The real number is much higher. These reports don't cover many African countries because they can't get enough information. And of course they can only rely upon the official police records, and upon media coverage of such events, which can be biased. So we see that the system is crushing the people that are a voice on behalf of their community and on behalf of their ecosystems. So what is essential is that they are protected to do their work, that we defend those who defend the Earth.

And the problem, as you've pointed out, is enormous. We're talking about really violent repression of people who dare to speak up — torture, rape, beatings, murder.

Totally. Absolutely. And of course what does this do to community, if you see people get killed because of standing up, protecting the environment? And also of course protecting their livelihoods, and their way of living, and their values as a community. And then you force people into submission, or into giving up — because who is brave enough to do that? But still people do it, still they do it.

So how do you defend them?

That's a big question, and I think you can answer that from a more civil society perspective. You see NGOs actually acting in solidarity with these environmental defenders. You see Greenpeace paying more attention to this problem, and Amnesty realizing that environmental defenders are human rights defenders — because they defend also the human right to health, to life, to freedom of expression and everything.

So part of the answer is by really giving public attention to the fate of environmental defenders. If there is an environmental defender under threat, you have mechanisms for a massive outpouring of support, like Amnesty tends to do with human rights defenders. You say to a country, This is someone who is threatened by human rights violations, and we are aware of this; we call upon you to act, and to honour your obligations in international law. Public opinion, pressure and naming and shaming can have a real effect on the personal safety of those environmental defenders. I would like that to become bigger. I would like this to become more on the conscience of people, that these people need our solidarity and support.

I now work at IUCN Netherlands as the Senior Expert, Environmental Justice for their new project Defending Environmental Defenders, a collaborative project together with Friends of the Earth International and Global Witness. Raising awareness of the plight of environmental defenders is an important element of our work. At the same time, we are also developing practical tools like security training (both digital and physical security) for environmental defenders, creating networks of legal support — so-called legal 'help desks' — and creating an emergency fund in case of acute threats. Another important part of my work is promoting the international recognition that environmental defenders are human rights defenders, and that they need to be protected under international law.

In that regard, increasingly you see that, for example, the Special Rapporteur on Human Rights and the Environment and a Special Rapporteur on Indigenous Rights — which are UN agents — and the Committee for Economic Social and Cultural Rights and even the Human Rights Committee are saying that the states have a duty to protect environmental defenders under international human rights law. Under the Universal Declaration of Human Rights, and under the International Covenant on Civil and Political Rights, we have the right of expression, we have the right of assembly, we have the right of association — and environmental defenders exercise those rights on behalf of the environment. They use these political rights to give expression to their concern about the environment — and states have the duty to protect them when they exercise those rights, and to provide an enabling environment for them to exercise those rights, and to investigate cases when environmental defenders are harassed, when their human rights are violated, when they are murdered. So we see UN bodies actually speaking up and saying there is an obligation under law, under international law for states to protect them.

And this is a growing development?
A growing development, yes. I think for a long time the international community wasn't aware that environmental defenders are facing so much violence. It had to come to their attention, and it had to be recognized that they are human rights defenders. Unfortunately, the murder of Berta Cáceres, an Honduran environmental activist, was one of the events that brought the need to protect environmental defenders to the awareness of UN bodies this year. It often takes a catastrophe to bring something to the awareness of the international community.

Framing the protection of environmental defenders as a human rights issue helps to draw in the support of international human rights law, and also makes it clear what kind of obligations the states have. Of course, having those obligations, and having special rapporteurs reporting on them is one thing, and states actually doing it is another. So it's always, how can we enforce those obligations? And that has to do with economic systems, with power relationships, etcetera.

I feel very strongly that the role that we individuals can play in this is very important. If I campaign to make ecocide a crime, that's also connected to environmental defenders, because they are often ecocide whistle-blowers. If ecocide becomes a crime, it becomes illegal for companies to make money in a way that causes an ecocide, and this will greatly help environmental defenders in their causes, because they are confronted with the effects of ecocides or very big scale environmental pollution and destruction. So in that sense it is connected to our ecocide campaign. It's connected to the people who work for rights of Nature.

We're back to the interlinking roots.
Absolutely.

Are there particular stories about environmental defenders that you have strong feelings about? Are there examples you would want to share?
Let me think. Well, in my TEDx talk, I talk about a farmer called Indra Pelani from

Indonesia, who was killed — probably by security forces — for defending the rights of farmers against the corporate takeover of their lands. He was just 22 years old and because of circumstances he found himself becoming an environmental defender. Environmental defenders are often just living their lives, but they're faced with these encroachments upon their community, their livelihoods, and their way of living, so they're forced by the facts to become defenders. It's often not a planned thing. So he started to raise awareness. He was part of an alliance of farmers and he was trying to ring the alarm and then he was killed. He was just 22 and he was just trying to protect the interests of his community. If you see his photo, you read the background, you're like, "Wow! It's a person who was working for the well being of the people, and he was killed." There was no prosecution, there was no real police investigation — and this is of course not acceptable at all that a human life is sacrificed for monetary interests.

I can work on this issue in peace and quiet, you know? I can write about this, I can talk on TV or on your website about this without any threats to my well-being and health. I like to remind myself that I have a privilege that I can do this also on behalf of others for whom it's very dangerous. I can only do my small bit, but together if we raise the awareness, it can change our thinking. And also, when we buy products, we have to become aware of the environmental costs and societal costs of what we consume. In the end it's all to feed the consumer market.

Which is us.
Which is us.

Something that we have in common, you as a Dutch person and me as a Canadian, is that our countries are responsible for quite a lot of this activity in the Third World. The normal villain in an environmental horror story in South America is a Canadian mining company. You've got similar international corporations headquartered here in this small country. What can we do in our own countries to help people who are suffering from the actions of our companies in their countries?
Well, several things — but certainly to put pressure on our politicians, on our representatives, to say that the rules of behaviour that those corporations have to follow when they operate in our country, when they deal with our Dutch citizens, those standards should also apply when they operate abroad. Companies have to respect universal human rights. They should use the same standards of behaviour when they operate abroad. They will not pollute our rivers on that massive scale, because they can not get away with it. How can it be that they can get away with it in other countries? Is life less valuable there than it is here?

The answer, I'm afraid, would be "yes."

That is the unacceptable reality. But our country has legislation in place by which these companies have to abide, and they should honour the rights of human rights defenders. The Human Rights Committee just recently, in March 2016, issued a resolution which calls upon both states and companies to honor their obligation under international law to respect the human rights of human rights and environmental and land defenders everywhere in the world. These obligations should not only be corporate social responsibility or soft law; there should be more hard law in place. So I think we must put pressure on our politicians to take a stand on ecocide. What do they think about it? If they are against it why are they against it? Give reasons.

How can you not be against massive damage and destruction of the environment? How can you argue that? I think another way is to join NGOs that are protecting the rights of human rights defenders, and be part of those petitions, be part of those solidarity campaigns. When the Dutch Greenpeace crew was arrested in Russia because they they boarded an oil rig — the Arctic 30 they are called — there was a huge campaign to support them and to urge the Russian government to release them. In the end, they were released. It was very professionally set up by Greenpeace of course — and I think the people who are suffering the most often don't have that organizational capacity, and they are not as well represented. They need better representation. They need more of our support. And that's what we are trying to do with our project Defending Environmental Defenders at IUCN Netherlands.

One of the big problems for a lot of these folks is that nobody knows about them. It's all happening silently in some remote place, and there's no media coverage. And, as you said of the Indonesian farmer, he didn't go seeking the problem, the problem came to him.
Exactly, but what we do see also with this global world, with the power of social media, we have so much information available. People that work at such NGO's often get alerts that something happened or something is about to happen. They get it instantly, and then they can mobilize their networks. Using satellites to mobilize is part of the globalized world we live in.

I think that everything counts — what you consume, the choices you make, how you vote. But also as consumers, we have huge power in how we invest our money. Which bank? Does our bank enable ecocides? Does our bank enable dirty energy, or does it invest in renewable energy? Of course the divestment movement is huge, it's really gaining ground, and it's using that argument to help shift towards a more sustainable economic system.

With the climate case we have this victorious moment. It was wonderful and the effects have been very positive, ripples of hope and inspiration around the world. A similar case has started in Belgium and in other countries too — in

France, for example. But the Dutch state has appealed because it thinks the judge overstepped his authority with his ruling. It was too political. It was too extensive an interpretation of the articles, so the Dutch state is appealing against the climate case. Until we have a decision from an appeal court, this verdict is valid. It's in place, so it should be acted upon.

But the Dutch state says, "Well, what we're going to do is we'll have a committee look at it — in 2016 probably." Then they will look at if we should do something, what we should do, how we could lower the emissions, if it's feasible, what about the economic risks, etcetera. In short, they are not really acting upon it right now. Then it's about the balance of powers, the Trias Politica *[separation of powers — ed.]* so the judiciary is here, but the executive branch of government is there, and what is the real authority of this verdict? So that is a very interesting subject, especially for political scientists and constitutional lawyers.

At the same time the verdict is there. There will be an appeal and they will have again a presentation of their arguments in court. The Dutch state didn't oppose the Urgenda's presented facts. It didn't oppose the information about the CO_2 emissions — that it needs to be lower, that we need to not go above the two degrees threshold. It didn't oppose those; it actually agreed that it's happening and that it's needed. The Dutch state itself has promised that it would do more, and a couple of years back it has said it's urgent — but it's not acting upon its own promises. I don't know if it's an answer to your question, but you asked about the enforcement of the rules, and the verdict. Of course that is the big issue. We have to wait for a Supreme Court decision, ultimately, to know what is the real ruling. But that takes years, and the whole problem is, we don't have that time. Really, that's the whole problem. They're taking a route now that will take many more years.

Since they didn't argue the facts, they didn't argue that the situation was as the Urgenda case described it, basically what they're saying, I guess, is, We agree that this is true, but we don't think that the court has the authority to direct us to do something about it.
That's right. They said that the court was treading on the field of politics, that this was a political issue and that the court should apply the law, interpret the law, but it should not make law. So they said the judges are acting too much as a legislator by telling us what we should do about this problem — and this is not the authority that they have, because we are the representatives of the people, and our legitimacy derives from the votes of the people. The judges are appointed here, so they have no democratic legitimacy, as we call it. But of course the judge is there to uphold the rule of law and to apply the law, and to make the legislation and the policy of the state align with the rules that we have, and our international commitments and treaties, with everything that is so-called hard law.

Roger Cox did a wonderful job in arguing that there is an existing obligation under hard law, under tort law, for a duty of care towards current and future generations with regards to CO2 emissions. That is of course what the state's attorneys were arguing with. They say there is not such a hard law, such a hard-core obligation. Urgenda said that there is, and they built their case very well.

It's interesting that just before the verdict of Urgenda, an international panel of highly esteemed judges and lawyers including the Attorney General of the Dutch Supreme Court, Jaap Spier, issued principles basically saying that there is a hard-law obligation under international law for states to lower their CO2 emissions and that states do have a duty of care with regards to the atmosphere. They said there is such a legal obligation under existing law. It's not futuristic, it's there. So this gave huge support for Urgenda's legal reasoning. This is also the power of the collective; they dropped that just two weeks before the verdict.

Would the response to the government's position not be to say that there is a theatre in which politics reigns, but there are limits to that? That's what rights are about. Just because you've won an election, you may not infringe human rights, infringe the basic values of the society.
Exactly, that is the whole reasoning. This political freedom to make the laws of the land, this democratic legitimacy they have in a rule of-law system, is limited by the fundamental rights and freedoms of humans. Those cannot be sacrificed to the will of the majority, because they are human rights. They are fundamental rights — and the right to health, or the right to life for sure is one of them. The judge is the one to uphold that framework, to ensure that the will of the majority doesn't violate those rights. So it's very much a human rights issue.

It's hard to see how you could argue too strongly with that, but on the other hand ...
I think it's all about how extensively or restrictively a judge can interpret provisions in the civil code. The judge just has to apply law, but he interprets law when he does so. What we've seen is that often judges interpret restrictively, so they are conservative in their interpretation of legal terms and words. What is duty of care? What does it entail? That's the whole question. What this court did — which was a surprise to me — is they dared to interpret more extensively; they dared to take the whole body of international human rights law and the interests of future generations and they managed to read that into the provision — or to have that inform the provision — of the duty of care. The existing case law about this duty of care — they applied that to the subject of the atmosphere, but I think quite well, with a good foundation, with good arguments. It came close to judicial activism. And the state says, "Well, this was overstepping the boundary."

It's an interesting question isn't it? This is the way the law responds to completely chang-ing circumstances.

I think lawyers in general are quite a conservative breed of people, willing to listen to authority. To have authorities' arguments is very important for lawyers. But law has to be in relationship with the reality of the world we live in, with emergent realities and emergencies, if it wants to be responsive to what is needed, if it wants to really protect human rights. Otherwise it just becomes a paper tiger that offers no real protection from the worst threats of our lives. That's impossible, because it's still in the service of mankind. It's something that should serve us, to live together more peacefully, harmoniously, safely.

MARJAN MINNESMA

Risk-taking for a New Sustainable Society

Recorded November 2015

Marjan Minnesma is the founder and director of the Urgenda Foundation in Amsterdam, which sued the Dutch state for its tepid record on greenhouse gas emissions. Urgenda was joined in the case by 900 citizens as co-plaintiffs in what Marjan describes as "crowd-pleading." It won a court order directing the government to reduce the country's emissions by 25 percent by the year 2020, and the impact of that success has rippled around the world.

On three occasions Marjan has been named the greenest, most influential entrepreneur in the Netherlands. Entrepreneur? Well, yes. Marjan has studied business management, law and philosophy and has worked at Royal Dutch Shell and Greenpeace, whose world headquarters is in Amsterdam, as well for the government and at universities. Unlike most foundations Urgenda doesn't rely on endowments or contributions; it relies mostly on the profits it makes from its activities, which it then plows back into the expansion of its environmental work. It advocates a circular economy where products are not necessarily owned but are leased and then returned to their manufacturers. It promotes sustainable activities in energy, transportation, food production, industry, and construction, and it believes that the Netherlands can be completely converted to renewable energy by 2030.

We caught up with Marjan in Noyon, France where she and a group of fellow activists were stopping between Utrecht and Paris. They were walking to Paris for the COP 21 climate change talks.

We are walking from Utrecht in the middle of the Netherlands to Paris, so that's more than 600 kilometers. We're walking the whole month of November to end there just before the Conference of the Parties starts, of the climate change treaty.

And it's a very carefully planned walk. You're touching on railway stations very frequently, and the number of people changes. Tell me a little about the planning — because it's not just a group of people getting together.

No, it's a major operation. We started in Utrecht with more than 500 people and in the whole first week we were walking through the Netherlands and there were every day 200 people, but every day there's new people coming and going, so we see thousands of people during the whole trip. We have arranged through the whole day a coffee break, a lunch, a tea break and a hotel, and we walk, as much as possible, from station to station so that people can hop on and off. Every day there's a new group, so every day you meet other people. It's a very broad social justice movement, so there's farmers but also teachers and people from local energy corporations, people from very big companies like Unilever and the Dutch national railway organization. It's a very big movement of both business, citizens and NGOs — and they all want that we make a quicker move towards a whole renewable energy society. No fossil fuels any more and only sun, wind and a few other sources. That's what this whole group wants. It's not just an environmental movement any more. It's a bigger social justice movement. We just want a new economy.

If you've got large corporations actually participating, that's quite a change, isn't it?
Yeah, I think 20 years ago that didn't really happen, but now this week someone from IKEA is walking with us and someone from a big grocery chain in the Netherlands is walking with us. It's a whole different group — people from the building sector, people from the mobility sector, so they all can make the switch, and we can all make the change to having energy-neutral or even energy-positive houses. We can drive electrically and so on. It's about building a new society, and it's not only about end of pipe solutions — that's also, I think, a switch if you compare it to 20 years ago.

It's a big switch — and you also designed this walk very carefully for the maximum impact, right? You have a show on Dutch TV every night?
Well, when I invented this at the beginning of this year, I just told my colleagues I want to walk to the conference of the parties [COP 21] the full month of November, and we didn't know yet that the Dutch TV would be willing to join us. So five months later, something like that, I had a conversation with the Dutch TV. I told them that I was going to walk to Paris and they said, "That's interesting" — and now they're following us and have a five-minute, a kind of a little show on TV that shows what we're doing. So they show us walking and they have some conversations with the people that are in our group. And every day it's another group, so every day they have all the people on TV, and it shows also for the Dutch people at home how broad this movement is.

It's like a continuing story that they can tune in every night. Where are they now and what's going on?
Yeah, and it's about mobility — but also about a Dutch designer who makes clothes in a more sustainable way, and about what we call a vegetarian butcher that makes

meat out of soy and other products, so they get the full range of what you can do if you want to move to a new society.

This is a wonderful use of resources, to cover so much at the same time.
We're very happy with it.

And it levers what you're doing. The awareness that's being built from this must be quite considerable.
Yeah, because every day there are 600,000, up to even a million people watching the show. We have about 17 million people in the Netherlands, so that's a very large proportion. Therefore, I think we now really are heading for more mainstream attention, and that's very good.

Let me turn our attention to what I've been calling Urgenda, but which, the real name is UrgHENda [Dutch pronunciation]. Am I getting close to right with that?
Yeah, well in English I would also say Urgenda, because it's a mix of "urgent" and "agenda," so in English we would probably say Urgenda, but we say UrgHENnda [Dutch pronunciation].

I'm trying to learn to say it properly. So you founded UrgHENnda. How did that happen, and why?
I worked together with Professor Rotmans, who was here yesterday to walk with us. We were leading an Institute for Transitions towards a sustainable society at the Erasmus University in Rotterdam, and we had a big program with 40 PhD students who all wrote books. And in the end I said, "Nice, all those books — but what are we really changing in society?" I challenged him a bit, and then he came up with the idea, okay, let's make this "urgent agenda" and have a vision for the future but also an action plan per year. Then we described it in a big newspaper article — and it became very big article with a front page part in a very good newspaper. So we had thousands of reactions of people that said, "Wow, are you really going to do this then? Because it's a nice Urgenda, but who's going to do it?" And then we felt challenged and we decided to make the Foundation Urgenda and to do what we wrote down in this newspaper article. That's how we started and in the beginning we were both working at the university and doing Urgenda on the side, so 40 hours one and 40 hours the other, but Urgenda became so big that at a certain point I said, "Well I'm going to quit the university and going to lead the Urgenda and see what we can do."

So you called for something to be done and then found that you were the one who had to do it?
[LAUGHTER] That's what often happens!

Absolutely. So what are the objectives of Urgenda?
Well, we started with a broader agenda, but I brought it down a bit. I want to go to a 100 percent renewable energy society in 2030, so we made a book last year in which we described how could you make this switch within about 15 years. It means that you make all houses energy-neutral, and that you drive electrically, and that industry uses less energy and tries to move to renewables, and that you eat differently, less meat and more from the season and more from the region. And if you do all these things together then it is possible to reduce the energy by 50 percent, and what you still need you can do with solar power, wind power and a couple of other solutions.

We described exactly how this pathway could happen towards 2030 and also what it would cost, and it would be about 1.5 percent of our gross national product, which is a lot of money, but it's only 1.5 percent. We currently spend 2.5 percent on oil and nobody knows it. So for a very rich country like the Netherlands — which is amongst the five most rich countries in the world and people are very happy here; we have nothing to complain — this is an amount that you can really still afford.

We're not saying that the Dutch government should spend this money, but that people together are going to do this. It will be both people making their own house energy neutral, driving electric cars, spending money on more sustainable products — and also the government, that tries to help this process, and the industry that makes the switch to two percent reduction of energy per year, year after year. If everybody takes their own part then we together spend the 1.5 percent and that's something we can afford.

So your role is what, education, promotion, convincing people?
No, we have a very broad role. We are on the one hand entrepreneurs, so a few years ago we did the first joint collective buying action of solar panels in Europe. I bought 50,000 solar panels and the inverters and everything needed to put it on your roof. That was a 20 million euros project, but I bought the solar panels straight from China, and if the boat with the panels would strike an iceberg I would lose my house — so I was really the entrepreneur in that case. And because we bought 50,000 at one time, we brought the whole price of the whole system down by one-third compared to the market price at that time.

We also introduced, together with a partner, an electric vehicle that was at that time produced in Norway. We sold it to a couple of Dutch cities and they thought, "Oh, now we have electric cars," so we should create charging points, so then that market started to roll.

And then when other entrepreneurs come in, we move out and do the next thing. At the moment we are making houses energy-positive for around 35,000 euros. This is the amount that an average Dutch family spends on energy in 15 years. So if you would take 15 years and you spend 35,000 euros on energy, then you could bring that amount forward and make your house energy-neutral — which means that you don't have an energy bill anymore. Then you pay it off in 15 years time. It's the same amount, so you don't have extra costs, but you do have a house without any fossil fuels — and after 15 years it's yours, and you have a house without an energy bill.

So we are in that case the entrepreneur but also the ones who show that it's possible, because very often if I propose something like that, they say, "Yeah, you can say that, but that's not true." So you really have to do it before people start believing you. The same [is true] with the electric cars. They were in Norway already for years, and we thought for many reasons that it was not possible, or not good enough, or whatever, until you just buy them and sell them, and show that it is possible. And then people see them driving, and they make no noise, and they think, "Oh that's funny," and then it starts to run.

But only talking is not enough. I also give almost 200 speeches a year in all kinds of different audiences, day or night, but that's — I would say — something on the side. I prefer, myself, to start projects and to really get things off the ground. But we're also trying to influence both governments and others. For the energy-neutral houses, we have a very small group who prepared this, but the normal installers and building sector in the Netherlands are not able to do this. So we are also educating them, to show them how they could do it. Because it's not my ambition to become a building company or something — I just want to show that it's possible, and then have the market come in and take it over. So we're doing many things at this time, we're not really some organization that you could easily put in a corner and say, you are an NGO or you are an entrepreneur or — we are a bit of a strange animal.

A very interesting hybrid.
Yeah. I don't see any other organizations that do the same. You see organizations who do something with solar panels or who do something on advocacy, or with the circular economy, but I don't see any organization that does all these things at the same time..

And your interest really is in seeing the entire transformation right across the spectrum for the whole society within 15 years, right?
Yeah, well because I started of course in this Institute for Transitions, which is an institute that does system thinking. You want to change the system, and therefore you need to push several buttons at the same time to make the switch. It's just this process of seeing which buttons to hit — and also to see which other organizations are already doing part of that job, and then we fill in the ones that are not done.

So we are working on concrete projects to show that it's possible, and try to help scaling it up, and on the other hand we're working on making this movement bigger. That's one of the things we do with this trip to Paris, because there's more and more people seeing us, there's more and more people joining us.

We also organize the Day of Sustainability in the Netherlands, that's since 2009. Every year, one day we declare this is the Day of Sustainability and then many companies, schools, organize something on that day. The first time we did this was in 2009, and there were about 30,000 people joining us, but now there are hundreds of thousands of people joining us. So this is something growing too. So we both work on the movement and on the concrete solutions.

It's a fascinating model. Now you must have some kind of financial partner here. If I'm going to go and convert my house, spend 35,000 euros on my house, and I don't have 35,000 euros, you must have some way of helping me to borrow that money, do you?
Well, in that case, because that's a specific project, we are now helping people to find the money. There's a couple of options in the Netherlands, and what I'm working on is that I hope that the pension funds at a certain point will say, "Okay, we make this fund." Maybe the government can say, "Okay, we back it up," and then they offer this — and they know they will have it back in 15 years time with, I would say, a small percentage of interest. That's something they didn't want to do when I started, because they said, "I don't believe you that you can do it for 35,000 euros." So I thought, "Okay, so I first want to prove it and then I'll come back." I think next year I'm in the phase of going back. What I would prefer is that every citizen could simply get this amount and then pay it back over 15 years time. And because I don't have a banking permit I'm not allowed to do it myself, so I have to find a partner that has this permit.

So who does this for even the experimental period?
We do it ourselves. Many of the things are things that I have seen that should be possible, and I just start. I look for a few people that can help me — but many things, like the solar panels, I do myself. I just found a partner in China, Dutch people that were working there for 15 years on checking out the solar firms and I asked them, "How many panels do I need to buy to get a substantial reduction in price?" They came back after a few months and said, "Okay, 50,000 and then we can have a reduction of 30 percent." And I said, "Okay, we'll do that" and I told that to a few journalists who put it on the front page of the newspaper, "Urgenda is starting with solar panels" — and then we got thousands of reactions from people said, "Yeah, we want to join you." And I had made an arrangement that people could say, "Yes, I want to join," and they paid up front 20 percent — but if we would not succeed in having enough to buy the 50,000 panels, they were going to get everything back. So it was kind of, you didn't buy until the 50,000 were reached, and then it

was really a buying agreement, but before that it was just an upfront payment but not really a sale yet.

I was surprised that thousands of people in the Netherlands, on my blue eyes, said "Okay, I believe you." I never sold one solar panel before and they just paid 20 percent, and that was very special. And actually I thought, when I had those millions in the bank, that it would be easy to go to a bank and say, "Okay I'm going to buy panels." Normally you have five weeks on a boat and then you offer it to your customers and so you normally need the bank loan for six weeks. So I went to the bank and I said, "Well, I have millions here, I need a bank loan for six weeks," and all the banks said, "Yeah, nice idea but do you have money of your own?" "No." "Did you do it before?" "No, no, no, no." And then all the risk committees said, "No, we're not going to give this." And I was surprised because I thought, Well, I have already sold it. It's a done deal, it's not an idea. I knew many bank directors and they all said, "It's a great idea," but I could not get it done. And until that time I thought that entrepreneurs who said it was difficult to get money were not handy enough, but at that time I knew, okay, they were very right. It's just not easy to get money from a bank.

So I went to China myself. I went to the solar panel factory, and the inverter factory, and I told them, "Look, I have sold your panels already, but I cannot get the loan." They were much more inventive than the Dutch people. They said, "Okay, this is a new business model. We think all subsidy schemes will go down, and this collective buying might be the new business model. So we believe in it, and we will give you a new arrangement. You have to pay us only after six weeks, after it has arrived in the Netherlands and we give you a few cents discount per watt peak." That's the jargon in solar-panel-land, if you really succeed. So we emailed all the clients again and said, "Okay, we made it and you get an additional discount of 50 euros if you pay us already now." And the funny thing is that everybody paid us even before they had any panel in their garden. So when the boat was still at sea I had 20 million [euros] in a bank account and I could easily pay all the Chinese without any bank, without any subsidy, nothing. So that was kind of special — and you don't invent that up front. That's just what happened while playing the entrepreneur and trying to find solutions for the things that get in your way.

It's a problem-solving process, and you almost created the money out of thin air, right? I mean the money sort of exists and sort of doesn't exist.
Well, all those people just were prepared to pay before they had to. It's all a matter of trust, in the end. They trusted that I would do what I promised, and I did. And if anything is wrong, we solve any problem within two days — we also promise that, we give the guarantee and so on. So far we still get a lot of emails of people

who say, "Oh, my solar panels are doing great, I had so much kilowatt hours this year," and blah, blah, blah. So it's really a community now that also follows us in all the other things, and it's a group of people that are very happy. They were the frontrunners in the Netherlands, and now you see many other people doing the same, or trying collective initiatives and so on. So the market really opened up after our initiative, and that's what we're doing in many instances, opening up markets, making it visual. We show that it's possible, and then others think, "Oh, if it's so easy, then we can do it too."

Terrific, terrific. Have the banks taken notice? Are the banks a little more friendly?
Well, afterwards some of them said, "Yeah, we didn't really understand you," and I said, "Well, that's nonsense. I have a business degree and an MBA, and we understood each other very well. You just didn't want to pay. Okay, fair enough."

But next time you come around they may listen a little more.
Well, they still have this risk committee, because I've now been trying to interest banks in those energy-neutral houses. If I do 100 of them I need 3.5 million euros, and it's still not easy to get that amount.

It could almost be like a mortgage on the house, couldn't it? Just a little larger mortgage on the house.
Yes.

But then they'd have to be satisfied that the house would bring a higher price if it had to be sold.
Yeah, and it probably will, but that's not proven yet, because there are no such houses yet being sold. It's always that they wait until they are one hundred percent sure. They don't have the inventivity to say, "Okay, this might be true, let's try."

It's interesting that you, whose motives are not financial, are doing the entrepreneurial thing very successfully — and those people, whose motives are financial, could be making money on these things, and they're not.
Yeah, there's many things very strange.

You've also talked about a sustainable society and a circular economy. Tell me about a circular economy.
A circular economy is an economy in which you try to keep the raw materials in the system. So if you make a table, make it in a way so that if in five years time you say, "I don't like the table anymore," you can get all the components and use them again in the system. So you're not bringing it to burn it somewhere, or put it under the ground, but you give it a second and a third life. One of the business models under that could be that a company says, "Okay I'm selling you the table but it stays

my table. I only give it for use for you and you pay for use for five years. And if after five years you think it's not a very nice table any more, you give it back and then we use all the components for next series of tables." There are a couple of companies in the Netherlands who do things like that. A company like Phillips says, "In the future I'm not selling light bulbs any more, but I'm selling light hours." So you pay for the use, and not for the substance.

And that's a new model that's now starting here. It's also that, for example, a waste company might select all the plastics out of the waste and make new plastic out of it, and that's what's happening in the northern part of the Netherlands. They make of this plastic a new — say, a coffee machine — from used materials. I told them, "You should call it 'vintage' or something and not 'recycled' because then people think it might not be good. But if you call it vintage it sounds much better." Things like that. So it's also a matter of marketing, so that people don't want a plastic coffee machine anymore that's made from oil — because that's what it is actually, plastic is made from oil. Well, we don't want to use oil any more. We want to use the materials that were already in the system.

There's many different angles to a circular society. It also means that the water company that is making the water clean after use gets everything out of it — and also from that part, you can make plastics, but you can also make other things out of it. So in all different ways you try to keep the raw materials in the system and do not burn them and then they're gone.

That also requires a new business model.
Yeah. It's both raw materials in the circle, and it is dually based on renewable energy, with an eye for biodiversity in your environment. So it's actually three components that are also a part of the circular economy.

You must have run into Ray Anderson somewhere along the line, at Interface Carpet?
Yeah, actually Interface was one of the companies that was joining us during the walk and a number of the people, the current CEO and the Sustainability Manager were joining us for a day.

That's been their vision for a long time. I remember Ray Anderson saying that his idea was that they would just constantly recycle the materials, that they would never take any more from the Earth, and they would run the whole thing on sunlight. And I thought, that is a magnificent vision.
Every day on our Day of Sustainability, Interface organizes the Ray Anderson event where some speaker in the Netherlands gives a speech about the circular economy or something that has to do with it. So, yes, I haven't met him personally when he was still alive, but I think he was a visionary.

Absolutely. I interviewed him, but not on camera, only in person. He was a delightful person.

I can imagine.

You've created a sense of adventure around a lot of this, and you're having fun. When I talk to the people that are walking with you, they're having a wonderful time. They're meeting new friends, they're playing with new ideas, they're seeing new countryside, it's not all grim and …

I think that's very important, that people start to see that the new economy, the new way of living is not something that you have five sweaters and eat a carrot in a corner. It's about a new economy and it's fun. It's with young people, it's hip. We should leave the idea that "it's only less, and it's difficult," and that we should move to "it's new and it's different." It's not necessarily more expensive. All these ideas that people have in their heads we should leave behind. There's a new economy and it's fun and it's about finding new ways to organize yourself without all the waste and without putting CO_2 in the air. But it's still a way of earning money, and it's not something that only costs money.

Yes, and you don't feel diminished, you may feel wealthier — because we have to redefine wealth too, don't we?

Yeah, it also gives usually more health, and it gives more fun and, if you laugh that's good for your health, too. It gives new societies, new people that work together in a different way. That's what you saw during our walk: every three minutes you're walking with someone else, because you're moving all the time. Everybody has another story, and there's many people with good ideas, or who know someone who you might meet or whatever. So there's many things happening while we're walking as well, and I saw many people that exchanged business cards and said, "Yes, we should meet each other after the walk and let's do this together or how can we help you?" And that's I think a nice additional thing that happens during all these days of walking.

It happened to me, I have three business cards I collected just from meeting people last evening. It's just lovely. That brings us finally to the case that actually brought Urgenda to our attention, the famous climate change case. I want to come back and talk about the origins of it — but you also did something called crowd-pleading, and that's a new one. Tell me about what crowd-pleading is, and how that worked.

That's also something I invented. I thought it should not be an organization against the state, but it should be of the Dutch citizens. I asked people, "Do you know of any court case, anywhere in the world, that could be helpful for us? Please think with us — or if you're a law student, and you have a very great argument, tell us, so we could make use of it. And you could be the co-plaintiff in our case. Any co-plaintiff can be added — and we pay for it, so you don't have to pay, but it would nice to go into court with a lot of citizens." So there were in the beginning more than a thousand people that were joining us and then the state asked everybody for a copy of the passport and so on, so in the end there were about 900 left, but still a great group. And they went every step along the way with us. Even if we only handed in a bunch of papers for the courts, they just went with us and we together handed in a bunch of papers — with children, and a lot of fuss around it. We had a very large group, and I think it's important that the government sees that it's not only Urgenda that wants this. No, it's a large part of society that is anxious to have a change, and that is afraid of what's going to happen if we don't make the change.

That's a very effective promotion also. It's a news item when 900 people go and say, we're presenting a paper — even if that's all that's happening right?
Yeah.

So tell me how the case began. How did it come up on your radar screen?
Well, we have kind of a think tank with Urgenda of people that we call "front-runners in society" — people from big business, but also from media, and professors from universities. It's a very large variety of people. One of them is a lawyer, Roger Cox, and he wrote a book called *Revolution Justified*, in which he described that climate change is a big problem, the whole fossil fuel world. And then he said, "We are not going to change quickly enough to give my children a future, and the only democratic way that I still see is to go to the judge because the judge looks at the facts, and the facts are very clear: 195 countries have agreed that we should stay underneath two degrees, but we're heading for four to six degrees. We have acknowledged that we want to stay below two, but we're not doing that."

Well, if a judge looks at that, he might say, "Yes, you should protect your citizens, because that's one of your roles as a state — and I, as a judge, can help citizens against their state if they're not doing what's necessary." That was the basic idea of his book. I thought, "Yeah, this might be a way to go, it's at least a democratic way." I agree with him that politics is too much right wing, left wing. Right wing thinks that environment and climate is something from left wing and therefore they don't want to change. It's stupid; I'm always saying, "Your right wing children also have a problem," but somehow it's still this division, and we should overcome it. It should be a matter for all of us. We all want a future for our children. So that was why I thought it was a good idea to try — and then I found another lawyer, and the two of them made the whole court case. They were very complementary and I think they did a great job.

But nobody in the Netherlands believed that we could win. A lot of journalists would phone up professors and say, "What do you think about the court case of Urgenda?" and they would say, "Ah, that's a PR stunt, and they will never win," and so on. I was kind of disappointed because it was clear from what they said that they had never read anything of what we had written, because most professors that were called were people in environmental law or public law and so on — but we are doing tort law, and that makes it different. You really have to read it before you give a comment on it, and nobody did. In tort law you have what's called an unlawful act, and an unlawful act can also be that you don't do anything. So if government doesn't act, it can be an unlawful act.

In this case that's what we said. We said, "Well, you have a duty of care towards your citizens, and you're clearly not taking your duty of care, because climate change is a very big problem and that's acknowledged by you as a country" — because the Netherlands was one of the three that started the climate change treaty in the 1990s, so then when we were still front runners. "You have acknowledged that all industrial countries should do between 25 and 40 percent CO2 reductions by 2020, but you're only heading for 16 percent and you might not even make the 16 percent" — because we're not really doing very well. So the judge clearly said, "Okay, you have acknowledged that this is a very big problem" and in the whole process, the Dutch state never said "We don't agree with that." They said, "Yes, it is very urgent, and we should stay below the two degrees," and so on and so on. So many things were not disputed — but the Dutch government simply said, "We don't want to be a front runner."

Well, that's a little bit to laugh at because we are in Europe way behind. We are between Cyprus and Malta. We were only, at that time, 3 or 4 percent renewables. We were the laggard of Europe — and that's what foreigners don't know, because once we were a frontrunner. But at the moment we are a real laggard in Europe; we have hardly any renewable energy, and we're not speeding up at all. So the judge also said, "Well, before you are a frontrunner you have quite a lot to do," and then the Dutch government said, "Yeah, we don't want to do too much because we might lose our position." Then the judge also said, "Well, the Germans are heading for 40 percent, and Denmark and England and a lot of countries around you are all heading for 35 to 40 percent, so you can do 25 in 2020. That should not be a problem." So many arguments of the Dutch state were just slashed by the judge and in the end he said, "You have acknowledged that it should be done between 25 and 40 percent. Maybe 40 percent reduction of CO2 is necessary, but that's your discretionary power, that is what the state can decide itself. But the minimum level, the 25 percent, that's what you should do." So that's why the judge said, "Okay, I'll give this to Urgenda. You should do 25 percent."

And all those professors that had looked at our case did not really read it and did not see that the main thing is that it's about a dangerous situation, an extremely dangerous situation that is actually acknowledged by the Dutch government. So it's not something about that we ask for money. That's why we also called it a court case out of love, because we just want a change. We don't want the money. We want new policies to still have a future for our children.

"A court case out of love," and also "a court case out of hope" was another phrase —
Well, that was something I only noted afterwards, because I hadn't really thought about that. But when we won, within half an hour it was all over the world. I was really surprised how quickly news travels in this case. We received thousands of phone calls, emails, letters of people that said, "Oh, I really thought that we would never get the change any more, but now I have hope that it will happen! I will go on now." It gave people hope to continue, because they thought, finally there's a judge that sees that this is a real big problem, and if this is one judge, there might be more. So it gave people hope to go on and I didn't really expect that. That was a new additional thing that is also very nice.

You seized on that right away too, when you suddenly realized that the world had taken notice. Probably nobody was paying much attention until the actual victory — but now they were, and then you published all the documents online in English. And you've been to Australia since, and it turns out you are a global frontrunner in this one. But you've really seized that opportunity too, haven't you?
Yeah, we had already translated most of the pieces while we were doing it, because we thought it might be useful for others, and Dutch is not a language that many people know. And the verdict was translated by the Court itself, so the day that the verdict was given it was immediately on their website in two languages, and that also made it possible to transfer it all over the world so quickly. We think that everybody that has a law system that's based on Roman law — and that's many countries — can use 80 percent of what we have produced. So that saves you two years of research, but it also saves you a couple of hundred thousand euros of finding it out and putting it in nice legal language. It's only the last part, putting it in your system, that you need to do yourself. Because, for example, in the Netherlands an NGO can go to court for the general well-being, but there are many countries where this is not possible. You cannot go for the general well-being to court. In that case you can have a class action of citizens or whatever, so that's a little bit different system, but 80 percent of what we have been doing can simply be copied — and that's why we translated everything.

One of the key things is that the Dutch government has already admitted that the problem is serious, and they've already said they have to take action. So you don't have to prove that, right?

When we started the case, we thought in case we don't win, we at least ask the judge to give statements of law that climate change is a big problem and that it's caused by us and so on and so on. So we asked for a number of things — and the funny thing was that he started his verdict with saying, "It's a big problem," and blah, blah, blah, but he said, "I'm not giving this statement of law." Well, he already said it in the verdict, so we were already very happy while he was reading it, because then we can skip all this discussion on, is climate change happening or not. That's a fact. Now we can discuss how are we going to fight it.

But the funny thing was he'd say, "I don't give these statements," but he already described them — and then he went on, and suddenly we were looking at each other like, Wow! it seems like he's going to give the 25 or 40 percent. At that time, while he was reading, I was doing the Twitter account to inform people outside of the court. And at a certain point I just stopped and I thought, "Wow! He's going to do it!" And then we were all like — we were not allowed to yell until the three judges had left the room, and there were other people of ours who were looking through a camera next door, who didn't have to wait, so they were already celebrating, and we had to wait. Because everybody thought we would never win. There was a large, how do you call that, unloading or something? Everybody was crying and yelling and — yeah, there was so much pleasure in the room of everybody who thought we would never be able to win it.

A fabulous moment.
Yeah, a very special moment.

I gather Roger Cox couldn't even speak for some time.
Yeah, he was crying and I actually, we all, the three of us, the two lawyers and myself that was in the centre of the whole period since 2012 — we were all emotional.

For sure. And this judge has found, as a matter of fact, that climate change is real, human-caused and needs to have a strong response.
It's the same all over the world.

So that's a huge obstacle that other cases wouldn't have to confront. There's another case going forward in Belgium?
They have already started, and there are a lot of countries that are now looking at our case to see if they could do the same. But it takes at least a year to write it, so I didn't expect that within a few months there would be many more court cases. The Belgian people had already started because they're close to us and they also

understand Dutch so that's easy. But in other countries people are now studying the verdict and seeing if they can do the same.

Do you have a sense of which countries are likely to follow the lead first?
No. I know there's people in Australia are serious and in Canada and a couple of people looking in USA and Ireland, or was it Norway or Finland? There's quite a few people looking at it — and you never know, because they all still have to find the money. It's not very cheap to do a court case. I think we have a very good system, because the one who loses pays in our case only 13,000 euros, so that's something you can afford. In other countries you have to pay all the costs of the lawyers of your opponent — and then it might be half a million. So if we had to pay that, then it would be very difficult for us — but this is an amount that you can afford, and therefore in the Netherlands everybody can go to court. But there are countries I think, like England and America where it's not so easy to do that.

Now let me make sure I understand that. So if you had lost, you might have had to pay 13 percent of the government's costs?
No. The government now has to pay us 13,000 euros. Well, that's only a fraction of what it really cost to me, because I have also spent a few hundred thousand euros in the whole process to pay lawyers and everything around it. But the Dutch government doesn't have to pay that to us. We have paid our cost, they have paid their cost, and they only pay 13,000 as a fine, which is really nothing. But if we had lost, we also would only have to pay 13,000 euros and that's something that you can still afford. If I had to pay the lawyers of the state, I wouldn't have had a half million left over. That's half of my year budget.

It's a pretty good budget though, all the same. [LAUGHTER] I think Roger says you were one of the first people to really see the importance of his book.
Mmm-hmm.

When I read it I thought, "The book is like a machine. It's so relentless."
For me he didn't write anything new. I knew everything that was in the book. He had only invented the idea, "Let's go to court and make it civil law, an unlawful act." I've studied law myself — I have several degrees, and one of them is law — and I graduated on the climate change convention, so I did international environmental law. So you read it also with the eyes of a legal expert, and I thought, "Yeah, it might not be easy, it's never been done before, but I see the opportunity that it might work if you make a real strong case." And it would make such a difference if we would be able to do that. As you've already noticed, I'm an entrepreneur. I take risks. So if I see a challenge, and I believe in it, I very much believe that I can do it. So then I'll try.

But you tried not to have to do it too, right? You gave away hundreds of copies of the book, and you also wrote a very detailed letter to the government saying, You should do this — and I can sense behind that letter that you were saying, If you don't react to this letter you'll face further action. And still, they obviously thought you weren't going to do much.

Well, I don't know what they really thought, but at least they thought that we were not a problem to them, and they didn't take it seriously. And even now they have decided to appeal — and we pointed out, you do not have to appeal to ask your questions to the legal system, because in the Netherlands' system you can say, "Okay, we accept the verdict; I'm going to do the 25 percent reduction by 2020, but I still have some legal questions." For example, whether the judge was able to do this — was this not something that's up to politicians? Because that's the main question that our politicians have. Well, you can go straight to the High Court and say, "I have a couple of legal questions; will you please answer them?" That is something they could have done — and then we would have been ready within half a year, and then they would have the answer to their questions and we would have our 25 percent, but they were not prepared to do that. So now they first go to the court one step higher, and the one who loses will certainly go to the High Court, and it takes two, three years. So now we're going to spend two, three years of quarrelling, of spending money, of actually retarding the process — for nothing, because they know that it's a big problem.

I also think that it is not strategically a very wise decision, because they are the chairman of the European Union in the coming half-year, and they will have a lot of fuss again with us. There will be a period that the Dutch government will hand in its complaint, and then we will react again — and that will all be in the period when they are the chairman. We'll make a lot of noise around it — and until our court case, the foreigners didn't know that we were laggard, but now everybody knows it. So I don't think it's very handy, what they have done, but they do it. We will just go on and we'll have another two, three years of legal process.

I've been told that while the court processes are going on the government has to respect the present finding, right?

Well it's a bit different. What it says is that, even if you lose, say after two or three years, then you still have to make the 25 percent in 2020. For that reason the government thinks that "Well, I cannot take the risk of just going on without taking any measures, and then in 2018 suddenly hear that I still should do 25 percent," because in two years they will never be able to make that. So they say, "Okay, we'll start to do the 25 percent," so they're making new policies now and as long as it's in the courts we will continue to do the 25 percent. But legally they could also say,

We do nothing until the last day of 2020 and then we close at once all coal-fired power plants and we do what's necessary. But usually it doesn't happen like that.

Yeah, but that would cause a great catastrophe within the Netherlands, right?
That's not the way a government works, so therefore they have said, "Okay, we're going to work on the 25 percent; that will be our new goal. Until the legal process is done, that will be our goal — and if we win, we'll see what happens then." But if they lose, they still should make it in 2020.

We have just had the experience in Canada of a government that in several cases did things that were clearly illegal, but just relied on the fact that the court case would take so long that by the time the case was heard it would be all over.
Well, in the Dutch system, it would cost them a lot of money, because at the end of 2020 they should make the 25 percent, and if they haven't, then we can go back to court and ask a fine for every day that they're not making it. And the fine will be high enough to make them act. It will not be ten euros per day. So this is the first case that you really have something to push them to act, because normally a government sets a goal or whatever, and if they don't make it, there's nobody who will punish them. They'll just say, "Ah, we wanted to do two percent end of year reduction, and we only made one, too bad," and nothing happens. But in this case if they don't make the 25 percent we go back to court and say, "Okay, we want a daily fine to make them act" — and then the fine will be huge and it will be paid to us. So that will be nice but it's not what I want.

It's paid to the foundation?
Yeah. Then we will build a lot of windmills, solar panels, whatever.

This is a also very strange thing for the government to do just on the eve of the COP 21 conference. What do you think accounts for that? Why would a government behave in that way?
Well, I think part of the government doesn't take it seriously still, and they think that they will win in the next instance. They still have the same kind of arrogant attitude, that this is nonsense. And the right-wing party was very angry that we won and they blamed the judges — which is stupid, because a Dutch judge, in our system, has to answer the question of citizens in civil law. It's not something they can say "Uh, this is too difficult or this should be up to government." If you put a question forward the judge is legally obliged to give an answer, and he simply says, "Is there a duty? Yeah, a duty of care is there." There's about five or six factors that he's checking, and if he finds yes, yes, yes, he simply says, "Okay, then there is an unlawful act and then you have to do something." He didn't invent anything. The 25 percent up to 40 percent was invented by the countries themselves, and

the Netherlands have signed for that. So many of the things that a judge has said is not something the judge invents. The judge just looked at all the details and all the facts, and said, "Okay, you have said this, you have said that and therefore I just simply tell you to do what you have said."

It's like he's in a narrow channel. In other systems I think somebody might say, "Well this is ultra vires, this is beyond the jurisdiction of the Court." I guess that's what the government in effect is trying to say...

Yeah, and that's not true. That's something we will quite simply win. If you as a citizen say there is a duty of care and it's breached, then it's a role of the judge to say something about it, so I'm not very worried about that argument.

What's next for Urgenda?

Well, first finish the walk — and we are very busy with those energy-neutral houses so that you don't have an energy bill anymore and you have your house 100 percent on renewable energy. We want to scale that up, so I'm trying to make a new company that's going to do that and is going to train people and so on. That's one of the big things at the moment. We are working on scaling up electric vehicles and building car ports with solar panels on top of it for companies that can have their own employees on electric cars and have the charging station at their factory. So we're doing many practical things that make the ball roll a bit quicker. I'm working on the circular economy in the region of Frisia, which is a region of the Netherlands. There's a lot of entrepreneurs there that really want to make the circular economy happen, and that want to work together, and that's something I think is very nice as well.

So you'll be spending a lot time in Frisia. What are some of the products that would be in that circular economy?

Well there's many, many. I talk already about the plastics and new [items] built of vintage plastic, but there's also a company there that says, along the road you have very often those steel bars, so that if your car goes too much to the right it makes sure that you're not falling over. Well, you can also do that with green hedges — and they catch the CO2, they catch fine particles and you can a few times per year prune them and use it as biomass in the circular economy. If you have a steel bar next to your road, it's only steel and you do nothing with it; if you have a green hedge, then you can use for it different purposes. There's three or four different purposes that governments want, because governments want to reduce CO2, and they want to reduce fine particles in the air and so on. So they have now been able to have connection with municipalities in this area and the first ones have said, "Okay, plant your hedges and we use that in the future." There's many different ways of how you can do this. There are also plants that are giving both protein, but also can be used in the car factory and can be used to improve the soil and so on. You have three or four different way to use one plant.

You're not just looking at it as a single thing. You're looking at it as one thing with many benefits and many different uses, right?
Yeah.

I ask that because it's helpful for people who want to understand what a circular economy actually means and how it might work. The more examples you have, the easier it is to understand it.
I understand, yeah. It's a fairly new concept still. We do have an interest in innovations. We are not the researchers ourselves; we are a very small company and I don't want to become much bigger than we are, but we look in the market. Where are the innovations? There is, for example, a small company in the Netherlands that had a new concept; if you have a big server company where there's many computers that do large accounting jobs, then very often they need a lot of cooling because it gets very warm. But they also need to be protected, because it might be important accounting jobs. And what they thought is "Well, if we bring all these big computers into smaller units and make heating systems off them, we sell them to customers and they have small computing units as free heating in their room — and we have free accounting, because we don't need cooling anymore." We don't need to put security in the room, and through a kind of wi-fi system it gets to a central point where all the details come together again. This has been picked up by a large company in the Netherlands which have paid the financial means for the next step — and we have said well, as soon as you are ready to fit in our energy neutral houses, we would be very happy with that.

So what would be in my house would be a bank of computers that even if I hacked them, it would do me no good because they only make sense when they're talking to all the other computers at the central hub. So it's secure, because it's a little piece that doesn't make sense on its own.
Yeah. And if it's for example an accounting job that's very difficult, or that you really want to be sure that you have the figures, then you could do three houses with the same thing. If one house gets robbed or burned, the others can take over. This is just another way of thinking, a new business model. We are looking at things all the time. I'm also, in my speeches all over the Netherlands, telling people about new things that happen so that people find each other. And we are testing ourselves, because now, in the northern part of the Netherlands, we are helping the islands to become energy and water-neutral. We have one house with a kind of rooftop windmill on

the top of the house, and it works only in areas with a lot of wind, and where the wind usually comes from one direction. Well, that happens on these islands, and we are monitoring that. If after a year it appears a good investment, then we might put it on other houses as well. Then we'll put it in a booklet, so people can see, "Oh, it's already working and they have tested it." Then we hope that we can let this market grow as well. We are always looking for new opportunities. We're not the inventors or the researchers, but we are looking for start-ups that have new ideas that can fit into the new sustainable society.

You said something very interesting just then. You said we are just a small company. You think of yourself as a company, not as an NGO, right?
Yes, because my first study was business. I have an MBA. So I'm looking at it from a business perspective and I don't want subsidies or whatever. I think it should be part of a new economy. We are non-profit and we are non-governmental, so in that sense we are an NGO — but we are a kind of entrepreneurial NGO. I run it as a company. I have 15 people on the payroll, so I have to pay them every month, so that's no different from another business. And we don't have subsidies from government. You can always give something to Urgenda, and we will be very happy — but so far that's not more than, I think, 15,000 euros a year. That's one-third of a monthly payment to all my employees. It's not much. We are supported by a few companies that like our frontrunning work and therefore donate a yearly amount.

You're basically driving the work of an NGO through operating an effective business — a business that's compatible with your objectives as an NGO. Is that right?
Yeah.

One of the things that we're running up against all the time is the corporate need to make a profit. That's the purpose of a corporation, and everything else is either an interference or a side issue. You, however, you're actually making a profit, but that's not your objective. That's a very unusual business model.
There are many companies, like Unilever — Paul Polman, the CEO of Unilever, he wants to run his business and he needs to make profits to do the next investment, but his purpose is not to make as much money as possible. They have another purpose. I think that's more and more like Ray Anderson — CEOs that think of themselves as running a company to help people to get an income, and at the same time make products that are useful for people, and that can be used again and again. I don't see business as bad, and I think that's also typically an old-school NGO thing. to think business is bad. Business is not bad. There are bad businesses, but there are also bad NGOs. I think an NGO should be viable, and it should not survive on

subsidy schemes. You should invent things that are good both to your organization and to the world, and then we are on the right track.

This is a very different model from what now would be considered an NGO. I think it's inspiring.
That's nice.

Well, it is, but you have to see the new possibility before you can really appreciate it. It's like Ray Anderson's comment about waste. He said, I've never done a waste reduction project that didn't make money, because you've been paying to make something that you throw away — and if you stop doing that, you save that money.
You probably also know then McDonough, who has invented this cradle-to-cradle concept. That's the same idea: there is no waste anymore, because waste is a raw material. Waste can be either kept in the technical sphere or it can be part of the non-technical sphere and used as compost, or to make green gas out of it, or things like that. You can reuse almost everything if you design more cleverly, because if you mix everything, it's very difficult to get the components out of each other — but if you design differently, you can use everything again and again. It's actually quite stupid that we, as extremely intelligent creatures that go to the moon and whatever, that we still make so many products that aren't useful afterwards. That's kind of stupid.

And it shows we're not paying attention to the natural world either, because the natural world operates exactly that way, right? The natural world is a circular economy.
We can do things so much more cleverly, and it's just a matter of other attention, other focus, other goals — but everything is already there. It's not something that we need to invent. We can do this already. It's just a matter of being more careful.

ROGER COX

Using the Law to Save Us

Recorded November 2015

In 2006 Roger Cox, a Dutch lawyer in private practice in the city of Maastricht, watched Al Gore's film *An Inconvenient Truth*. He was horrified at what he learned. With his law partners, he acquired the Dutch distribution rights to the film, and organized free screenings all over the Netherlands. Like many others, he had high hopes for the Copenhagen climate change talks in 2009 — and he was bitterly disappointed at their failure. The nations of the world had already agreed that climate change directly threatens the human rights of all people and all societies — but the failure of Copenhagen showed clearly that the political process alone couldn't possibly avert the looming climate catastrophe.

Well then, could citizens sue their governments for failing to take dramatic and timely action to protect their people? That idea is at the heart of Roger Cox's 2011 book *Revolution Justified: Why Only the Law Can Save Us Now*. In 2012, in concert with 900 citizens and a remarkable Dutch organization called the Urgenda Foundation, Roger Cox took the government of the Netherlands to court. Their objective: a ruling that the government had a duty to cut emissions far more dramatically than it had intended. In June 2015, they won — and the ripples of their victory are being felt in courtrooms and legislatures all around the world.

Well, 2009 was the much-anticipated climate summit in Copenhagen and everybody expected a lot from that summit. Basically everybody agreed that that was the final point where we had to agree on an international convention on burden-sharing with regard to emission reductions, and if we wouldn't be able to reach such an agreement in Copenhagen then staying below two degrees would become almost impossible. And then Copenhagen failed. It became clear that nation states were not yet up to the task to keep us below two degrees. And then I thought, let's see if there is a way that we can use the law in pressuring governments into more climate action — because without them and without their lead and coordination such a transformation is almost impossible. That's when I started thinking about writing a book about the issue of climate change, and why there's this stalemate.

It's a brilliant idea. You say, if I can't come in the front door I'll come around the side door — but I'll still get into the room, using the courts as opposed to the legislatures.
Yeah and also a historic perspective, I thought there is no proof whatsoever that large scale transformations in the energy sector can happen without a leading role of governments. If you look at our energy infrastructure in Europe, for instance, all our electricity networks are built by governments. They're not *subsidized* by governments; they're *built* by governments. If you look at the power generation, the gas-fired power plants and coal-fired power plants, they've all been built by governments. Only in the recent 10 to 15 years we have been starting to privatize certain coal-fired power plants and gas-fired power plants, but up to that point it was the governments that built those infrastructures. So that shows you that you need them for implementing such a transition.

You have a wonderful anti-neo-liberal passage in the book where you say companies don't build economies; governments build economies. Governments do the big things, and then the companies work within the framework the governments set up. It's not a popular viewpoint in North America at this point.
Yeah, the western world has become quite neo-liberal in its view on how to develop, evolve and create society. Most people believe that you can leave that up to the markets, and business will run society, but from a historic perspective, that's absolutely not the case. The incentives for businesses are not to build a society. The incentives for businesses are to create profits for shareholders, basically, and look at the short-term interests of the company as such, within the context of society. All large infrastructures, whether it's our roads or our airports or our ports or our electricity networks or our health-care systems, our schooling systems — they've all been built by governments. And from those large infrastructures, companies and citizens can start to prosper and develop their own activities.

Your book is quite relentless in its arguments. You went right back to the issue of the oil decline, and you have a thoroughly relentless passage on that, arguing "the oil decline has the potential to unleash a complete breakdown of western society economically, socially and politically." Tell me about that.
Well, if you look at oil crises in the 1970s, you will see that that immediately had quite a negative impact on our economies, and on mobility within our countries. We've now seen that we have to start using tar sands and drilling in the Arctic and other deep sea places, for instance, to find the last parts of oil that are available because the large oil fields are now mostly in decline, and in our western countries, they are heavily in decline already. If you look at the oil reserves of the Netherlands

or Norway, or most developed countries, these reserves are drastically declining, as are reserves also in other parts of the world. The United States have an increase now in oil development but these are mostly reserves that are very difficult to develop. They need a lot of investments, they need high oil price, and it seems that this is just a short term increase. Most prognosis are that around 2020 we'll see a decline in those new-found reserves as well. We have to understand that, basically, our whole globalized world is still running on oil. That's the basic fuel that we use for mobility around the world. So once we will find ourselves in a perpetual decline of oil exploration, then that can lead to harsh consequences for our society.

When you wrote the book you were clearly expecting the decline to happen much sooner than that. I gather you see a delay, but not a change in the structure of the situation.
Absolutely, yeah.

But you also see it as having the potential to cause great human rights violations. Tell me how declining oil leads to human rights violations.
Well, the situation is this. Once a heavy decline of oil exploration would occur, you will find that transporting our goods around the world will become much more expensive. If you look at agricultural production, we use oil at all levels of production, be it from using a fertilizer as oil-derived product to using the machinery to harvest the land, the transportation of the goods to markets, the use of freezers for keeping them stored for a certain period of time, the plastics to pack it, people running their cars to the supermarkets to fetch the food, etcetera. So once oil would become more expensive, within all those aspects costs will rise, and that will make food and other products — obviously, in the first instance — a lot more costly, and if that would drag on, mobility would shrink because you would have not enough oil available for getting all the goods transported around the world. And that could lead to shortages in food and other basic needs for people, for instance, which would in itself create health effects or other impoverishment of societies.

Basically the right to live a reasonable and comfortable and secure life is what's at risk, right?
If we don't transform in a timely way to another fuel that could be used as an alternative for oil, then in the next decades ahead, we will definitely hit a wall with oil production, and oil decline would certainly have grave impacts on societies around the world.

Which might lead to things like food-based or climate-based refugee floods, such as Europe's experiencing now from the Syrian war, right?
With the Syrian refugee crisis, there's already proof that it's partly related to the changing of our climate. Between 2007 and 2011, Syria was hit by the longest and

heaviest drought that was ever recorded in Syria, making a lot of farmers have to leave the rural areas of Syria and go into the cities. They ended up in poverty, creating a hot-spot for social unrest, and that social unrest in itself has led to instability within Syria — with all the consequences that it has now. Obviously there are also other causes in the relation to the crisis in Syria that might even be more predominant than climate change — but there is already some scientific proof that climate change does have an influence on the situation in Syria, and the resulting refugee crisis. You can expect to see a lot more of this happening in decades ahead.

What we really need to understand is that what we see happening in the world today — like the crisis in Syria which is partly related to climate change, like the melting of our polar ice cap and the melting of our glaciers, and the more extreme droughts and intense heat waves, more bush fires etcetera — those are all the results of emissions of about up to 1980. There's a delay between emissions, on the one hand, and the warming of our world, on the other hand. It's a delay of about 30 to 50 years. So what we see now is the result of the emissions of up to 1980 — and what we will see happening in the next decades will be the results of the emissions that have been emitted after 1980 and until today, which will warm our world a lot more even than has already occurred.

And we also know that in the next decades we will discharge a lot more emissions into the atmosphere because basically we haven't started with our energy transition yet. We'll be relying on fossil fuels for decades, emitting a lot more CO_2 and other greenhouse gasses to the atmosphere. That's why we almost know for sure that if we don't start reducing emissions in large quantities — and start doing that now — that our world will be a lot warmer than two degrees at the end of this century. The outlook for refugee crises and other extreme events in our weather patterns around the world will be so much more visible and extreme than what we are experiencing today. That's basically what we need to prevent.

In the book, you said, "The western world's addiction to oil means that we are in effect at war with ourselves when we talk about wars on terrorism." And you also talk about selling out the constitutional state. Can we just touch on those two points?

Sure. Except for the situation now in the United States, our dependence on oil it makes us more and more reliant on the Middle East states and North African states which are the most unstable states right now in the world. Also the main source of Islamic extremism is found in Saudi Arabia and Iran and other countries in that area — and we keep on feeding them a lot of money because we're so reliant on their resources. The extremism in itself is a result of our past interventions in those countries because of those oil reserves. Our oil companies and our governments did want to have a grip on those Gulf reserves, and therefore also wanted power and influence on the governments within those countries. So we've even been overturning governments in that region of the world, because that made it possible for us and our oil companies to explore and exploit those oil reserves.

So we're paying radical governments, which are in turn financing Islamic fundamentalists — with whom we are in conflict on the other side of the coin?
With whom we are in conflict, yes. That's why we must make a transformation to renewable energy, for instance. Wind and solar and tidal energy makes us a lot more independent from those regions than we are right now — and that would create more stability in the world.

Now the tendency in the neo-liberal world is to say the market will deal with this. I think you show quite convincingly that the market is structured in such a way that it can't possibly deal with this.
The oil market as such is not a free market at all. It's heavily regulated by governments. If you look at the history of oil companies, they obviously were in a position to explore within other territories in the world because at the end of the nineteenth and the beginning of the twentieth century, we had all those colonies around the world — and within those colonies, our governments gave free way to the established oil companies to do their thing. So there's been a lot of cooperation between our governments and oil companies in creating the oil business. Oil is very heavily subsidized around the world. It's the most subsidized energy source that we have. The estimates are about $400 to $500 billion per year on subsidies. It's not a free market at all.

You also quote Lord Stern, who says this is the greatest market failure in history, because the consequences of the actions are so far divorced in time and space from the benefits of it that the costs are away down the road and paid by somebody else.
Yes. I think that what Stern meant is that because of the delay in emissions, on the one hand, and the warming effect 30 or 50 years later, on the other hand, that means that whatever we do at this point in time, it will not change what will happen in the next few decades. What will happen in the next few decades will be the results of the emissions of the last few decades. So whatever we do, the warming that we will see in the next few decades will be there anyway. Even if we take drastic action and reduce our greenhouse gas emissions, we will still see a lot more warming in the next few decades. But markets and politicians are obviously very much reliant on seeing results within one or two or three years, because you want to be re-elected — or you want to show to your shareholders that you did well as management, and that you generated profits.

The problem with climate change is that what we will do now will only bear fruit in the second part of this century. That is such a long term perspective that it's not a very interesting incentive for markets or politicians to start acting upon it. It will be other politicians down the road and other governments down the road and other managements within those companies down the road, in 30 or 40 or 50 years time, that will see the fruit of the actions that we will implement today. And that is why Stern indeed said that climate change is the biggest market failure there is, because markets are not up to the task of coping with such a long-term problem, which only generates the effects intended in the long term, and not in the short term.

So our prices are too low now, because they don't take in to account the full costs. Those costs are far away and will actually be borne by somebody else. If we were paying the true cost of oil, it wouldn't be even $100 a barrel right, it would be …
A lot more, that's for sure.

All right, so the market's not going to solve it. You have a whole section in the book called "The Failure of Democracy." Let me quote your book: "It is not technology that has failed western society, but first and foremost the market and the democratic system."
The problem with these long-term issues, like climate change is that our focus in this neo-liberal world is very much short-term based and it's very much based on individual action. Our basic idea of governments is, strangely enough, that governments should be as small as possible and have as least influence as possible on society, because markets can rule the world. Markets react on individual interests, and if everybody would be looking for his own individual interest, that would generate the most efficient world there is — and that would create a prosperous society for all.

That whole system obviously makes it very difficult to cope with a long-term problem where you cannot generate the outcomes that you're looking for in the short term but only in the long term. So that's the first problem that you have with our current system — and the same goes for politics. Politicians get elected every two, four or six years, and once they are in office, they want to show results immediately because only by showing results do you have a shot of becoming re-elected again. So that's the first hindrance for addressing a long-term problem like climate change.

The other problem obviously is that our governments together with the fossil fuel industry have been creating the world that we're currently in. They've been doing so the last 150 years, making the fossil fuel industry the biggest industry that the world has ever seen. Many of the fossil-fuel companies have turnovers that are a lot larger than most national incomes of countries. They have an enormous amount of revenues. They have an enormous amount of political power, and they have enormous resources to lobby, to work on our political system. There are five to ten times more lobbyists in the car industry in Brussels than there are civil servants in Brussels, for instance. There's also enormous societal power, because obviously they're also one of the largest employers in our society, so once their business is threatened, these companies threaten to lay off people, which in turn creates a lot of pressure from employees in the direction of politicians to do something about the issue. Our banks are also heavily invested in the fossil fuel industry, because they are the biggest industry and they have the biggest outstanding loans. They also have the biggest capital goods that need to be financed, like oil refineries or oil rigs, pipelines, oil tankers etcetera. Those are the biggest capital goods we have. So our banks also are very much involved in the fossil fuel industry.

So looking at that triangle, if you will, between our big banks, our big fossil-fuel companies and our governments, that obviously is a system that has no incentive whatsoever to turn over the fossil fuel system, and create a new renewable energy system. That is contrary to the interests of the fossil fuel industry. So now looking at this particular triangle, looking at the short-term interest that is still the driving force behind our political and business actions — that makes it almost impossible to address this long-term climate change problem. Climate change needs the oil industry to be phased out in the next decades, which creates a conflict between the biggest industry that we have, and our banks and our governments, on the one hand, and this long-term interest that needs to be served, on the other hand.

And that is why, looking at the climate problem, we have a UN climate convention already in place since 1992; we're 23 years down the road now, and the problem has only gotten worse. There seems not to be a solution yet to the problem, while the window of opportunity for addressing that problem is rapidly closing. That's why I think that the system is failing us. We need in fact pressure from civil society, on the one hand, and pressure from the third power within our society, the judiciary, on the other hand, to create enough pressure on our governments to start implementing adequate climate policies that serve the long-term interest.

This is, I think, where you've had the brilliant perception that has brought us together here. A lot of people would understand what you just said in terms of the triangle of large bodies that form the system, and it makes people feel quite desperate. This looks like a prescription for disaster, and there's nothing within that system that helps you to change that — but you've seen a long-term approach through the judiciary. That's a really fabulous insight. Tell me how that works. How do you get leverage within the judicial system to deal with an issue like this?

Yeah, everybody would think that climate change is basically a political issue, because of all the consequences that addressing the problem will have on society. That was my starting point also, but we are in this stalemate situation right now where we know — based on science — that something drastically needs to shift and change within society, but you also see this mechanism that prevents this change from happening. And then you start wondering, okay if this system is failing us and if it creates this big of a danger, a danger that will create a lot of casualties in the second part of this century, which will create a lot of damage within society, then you start to enter into the legal domain — because damages and casualties and other dangers are definitely something that the judiciary can cope with.

So that was the starting point, I think, for myself to start looking at what the law and the judiciary could mean for helping to create this transition. Once you see the triangle and the power that this triangle has, then as an individual, if you want to do something about it, you have to look at another power structure.

Then looking at our legal system and at the judiciary, I thought, well, there's a lot of wisdom within that system. It's a powerful system, because our democracies are based on the rule of law. Law is one of the three powers within our society, next to the legislative and the executive power. So why not find a way to get this third power involved in this climate change debate? Well, the only way to get them involved is to find a way to bring a suit to court, because the judiciary can obviously not become active on behalf of itself. It needs cases that are brought before courts for it to become active.

Then looking at the legal system your basic idea would be to rely on environmental law or international law, but basically you apply environmental law once you see that certain industrial activities, for instance, are not in compliance with the legislations and other rules that are made for protecting the environment. But with climate change, there are actually no adequate environmental regulations in place that you can rely on. You can maybe use environmental law to postpone new coal-fired power plants, for instance, because the developments do not comply with certain regulations — but basically it will give the operator the opportunity to correct it, and once they can comply again with the regulation then these coal-fired power plants will still be built. You can postpone certain action by using environmental law, but you cannot deny those developments. So environmental law, I thought, is not up to the task because we do not have environmental regulation that has the purpose to prevent dangerous climate change. So that was a road that I thought could best not be traveled.

Looking at international law — let's see what international law can do for you. But international law can only be activated by nation states, so that would mean that citizens or an NGO could not activate international law directly. So that was also a road that I thought was not the way forward.

A third road that we best not travel, I thought, is the road of arguing that there needs to be new regulation in place. New regulation that creates the possibility of a really large shift within society, and will therefore hurt the conventional interests of the fossil fuel industry and other industries, will be so heavily lobbied that they probably will never be enacted anyways. So that's also a road I thought that we best not take.

So that leaves you with looking at the existing law to be used as a lever for pressuring governments to more climate action. Now if you want to activate a judiciary and give the judiciary as much manoeuvring room as possible within the legal system, then you had best look at open legal norms that can be implemented by the judiciary by looking at all the circumstances in the particular case. And that's when I thought, well, the best open norm that I can think of is the basic legal notion of the duty of care. It is not allowed for anybody within society — not for us as citizens, not for a company, but also not for a public or political institution like our nation states — to create harm for others that has a certain gravity to it, and that can be prevented without being too onerous for our states to act upon it.

That's when the whole idea started. We could institute legal proceedings against nation states based on their violation of the duty of care to prevent future drastic and grave harm from happening by keeping on contributing to dangerous climate change.

The counterpart of that is human rights, isn't it? Seen from the one side, the nation state has a duty of care, and seen from the other side, the human being has rights.
That's exactly right, because the basis of the whole case is the duty of care — but looking at the effects that climate change will have, you will see that the effects of climate change within every region of the world, including our own region, will indeed be the infringement of basic human rights such as the right to life, the right to water, the right to an undisturbed private life, etcetera. And all our nation states, all 195 countries that are a signatory party to the UN climate convention, have also acknowledged this in 2010, in the Cancún agreements. Those Cancún agreements are also very relevant in another way, because it has also been established that a two-degree warming of the average temperature of the Earth will indeed become dangerous for humankind and the ecosystems that humans depend on. So taking them together, you know that bringing us over the threshold of two degrees will constitute large scale infringement of human rights all around the world, including within our own western countries. And that gives you a good starting point for legal action.

The interesting part, then, is using this open norm of the duty of care, and pointing out the real and imminent threat of human rights infringements around the world. This also gives the court the maneuvering room to start implementing indirectly the agreements that have been made on an international level. With the open norm of the duty of care, you can start to look all circumstances of the case, including what consensus has been reached in the international community on certain aspects of climate change, like the two-degree threshold, for instance.

It almost sounds as though at Cancún everybody said, "Well, yes, we can agree this is what the science says; yes, yes, we stroke our chins, and this is the implications of it; yes, yes — but we don't have to do anything." And nobody realized that somebody could come out of Maastricht and say, But you do have to do something about this.
Yeah, I don't think that was expected. And it's not that they have agreed on all these aspects, for instance.

But they have agreed on the facts that are relevant, right?
They have agreed on the facts that are relevant — and if everybody is in agreement in the world on a certain fact, then that fact does have some legal relevance, obviously. If the whole world agrees that a warming of two degrees of the average temperature of the Earth is a danger for mankind, then there's no other possibility for a court than taking that as a starting point. "Okay, everybody seems to be in agreement that we should be below two degrees so let's take that as a starting point."

Including the defendant government, which has also agreed to that.
Including the defendant government. Also something that I've already been stating in my book is that one of the best reasons to go to court is to get rid of this silly media discussion around climate change and climate science — that it's not settled science yet, that it's all up in the open still if it's man-made, if it constitutes a danger, if it's related to greenhouse gases or not. I already said in my book, there will be no discussion on the climate science, because the climate science is clear, and courts are maybe the best organizations that we have within in society to look at evidence, because that's what courts do — they look at evidence. So I always said, let's bring the climate science to court, and you will see that in the courts the climate science will be accepted as it is, because the certainties around climate change are at a very, very high level. And indeed, there was no room for our state to deny the climate science as presented by the IPCC, and the Dutch state didn't even try to deny that science. It accepted that science fully and completely.

Which is not very strange, because if you look at that science we know for 100 percent sure that the Earth is warming since the industrial revolution. We know for 100 percent sure that greenhouse gases and CO_2 have risen quite dramatically since the industrial revolution. We know for 95 percent sure — or more — that those two 100 percent certainties are connected to one another, meaning that the warming that is observed in the world today is indeed the result of the increase of man-made greenhouse gases in the atmosphere. So those are very high percentages of scientific certainty — and we also know for more than 90 percent sure that a two-degree warming of the world will have adverse effects in all regions of the world. Now in court that is pretty convincing scientific evidence, so you can build a case on that.

So what are you asking the court to do?
Basically, you ask for two things. First of all, look at the science. Look at what has been acknowledged on the world stage as being dangerous. Look at what the derived reduction targets should be based on science and also as acknowledged by all industrialized nations in the world. So make a declaration that not doing your part as a nation state to keeping us below two degrees constitutes a tort and is a negligent action. So first you ask for a declaration that current climate policies by, in this case, the Dutch nation state are inadequate, and therefore also unlawful, and ask the court to label them as hazardous negligence and that's a violation of the state duty of care.

And then secondly, we requested to impose a duty on the state to start reducing greenhouse gas emissions in a rate that is consistent with what is necessary based on science, and as acknowledged by the nations of the world as being necessary to staying below two degrees.

And when you come to a specific ruling, what do you actually demand?
What we actually asked for is reductions between 25 and 40 percent in 2020 relative to the levels of 1990, which are quite ambitious reduction targets. However, these reduction targets are necessary from all developed countries in the world if we want to have a 50 percent chance of actually staying below two degrees. These numbers have also been acknowledged by all developed countries, so each developed country knows that this is something it should do, or the countries as joint parties should achieve before 2020 — but none of them are. A few exceptions are there, like Denmark and Germany, for instance, they have voluntarily have set targets of 40 percent reductions in 2020, and they're well on their way to achieving those targets. So it's also possible. We have proof that nation states can reduce within this target range, and even in the upper target of 40 percent, and prosper as an economy, have prosperous companies etcetera. So there's proof that it can be done but most nation states aren't. The Dutch aren't, the Canadians aren't, the US isn't. The same for Australia and most European countries. Except for a few frontrunners, nobody's doing what needs to be done and therefore that's what we're requesting the courts to impose on our states.

Now how does a government respond to that? As you lay it out, I'm struck by the same

thing I was struck by in reading your book, which was is that the structure of the argument is just relentless. There's no holes in it, there's no wiggle room; it's based on scientific fact that's been well established and acknowledged even by the people who are not paying attention to it. What kind of a defense can the state mount against a lawsuit like that?
States will say anything that's necessary to keep them from getting a negative ruling. Our state said a few things. First of all, they acknowledged the climate science, which obviously is a first big step also for the court because the life of the court is a lot easier because there's consensus by both parties, the state and the claimants, on the climate science. So that's a good starting point.

But from there on the state has mainly argued that it didn't feel that this was a legal question, and that it's political discretion to deal with climate change and to set targets; that there's no such thing as a binding international rule, and that although certain things in fact have been acknowledged, the acknowledgment as such cannot create a legal obligation. So that was a main argument. And obviously they will state that all requirements that need to be addressed before a court can say that a government acts in a tortious way were not met from a legal perspective. That whole legal discussion becomes too detailed from a legal perspective to discuss this now, but you have to address certain requirements before a court can conclude that there is indeed a tort of negligence or any other infringement of the law. We were able to convince the court that all requirements are met based on very sound, solid factual and legal reasoning. I don't think that it's a very exotic legal exercise. The exotic part is only that it is related to one of the biggest questions that we have.

Obviously it is an international dilemma, an international problem, and it should be solved on an international scale — which was also one of the main arguments of the state. Even if the Dutch would do what is necessary, the climate problem will still evolve in a way that climate change will become dangerous for mankind, so there's no causation between the actions of the Dutch government on the one hand, and the development towards dangerous climate change on the other hand. But here again — as the Supreme Court in United States has also already said — the Dutch court ruled that it is obvious that it is an international problem, but it can only be solved if every country takes its individual responsibility. So there is no excuse to be pointing to other countries. There is an individual responsibility to do your part within your national boundaries.

Now the argument that this is a matter for legislative decision-making rather than legal decision-making, would it be right to say that that escape hatch for the state is blocked by the fact that this has to do with rights? Democratic processes don't alter inalienable rights.
Exactly, and that's also what the court said. When looking at the separation of powers, we have as a court a constitutional duty to answer legal questions, so our first

main task is to define whether there's a legal question raised or not. With regard to the dangers of climate change, and whether or not you can contribute to knowingly and willingly creating that danger, that does pose a legal question, according to the court. Once a legal question is raised then the court has to answer that question. And courts also have democratic legitimacy because our statutes do create this legal obligation for our courts, and these statutes and legislations have been created by our parliaments of the past. That's basically what our laws are — decisions of our parliaments of the past and — therefore they have a democratic basis.

By ruling the way the court did, you create a lot of consequences for society as a whole, not just for the Dutch state. And the court did say that that we have to take some caution into account, because of these external effects that this ruling will have for other parts of society as well. But we have to balance that against the risk that a two-degree warming of the average temperature of the Earth poses for the Dutch society, and societies around the world. Looking at the gravity of that danger, we do not feel that we have to restrain ourselves by not imposing a duty on the Dutch government to do its contribution. So it's a sort of balancing act. You have political discretion on the one hand, but political discretion does not mean that you can actively and knowingly and willingly create humongous danger for the society that you're ruling. And that's basically what the court found.

It's a deeply moral finding isn't it? You were elected to ensure the safety and security of these people, and you haven't done it.

You haven't done it, yeah, exactly. That's also what some political parties said after the ruling as well: we should be ashamed that we need a court to point out to us that we have an obligation to protect our citizens against such grave danger. That was maybe the most optimistic part of it all, I think, is that after the ruling a lot of political parties in Parliament said, "Well you know, let's not appeal this case. It's pretty clear what needs to be done. We've always acknowledged what needs to be done, so let's just get on with it and start implementing these emission reductions."

But there is an appeal all the same.

There is an appeal. There's a parallel course that the government is now following. First of all, there is an appeal principally on legal grounds, but on the other hand they will comply with the verdict. They have said to Parliament that they will present a plan in the beginning of next year — in the beginning of 2016 — to show how they will meet this new set target by the court in 2020. So our climate policies have already changed due to this court ruling, because first we had a 16 percent reduction target for 2020 and now we have at least a 25 percent reduction target.

So they're saying, we think the court overstepped its authority in forcing this upon us. Since

they have, however, we're complying, but we still want to settle the legal question anyway.
Yeah, the government is afraid that this intervention of the court might also spill
over to other policy fields, and that's why they feel that some questions of principle have to be raised before a higher court. My personal opinion is that I don't
think it will spill over to other policy fields, because climate change, I think, is a
very unique issue for several reasons. First of all because of the scientific status of
climate change, which is pretty much settled. Then there's the consensus around
the world on what constitutes dangerous climate change. Again, there's the two-
degree threshold and the acknowledgment of what needs to be done by industrial
nations to keep a good chance of staying below two degrees. Then — maybe the
most important part — there's only one measure you can take for keeping us below
two degrees, and that is mitigating greenhouse gas reductions. So there's not much
political debate possible on what the solution to the problem is. However, if you
look at other policy fields like health care or education or what have you, there
will certainly be very relevant questions that can be raised within all those policy
fields, but there will never be one single solution to that question. And that, I think,
makes climate change such a unique issue. So personally I'm not afraid that this
ruling can spill over to other policy fields.

*You went to court on behalf of a foundation and 900 plus citizens, right? And that's an
aspect that we skipped over. There was something new called crowd-pleading, and from
a lawyer's point of view this must have been a very complex clientele. How did that work?*
Well, the idea of crowd-pleading was that everybody who thought he had relevant
input that could be used in this particular case could bring that forward, and then
we as a legal team would have a look at it, and see if we could integrate it. So we
made a draft of the summons that would be served on the State, put it online,
and gave everybody who wanted to have input the possibility to point out things
that we should maybe integrate, or point out certain reports that we not used yet
etcetera. We generated quite some valuable information via that route, and then
adapted our draft along those lines before we served the summons upon the state.

*This is a really democratic legal procedure, isn't it? There's a democratic aspect to it right
at the foundation of it before you even go to court. And of course if you don't have a body
of citizens that are willing to do something about this, the courts hands are tied right?*
The court's hands are tied because if there is no case that's brought before the
court, courts can not intervene into the debate. I think the basic moral duty is to
at least bring a case to court so the judiciary, as a power within our democracy,
can be involved in this issue of climate change, which is the biggest issue in this
decade, and in this century. And however the court may rule, the court will rule.
It's not upon us to decide what the outcome of the case should be. Obviously we

have our preference, and we will do our utmost to get the ruling that we want — but the basic success of the case was already bringing a case to court so we could get the judiciary involved. Even if we would have lost the case, we would still feel pretty good about what we did because at least we gave the opportunity of courts becoming engaged and involved in the climate change debate, and I think that's maybe the most important part of our initiative.

And that's a broad lesson that we can all learn something from, right? Climate change is unique as a case, but it's not the only issue that we face — and maybe not the only issue that should be ventilated in court.
Yeah, it could be, it all depends on what cases it would be. Obviously I do feel that climate change has a few unique aspects to it that make it urgent to bring those cases to court. The gravity of the danger is certainly one of them.

There might also be actions taken against companies, right? Where a company is knowingly endangering the health and well-being of people that its action affects?
Yeah, absolutely. I think that we are reaching the point where we'll be able to get a positive ruling against companies as well. A lot of fossil fuel companies have now, in the last one and a half years, sent open letters to society in relation to the carbon bubble debate, meaning that if we want to stay below two degrees, then four-fifths of all the fossil fuel reserves that are already on the balance sheets of fossil fuel companies need to stay underground. A lot of the assets of fossil fuels companies will become stranded if we really work toward the two-degree target. That affects the financial valuation of fossil fuel companies, and these new facts also make it almost a necessity for them to react.

They did not deny — if you look at the open letter from Shell Oil to society you see that they don't deny these facts. They don't deny the two-degree target that is necessary to stay below. They don't deny the science. What they're basically saying is, "Our assets will nevertheless not become stranded, because governments around the world will not be able to regulate us quickly enough to stay below two degrees. So we expect the world to be a lot more warmer by the end of the century than two degrees, and because governments can not regulate us that quickly, our assets will not become stranded and we will keep on doing business as usual."

I think that position already creates more liability for fossil fuel companies, because on the one hand they accept the science, they accept the danger and their only excuse is, Well, we will not act unless we are regulated upon and since there will be no regulation in place quickly enough, we feel free to keep on with business as usual trajectory and do as we please. I think that might create liabilities for those companies, because if you look at, for instance, asbestos and the asbestos liabilities of the past, companies were already liable as of 1969 for not protecting their employees against asbestos. Once you inhale asbestos particles it creates diseases that are quite deadly. In 1969 there was no regulation in the world whatsoever with regard to asbestos, but the fact that companies did know about the danger was enough for Supreme Courts later on, in the 1980s, when all these people actually became ill, to rule that companies had already a duty to protect their employees, notwithstanding the fact that there was no governmental regulation in place. The fact that there is no regulation in place will prove to be not a good defensive argument, I think, for fossil fuel companies to keep on doing what they're doing. In the near future I think we will definitely see successful climate cases against fossil fuel companies as well.

That's a scandalously immoral position to take, isn't it? The only reason for a corporation to exist is because it is serving the welfare of human beings — and if it's knowingly serving profit over real human beings, does it have any right to continue to live?
Well, companies themselves will argue that they have this right to live, and that they actually have the legal right, and even the legal obligation, to look after the interests of their shareholders and their employees. So there's a counter argument to be made. But I think because of the gravity of the situation, and the fact that these companies know about this situation and know that these consequences will be grave for humanity, that they have in the end a legal obligation to start taking their own individual responsibility to transform as a business to a new perspective, and become a new energy company which relies on technologies that will be beneficial to mankind and will not hurt mankind in the long run.

One last point — and I'm not quite sure that I have a good precise question about it — but you're quite indignant about the fact that the media, who should be informing us, are actually obscuring the real situation by pretending there's still a debate when really, in the scientific world, there is no such debate. That's another dereliction of duty, isn't it? Is there any way that a case such as this could roll out to basically say to the media, you guys have a responsibility here too. Is there any way to use this to do some correction with the media?
Well, we've been arguing quite publicly and openly, once we had the successful verdict, let's now stop having these discussions in the media whether climate change is real, and whether the climate science is settled, whether it's man-made or not. This court ruling shows us that the evidence has been evaluated by our courts, and the ruling is quite clear on that aspect. It is man-made and it will have huge consequences for society. So let's skip the whole debate on the climate science, and let's now start having media discussions on how to transform society to a carbon neutral society in the next decades. We've definitely tried to use that verdict to get that message across to the media also, to stop this debate. There is no debate any

more. This is just media fun, having a discussion where people are set up against one another and have different opinions. That's mostly what talk shows are all about, is to have discussion. But there is no discussion in climate science, on what causes climate change and what the gravity of the situation is.

It's a bit like having a discussion of whether or not you believe in gravity.
It's a perfect example. That's basically what it is. It's similar to denying gravity, I agree.

When that decision came down, it must have been an incredibly powerful moment for you.
I think it was, for everybody involved and attending that courtroom in that moment. It was a huge victory and very impressive moment. Also the way that the court had built up its reasoning and that it made public a sort of summary of the written verdict. It was a very powerful way the court pronounced that verdict. We knew that it could become a historic moment if the court would rule in our favour — and once it became clear that the court *would* rule in our favour, that obviously stirred the emotions quite a bit with all involved. Including myself, yeah.

POLLY HIGGINS

Making Ecocide an International Crime

Recorded November, 2015

Polly Higgins is known as the lawyer for the Earth. She's a barrister, an international lawyer, and the award-winning author of *Eradicating Ecocide* and other works. "Ecocide" is damage, destruction or loss of ecosystems so extensive that peaceful enjoyment of a territory by the inhabitants is severely diminished or lost — and that includes all the inhabitants, not just the human ones. Polly Higgins is out to make ecocide a new UN-recognized crime against peace, just like crimes against humanity, war crimes and genocide.

She calls these UN-level international laws "super-laws:" laws that supersede everything else, so that all other laws must conform to them. Ecocide clearly is, she argues, not only a crime against peace, but also a crime against humanity, against Nature, and against future generations. An international ecocide law would trump the national laws that give the highest priority to profit and would substitute an overriding duty of care for people and the planet. She proposed such a law to the UN in 2010, and she's been organizing support for it ever since. No small ambition — but I wouldn't bet against the strength and passion of Polly Higgins.

Polly, let me say it's a pleasure to meet someone who's been described as "one of the top unreasonable people in the world." (LAUGHTER) Who called you that, and why?

Well, that really is my greatest accolade. I can't remember — it was an American magazine, some big American magazine, a few years ago. They listed me as one of the world's top ten most unreasonable people. That really spoke to me because reasonable people just say, "You've got to be reasonable. This is the way things are." But the problem is, if you remain reasonable, you remain complicit in an existing system, and if that existing system is causing harm, then it's not about whether or not you're reasonable. If anything, it's about standing up and saying, "No! I refuse to remain reasonable about this! I refuse to remain complicit in a system of harm." So for me, this really does speak very loudly. There's a wonderful TED talk somewhere about how if the world is going to change, all it requires are a few fundamentally unreasonable people, because they refuse to accept the existing normative standards. And that's precisely what I'm doing.

Well, in a way that's your "Dare to be great" theme, isn't it?
Yeah, exactly. It is, in a way.

You can't be reasonable and be great.
Precisely, precisely. You've got to rock the boat sometimes. You've got to disrupt the system to effect greater change.

And you're trying to upend the system in a very serious way, calling for a law of ecocide that would override the obligation of corporations to make profits.
Yes, that's right. I'm not anti-profit. What I'm doing is, I'm addressing profit that causes significant harm. A law of ecocide creates a legal duty of care to put the health and well being of people and planet first. So that's an overriding legal duty. That comes first, and then profit can flow from that. So what it does is, it restricts — and in fact it prohibits — dangerous industrial activity. But it enables industrial activity within a corporate context to move into innovation of a different kind, based on a first-do-no-harm principle. So actually it's very exciting. Laws restrict, and they also enable. By restricting or prohibiting on one side, you're enabling innovation in another way to evolve. This is very important, especially when we're looking at corporate-driven ecocides, human-caused ecocide on a major scale. It's about changing the decision-making in the boardroom at the very top end, the principle known in international criminal law as the principle of superior responsibility. Those who are at the very top, the decision-makers, then have to fundamentally change the questions they ask themselves, and rather than asking the question, "How do we maximize our profit out of this energy company?" they're asking, "First of all, is this going to ensure that we do no harm?" And then what happens is you make very different decisions about who your energy's being sourced from, and that creates a very dynamic energy and a very different direction, quite literally, as well as metaphorically.

You don't even get to make the business decision until you're satisfied that you're within that limitation.
And in one way, yes, it's a limitation — but in another way it's an enabler, because if you really want to go beyond petroleum today, it's actually almost impossible. At the moment you're stuck in a legal framework that says that you have to put the interests of the shareholders first, which is to maximize profit. So of course it becomes a huge hindrance that you have to deal with environmental issues. That fundamentally undermines your profit margins. But if you start with an overriding legal duty of care that puts the health and well-being of people and planet

first, then it frees you up to make fundamentally very different decisions at the boardroom level.

It's bizarre, when you think about it, that shareholders outrank everything else on the planet.

Well, we put in place laws as we evolve over time, and one of the fundamental laws that we have actually dates back to a case in, I think, 1886, in America, the Santa Clara case. The Fourteenth Amendment had just been put in place, and the recognition of rights of former slaves, and it was announced at the beginning of the case, without any legal determination, that in fact companies have the same rights as Blacks do. It was the first time ever that a company, a fictional legal personhood, had the same right as natural human beings. The problem is that a company is actually just a piece of paper — and granting rights to a piece of paper has created a huge amount of problems because the fictional person who does not have the same duties and obligations. Human beings carry duties and obligations, but ultimately, at the end of the day, if a company does wrong all you can do is sue the company, the fictional personhood, and there's no point putting a piece of paper in prison. All you can do is leverage a fine, and the company can continue as normal. So this is really a fundamental flawed imbalance, an injustice in its own right. You could say the scales of justice are out of kilter here, because it's the absolution of responsibilities within the corporate entity. So in a way, what I'm doing with international criminal law is putting back those responsibilities.

I'm in favour of the death penalty for companies. One thing we could do — but for some reason we don't — if the offense is sufficiently egregious, you could dissolve the company.

Well, actually, under criminal law what happens is — because you're leveraging a crime against a person, so that would be a CEO or director — the court then has the power to close down the company as well. When something is a crime, then you are enabled to actually stop what's happening. Under civil litigation you can't do that. All you can do is leverage a fine, and business can continue as usual. I call civil litigation catch-me-if-you-can laws because often a company can litigate for many years, can throw a lot of money at it, can settle it, and can still move on with business as usual. But criminal law is about prohibition. It's about prevention as well, and it's about pre-emption. It's about stopping something before it escalates, and that's very important.

And your view of this would also pierce the corporate veil as they say. So instead of saying it's the company that's responsible, you're saying, "No, no, there are people within the company making these decisions, and they need to take responsibility, not slough it off on the company."

That's exactly right. Piercing the corporate veil is absolutely crucial here, so that there's no hiding behind that. It's about dealing with individual responsibility at the very top end, and holding those individuals to account. That actually acts a very powerful lever. If you're sitting on a board of directors, and you think that company is about to commit ecocide or contribute to ecocide, then you as an individual, you have responsibility for that decision-making, and what you'll find is many CEOs and Directors will say, I don't want to go there. That's a crime. We don't want to be in that business because actually we're unlikely to get the permits for what we want to do, and our shareholders would find it untenable, and investment will no longer flow to this — and actually that will damage our bottom line in any event.

But also, if we go ahead and do this and I am directly responsible, I will personally face the consequences — and that also is a real incentive not to do it, right?
Huge. Absolutely.

Let's go back a moment to talk about what "ecocide" actually is. When I first heard the word, I took it to mean the overall decline of the planet that we're going through — in a sense, almost like an extinction, that ecocide equals a harm that broad. But your use of the term is more constrained and more condensed than that.
Well, it's giving practical application and a legal definition to the word "ecocide." So I have defined ecocide in law as extensive damage or destruction to, or loss of ecosystems of a given territory. There are two types of ecocide here. There's human-caused ecocide, which is largely corporate ecocide. You can identify mass damage and destruction, and say that is an ecocide caused by that particular industry's activities, which has been caused by decision-making by individuals at the very top end, and you can identify those people that are responsible for what has played out.

There's also a second type of ecocide which is equally as important, and that's naturally-occurring ecocide, rising sea levels, tsunamis, typhoons, floods. This is very important. What happens here is actually about creating a legal duty of care to give assistance and to stop, first of all, the dangerous industrial activity that is helping trigger the unnatural or the naturally-occurring ecocides. So it's two-fold. You could say that it's climate crime if you like, and that the criminality lies in those states who are allowing those companies to continue with the dangerous industrial activity that contributes and triggers climate change. But the second side of it is the creation of a legal duty of care to make it mandatory for other states to give assistance to those who are adversely impacted by climate change. And that's very, very important, especially within the context of the failure of climate negotiations to even begin to address this.

For instance, in the climate negotiations there is currently no lifeline for Small Island Developing States and other countries that are looking at catastrophic events such as rising sea levels and so on. How do you ensure migration with dignity, where your properties and land have been washed away through some catastrophe? Where do you turn?

What I'm proposing with ecocide law is another way. An amendment can be made to the *Rome Statute* to put in place a crime of ecocide that has that two-fold mechanism. It places a duty on the states to close down the dangerous industrial activity that's triggering climate change, and it creates the legal duty of care to give assistance in times of emergency.

So it's an orderly way for people in a state whose territory is disappearing to move on to whatever may be next.

And the important thing here is that it becomes a mandatory duty, an overriding duty at the very top end. There is a hierarchy of law, if you like, and international criminal law sits at the very top. You cannot override international criminal law with bilateral treaties, for instance. What I'm proposing through an amendment to the *Rome Statute* is very simple. It's a fast track, if you will, where we're not having to create a whole new treaty or agreement. In fact we're putting in place something that has legal teeth at the very top end — and that's absolutely necessary, especially when you're dealing with something like the climate negotiations, where there is no enforcement mechanism to ensure that what is absolutely required in times of emergency is given that legal weight. And in fact the mechanism that's required is being removed in any event, so it's left completely toothless.

Now let me again go back a little bit. The Statute of Rome is really a treaty more than a statute; it's not a statute of a parliament, but a treaty arrangement, right?

Okay, you've got two things at play here. You have the Rome Treaty — it's a completely different document — and you have the *Rome Statute*. The *Rome Statute* originally was called the code of offences, the International Crimes against Peace. The *Rome Statute* is a codification document, and it happened to be signed off in Rome in the end. What it does is, it codifies the existing International Crimes against Peace — that's genocide, war crimes and crimes against humanity — and it makes provision for new international crimes against peace to be added to it. So crimes of aggression was tabled for amendment in 2010. What I'm saying is that now there's another tabling for an amendment required here, for ecocide to be added alongside genocide and the international crimes. *The Rome Statute* also sets in place the International Criminal Court, which sits in The Hague, in the Netherlands.

The important thing really with this document is that to have an amendment put in place, all it requires is for one signatory state to call for that amendment and then it uses the normal United Nations process where it's signed off after you have a two-thirds majority of signatory states. It's one vote per signatory state, unlike the climate negotiations where you have huge power imbalances. For instance I was in Bonn for the interim climate negotiations, talking to negotiators there, and what I saw was a system where there were over 700 negotiators from America, but for the Small Island Developing States, and there are 54 of them, some of the negotiators were doubling up. Some of them were even representing five states — and when you have 32 working-group meetings running in tandem and you've got one person representing five countries, you have real difficulty in deciding which meeting you're going to go to and trying to cover the others. So this is really problematical. It's basically a power struggle. It's a huge imbalance.

But the avenue I'm proposing doesn't work on that system. The climate negotiations work on a very unusual system. It's not the normal system. What I'm saying is that there is a just system that can be applied here by using the normal way through the United Nations by getting an amendment to the *Rome Statute*. You can call for that, and then when it's tabled it's just simply an addition of signatories. It's not a be-all or end-all vote in one day, as we have with climate negotiations. You have to get something sorted by the end of the two weeks in Paris. This other process doesn't work like that. Once it's open for signatories, it remains open, and you just simply accrue the signatories over time.

And it's not political in the sense of a whole bunch of people getting together and lobbying and voting. It's a very precise legal process.
Absolutely right, yes.

And that actually bring us to why we're pursuing all this. We at The Green Interview have seen a number of cases where legal processes have compensated for the failure of democratic processes to actually reach conclusions.
In a way, what's happening here is, where political will fails, then the rule of law prevails, and we get to a certain point where we recognize that we have to turn to the rule of law. What is also very interesting here is that ecocide law is about state crime and corporate crime, really. This is very important here, especially when you have 31 countries having their oil interests under state ownership. If those countries refuse to abate their dangerous industrial activity, then ecocide law becomes very a powerful instrument to ensure that the state adheres to international criminal law. Suddenly ministers and heads of states become accountable in an International Criminal Court of last resort. So that's really about the check and balance of political will as well.

Now tell me how this works in practice. Let's say we have the ecocide law, and I am running a small oil-rich state irresponsibly. Essentially the law says, "Cease and desist, you can't be going on this way." I say, "Make me." What happens now?

Well, imagine this. You aren't even signed up to the *Rome Statute*, so you're not a signatory. We can't touch you if you continue with your operations within your own country, but as soon as you step out of that country, action can be taken. If you step into a signatory state, then you can be prosecuted. I'll give you an example of a precedent when we've done this before. Back in 1998 General Pinochet came to my country, to the United Kingdom. In fact he was there to see his doctor; he wasn't well. A Spanish prosecutor came over and indicted him on the spot for crimes again humanity. Baltasar Garzón was the Spanish prosecutor.

What happened there was that Pinochet was indicted on crimes against humanity and his legal team argued, "You can't touch us. We haven't signed up to the *Rome Statute*. We're not signatories, and therefore this doesn't apply." That went up, all the way up to our House of Lords — it's now called the Supreme Court — and in a nutshell judgment was given saying, "Tough. Yes it does." The principle in law is called *erga omnes*, it applies to all and if you step into a signatory state we are perfectly entitled to prosecute you for this. Now the International Criminal Court at that time was being set up, it wasn't fully operational. So he actually was given a choice: you can stay here and be prosecuted in the UK, or you can go back to Chile and be prosecuted over there. That's because the International Criminal Court acts a court of last resort; you should be prosecuted on national territory first and foremost, and where a state is either unwilling or unable, then it will step in.

Essentially what was happening was that the legal system within the UK was stepping in and saying, You can be prosecuted here on our territory if you're either unwilling or unable to be prosecuted in Chile. Actually the Chilean government did prosecute him over there, or set up to prosecute him, and in fact he pleaded guilty two days before the court trial started, and he died. What's important here is that it set a precedent. We know how this can apply for the future, so even if you are a state that isn't a signatory — such as America, interestingly — you can be prosecuted once you step out of your own territory. So what the *Rome Statute* does is it significantly marginalizes your operations. At the moment we have 123 signatories to the *Rome Statute*. If you are a global player in whatever business we're talking about that for purposes of ecocide is a dangerous industrial activity, you will either become significantly marginalized in what you can and cannot do, or you will want to go with the new rules of the game so that you can continue with business as usual and operate in a new way.

So you either have to sign up and change your ways, or face the possibility of prosecution anywhere in the world anytime you leave your own country.

Or just scale down your operations — but business of course always wants to grow. It doesn't necessarily want to reduce itself to a marginal player. So choices then have to be made.

Let me be sure I understand the extraterritorial character of all this — because although the United States is not a signatory, there's a credible body of opinion that argues that at least one of the past presidents of the United States is a war criminal. Does that mean that when George Bush travels, he could be charged with war crimes in whatever country he visits?

Yes, that's right. It's stepping into signatory states, yes. All it requires is actually for a case to be up and running and ready for him to step into a country. So the evidence has to be garnered; it's a bit pointless trying to indict someone if you don't have the case to back it up. So this is about having the evidence and the facts to hand, this is what Baltasar Garzón had ready and prepared with General Pinochet — ready to go, boom! Indict! Move fast!

So he had the trap laid before the quarry came anywhere near the territory.
He had the case ready to go.

So if one had prepared a similar case against someone like George Bush and had it ready to go whenever Bush went to any signatory state, this is something that he would really have no way of avoiding, would he?
Absolutely right. That's correct.

So the effect of the ecocide law would be very powerful even in non-signatory states. It would marginalize them, make them outcasts and it would specifically endanger the corporate officers personally, not just the corporate entity.

It has huge power to really change the rules of the game very, very fast. But it goes actually further than that, because in fact it adversely impacts those countries who aren't signatories, pretty much from the outset, as soon as it's on the table for amendment. All laws have a transition period: national laws are usually between six months and two years, European directives usually around two years, and I advocate for a five-year transition period for the ecocide law. That allows corporations and politics to realign their priorities — and more than that, it creates long-term investment signals. So the investment world says, okay, in five years time this is going to be criminal activity, so we no longer want to invest in this. In fact the low risk and even no risk, zero risk, investment is going to be innovation in the other direction — renewable energy as opposed to fossil fuel energy, for instance. And suddenly you'll see that the flow of money shifts very quickly, and of course once money starts shifting in another direction you get new institutes coming in and you get skilling up. You're building a resilient economy, and you're basically creating jobs very fast.

In truth, those countries that are not signatories will find that there's not only a brain drain, but also there's a financial drain. No longer will major investment want to go into an old way of doing things that's actually becoming obsolete very fast. So it becomes more difficult to actually receive permits in countries that are moving in that direction. The finance and investment lobbying in those countries is no longer pulling the same kind of leverage, because you'll have ministers saying, "I can't give you those permits, because this is going to be a crime in so many years time, but we're more than happy to assist you if you want to move in a different direction." And we're such a globalized world that if you're a shareholder of a big transnational corporation, and you see that the rest of the world is moving into another direction, but your company's evading responsibility, you're not going to want to put your money in there either. So it changes the playing field overnight, and it creates a level playing field for everyone to come in and move in a different direction. Remember, law serves to restrict on one side, but it enables on another, and that's what's so important here. It has a dual purpose, if you like.

It's quite fascinating, isn't it? It's not just the legal process; it's the knowledge that the legal process exists. And you've said that you'd like to be quite severe and quite tough, and have fairly stringent penalties for individuals behind the corporate veil — but you'd also like to see no prosecutions.

The success is actually how it moves, and because everything shifts in a different direction, it's ultimately is about the flow of money. It's enabling money and investment to go in the other direction very, very fast. Corporations work very well with very clear-cut boundaries. When it's known that actually to go that way has significant consequences at a personal level, you'll find that very few people do want to undertake the dangerous industrial activity. And suddenly the problem becomes a solution, we want to go in that direction. There's a good story to be told there.

Now if I were your tough Texas oil baron, I'd say, "Now Polly, this is all very well, but you know we can't make that big a transition that fast, and fossil fuel is going to be part of future for as far as the eye can see." What do you say to him?
Well, I'd say look to your own country, how often it's happened before. For instance, your country decided that you wanted to come in very late into World War Two, and you wanted to scale up with airplanes. The problem was that in America the aviation industry wasn't set up for mass production. So the likes of Henry Ford were asked, "You know, you're doing mass production of automobiles: why don't you just make them larger and make airplanes?" And of course Henry Ford said, "No, I don't want to do that. I'm busy pulling up railway lines, so that nobody uses trains and they use my cars instead."

So your government, the American government turned around, scratched its head that night, came back the very next day and said, "It is now illegal for you to make cars. You are now, by law, going to have to make planes, and we will make it financially worth your while." And the amazing thing was that over a period of just 18 months — I forget what the exact figures are — but say about 5,000 planes were required. In fact the problem wasn't the scaling up of industry; it was the training up of engineers. Huge numbers of engineers were required very quickly. Usually it took five years to train engineers — so what America did was it took the best up-and-coming students and very bright existing engineers and said, "Okay, you're going to train them up in seven months." Now your country didn't get 5,000-odd planes, it got ten-fold — 50,000 within 18 months.

That scaling-up in times of emergency and that can-do mentality that created the oil industry in the first place, that mentality can be applied just as it was during war time to really move very, very fast. And the enabling conditions were set as a result of the laws that were put in place. And of course the the investment that went into it went in very quickly, because this was going to be highly profitable. What's more, it had knock-on secondary industries. America was the one country after World War Two that really flourished financially. It created a can-do mentality that exists to this very day.

You're right, that's an astonishing transformation. Let me come back again briefly to ecocide before moving forward again with the question of how we get from here to there. You've described ecocide as being a crime against Nature, against human rights and against future generations. Can you tell me how it works on those three fronts? For example, on human rights?

Well, where humans are put at risk of injury or harm — or worse yet, loss of lives — then those states that are failing to stop the dangerous industrial activity that's triggering climate change, if we're looking through the context of it being climate crime, or are failing to give assistance, can be held to account. That's very important, and most particularly when it comes to prosecution, you're looking at the individuals who make the decisions. So you're looking at key ministers and key heads of state.

This is really about governance and protection, duties and obligations to ensure and uphold the human right to life if you will. We already do that on a one-to-one level, you know; your human right to life is governed and protected by the crime of murder. In America you call it homicide. What that means is your life is protected, and I have a duty and obligation to ensure that I do not destroy your life. Now that doesn't mean that we have no murder happening, but what it does mean is that we can take action to either prevent or pre-empt or prohibit, so if I take your life I can be prosecuted, and my rights as a citizen are then withdrawn and I'm duly imprisoned. This is about justice, retribution, but it's also it's about messaging out to society that it is absolutely untenable, and not just morally wrong but legally wrong to take another's life. What it does is it serves to significantly abate it. Society at large recognizes that is a wrong *per se*. Believe it or not, there was a time when it was not a crime to take another person's life.

So with ecocide we're dealing with collective harm at the very top level. This is very much about not just one human life but many human lives being put at risk of injury or harm, or even loss of life. Of course if your small island state is going underwater, and there is no life line and you're just stuck on boats, what happens? You could be just left to die, or in camps and so on and so forth. That creates a legal responsibility, a duty and obligation on states to ensure that that does not happen, to ensure that there is in fact migration with dignity, to ensure that states come together and say, "Okay, we need to allocate land here, we need to allocate provisions, we need to allocate assistance under trusteeship principles." So that's how ecocide law creates a collective duty, a global commons duty for humanity at large.

Now, a crime against Nature: ecocide is a crime against Nature, of course. This is mass damage and destruction of land, of water, of the atmosphere. A heavy extractive industry such as oil extraction is a dangerous industrial activity that causes significant harm. You know, ancient arboreal wetlands, peat lands and forests are destroyed — and for what? A quick fix of fossil fuel, and another carbon sink is destroyed.

And crimes against future generations? Well, this is really about ticking time bombs, if you will. What is it that we do here and now, that may not have a significant adverse effect or long-term harm playing out until a future date? Say, nuclear waste, nuclear energy. What are we setting up and storing up where it can go very, very wrong further down the line, or the use of — dare I say it? — you know, genetic modification, chemicals, pesticides on our land that can play out for generations far later on. And that in itself is, once we know that there are potential adverse consequences than it is our duty and responsibility to ensure that stops and we find better ways of addressing it.

So if you had ecocide on the books as an international crime, presumably chemical companies like Monsanto or Bayer would be very, very careful about what they released into the environment, right? Whereas now they tend to say, "Well, we think it's good and there's certainly a profit in it and we're going to spray it all over the place."
You have to look to the consequences, so decisions then have to be made in a very different way. If a company comes along and says, actually this is perfectly safe, fine not a problem. If you end up being prosecuted for a crime of ecocide, because it has demonstrated harm, then the burden of proof shifts; you have to then disprove that

it caused harm. So this comes down to evidence, and it's also it's creating longer time spans. You're looking into the future. How does this play out maybe 5, 10, 15, 20 years down the line?

Of course if a company is not causing harm, they have nothing to fear from ecocide law. It will help and benefit them greatly to advance and move forward with something that is non-harmful. It also allows those companies to think outside the box, to be the true innovators, maybe to get into more bio-diverse ways of engaging with farming practices such as permaculture, biodiversity programs such as biodynamics. There's a different way of engaging with agriculture that needn't be harmful.

There's another huge theme that you just touched on too, which is that if you're dealing with things in this manner it doesn't become a matter of PR, or of people's opinions, or of votes. It becomes a matter of evidence. And isn't that one of our great problems with the whole ecological theme? So much that goes on is not based on evidence. It's based on stuff that can be easily manipulated.

Absolutely right, and this is one of the biggest problems we have. We don't have a proper forum to give proper assessment — and of course a court of law, a criminal court of law does do that. It is not a defense in criminal law to say, This is good for society at large. If it causes a harm, it's a harm and it must stop. There is no such thing in criminal law as a good harm. For instance, beating up children and then saying, "Well, my defense is that the child needed a good beating up, so that they would do as they were told." In a court of law this is not recognized as a valid defense. Likewise, to be able to stand up in court and say, "Yes but it's good for society that we feed them with crops that are sprayed, and cause illness, and create massive soil depletion" — that's not a valid defense. The good harm defense does not exist in criminal law.

Of course the goods you've just intimated aren't goods, right?
Well, precisely, precisely, yeah. It's too narrow a view. It's recognized that harm can play out in many different ways and can be hidden. When a criminal court of law brings that to the fore, it's no longer a hidden harm.

This whole business of having decisions based on evidence, and having an objective hearing — that strikes me as a key way forward in so many issues. I'm particularly sensitive to this because we in Canada have just dismissed a government that was hell-bent on getting rid of every possibility of solid evidence, right? Muzzling the scientists, getting rid of the long term census — there was a real war on knowledge, because if you have knowledge then you have the possibility of using a route of evidence and judgment rather than of sheer power or popularity. That's not something these guys wanted.

No. When I see how fast things can change, this is very exciting. Your new Prime Minister Justin Trudeau is really daring to be great, I suspect. He's standing up, and he's flipping normatives very quickly. That's very exciting, because it demonstrates that nothing is set in stone. The rules of our world, our laws, can and do change, and they can be changed very, very fast. Every country in the world can pass emergency legislation over-night. George Bush shored up Wall Street at 3:00 in the morning, for instance, by writing new laws. It's just a question of whether or not we consider it now an emergency. For many Small Island Developing States, yes, it is. Absolutely.

There was a point back in the 1990s when ecocide almost made it onto that very short list of international crimes. What happened there? Do we know?
Well, it's kind of missing. There are gaps in our knowledge. What we do have are some of the minutes of meetings from that time. It's a mystery that's been pieced together bit by bit. What we do know is that ecocide was to be the fifth international crime against peace under the *Rome Statute*. That was watered down; the word itself was taken out, both as a war crime and a peace crime, and even the war crime was watered down to a very restrictive test. We do have during wartime what's known as a disjunction test, an either/or test to establish whether or not significant harm is playing out. That's set out under the Environmental Modification Convention, which sets out a size or duration or impact test, so it's a disjunctive test. But what we see under the *Rome Statute*, under article 82B, is that that test was put in place there for environmental harm and at the very last minute the word "or" was removed and the word "and" was inserted instead — and what you have then is a conjunctive test, size *and* duration *and* impact. This has been such a high test that absolutely no prosecutions have ever been brought for environmental harm during peace time.

Now as a lawyer I know the difference that can make, that one word being removed, "or" to "and." That closes the door to being able to do anything about it. So what I'm advocating for ecocide is that it's put back in its rightful place as it had been in the first place. In the first drafts it was in there — and remember this: it has been noted that over 50 countries at the time supported it. It was only four or five countries that had objected behind the scenes and had it removed without vote, and many of those other countries objected to it being removed. Those four countries were the US, UK, France and the Netherlands.

What we do know from the records that we have is that the UN Rapporteurs at the time actually wrote their opinions on why this had happened and logged the documents into the United Nations basement. Now they've been discovered and we know that in their opinion — it's not mine, I wasn't there — this was as a result of corporate lobbying behind the scenes by oil, genetic modification and nuclear interests because it would stop business as usual.

So we have a very interesting thing here in the Netherlands, where I'm based for the next week or so. There's a documentary that's just gone out about my work — and not just my work, other lawyers working this area — called *An Advocate for the Earth*, and this has triggered a huge amount of activity in the Dutch Parliament. Questions were asked immediately in the Parliament. Why was it that the Netherlands had ecocide law removed? This is really fantastic, so this should be flushing out something. And in fact just yesterday a motion was expedited in through Parliament to demand support for ecocide law to be put forward once again. So it's triggering a whole lot of activity in a lot of different ways here. Of course this is very important because The Hague is the seat of the International Criminal Court as well, and I've just been speaking there along with other lawyers about the whole idea that this is really a legacy issue. You know, what is it that we choose to put in place? There is a missing crime here, there is eco-crime, climate crime if you like missing, and that crime is ecocide.

You've been speaking at the Peace Palace in what context?
Well, I was actually speaking at the International Criminal Court. We have the annual Assembly of State Parties meeting happening this week and last week, so I was speaking there just yesterday along with various others about ecocide law and the practicalities of how an amendment can be put forward, and how this could move very fast. This is in the run up to the climate negotiations that are happening next week in Paris, and the fact that there is another legal route that can fast-track and expedite what is really required for those countries that are most adversely impacted by climate change.

That reminds me of another sentence that I picked up in my research on Polly Higgins, and the sentence was this: "In April 2010, Polly proposed to the United Nations that an international law of ecocide be made the fifth crime against peace." I thought to myself, "Polly proposed to the United Nations." How does a person get to do that? If Donald wants to propose something to the United Nations, how does he do that?
Well, I think it helps to be a lawyer.

I'm sure it does.
As a barrister, as a lawyer, I have a mandate. I am able to submit a fully-proposed legal document into the United Nations Law Commission, which is what I did. So I had the requisite mandate to be able to do that.

Can any lawyer do that?
Yes, actually. Any lawyer can do that.

So if I actually wanted to propose something to the United Nations, what I'd need is a partner lawyer who will go forward and do that with me or on my behalf?
There are other routes as well. It just so happened that I'm dealing with a proposal

for a legal amendment, so as a lawyer I can put a legal amendment proposal forward. For instance, if you wanted to bring a case in The Hague, under existing law you could do that as a citizen. There are a number of routes to bring a case in the International Criminal Court, and indeed the first four court cases were brought by citizens quite literally writing to the ICC and saying, "We have genocide playing out, and our country's complicit in it and we want you to investigate this and bring a case" — and indeed that is what happened for the first four cases. So it depends how you want to engage with what the United Nations is doing.

I was struck by the disparity between one person and this huge international structure — but I think it's a very useful reminder that the legal system actually is quite accessible even at that level for even one person.

Yes, but actually I think we often forget that within society in general we have a real mandate, if we choose to speak out. Often there's a sense of disempowerment, of, you know, what can I do? I can't do anything. Actually you can; you can do a heck of a lot. And even just speaking out and saying that I refuse to engage with a system of harm is very powerful. The more of us that do that and say "I'm calling for whatever" — say a law of ecocide — it creates a sort of momentum. The beauty is for me is that I'm not a solo lawyer saying there is climate crime. There is state crime, there is corporate crime. Baltasar Garzón, the state prosecutor from Spain who indicted Pinochet, he's standing up, and he's really calling for this in a big way. Bolivia as a state is calling for crimes against the environment to now be recognized. The Pope, Archbishop Tutu are all speaking out about the moral duty of care and how there really should be climate liability in law.

So there are many different actors in this. NGOs are ready to really run with this whenever any head of state stands up and speaks out. We're not short of people that are already recognizing that there's a missing crime. The legal community, particularly internationally, are recognizing that is this the natural next step, that it just gives weight and governance and legal teeth to all those hundreds of legal environmental treaties. These are obligations that we already have in place and agreements that just haven't got the force of criminal law and the weight behind them to become operable.

Within the last six years a huge amount has happened. It's not just been about writing three books about ecocide law. There's been an awful lot more involved, and it's seeded right across the world. I think this happens when an idea has its time. It resonates very deeply right across the world very fast.

Well, the idea that the natural world has rights, you know — Christopher Stone was writing about that way back in the 1970s.

Yes.

Those of us who blundered across his work were electrified — but there weren't many of us, you know. But now when you start to say the natural world should have rights, there's quite a large group of people to whom this is not a totally unfamiliar idea and certainly not an unwelcome idea.

And in fact this is something that the Indigenous world really gets. That fundamental relationship between human life and the natural world is something that's understood by millions of people in the world, Buddhists as well. This is not really an alien concept. If you look at the timespan that we're looking at from the 1970s, with Christopher Stone, as you say, first positing that key question, *Should Trees Have Standing?* — legal standing — and moving on from there, there's been really over 40 years of legal engagement around this. So this is an idea that — it's time, and the legal weight behind it is there. The momentum is absolutely huge to take this to the next point and just have it put in place.

So how far are we from doing that? Are we waiting for a state to propose this under the Rome Statute?

That's a very interesting question. I think we have a huge window of opportunity here, in particular with the climate negotiations. If the climate negotiations fail to put anything in place that gives assistance where it's really required — and by that I mean to stop the dangerous industrial activity that's really triggering climate change, and creating the mandatory assistance that's required for those who are most adversely impacted by climate change — then it's a window of opportunity. It's an opportunity for those voices that are normally marginalized, such as small island states and Central and South American countries such as Bolivia, to speak out and say, "There is another way. We are calling for recognition of climate crime." And that is ecocide.

So I think what we're seeing is a distilling and crystallizing of a narrative emerging here. It's a great turning point, a critical junction point where the eyes of the world will be on many people in Paris, and press agencies from around the world can hear those voices. When they stand on their own, small island states, and say, "Help us, we've got ecocide playing out," they're not heard. Reuters isn't there. But over 4,000 press agents are going to be in Paris in the next few weeks. So now to stand up and say, "We call for another way to be taken here. We call for this to become an international crime" — that could be the most powerful of thing of all. And for civil society to come behind this in a really big way — the grassroots movements, the Indigenous communities, the NGOs, the faith world, and the lawyers — for those voices to come together, these unlikely alliances to speak out as a unified voice and call for a very different route to be taken, one of climate justice, that would be very powerful.

But we still need a nation to say, "Let's make this the fifth crime." You would think that Bolivia would be a very good candidate since they've passed that law that Mother Nature has rights — and they've been very brave on the international scene in going alone against some of the compromises on climate. Do you think they might be the ones to do it?

Certainly there's a huge amount of discourse around this happening. And the more people who stand up and speak out, the more strength it garners as it moves forward.

Well, the Global Alliance for the Rights of Nature has already done a tribunal, and you've overseen a mock trial in London about this, right?

Yes, on ecocide law, and of course in Paris a similar mock tribunal is being set up to look at Nature's rights and ecocide as well, to see whether or not there is evidence to establish that there's a crime here. That's very good, because it's not about waiting for the governments to do something about this. It's actually civil society themselves taking action and saying, okay we're going to show how this could work in law before it's even put in place.

I wanted to come back to your sense of the potential that each of us has. And also, you've talked about "internal ecocides." That's a fascinating concept. Tell me about internal ecocide.

Well it's my term for the patterns of harm that play out in our own lives, our own ways of being, and how we can actually set in place cycles that take us to a place that does not serve our best interests. Negative belief patterns, you know? I'm not good enough. Who am I? I can't stand up and speak out. It closes us down, it disempowers us. These are our inner ecocides, these patterns of harm that prevent us from moving onwards and forwards and actually stepping into our own greatness, if you will.

I'm very interested in how we can disrupt our own inner ecocides. It's not about allowing those thoughts to come to us a little less; it's about actually saying, Enough. No more, I'm not having it — just as we do with ecocide law. This is about self-governance. How do we choose to govern our own lives? How do we choose to govern ourselves, our very being, which is then reflected out into our doing? It's not an accident that we're called "human beings." We're not called "human doings." So it starts with the being. Whom do we choose? What is our belief system? What is it within ourselves that we choose to be, which then informs whatever we choose to do? And what is it that's no longer serving our best purpose? What is it that actually prevents us from standing up and speaking out, and daring to be great, in effect?

You made a reference earlier on to the unlikely alliance that's coming together around a whole constellation of issues and approaches, arising from a shared and growing global consciousness. I was struck that you mentioned the faith community, because you would expect the faith community to be rather more prominent than it is in this. The faith community as a whole seems to be harder to mobilize than the lawyers, even.

I think the reason behind that is because often, not just the faith community, but many people feel they don't have permission to speak out about climate change because they're not a climate expert. But this isn't about knowing your science. That's for the scientists to come and give that evidence. I'm not a climate expert, I'm not a scientist; I'm a lawyer. But I can see that there is significant harm playing out and I refuse to be complicit in that harm, so I will speak out against it.

From my position as a lawyer I can see there is missing law and that there's a legal framework required so that the scientists can come in and give that evidence. But often I think we get trapped in this idea that it's not for us to speak out about something we don't know about. Actually we know a lot about climate change. We see it on the news, and we can see that people are being harmed. You don't have to be an expert or a rocket scientist to say, "This must end." In a way, the Pope has given permission to the faith world to start speaking out from a position of care, and indeed that's about exercising their role as moral leaders in the world to say there is a moral duty of care here. Absolutely right. That has to be heard from the faith community, and I was very excited to hear and see the Pope mobilizing for that. I was in Paris just a few months ago where President Hollande had brought together faith leaders of the world to speak about that moral duty of care for climate issues. So there's very much a heightened awareness now, and I think what's happening here is giving other faith leaders permission to stand up and speak about this and to recognize that they don't need to be some climate expert or scientist to be able to say "This is wrong. Enough! No more! We owe a moral and therefore legal duty of care to protect our Earth."

And if they aren't experts on moral matters, who is?

Well, I think we all are, in truth, and you don't need to be expert on that. This is actually quite simple stuff. Ask a child, "Do you think it's right that we destroy the world?" Most children will turn around and say, "No." "Do you think it's for the best that we do something, that we put the people and planet first?" "Yes." You know, this is not rocket science. I sometimes get contacted by kids who say, "This is right; thank goodness you're an adult speaking sense on this." So I'm a lawyer, and I've got a kid telling me this — and that's good. Obviously my message is being heard. I think this is true of universal truths: they are inherently simple. They needn't be complicated. It's just lawyers that make things complicated. Once you pare it down and distill it to, what is it that we're really addressing here, what is climate justice, what is climate care, what is it? It really comes down to, it's about a duty of care. It's about our responsibilities to the collective. We have a common and joint responsibility here. This is a global commons issue.

Isn't there internal ecocide that has to do with what specialization has done to our ways of thinking about ourselves? Somebody said to me — I think with relation to the Urgenda case here in the Netherlands — what does a judge know about climate change? To which my response would be, "Well, a judge knows how to evaluate evidence and that's really what's required." It's up to others to present the evidence. But I think a lot of us feel that if we don't have some kind of specialized knowledge we're disqualified from speaking. And that's your internal ecocide, isn't it?

Absolutely right, and in fact it's missing the point of what happened with the Urgenda case here in the Netherlands. The judge there was proclaiming that there is a state legal duty to ensure that harm does not occur. He doesn't have to be the expert on that. He has heard evidence from the experts and he is satisfied, so he is sure that there is a missing duty here. So this is about state responsibility.

Interestingly, we've just discovered that when ecocide was removed from the *Rome Statute* back in 1996, at the same time there was a drafting of another document for state crimes which stated what the state responsibilities were — and that document had ecocide as a crime against the state in it, and it was removed at the same time as it was removed from the *Rome Statute*. So it was removed as a crime against peace and it was removed as a state crime. How come that happened at the same time? What was going on there? We don't really know, but it was removed on both sides. We actually do have a very limited document that states what a state crime is, but what is absent from it is any form of responsibility for people and planet, for environmental issues, for climate issues. So all this judge is doing is giving voice to something that hasn't been put down in paper form. And quite rightly. I mean, it's common sense at the end of the day. He's saying the state which represents civil society at large has a common and joint responsibility for their citizens, and for the citizens of the world as well. It's not just a sovereign duty. It's a global duty as well.

It's a terribly moving case.

Oh, it's very exciting! It's being appealed by the government, and of course this is about the wisdom of the rule of law at the end of the day. So it will be very interesting to see whether or not this is substantiated. It's just been announced here in the Netherlands — just yesterday — that they're now calling for a climate act, and what is so truly radical is that there's a coalition government. For the first time in 35 years members of opposing political parties have come together to call for this climate act, which of course creates even more leverage and support for the judiciary saying Yes, there is a missing duty of care here. There is an implied duty of care, a legal duty of care that now needs to be put in place through law.

We're living in a scary period — but when we have a conversation like this, you realize that we're also living in a tremendously exciting period.

Absolutely. Yeah, absolutely! And it's not about allowing the fear to close us down and getting stuck in negative thought patterns. I was hearing this just yesterday — how it's not possible, we can't do this, we've got too much work. Getting an ecocide law in place will be too much to do. Well, actually this is a legacy issue, you know? We make the space. We make it happen. This is about saving lives, about ensuring the health and well-being of our very planet and future generations. It's not about allowing the ticking time bombs to keep on exploding as we move forward. It's about actually dismantling and stopping the ticking time bombs here and now.

And if you don't have time for that, what do you have time for?
Well, hey, you just make the time. I decided to take a year off from being a court advocate to work this out. As a court advocate my tools of my trade are laws, and I could see there were missing laws, and I also know how fast a law can be put in place. Every country in the world can pass emergency laws overnight. We can make the time for this.

About the
Green Interview

The environmental movement, says Paul Hawken, includes more than two million organizations. It is the greatest social movement the world has ever seen.

Meet the folks who are driving it.

At TheGreenInterview.com, we interview green leaders from around the world — but for us "green" is a very inclusive term. We have painters and poets and pranksters. We've talked to a race-car driver who's reinventing the car industry, and an economist who lives without money. We've visited the then-Prime Minister of Bhutan, whose government was pursuing Gross National Happiness instead of Gross National Product. We talked with the man who measures GNH, and the man who created ecological footprint analysis.

We interviewed a classical composer who provided us with a full-length orchestral concert, an 84-year-old great-grandmother who spent three years in the slammer for tree-hugging in the British Columbia rain forest, and a couple who live sustainably and permanently on a 35-foot boat, sailing all over the world.

The Green Interview exists to promote the wisdom and passion we need to create a truly sustainable future. The practical visionaries we interview are inventing that future — and they're already living in it. They have a radically different vision of life and society, and they embody that vision in their actions.

Our in-depth conversations are usually about a hour in length. They're designed to bring flesh and blood and passion and personality to the dry bones of great ideas and astounding experiences. It's one thing to read about Jane Goodall, Paul Watson, George Monbiot, Vandana Shiva and other famous environmental figures. It's a completely different experience to see them, hear them, watch them exchanging ideas in conversation.

We publish the interviews in audio, video and transcript forms. Here are green giants like James Lovelock, who showed us that our world is a living thing; Farley Mowat, the legendary environmental writer; Sir Tim Smit, creator of The Eden Project; and Satish Kumar, editor of Resurgence, who once walked from India to Moscow, Paris, London and Washington to protest nuclear weapons.

The host of The Green Interview is noted author, speaker and educator Silver Donald Cameron (www.silverdonaldcameron.ca). The producer and director is master videographer Chris Beckett. We post excerpts on YouTube (www.youtube.

com/thegreeninterview) and complete interviews at www.TheGreenInterview. com. The interviews are accessible in libraries worldwide through Gale Cengage Learning and Bibliolabs; in educational institutions globally through their inclusion in the Films On Demand and Kanopy Streaming services; and in Canadian institutions through McIntyre Media Inc.

Fundamentally, however, we rely on our individual subscribers. If you like what we do, we hope you'll consider subscribing. We publish a new interview every month — and a subscriber's first month is free.

Please join us!

About
Silver Donald Cameron

Silver Donald Cameron, one of Canada's most versatile and experienced professional authors, is currently the host and executive producer of TheGreenInterview. com, an environmental website devoted to intense, in-depth conversations with the brilliant thinkers and activists who are leading the way to a green, sustainable future. Dr. Cameron is also the writer and narrator of The Green Interview's five special documentary presentations: *Bhutan: The Pursuit of Gross National Happiness* (2010), *The Celtic Mass for the Sea* (2012), *Salmon Wars: Salmon Farms, Wild Fish and the Future of Communities* (2012), *Defenders of the Dawn: Green Rights in the Maritimes* (CBC, 2015), and *GreenRights: The Human Right to a Healthy World* (2016).

His literary work includes plays, films, radio and TV scripts, an extensive body of corporate and governmental writing, hundreds of magazine articles, and 18 books, including two novels. He has won awards in all these forms of writing. His non-fiction subjects include history, travel, literature, politics, community development, ships and the sea, education and public affairs, as well as nature and the environment. From 1998 to 2011 he wrote an influential weekly column for the Halifax *Sunday Herald*. His most recent books are *Sailing Away from Winter: A Cruise from Nova Scotia to Florida and Beyond* (2008); *A Million Futures: The Remarkable Legacy of the Canada Millennium Scholarship Foundation* (2010) and *Warrior Lawyers* (2016).His classic book on shorelines, *The Living Beach* (1998), was re-released in 2014.

Silver Donald has been Writer-in-Residence at the Nova Scotia College of Art and Design, the University of Prince Edward Island, and Cape Breton University. He has been a member of numerous Canada Council juries. His consulting clients have included four federal government departments, five provincial departments, several important corporations and major charitable foundations. He was the founding Chairman of Telile, the community television station in Isle Madame, Nova Scotia, his main residence since 1971, and was also a founding director of Development Isle Madame. He has served on many other volunteer boards, including several terms on the executive of the Writers Union of Canada, of which he was recently Treasurer.

A distinguished educator, Dr. Cameron was the first Dean of the School of Community Studies at the University College of Cape Breton (now Cape Breton

University). He has taught at Dalhousie University, the University of British Columbia, the University of New Brunswick, and the Banff Centre. He holds a BA from U.B.C., an MA from the University of California, and a PhD from the University of London, England. In 2004 he received an honorary Doctor of Civil Law degree from the University of Kings College, and in 2007 Cape Breton University awarded him an honorary D. Litt. In 2012 he was appointed a Member of the Order of Canada and also a Member of the Order of Nova Scotia. He is married to Marjorie Simmins, also an award-winning writer. The pair divide their time between Nova Scotia and British Columbia.

Silver Donald Cameron continues to accept contract writing assignments and public speaking engagements. His professional web site is www.silverdonaldcameron.ca .

Thanks and Acknowledgments

Because this book is part of a multi-year, multi-media project (www.GreenRights.com) which in turn is an outgrowth from a digital serial publication (www.TheGreenInterview.com), an unusually large number of people have been involved in bringing it to fulfillment, and the chances of overlooking someone are spectacularly high. I apologize in advance to anyone I may have missed.

I want to thank the whole team at The Green Interview — our transcribers, particularly Kelly Lane and Carolyn Gibson; our researchers and editors Laura Landon and Linda Pannozzo; our web wizards Robert Samson and Neil Kenny; and the partner organizations that distribute our productions to schools, universities and libraries across the continent and around the world: Films on Demand, Kanopy Streaming, Bibliolabs, and particularly our long-time partners Gale Cengage Learning. In the earliest days of The Green Interview I was fortunate to have Samantha Peverill as an intern and full-time assistant, which gave an enormous lift to a fledgling enterprise. I especially want to thank my own family, notably Karin Weiss and my brothers David and Ken, who have hosted the OFIAS collective repeatedly in Ottawa, Toronto, and Vancouver. We are also deeply grateful to all the environmental leaders we've visited for The Green Interview. It continues to amaze me that we can simply ask a James Lovelock or a Vandana Shiva or a Jane Goodall for an interview, and be warmly welcomed.

With respect to the GreenRights project, I'm greatly indebted to the Sierra Club Canada Foundation and its two recent executive directors, John Bennett and Diane Beckett, especially for adopting GreenRights as an SCCF project and handling charitable donations on its behalf. I'm profoundly grateful to our donors, particularly the legendary Rudy Haase, whose passion for the environment and whose faith in our project remain undiminished as he charges into his mid-nineties. In addition, we've been fortunate to have the moral and financial support of a small "cabinet" of advisers and contributors, notably Graham Smith, Fred Blois, Henry Hicks, Ifan Williams, Lil MacPherson, Susan Kerslake, and Ann and Craig Bannon.

We couldn't have negotiated the swamps of film financing in Canada without the knowledge and generosity of John Wesley Chisholm, David Perlmutter, and Len McKeigan. I'm grateful to Scott Macmillan and Jennyfer Brickenden and to Stephen Augustine of Unima'ki College for their contributions; to Peter Hall and Stewart Young of the Canadian Broadcasting Corporation and Kevin Matthews for permitting us to use footage they own; and to Ossie Michelin for allowing us to use his iconic photo of Amanda Polchies confronting the storm troopers at Elsipogtog. Miles Howe gave me an advance copy of his book *Debriefing Elsipogtog* and also gave us the use of his remarkable collection of still photographs. Larry Evans provided legal services, and Paul Lipkus eased us through the bramble bushes of film insurance. And again, we're grateful to all of those who talked on camera about environmental rights, from Manhattan to Manila to Maastricht to Moncton, and a good many places in between.

When the time came to make a book from all this research, I was blessed to have the amazing Elizabeth Eve to edit the book and quarterback the whole process of publication. Brenda Conroy did an admirable job of designing the book's interior, and Denise Saulnier designed a superb cover. My deep thanks to all three.

Finally, the three people who share the dedication have been so deeply involved on a day-to-day basis that it's hard to imagine getting any of this done without them. Erika Beatty is a brilliant blend of administrative know-how, dedication to the arts, dogged determination, diplomacy and patience. She was also our budget director, second-unit camera operator, occasional transcriber, and ambassador-at-large to the federal and provincial bureaucracy. She has moved on to become executive director of Screen Nova Scotia. They couldn't have made a better choice.

Chris Beckett and I have jointly created more than a hundred hours of programming and travelled tens of thousands of miles together. I am constantly astonished by his taste, talent and energy. At the end of every film, you'll see a long roll of technical credits for people playing mysterious roles like producer, director, cameraman, foley operator, drone operator, editor, sound effects, best boy, key grip, and much more. In this operation, Chris does all those things, and does them all superbly. Metro and Goldwyn and Mayer, all in one.

And finally, always and everywhere, there's Marjorie, who has put up with the vagaries of a restless husband, living (with two dogs) in the country, in the city, on a boat and in a motorhome — and has contrived to write two wonderful books of her own in the middle of the maelstrom. To her, my gratitude is boundless.

CPSIA information can be obtained
at www.ICGtesting.com
Printed in the USA
LVOW03s0232160218
566741LV00011B/824/P